# Foreign Policy of India

## Continuity and Change

# Foreign Policy of India

## Continuity and Change


***Edited by***

Mohanan B Pillai
Professor and Head,
Department of Politics and International Studies,
Pondicherry University, Puducherry

**and**

L. Premashekhara
Associate Professor,
Department of Politics and International Studies,
Pondicherry University, Puducherry



New Century Publications
New Delhi, India

NEW CENTURY PUBLICATIONS
4800/24, Bharat Ram Road,
Ansari Road, Daryaganj,
New Delhi – 110 002 (India)

Tel.: 011-2324 7798, 4358 7398, 6539 6605
Fax: 011-4101 7798
E-mail: indiatax@vsnl.com • info@newcenturypublications.com
**www.newcenturypublications.com**

*Editorial office:*
LG–7, Aakarshan Bhawan
4754-57/23, Ansari Road, Daryaganj,
New Delhi – 110 002

Tel.: 011-4356 0919



First Published: **July 2010**

ISBN: **978-81-7708-243-2**

Published by New Century Publications and printed at Salasar Imaging Systems, New Delhi

Designs: Patch Creative Unit, New Delhi

PRINTED IN INDIA

# Foreword

This volume on India's Foreign Policy is a brilliant, thought provoking crystallisation of ideas in the post-Cold War era in the light of Nehruvian legacy. Not only does it help understand the vision and the ideas that have moulded India's foreign policy, but also it sheds light on India's economic policy, which is joined umbilically to the former.

The book is set in the backdrop of the current decade. This renders the present work vitally relevant today. The present decade is not only marked by contradictions, it is also reflective of the benchmarks touched upon by Indian democracy. India has celebrated her post-sixtieth Independence and Republic days with exuberance and great vigour and has also stabilised itself in the face of financial reforms introduced a decade ago and the subsequent forces of globalisation unleashing on her shores. Thus, India has showcased itself as not only an evolved democratic polity but also an equally matured economy. It has stood tall and robust as a mammoth, if I may put it so, amidst the domineering global financial meltdown and an equally contagious disease—authoritarianism—in the neighbouring developing world. India's endeavours are denotive of the convoluted contours shaping it. On the one hand there is an intense support to Nehru's passionate implementation of ethics and morality in India's policy-making and on the other there lies a tussle and a half-hearted consensus in letting them go under the pressure of a changing world order. Whatever be the nature of engagement with Nehru's legacy in India's foreign policy-making—as an urge to usher it into the future unaltered or as a critical engagement advocating a marked shift—that distinct Nehruvain flavour to India's foreign policy is retained. And it is perhaps this itself that helps us confront adverse international political situations.

Despite compelling circumstances like the Iraq war or the war in Afghanistan on the one hand and India's Nuclear Deal, India has striven to maintain her Non-aligned stance. Similarly, conflicts and strife in the territories of immediate neighbours as well as towards distant neighbours such as the ASEAN or West Asian countries has called for a much more serious and responsible role to be played by India. Under such circumstances an intermix of a hesitant shift from the Nehruvian legacy as well as an attempt to utilise it as a marker of India's distinct foreign policy making remains a reality. The present work is a collation of the views of noted academicians and practitioners of India's foreign policy and policy-making.

The compendium dishes out variegated perspectives on India's foreign policy underscoring the importance of regional cooperation—especially among South Asian countries—and engaging insightfully with the debate over the Nehruvian legacy, shimmering on the horizon of India's foreign policy making. A must read for students of international studies, the work appraises and ignites an interest even in those lying beyond its ambit. Such an effort is awe-inspiring and rightfully deserves felicitation.

**Professor J A K Tareen**
*Vice-Chancellor*
*Pondicherry University*

# ABOUT THE BOOK

Professing and practicing Non-alignment has been the hallmark of India's foreign policy since Independence in 1947. The initiative for Non-aligned Movement (NAM)—the biggest independent and informal association of countries on a *sui generis* basis—came from three nations, viz. India, Yugoslavia and Egypt, represented by the three statesmen Jawaharlal Nehru, Joseph Tito and Gamal Abdel Nasser respectively. From its modest beginnings at the Belgrade Conference in 1961 with a participation of 25 nations, the NAM has expanded to include 119 members at the Sharm El Sheikh (Egypt) Conference in July 2009.

The fall of the Berlin Wall and the collapse of the Soviet Union ushered a new era in Indian economy and polity and consequently in India's foreign policy. India unveiled the *Look East* policy in 1991. East Asia—including Japan, China, South Korea and ASEAN—is today India's largest trading partner, ahead of EU and the US.

India's foreign policy posture in recent years, particularly towards the region of West Asia and North Africa (WANA), has been a subject of intense debate. India's growing relationship with the US and Israel, and its *lukewarm stand* on Iraqi crisis and Iranian nuclear issue is seen as a fundamental shift in the Indian foreign policy exercise. Critics have accused the succeeding Indian governments during the past two decades of abandoning its *independent* foreign policy, of deviating from Nehruvian national consensus in foreign policy matters, and towing the pro-American line. Others have argued that the radical shift in the orientation of Indian foreign policy in terms of its pro-American tilt bears the mark of *realism* and *pragmatism* that is dictated by the demands of globalisation.

The present book contains 28 scholarly papers—contributed by experts in the field—which provide deep insights into the various dimensions of India's foreign policy, focusing on recent developments.

# ABOUT THE EDITORS

**Mohanan B Pillai** is Professor and Head of the Department of Politics and International Studies, Pondicherry University, Puducherry. A teacher of repute for more than three decades, he is the founder Editor of ISDA Journal—*Studies in Development and Administration,* Trivandrum. He is also the founder Editor of *International Journal of South Asian Studies,* Pondicherry University. Specialising in development studies, South Asian studies and political theory, he has published several books, research papers and articles in these areas. His major books include *Politics of Regionalism in South Asia* (1991); *Globalization of Economy* (1995); *Gandhi's Legacy and a New Human Civilization* (1999); *Quest for a Just World Order* (1999); *Women and Law* (2003) and *Decentralised Governance and Participatory Development* (2005). He has travelled widely in India and abroad to participate and present papers in several international and national conferences, seminars and workshops.

**L. Premashekhara** is Associate Professor in the Department of Politics and International Studies, Pondicherry University, Puducherry. He specializes in Pakistan and China Studies. He has participated and presented papers in several international and national conferences, seminars and workshops in India and abroad.

# CONTENTS

## PART III: INDIA, PAKISTAN AND WEST ASIA



## PART IV: INDIA AND SOUTH ASIA

## PART V: INDIA AND SRI LANKA



## PART VI: INDIA, US and EUROPE

## PART VII: INDIA AND AFRICA

# CONTRIBUTORS


| | |
|---|---|
| **K.S. Pavithran** | Head, Department of Political Science, Calicut University. |
| **Shaji. S** | Assistant Professor, Centre for Multi-Disciplinary Development Research (CMDR), ICSSR Institute, Dharward, Karnataka. |
| **M. Basheer Ahmed Khan** | Senior Professor and Dean, School of Management, Pondicherry University. |
| **A. Subramanyam Raju** | Reader, Centre for South Asian Studies, Pondicherry University. |
| **Suresh. R** | Reader, Post-graduate and Research Department of Political Science, Sree Narayana College, Kollam, Kerala. |
| **Jigar Patel** | Gujarat National Law University, Gandhinagar. |
| **Hardik Mehta** | Gujarat National Law University, Gandhinagar. |
| **Sudhir Jacob George** | Formerly Professor and Head, Department of Political Science, University of Hyderabad, Hyderabad. |
| **R.S. Vasan** | Head, Strategy and Security Studies, Centre for Asia Studies, Chennai. |
| **Mohanan B Pillai** | Professor and Head Department of Politics and International Studies, Pondicherry University. |
| **G. Supriya** | Research Scholar, Department of Politics and International Studies, Pondicherry University. |
| **Amal Sarkar** | Head, Department of Economics, Narasinha Dutt College, West Bengal. |
| **A.K. Pasha** | Professor and Director, Gulf Studies, Centre for West Asian and African Studies, School of International Studies (JNU), New Delhi. |
| **Sudhir Singh** | Department of Political Science, Dyal Singh College, University of Delhi, New Delhi. |
| **L. Premashekhara** | Associate Professor, Department of Politics and International Studies, Pondicherry University. |
| **M.D. Nalapat** | Professor of Geo Politics, Manipal University. |
| **V. Suryanarayan** | Formerly Senior Professor and Director, Centre for South and Southeast Asian Studies, University of Madras. |
| **P.M. Joshy** | Deputy Director, ICSSR Project. |
| **Deepa Karthykeyan** | Research Fellow, Centre for Asia Studies, Chennai. |
| **Jayaraj Amin** | Reader, Department of Political Science, Mangalore University. |
| **R. Swaminathan** | President and DG, International Institute of Security and Safety Management, New Delhi. |
| **S.Y. Surendra Kumar** | Reader, Department of Political Science, Bangalore University, Bangalore. |

| | |
|---|---|
| **Ramu Manivannan** | Reader, Department of Politics and Public Administration, University of Madras. |
| **Jacob Ashik Bonofer** | Research Fellow, Centre for Asia Studies, Chennai. |
| **M.J. Vinod** | Professor, Department of Political Science, Bangalore University, Bangalore. |
| **B. Krishnamurthy** | Reader, Department of Politics and International Studies, Pondicherry University. |
| **D. Purushothaman** | Assistant Professor, Centre for South Asian Studies, Pondicherry University. |
| **Vijay Prakasam G. V.** | Associate Member, Institute of Defence Studies and Analysis. |

# INTRODUCTION

*By Mohanan B Pillai*

The kaleidoscopic disposition of the realm of international relations is compelling in more than one sense. Bringing out the overwhelming inadequacies weaved into the prevailing leitmotif, it necessitates an introspection of conventional vocabulary and established patterns of contemplation. It is in the face of this undeniable veracity of the protean visage of international relations that the present work carves out its niche. Engaged in etching out the continuities, rifts and the consequent shifts in foreign policy, the compendium puts forth motley of ideas that effectively permeate existing gulfs and unseen crevices.

Professing and practicing Non-alignment has been the hallmark of India's foreign policy since Independence in 1947. The initiative for Non-aligned Movement (NAM)—the biggest independent and informal association of countries on a *sui generis* basis—came from three nations, viz. India, Yugoslavia and Egypt, represented by the three statesmen Jawaharlal Nehru, Joseph Tito and Gamal Abdel Nassar respectively. From its modest beginnings at the Belgrade Conference in 1961 with a participation of 25 nations, the NAM has expanded to include 119 members at the Sharm-El-Sheik (Egypt) conference in July 2009.

In the words of Nehru, the Non-alignment was not being neutral or being passive but entailed staying away from military alliances of the superpowers geared against each other and their camps. This was done to protect the fragile economic interests of the infant nation. Help would be accepted from quarters which provided it without any strings attached. As it turned out, erstwhile USSR made deep inroads into India's life and because of the noted 'sympathetic attitude' that it showcased towards India, many analysts believed NAM actually to be Non-aligned to the US.

The fall of the Berlin Wall and the collapse of the Soviet Union ushered a new era in Indian economy and polity and consequently in India's foreign policy. India unveiled the *Look East* policy in 1991. East Asia—including Japan, China, South Korea and ASEAN—is today India's largest trading partner, ahead of EU and the US.

India's foreign policy posture in recent years, particularly towards the region of West Asia and North Africa (WANA), has been a subject of intense debate. India's growing relationship with the US and Israel, and its *lukewarm stand* on Iraqi crisis and Iranian nuclear issue is seen as a fundamental shift in the Indian foreign policy exercise. Critics have accused the succeeding Indian governments during the past two decades of abandoning its *independent* foreign policy, of deviating from Nehruvian national consensus in foreign policy matters, and towing the pro-American line. The significance of WANA for India in terms of oil, gas and labour remittance is too well known to be repeated here. Others have argued that the radical shift in the orientation of Indian foreign policy in terms of its pro-American tilt bears the mark of *realism* and *pragmatism* that is dictated by the demands of globalisation.

The fall of the Berlin Wall and the collapse of the Soviet Union ushered a new era in Indian economy and polity and consequently in India's foreign policy. The 1990s saw the dismantling of the *licence raj* and heralded a new age of liberalisation. This opening up of the economy to the world and its closer integration with the world capitalist system, symptomized by an increasing transaction of people and ideas, has brought India closer also to the capitalist giant heading this system, viz. the USA. The culmination of this is the civil nuclear deal.

Somewhere in the midst of all this, lies India's struggle for autonomy in guiding her foreign affairs, which surfaces as intermittent, ambiguous and ambivalent calls for a revival of the NAM or it being reflected in certain policy actions of the nation-like that of the refusal to send troops to Iraq-which are oft cited as NAM successes. Through another lens one may view foreign policy makers and elites propounding Indian success through its subordination to the US, in this unipolar world. To them, Non-alignment has ceased to occupy its historical pedestal, its warranted place of prominence in Indian foreign policy making.

The present book contains 28 scholarly papers—contributed by experts in the field—which provide deep insights into the various dimensions of India's foreign policy, focusing on recent developments. The editors are grateful to each of them for their brilliant contributions.

Despite the resplendence of views expressed, the running strand may be singled out with comfortable ease. The trust that the authors repose in South Asian co-operation so as to overcome looming perils—economic, political, social and defence, especially from China—reverberates clear and crisp. The rise of the Dragon grips everyone, which makes them fume and fret of the possibility of being engulfed by its ruthlessly deleterious fire. South Asia is no exception to this paranoia. And this abundantly flows out of the streams of thoughts.

The panacea to this, they vociferously voice out, is a South Asian solidarity that would help not only resolve issues more painlessly on the domestic front but also would lead to keeping external powers, playing in this region, at bay. This would require these nations to settle their qualms amicably or push them into the oblivion so that they may not hinder their co-operation on a larger level. To do this, India has an important role to play. It has to act responsibly and conscientiously—something that its smaller neighbours are waiting for with bated breaths.

*Puducherry*
May 2010

**Mohanan B Pillai**

# PART I

# INDIA'S FOREIGN POLICY: GENERAL

# 1

# Understanding India's Foreign Policy: Non-alignment and the Way Ahead

K.S. Pavithran

## Introduction

As an impulse and an idea, Non-alignment is rooted in the ethos of world politics that developed as a consequence of the great collapse of the hegemony of the West European imperial system after the World War II. During the Cold War era the super powers—USA and USSR, by their very nature, tended to divide the world into their own spheres of influence. However, the disintegration of the USSR and the end of the Cold War has radically changed the international environment. The United States became the only dominant power in restructuring the international political and economic order. The dominant position of the USA and the continued tendencies of political and military expansion demonstrated by the United States and its Western allies, in different parts of the world, stand in sharp contrast to world trends characterized by the strengthening of multilateralism and of open, mutually beneficial international cooperation. Then there is the interface between global and regional organizations in the context of globalization. Sometimes these accounts are concerned with the implications for sovereignty of the increasing permeability of national borders, a symptom of globalization, with what are seen to be transnational systems of accountability and authority [Taylor 2006:25]. In this largely chaotic situation, international relations have become extremely complex and unpredictable due to the new distribution of military and political might, the domination of United States as the only super power as well as the emergence of many countries, varying in size and strength, which do not try to conceal their ambitions to create their own respective spheres of influence. These new realities are particularly important for the Non-aligned Movement (NAM), the biggest independent and informal association of countries on a *sui generis* basis created by disavowing bloc divisions and the bipolar domination of two super powers. The present paper has been largely an attempt to conceptualize NAM and analyze the factors, which shaped India's independent foreign policy.

**Emergence of India's Foreign Policy and Non-alignment**

With the end of the Second World War, the dominant nations of the world grouped into two power blocs, one under the United States and the others under the USSR. Emerging from the nightmare of global war, the world found itself on the threshold of an era of escalating international tensions and Cold War politics. It was against this background of a rapidly deteriorating international situation, contributed by Cold War rivalries, that a number of nations of Asia and Africa became independent. The newly independent states vibrating with nationalist spirit were eagerly looking forward for their rightful and honoured position in the community of nations.

The aim of the Asian-African nations was a progressive revision of international order and the internal set up. They saw the Cold War as a struggle for power between two super powers for world domination. Non-alignment as an idea was a concerned appeal to the nations of the world for a retreat to peace and security. The initiative came from the three nations-India, Yugoslavia and Egypt, respectively represented by the three statesmen Jawaharlal Nehru, Josip Broz Tito and Gamal Abdel Nassar. [1] From its modest beginnings at the Belgrade Conference in 1961 with a participation of 25 nations the NAM has expanded to include 119 members at the Sharm-El-Sheik (Egypt) conference in July 2009.

Originally as projected in India's foreign policy, Non-alignment implied a country not joining any of the Cold War power alignments while trying to maintain friendly relations with all kinds of nations and helping the preservation of world peace. Historically, the foreign policy of India to a certain extent emanated from the past legacy of India, her national urges and objectives, her way of life and cultural heritage. The Indian National Movement which drew its inspiration from the Indian Renaissance of the 19th century was a national experience and successfully wrested independence from the Britain and exemplified the political tradition of the country which is an important constituent of the country's foreign policy. The Non-aligned policy symbolizes the Indian national ethos, sporadically springing out our struggle for freedom. Non-alignment was the only credible and viable alternative for India after Independence.

Besides these factors the public opinion in India did not show any special enthusiasm for any one of the ideologies-capitalism or socialism. Public opinion at the base and at the higher level of leadership was largely conservative. No doubt Nehru was the undisputed leader, with leanings to the Left, yet his authority over the Indian National Congress was by no means unquestioned. In the centre of the spectrum of public opinion were the dominant sections of the Congress, Praja Socialist Party and Socialists; the Jan Sangh and the Swatantra parties were on the Right, the communists were on the Left. Naturally the foreign policy of India could not ignore the views of the middle sectors, which obviously had no special affection for any of the super powers. Thus it appeared that Non-alignment imparted to the foreign policy of India, the character of a national policy.

Furthermore, the question of stability of foreign policy of India can be seen in contexts like the gigantic social problems after the Partition from 1946 to 1954 and the tensions expressed through linguism, provincialism and communalism during 1956-62. Another important factor that influenced the shaping of India's foreign policy was her perceptibly precarious economic situation. The British had ravaged Indian economy and when they left there was rampant poverty and misery; the social and economic system had lost its vitality and viability and life, for the common man, had become almost stagnant. India had been watching the simmering international situation in which conflicting ideologies, confrontationist ambitions, economic self-interest and a host of territorial, racial and religious disputes posed a danger to world peace. It was in the midst of this unsettling and unstable environment that India had to adjust herself with the power blocs without in any way compromising on her fundamental policy objectives. It is an undeniable truth that the economic imperatives of independent India had pre determined the colour of her foreign policy.

Thus, Nehru said in 1947 "ultimately, foreign policy is the outcome of economic policy and until India has properly evolved her economic policy the foreign policy will be rather vague, rather inchoate and will be groping" [Nehru, 1961:24-32]. In this context Michael Brecher, one of Nehru's biographers wrote in the 1950's, "Non-alignment is considered essential to the fulfilment of India's economic revolution and avoids alienation of India's two powerful neighbours-China and Russia. Beyond that is the conviction that it contributes to the maintenance of peace and relaxation of tensions. Indeed, the possibility of total destruction and international balance of power impose a moral as well as practical obligation on India to remain uncommitted" (Brecher 1969:266-68). K.R Narayanan writes, "it [India's foreign policy] is really an alchemy or shall I say a chemical combination of certain attitudes, the thirst for Independence, the determination to be independent, the desire to safeguard our national interest, the desire to pursue peace and cooperation in our environment and in the world as a whole and if I may put it more simply, it is a chemical combination between Nationalism and Internationalism and this is where the uniqueness of Non-alignment comes in the manner in which these two considerations are combined and projected in our interest and the interest of the world as a whole..." [Narayanan1986:23]

It is in the early phase of Non-alignment that the fundamental objectives of India's foreign policy were determined. These are to maintain national identity in world politics instead of becoming cogs in the wheels of great power politics, to help the preservation of world peace and promotion of international cooperation antithetically to the Cold War for the sake of a pluralistic and just world order; to seek the liquidation of colonialism and racialism in international politics; to promote disarmament, conventional as well as nuclear, to work for riddance from economic backwardness by putting the pressure of persuasion on the advanced nations for economic and technical aid and for relaxed trade terms; to promote and help sustain egalitarian and democratic trends in world politics against hegemony. The idea is that, Non-alignment seldom if ever means isolationism or neutralism. It signifies not a way of withdrawing from world politics, but of avoiding permanent or certainly onerous prior and continuing commitments to a particular multinational military team led by a super power. Jawaharlal Nehru elaborated the idea while replying to the debate on foreign affairs in the Lok Sabha on December 9, 1958. He said,

"When we say our policy is one of Non-alignment, obviously we mean Non-alignment with military blocs. It is not a negative policy. It is a positive one". He further said, "....we do not align ourselves with either bloc....the policy itself can only be a policy of acting according to our best judgment, and furthering the principal objectives and ideals that we have..." (Nehru1955-1963:381)

Nehru's concern after attaining Indian independence was peace and economic development. He described Non-alignment as a policy which is nationally profitable for any country. Nehru successfully emphasized that Non-alignment is an instrument for catering national interests and every Non-Aligned nation is certainly guided in whatever it does by the considerations of its national interests. In this respect, it is important however that enhancing the prospects of world peace and international cooperation has come to them as something akin to their common interest of gaining political and economic stability. At the same instance, Non-alignment as a universal movement, is directed towards universal democratization of international relations or as Marshall Tito said, "Active Non-alignment means an increasingly broad and active participation in the struggle for the triumph of the principles of the United Nations" (Schou and Brundtland, 1971:103).

Elucidating the opposition of Non-alignment to imperialism and colonialism Nehru asserted, "Where there is continued domination, whether it is in Asia and Africa, there will be no peace either there or in the people's minds elsewhere, there will be a continuous conflict going on, continuous suspicion of Europe in the minds of Asia and therefore the friendly relationship which should exist between Asia and Europe will not come about easily. It is therefore important that all these areas of colonial dominations should be freed and they should be able to function as free countries" (Nehru 1961: 44-48).

India gave its lead further, in elaborating the concept of Non-alignment and in causing the evolution of its new dimensions by working out with People's Republic of China, the five principles of peaceful co-existence [2] governing bilateral relations between two sovereign countries following different social ideologies and political systems. These principles were first enunciated in the Sino-Indian agreement on Tibet and then in the Joint Statement by the Prime Ministers of India and People's Republic of China in 1954. Both India and China had credit of giving birth to *Panchsheel* or the five principles of peaceful co-existence.

In an address to the United Nations General Assembly on November 3, 1948, Nehru said, "I should like to state in this General Assembly on behalf of my people and my government, that we adhere completely and absolutely to the principles and purposes of the United Nations Charter and that we shall try, to the best of our ability, to work for the realization of these principles and purposes," Nehru 1946-49, 1958:323]. Thus by challenging the monopoly of the United States and USSR and their blocs in the world organization, the Non-Aligned Movement made an important contribution to preserving the universal nature of the United Nations [Jevremovic 1996:293].

### NAM and Changing Manifestations of Imperialism

In the course of its rapid development as an international movement, Non-alignment has changed in a significant way. From a primarily political strategy against imperialism and colonialism individually and collectively followed by the new states, it has transformed itself fundamentally into a collective economic movement of the third world countries, entered forcefully into the North-South economic confrontation and spearheaded the demand and the struggle for a New International Economic Order (NIEO) based on equality and justice. While direct political imperialism is by and large only past experience, economic and cultural imperialism practiced by the same imperialist powers is an obnoxious contemporary reality. Today, the whole international system itself is in a state of crisis and the cohesions-political, economic, social, cultural and otherwise which have held it together are coming unstuck at an alarming rate. The fact of the paradigm shift is that the global strategic situation continues to be dominated by the United States. It shows a greater inclination to stimulate, encourage and control conflicts in the Third World to serve its own strategic goals. Consequently military interventions and exertion of direct and indirect pressures by the super power have significantly increased. The United States has seemingly arrogated to itself the role of policing the world as it was articulated in its policy of New World Order. [3] Zbignien Brzezinski [4] has spelt out better than anyone else the geopolitical requirements for establishing American hegemony-domination of Eurasia — a chain of military related bases, over 730 in over 135 countries-far more than at the peak of the Cold War era. [Vanaik 2008:68-73]. Unless the developing countries, who are also the members of NAM put up united resistance against these onslaughts by the US, the world prospects of peace, security and equality of status for nation states will remain a distant dream.

The process of globalization, the use of World Trade Organization (WTO) for forcing developing countries to reduce tariff walls and observe labour standards, while continuing to protect the economies of developed countries by tariff barriers and other no-tariff measures, is another case in point. Joseph E. Stiglitz, once chief economist of the World Bank, in his critique of globalization has observed that the financial institutions [World Bank and the International Monetary Fund] have pushed a particular ideology-market fundamentalism-that is both bad economics and bad politics; it is based on premises concerning how markets work that do not hold good even for developed countries much less for developing countries. The IMF has pushed these economic policies without a broader vision of society or the role of economics within societies. And it has pushed these policies in ways that have undermined emerging democracies [Stiglitz, 2002:0114). Consequently globalization itself has been disadvantageous to developing countries, especially the poor within those countries [Loomba, 2007:221].

The situation calls for a common strategy from the Non-aligned Movement to deal with the crisis of the international system and to adjust the terms of its dialogue for global negotiations to new conditions, integrating the security and economic as well as developmental aspects of problems through a set of regional approaches, within a global perspective. It is obvious from the current developments in world affairs that there is a dialectical relationship between the imperialist economic order and imperialism, and the Third World can never hope to alter the one without the other In this era of global change, old alignments are yielding to new arrangements that may not be always palatable but their appraisal and understanding has to be the first task before Indian foreign policy. In a situation where the IMF and World Bank prescriptions are further tightening the noose it is imperative to work to release us from debt traps and economic degenerations. Priority should also be given to consolidate and update India's cooperative relations with the neighbours. Any kind of military and strategic partnership with the United States will create unnecessary complications in our relations with our neighbours. K.R. Narayanan has succinctly remarked, "That politics is the soul of the movement (NAM) and even when you are following questions of global economics or elimination of economic disparities, it is this political attitude, which is propelling, which is giving vital life to this movement even though the problem has taken an economic shape" [Narayanan, 1986:20]. Hence the battle for a new economic order is the battle against neo-imperialism.

On the surface it does seem logical that with the disappearance of bloc divisions and rivalry between the two nuclear super powers, there was no longer any reason for countries wishing to stay away from these divisions to remain together hence the relevance of Non-aligned Movement. It may seem paradoxical that the first serious dilemmas concerning the future of the NAM were voices, both within and outside it, as *detente* evolved between United States and USSR. It was said in various quarters that the Non-Aligned Movement has become superfluous. Now, it is alleged that during its decades of existence Non-alignment has proved to be ineffective. However, at the same time the NAM maintains its regular schedule of periodic summit meetings, while increasing its number of member countries. The steadily growing membership of the NAM eliminates all doubts as to the relevance of the NAM. However, one should note that the existing contradictions making the Non-aligned movement itself, which could be to a great extent reduced to a discrepancy between theory and practice, between declared goals and behaviour in practice-weaken the capacity of NAM to carry out more successfully its historical mission.

The fact is that the collapse of the bipolar system and emergence of unipolarity in political, economic and military terms is leading to further inequality and injustice and hence, the role of Non-alignment becomes much more important as a counterforce to unilateral military and economic coercion [Dutt, 2001:62).

Politically as Ngaire Woods suggests that the impact of globalization differs not just according to the sector of the economy being examined but also according to the character of each state. Strong states have not only influenced the nature and pace of globalization, but, equally, have controlled their own integration into the world economy. Their sovereignty may well be qualitatively changing, but it is surely not being eroded. Weak states by contrast risk being further weakened by globalization. At the same time however, globalization is opening up new kinds of governance (such as regional institutions) and adding new actors to the process (such as non-governmental organizations and transnational arbiters and regulators) [Woods 2000: 2-3]. This is because capitalism's globalizing tendencies have been substantially realized in particular historical contexts, and this has been the political project of the tangentially transnational-if also US led-historic bloc comprised of particular fractions of the capitalist class, state managers and international bureaucrats, journalists and mainstream labour leaders [Rupert, 2003:190].

The above naturally reminds us of the 'World System' theory of Wallerstein which means in a nut shell, the following: Capitalist accumulation (and its attendant exploitation) has created global inequalities based on the domination of the core capitalist states of the West over non-western peripheral countries. [5] This surge of inequality especially in the conditions of extreme economic instability such as those created by the global free market in the 1990's is the root of the major social and political tensions of the new century. In so far as international inequalities may be under pressure from the rise of the new Asian economies, both the threat to the relatively astronomic standards of living of the peoples of the old north and the practical impossibility of achieving anything like it for the vast populations of such countries as India and China, will produce its own domestic and international tensions [Hobsbawm, 2007:3].

In the absence of countervailing forces which existed in a bipolar world the Allied forces under the hegemony of United States are using unrestrained force in Afghanistan, in Iraq or in Kosovo. The use of military power to settle disputes is required to be restrained. There are still many areas of conflict-in Sri Lanka, Angola, Bosnia, the Democratic Republic of Congo, Rwanda, Sudan and Somalia. The NAM does not appear to be doing anything to settle these disputes. In all these cases, armed intervention has come from US led coalitions. This proves that the international system is potentially unstable and the disintegration of the USSR and the East European communist models increased this instability. In this situation Non-alignment has to be reformulated and revitalized to be able to respond more effectively to the needs of the Third World's national security that are overgrowing in magnitude and complexity. Unless the NAM pays adequate attention to these matters, it may not be able to halt the present drift or resist erosion.

**Conclusion**

In the present context of the collapse of east bloc led by the Soviet Union and the consequent globalizing capitalism and neo-imperialism, the notion of Non-alignment appears more problematic. However the Movement constitutes an integral part of the profound changes in the structure of contemporary international relations. The only way to strengthen the role of Non-aligned Movement as the greatest independent and biggest peace movement in the world is to reinforce the Non-aligned countries' unity. The basis of such an approach can be cited in the idea of democratization of international relations as an imperative necessity of our times, which will lead to the realization of the unfettered development and genuine independence of all states. Democracy then requires the collective public regulation of these activities responsible for our social reproduction, which in most parts of the world are currently affected through the capitalist market [Colas, 2003:97]. This means that the uni-dimensional and unipolar versions of the new international system need to be contested by the NAM as a whole. Unity and solidarity among the Non-aligned countries are all the more necessary in the present crisis in international relations. In the new situation with issues of military occupations, human rights, new dimensions of North-South conflicts, restructuring of the United Nations and nuclear disarmament, it falls on the NAM to survive meaningfully and not just ceremonially as a movement. This would require a newer unifying rationale [Vanaik: 5047] to strengthen the United Nations, to ensure security of smaller states, to settle disputes among the member states and to defeat the Neo-con ambitions globally.

It is difficult to discern the future political profile of the Non-aligned Movement in the turbulent present day world. Notwithstanding, all the development occurred in the international arena with the last decade of the 20th century, the world situation is still in a state of transition. It is, therefore, incumbent on the Non-aligned Movement to ensure its full participation in the building of the new world order, this more so because a new international order has proven to be elusive and what transpired to date is a little more than a new international realignment. One of the greatest living historians of the world, Eric Hobsbawm was poignantly prophetic in stating, "that the US has failed and will inevitably fail, to impose a new world order (of any kind) by unilateral force, however much power relations are skewed in its favour at present, and even if it is backed by an (inevitably short-lived) alliance. The international system will remain multilateral and its regulation will depend on the ability of several major units to agree with one another, even though none of these states enjoys military predominance. How far international military action taken by the US is dependent on the negotiated agreement of other states is already clear...." The era of wars ending with unconditional surrender will not return in the foreseeable future (Hobsbawm, 2007:27). It is therefore imperative for the NAM to play its role in defining and shaping international realities, to adapt to change and to articulate and implement appropriate strategies and approaches in the new millennium.

**Notes**

1. Non-alignment first sprang into popular use with V.K. Krishna Menon, while articulating the

aspirations of the newly independent countries in the United Nations. see, Peter Lyon (1980), 'Non-alignment at the Summits: From Belgrade 1961 to Havana 1979- a Perspective View", *Indian Journal of Political Science*, Vol. 41, No. 1, March, p. 149., also see K.R. Narayanan (1986), 'Relevance of Non alignment', *Kerala Journal of Political studies*, Vol.1, No.1, January, p. 16.

2. The five principles as they originated in the sino-Indian Agreement on Tibet were: 1. Mutual respect for each other's territorial integrity and sovereignty; 2. Mutual Non-aggression; 3. Mutual non-interference in each others internal affairs; 4. Equality and mutual benefit; and 5. Peaceful co-existence.
3. The idea of a 'New World Order' was camouflaged by president Bush as "a new era, free from the threat of terror, stronger in the pursuit of justice, and more secure in the quest for peace, an era in which the nations of the world can prosper and live in harmony". For full text of president George Bush's statement of 11 September 1990 see, US Department of State (1990), *Current policy Documents*, No. 1298, Washington DC.
4. The two important works of Brzezinski are '*The Grand Chess Board*' (1997), Basic Books, New York and '*The Choice*'(2004), Basic Books, New York.
5. For a detailed analysis see, Immanuel Wallerstein (1979), '*The Capitalist World Economy*', Cambridge University Press, Cambridge.

**References**

Bandyopadhyaya, J. (1977) 'The Non-aligned Movement and International Relations', *India Quarterly*, Vol. XXXII, (2) April-June.

Brecher, Michael(1969), *Nehru: A Political Biography*, 2nd Edn., Bombay.

Colas, Alejandro (2003) 'The Power of Representation: Democratic Politics and Global Governance', in David Armstrong, Theo Farrell and Bice Maiguashca (eds), *Governance and Resistance in World Politics,* Cambridge University Press, Cambridge.

Dutt, Ruddar (2001) 'NAM – Its Relevance in the Unipolar World', in Pramila Srivastava (ed.) *Non-Aligned Movement: Extending Frontiers*, Kanishka Publications, New Delhi.

Hobsbawm, Eric (2007) *Globalization, Democracy and Terrorism*, Little Brown. London.

Jevremovic, Pavle (1996) 'Non-aligned Movement: The End or a New Beginning?' *International Studies*, Vol. 33 (3), July-September.

*Jawaharlal Nehru's Speeches*: September 1955–April 1963, Vol. 4 (1964) Delhi: Government of India, Publication Division.

Loomba, Ania (2007) *Colonialism / Post Colonialism,* Rutledge, London.

Narang A.S. (2001), 'NAM in the New Millennium: Challenges and Issues', Pramila Srivastava (ed), *ibid n..3.*

Narayanan, K.R. (1986), 'Relevance of Non-alignment', Kerala Journal of Political Studies, Vol.1, (1) January.

Nehru, Jawaharlal (1961) *India's Foreign Policy* Publications Division, Government of India.

Rupert, Mark (2003) 'Globalising Common Sense: a Marxian Gramscian (re-) vision of the Politics of Governance/Resistance', in David Amstrong et al; (ed.) *Governance and Resistance in World Politics*, Cambridge University Press, Cambridge.

Schou, August and Arne Olav Brundtland (eds.), (1971), *Small States in International Relations*, New York.

Stiglitz, Joseph, E. 'Globalism's Discontents', American Prospect, 12 January, 2002, accessed at: *http:// www. Globalpolicy.org/globalitz/econ/2002/0114 Stiglitz.htm* on November 24, 2004.

Taylor, Paul (2006) International *Organization in the Age of Globalisation*, Viva Continuum Edition, London.

Vanaik, Achin (2006) 'National Interest: A Flawed Notion, Indian Foreign Policy Since 1991', *Economic and Political Weekly,* Vol. XLI (49) December 9: 5045-5049.

Vanaik, Achin (2008) 'Post Cold War Indian Foreign Policy', *Seminar*, No.581, June.

Woods, Ngaire (2000) *The Political Economy of Globalisation*, St. Martin's Press, New York.

# 2

# Technology Transfer and India's Foreign Policy

Shaji. S

---

The role of technology and trade has been increasingly crucial in the shaping of international relations, especially after the disintegration of the Soviet Union and the consequent end of the Cold War in 1991. Against this backdrop, the present paper discusses in brief a few aspects pertaining to India's foreign policy vis-à-vis technology and trade since 1990s which is characterised by the ascendancy of globalisation. In the process it raises certain significant questions, such as: what are the major trends associated with technology/trade and its linkages with international relations under the ongoing process of globalisation? What impact has technology/trade had on India's foreign policy in the post-Cold War world? In the process, what are the new strategies and initiatives India undertook to address these issues.

The sequence of this paper is as follows: to begin with, a modest attempt has been made to locate India in the context of global economy. The analysis is carried out through the prism of the concepts of 'Hegemony' and 'Counter-Hegemony', a Gramscian theoretical framework. On the basis of the discussion, the paper analyses major shifts and changes pertaining to India's foreign policy vis-à-vis technology. The final part of the paper throws light on India's emerging relations with the developing world, with special reference to its regional and trans-regional alliances involving South Africa and Brazil as evidences of counter hegemonic alliances/tendencies. The discussion on these two countries assumes manifold significance because: like India, both South Africa and Brazil are middle level powers and emerging economies with apparently similar developmental experiences, possessing preponderant power status in their respective regions.

## General Setting for Change in India's Foreign Policy since the 1990s

After the collapse of the socialist bloc and the subsequent end of the Cold War on the international front and the launching of economic reforms under the process of globalisation, economic issues increasingly began to dominate foreign policy debates in India. In such a scenario, acquisition, development and trade/transfer of technology began to acquire significance, which in turn, impelled unprecedented changes in the major contours of India's foreign policy. Such contours of foreign policy called for new strategies that involved new alliances/linkages at the international level to leverage maximum economic benefits for the nation. In fact, the underlying assumption behind such changes is the fact that there is a strong hegemony in the realm of trade and technology in favour of the developed countries as global trade and transfer of technology is predominantly controlled by the global bodies such as the World Trade Organisation (WTO). Some of the prominent tools these global institutions employ to perpetuate hegemony include Trade Related Intellectual Property Rights (TRIPS) and Trade Related Investment Measures (TRIMS) and so on. The presence of hegemony in turn induces 'counter hegemonic' actions/tendencies in the system, which in turn shapes the contours of hegemony further.

In this context, the concept of hegemony helps us perceive the ongoing international power struggle between developed and developing countries vis-à-vis technology, both explicitly and implicitly, as evident from the formation of a hegemonic alliance/hegemonic order of transnational capitalist classes, predominantly concentrated in the developed states. To put it tersely, a hegemonic order is one where consent rather than coercion primarily characterizes the relations between states and civil societies, and trans-national capitalist classes have been seen to employ tools such as global trade rules, practices and patent regimes to hegemonize developing countries. In order to counter this hegemonic bloc, developing countries mobilise like-minded countries through several networks and alliances at the international level while restructuring their economy at the domestic level.

Although Gramsci initially conceived hegemony in the domestic context of state-civil society ties, the notion of hegemony has also been deployed in international relations. Prominent scholars including Stephen Gill and Robert Cox analyse international relations through the prism of Gramscian theory. Admittedly, there is no World State and the notion of the so-called international civil society is also in its embryonic form. Thus, stretching the concept that emerged in the context of domestic state-civil society ties across state boundaries is not free from complexities. Moreover, hegemony is organised by class forces. In this context, whether transnational class alliances constitute hegemony, is a doubtful proposition. Having spelt out the limitations of the Gramscian perspectives on international relations, it may be worthwhile to look at the arguments put forth by the Italian School of Marxism.

**Hegemony, Trade and Technology and Developed Countries**

In general, hegemony as a political concept was analysed and explained for the first time by the Italian Marxist theoretician, Antonio Gramsci. According to Gramsci, the concept of hegemony can be employed to analyse relations of forces in a given society. In a hegemonic set-up, the power of the ruling class, or class fractions, which dominate over the others, is partly exercised through the state. It is not simply a case of dominance through sanctions, punishments or inducement; it also involves intellectual and moral leadership. In fact, hegemony is exercised within a wider social and political constellation of forces or 'historic bloc'. The latter refers to a historical congruence between material forces, institutions and ideologies, or broadly, an alliance of different forces. Thus, a historic bloc refers to the organic link between 'political' and 'civil society'—a fusion of material, institutional, inter-subjective, theoretical and ideological capacities. [1]

In fact, such a historical bloc functions in this setting of the contemporary period, characterised by globalisation, information-based economies and transnational interdependence wherein power is becoming less transferable, less tangible, less coercive and more consent-based. Accordingly, technology, capital and knowledge have become prominent tools of 'consent formation', which in turn, relates to power equations in contemporary societies/states. In fact, there are many agencies within capitalist forces, which construct the contours of hegemony. As mentioned earlier, the widely accepted perception is that world trade regulating bodies like WTO and financial bodies like IMF and the World Bank act as the agencies of capitalist forces that have a well-knit nexus, which invariably favours developed states.

In a world, where capitalism dominates over other modes of production, several tools are employed by global corporations and other international trade and financial bodies, the major actors in a capitalistic system, to exercise hegemony over the developing states. This is because a cluster, which owns a certain means of production, is influenced by like-minded class fractions whose manifestation can be discerned in global corporations and other international organisations that represent the interests of developed states. Stephen Gill argues that these global corporations lobby with their governments in order to obtain policies favourable to their operations overseas. Such lobbying also takes place with regard to host governments, as well as international organisations, such as the World Bank (WB). Transnational financial networks are particularly well-developed and links between commercial banks, central banks, the International Monetary Fund (IMF) and the World Bank are evident in a number of international forums such as the Bank for International Settlements. [2]

In brief, if we apply the Gramscian concept of hegemony, the capitalist bloc evolves a particular type of consent among all sections or classes of people, through which hegemony operates. Technology (both military and civilian) is one of the major pillars of any form of production that no state can afford to lose. Technological capability determines the position of each state in the current global scenario. The international patent regime, envisaged in the provisions of the WTO which is in vogue since late 1990s is plausibly intended to help states to protect their patent rights over newly developed technologies. This aspect assumes added significance since technology has emerged as one of the major determinants of economic growth and competitiveness, which in turn consigns a state a place in the contemporary architecture and hierarchy of power. Currently, the role of technology is much larger than it was two or three decades ago. The next section examines the notion of counter-hegemonic strategies and their emergence in the present setting.

**The Concept of Counter-Hegemony**

The organisation and operation of hegemony under a historic bloc simultaneously stimulates hegemonic and counter hegemonic tendencies. [3] Interestingly, the formation of hegemony is dialectical in nature with the inherent capacity to absorb even the counter-hegemonic forces. Therefore, counter-hegemonic forces are also responsible for the shaping of the content and contours of hegemony. A counter-hegemonic force emerges against any historic bloc that stands for hegemony in capitalistic society. In fact, every historic bloc that stakes its claim for the hegemony in any social formation, leaves room for the development of a counter-hegemonic project. Thus, in the context of capitalistic hegemony, the discordant elements within the subaltern or subordinate classes rise to organize their counter-hegemonic project. [4] In substance, the major method of counter-hegemony is to expose the theoretical base of imperialism or world capitalism and to build resistance and strategies to nullify the effect of hegemonic tendencies. [5]

At the global level, there have been several such resistances against various manifestations of globalisation, especially against the WTO. For instance, the massive protest staged by people regardless of class, race, gender and region, against globalisation at the venue of the Third Ministerial Conference of the WTO on 30 November 1999 at Seattle and in subsequent Ministerial Conference such as Doha, Cancun and so on can be broadly counted as some instances of emerging counter-hegemonic projects. The 'battle in Seattle' and mass protests in other Ministerial Conference venues may be linked to new patterns of political agency and a movement that goes well beyond the politics of identity and difference. It encompasses aspects of gender, race and class. It is connected to the issues of ecological and social reproduction, and most importantly, to the question of democracy. [6] In sum, these movements are beginning to form what

Gramsci called an 'organism', a complex element of civil society, which resists the historic bloc in a capitalistic hegemony.

With a reflection of such a trend, at the supranational level, states began to weave counter hegemonic strategies such as restructuring domestic economies while reformulating their major premises of foreign policies as well as building alliances with likeminded countries through regional arrangements, in order to nullify the effects of globalisation and to maximize their leverages by sharing technologies and other developmental experiences. India, Brazil and South Africa initiated such strategies at their domestic and external fronts.

Looking through the prism of counter-hegemony, one can see several trends pertaining to India's new strategies at the domestic level and at the international level. At the domestic level, these strategies included India plunging into globalisation by initiating economic reforms and opening its door to FDI, relaxing licensing and so on. On the international front, India reformulated its foreign policy strategies such as Non-alignment by shedding its political emphasis and adding to it, economic aspects. Besides this, India forged new alliances, engaged in multi-directional linkages with major powers and gave new dynamism to regional groupings while breaking new pathways.

In view of the above discussion, the following section discusses in detail India's counter hegemonic strategies in the realm of foreign policy-the issues pertaining to interventions in global trade and financial organisations, Non-alignment, bilateral ties and regional arrangements involving likeminded countries from the region and other continents such as Africa and Latin America. However, this paper does not delve into the counter-hegemonic strategies at the domestic level. Though it is an important intellectual exercise, it forms the theme for a separate research paper. The section will discuss India's strategies in global financial/trade bodies, its ties with major powers and prominent regionalisation initiatives.

### India's Foreign Policy and Counter-Hegemonic Initiatives/Strategies

Developing states such as India began opposing the hegemonic tendencies of the developed states at official-level trade negotiations, especially the WTO. In case of India, there are several instances wherein India formed counter-hegemonic alliances at the international level. India allied with states from the developing world to fight against developed states regarding trade discrimination as evident from the solidarity in the Doha (2001) and Cancun (2003) rounds of the WTO negotiations. India mobilised developing states against certain discriminatory proposals like provisions on Agreement on Agriculture (AoA), General Agreement on Trade and Services (GATS) of the WTO, which plausibly favoured developed states. The triangle of India, South Africa and Brazil (IBSA) is an attempt to counter the hegemony of the capitalist bloc. Similarly, WTO related issues are now being taken seriously by regional groupings from the developing world such as the SAARC. A joint statement towards this end was released by the SAARC Commerce Minister in Male in August 1999. This was issued with a view to adopting a common position before of the Third WTO Ministerial Meeting at Seattle in 1999. At the same time, India makes use of certain provisions in the WTO to benefit from global trade. For instance, the WTO provision allows regional trading arrangement. This provision is being used by India to enter into new alliances to further its trade interest. Having stated India's strategies at the international level in brief, let us examine trends pertaining to changes in various contours of India's foreign policy vis-à-vis technology, so as to benefit from the present international economic system.

**Shifts in the Practice of Non-alignment**

In the realm of Non-alignment, the global factors that prompted India to adopt it included the Cold War, military alliances such as NATO, and the fear of imperialism, colonialism and war. In fact, Non-alignment has been widely seen as the singular feature of India's foreign policy since Independence. [7] But the fall of Soviet Union and the consequent end of Cold War substantially changed this scenario. This has deprived developing states like India the strategy of manoeuvring between the two super powers to defend their vital interests and bargain for the best deals for economic development. According to C. Raja Mohan, the end of the Cold War put India's attachment to the idea of Non-alignment into an unforgiving political spotlight. [8] The altered world forced India to examine the relevance of Non-alignment in the conduct of its external relations during the 1990s. As India reviewed its commitment to Non-alignment, it had to reconsider its earlier rejection of formal alliance with great powers. The decade also brought up the deeper questions of where India stood vis-à-vis the West, while the East and its economic model stood shattered. Consequently, India has had to redefine its relations with the Western powers on a more pragmatic basis.

Hence, there was a 'de-emphasis' on Non-alignment as the core principle of India's foreign policy in the 1990s. This can be discerned from India's increased proximity to the United States and other European powers, which had been hostile to India during the Cold War days. There is a widely held belief that though India has de-emphasized Non-alignment in practice, theoretically, it continues to be the official foreign policy plank.

### Multi-directional Engagement with All Major Powers

Similarly, India's relation with major powers became multi-dimensional in the 1990s. According to C. Raja Mohan, crafting an alliance-like relationship with the United States without giving up its special ties with Russia, exploring deeper relations with the European Union and Japan and managing the complex ties with China became the national objectives. [9] For instance, India's relations with the United States improved in the first half of the 1990s and then suffered a great deal after India's nuclear explosion in 1998. But the recently concluded Indo-US Deal has brought about a drastic shift in US policy towards India. Consequently, the US withdrew certain restrictions imposed on the transfer of nuclear and other rare technologies. As far as Russia is concerned, the erstwhile Soviet Union was the prime source of technology through their investments in heavy industries like iron and steel. It also contributed in the form of Foreign Direct Investment (FDI) to the infrastructure sector of India. Soviet Union also transferred technology and other required resources for the establishment of India's space programmes. All these facts did underscore a measure of Soviet influence in the economic and scientific domains. Because of strong Soviet influence on India's industrial base, the sudden breakdown of Soviet Union left India hapless. Despite the disintegration of the Soviet Union, India is still considerably dependent upon Russia for its defence and space technologies.

Similarly, India's ties with China improved significantly since the beginning of nineties, resulting in a substantial expansion of trade between India and China, which in turn provided a stabilising element that had not existed in the past. Starting from a few hundred million dollars in the mid-1990s, bilateral trade touched US$ 7.5 billion in the year 2003. [10] In 2008, China emerged as the largest trading partner of India with trade value surpassing 41.5 Billion in January-November 2008. [11] Coupled with India's commerce with Hong Kong and Taiwan, Greater China today has emerged as the prominent trading partner of India. While Sino-Indian trade has many structural limitations, it has not showed any sign of slowing down and continues to grow rapidly. The most interesting feature of Sino-Indian relations is that New Delhi and Beijing no longer consider each other as potential enemies but as partners and are involved in new initiatives wherein they cooperate in trans-regional energy and economic projects. The national oil companies of India and China today bid for equity oil all around the world and occasionally find themselves in the same consortium, for example in Sudan. [12]

### Breaking New Pathways

Since the 1990s, India has engaged with several states that were at the other end of the ideological spectrum during the Cold War period. For instance, India established relations with Israel for the first time in 1992. India had not recognised Israel until then on account of two reasons: first, India did not want to support Israel as the latter was an ally of the United States during Cold War. Second, India was an ardent supporter of the Palestinian cause. Nonetheless, the association of India with the Jewish state since the early nineties resulted in large-scale technology transfer, especially in the Defence sector. This led to the exchange of visits by high ranking officials and Heads of Governments and States. [13] Likewise, India's relations with South Africa reached an all-time high in the 1990s after the abolition of apartheid. This resulted in cooperation in the realm of trade and technology. Further, India's quest for energy security prompted India to further its ties with states such as Venezuela, Nigeria, Algeria, Angola, Sudan etc, especially in the oil sector, while tying up with Iran for natural gas. This all-comprehensive relation resulted in dynamic economic and technology cooperation.

**Increased Dynamism in Regional Cooperation**

In the 1990s, there was an enormous rise in the flow of capital to these emerging markets, which in turn brightened their economies while propping up certain problems. One of the consequences of this development was the intensification of interdependence among states and heightening of the perception of interdependence. Regional economic integration efforts such as the European Union (EU), the North America Free Trade Agreement (NAFTA) and the Asia Pacific Economic Cooperation (APEC) are just a few examples of this heightened perception of interdependence. In the South Asian region, regional integration has taken solid shape through the process of the South Asian Association for Regional Cooperation (SAARC), generating a new partial free trade arrangement called the South Asian Preferential Trading Arrangement (SAPTA) in the year 1997.

Another prominent regional grouping in which India joined in the period of reform was the Indian Ocean Rim Association for Regional Cooperation (IOR-ARC) in 1997. This policy was envisaged to enhance cooperation at the bilateral and at the multilateral levels, especially in economic matters. In view of the progress and the growth of this organisation in the last ten years, one can confidently say that IOR-ARC can take huge strides towards technology cooperation among Indian Ocean States.

On similar lines, the 'Look East' policy of India assumed greater significance in this period. This was yet another consequence of India's economic reforms, initiated in the year 1991. The scope and density of relations between India and the ten-member, Association of South East Asian Nations (ASEAN) has been steadily growing. India became a sectoral dialogue partner of ASEAN in 1992. The sectors wherein India joined for dialogue were trade, investment, tourism and science and technology. [14] Mutual interest in wider engagement led ASEAN to invite India to become a full dialogue partner of ASEAN during the fifth ASEAN summit in Bangkok in December 1995 and a member of the ASEAN Regional Forum (ARF) in July 1996. Consequently, India is engaging with ASEAN through ASEAN-India Summits the first of which was held in Phnom Penh, Cambodia in November 2002. India strengthened its ties with ASEAN through various bilateral summits and a recent free trade treaty with ASEAN, signed in 2009, is quite noteworthy, notwithstanding the criticism it received from various quarters.

Among the regional groupings outside South Asia, the contribution of the European Union (EU) in technology transfer deserves specials mention. Indeed, the European Union is one of the largest trading partners of India. The First Summit between the European Union and India was held at Lisbon, Portugal on June 28, 2000. In the summit, both the parties resolved to continue trade links in mutually beneficial areas and recognized the significant growth achieved by India with respect to Information Technology (IT). The summit went on to recognise the mutual benefits of a substantial increase in the flow of investment, technology, expertise and services between the European Union and India in this knowledge-based economy. [15] For instance, the European Union has decided to establish an Institute of Environmental Technology in India as a token gesture for promoting technological cooperation between India and the European Union.

From the above discussion, one can draw certain conclusions. India has increasingly involved in the regionalisation process at various levels-within the region as well as inter-regional-in the post-Cold War era. Such a process of regionalisation, besides its strategic, geo-political and foreign policy dimensions has been a major plank for development cooperation and integration with other parts of the world. In order to compete with other states with regards to the acquisition of technology under globalisation, regionalism as a strategy is being widely employed by India. In a way, the end of the Cold War coupled with the process of globalisation, has prompted India to effectively formulate policies and participate in regional groupings. These groupings can act as a viable medium to control the onslaught of free markets, guided by global financial and trade bodies under the ongoing march of capitalism. In addition, technology and capital can be traded among member states of a regional grouping, which reduces costs of purchasing technology from transnational corporations and developed states.

Having discussed major changes in various aspects of India's foreign policy at the macro level, the next section analyses India's involvement in regional arrangements with like-minded countries such as South Africa and Brazil, two prominent states from the continents of Africa and Latin America, in the realm of technology/trade, as an evidence of its counter-hegemonic strategy. Here, the paper focuses on two regional arrangements in which India and South Africa share a common platform while the third one highlights an arrangement wherein India and South Africa align with Brazil in a trans-regional integration.

**India, South Africa and Brazil: Regional and Trans-regional Alliances**

There are several opportunities for India to have trade and transfer of technology with countries from Africa and Latin America, which can be channelized through durable arrangements built on the principle of mutual benefits, which in turn can promote economic growth in their respective regions. Apart from the larger goals of South-South cooperation, creation of larger and more integrated markets, facilitation of cross-border investment and allowing the free movement of people and exchange of ideas, carries economic as well as political benefits. It serves two basic purposes when states involved in cooperation belong to the developing world. First, these linkages promote South-South cooperation and secondly, it gives developing states a strong voice while urging advanced economies to reform their trade practices and thereby act as counter-hegemonic blocs. With these parameters in view, in the present paper three regional groupings are taken for discussion. These are: the Indian Ocean Rim Association for Regional Cooperation (IOR-ARC), India-South African Development Community (SADC) Forum and the India-Brazil-South Africa Alliance (IBSA).

**Indian Ocean Rim Association for Regional Cooperation (IOR-ARC)**

In fact, India's participation in the IOR-ARC has been inspired by the Nehruvian vision of Afro-Asian solidarity. The alliance with IOR-ARC gives an additional dimension to growing bilateral relations between India and South Africa. For Indian exporters, South Africa can eventually serve as a transit point for markets in the neighbouring African states as well as in South America. In this context, efforts have been made to make the Indian Ocean Rim Association a reality. This would not only be beneficial for over fifty littoral states but also boost India-South Africa economic interaction. Agreement has been reached to give the IOR initiative substantive content through practical cooperation in various projects. [16] Against this backdrop, India and South Africa played an important role in the successful launch of the IOR-ARC in Mauritius in 1997. The basic founding principle of this organization was to expand trade and investment among the states of the Indian Ocean region. [17] Its membership includes Australia, Bangladesh, India, South Africa, Indonesia, Iran, Kenya, Malaysia, Mozambique, Madagascar, Oman, Sri Lanka and so on. There have been several initiatives by India as well as other members to strengthen the organization. A high Level Task Force (HLTF) was set up by the Council of Ministers of IOR-ARC to look into organizational issues, such that economic and trade relations could be strengthened. [18]

Under the institutional setup of the IOR-ARC, FICCI [19] has also established an Indian Ocean Rim Business Centre (IOR-BC). Furthermore, this initiative has created an online business community, called IOR-NET, to allow interactions among the participating community. IOR-NET is also managed by FICCI. In addition, India has facilitated the conduction of workshops on IT and E-Commerce for trade facilitation. India has also undertaken workshops on Maritime transport issues and disaster mitigation and management in the IOR-ARC summit meeting on the 7th and the 8th of April in 2001, at Muscat in Oman. [20] The IOR-ARC member states account for about 7 percent of the world trade. Currently, South Africa is involved in two projects: a regional ports initiative and a financial systems harmonization initiative. At present, India is involved in the core group of the IOR-ARC, which intends to carry out a feasibility study for the establishment of a Preferential Trading Agreement (PTA), among the IOR-ARC states. [21] The next section discusses India–Southern African Development Council (SADC) Forum, a prominent economic grouping in the region.

**India-Southern African Development Community (SADC) Forum**

The Southern African Development Cooperation Council (SADCC) was formed in 1993 on the principle of greater South-South Cooperation. In 1997, Southern African Development Cooperation Council (SADCC) was renamed as South African Development Community (SADC). The renaming was warranted in the context of South Africa entering the organization. In fact, it strengthened the trade relationship of SADC states with other states, including India. India too realized the potential of such relations through regional cooperation. Consequently, a Memorandum of Understanding on cooperation between India and the SADC was concluded on October 14, 1997, which envisages both government and private sector cooperation and includes short and long term training, participation in joint ventures in areas like infrastructure, telecommunications, agriculture, automotive parts and leather products, and assistance in the development of small and medium enterprises in the Southern African region. [22] India-SADC Forum was formally launched following the approval of India's proposal by the SADC Ministerial Meeting in Luanda in 2003. [23] By this decision, India furthered its relations with all the members of the SADC. Simultaneously, India has also tried to further its relationship with other members of the SADC as a counter alliance to the hegemony of the First World.

A study by EXIM Bank notes that India had robust trade relations with SADC states, with the trade turnover more than doubling from US$ 1.5 billion in 1997-98 to US$ 3.4 billion in 2003-04. India's trade balance however, has changed from a surplus of US$ 68 million to a deficit of US$ 818.1 million over the same period. This is primarily due to almost a threefold increase of Indian imports from SADC over the period, while exports have not varied significantly over the years. [24] According to the study, potential exists to further enhance exports to the region, based on the import demand in these states and India's export capability. The SADC states offer potential for a wide range of products which include, among others, transport equipments, machinery and electrical goods, textiles, iron & steel, rubber & plastic products, road vehicles & parts, and wood & wood products. These states can also be important sources for import of copper & nickel, meat & meat products, diamonds, raw & processed cashew nuts, gold, coffee and electronic goods. [25]

Against the backdrop of the discussion on emerging trends in regional groupings in Africa and Asia in which India is a major partner, the next section analyses initiatives of India and South Africa for global alliances with particular reference to India-Brazil-South Africa Alliance (IBSA).

**India, Brazil and South Africa Alliance (IBSA)**

India and South Africa are members in a tripartite global alliance, along with Brazil from Latin America. In fact, the idea of IBSA had emerged out of the absence of an effective forum for South-South Cooperation. Another major objective of IBSA was to build a credible counter coalition against the hegemonic practices of the developed states at the international level. Broadly, this setup is an attempt to resist the imposition of a world order that seek the disempowerment of the developing states.

India, Brazil and South Africa established a Trilateral Dialogue Forum in June 2003. In fact, this forum was formed to boost trade and pool their political muscle in talks with developed states. [26] It was also decided that the three states would collectively address the issues of global concern. These include issues in the areas of socio-economic development, technology and those pertaining to global governance. [27] Indeed, this trans-continental dialogue forum has enhanced the space of South-South cooperation. In the words of the former President of South Africa, Thabo Mbeki these three likeminded states from three different continents represent large vibrant democracies with strong economies and rich human and natural resources. By providing an avenue for utilizing the potential synergies among the members, it is expected to contribute to the revitalization of South-South cooperation. [28] Developing states such as India, South Africa, Nigeria and Brazil have been playing an active role in defining the parameters of the World Trade Organization's (WTO) future programs. In the process, the issue based coalitions of developing states is supposed to add to their bargaining leverage and permit them to participate in world trading arrangements on better terms. [29] In fact, IBSA together with other important developing states were able to work effectively in the negotiations of G-20 or G-21 on the question of subsidies and through G-16 on the issue of new agenda items introduced in the Singapore Declaration of the WTO. In the WTO Ministerial Conference, this triangle opposed the existing Trade Related Intellectual Property Rights (TRIPS) Agreement on drugs and extracted a declaration by changing certain discriminatory provisions. The declaration clearly states that the TRIPS Agreement should not prevent members from taking measures to protect public health and, in particular, to promote access to medicine by all. [30]

Besides, this coalition has helped developing states in building resistance against the bulwark of developed states, as evident in the WTO negotiations in Doha in 2005 and in Hong Kong in 2006. The efforts of this tripartite alliance to resist the attempt of developed states to impose Trade Related Intellectual Property Rights (TRIPs) on developing states through the WTO are noteworthy. South Africa also adopted the 'New Delhi Agenda for Cooperation-a South-South cooperation agreement with India and Brazil in 2005.

In fact, IBSA identified a set of issues such as UN Reforms, proliferation of Weapons of Mass Destruction and terrorism as the core concerns of the forum. [31] Similarly, on trilateral cooperation, South Africa mooted the idea that India, Brazil and South Africa could consider starting a joint program to produce medium-sized passenger aircrafts, a venture which could pool India's expertise in military aircraft, Brazil's capabilities in producing passenger planes and South Africa's expertise in electronics. [32] The initiative shows eagerness on the part of three nations to develop an alliance for sharing technology for tangible benefits for all the parties involved.

Similarly, IBSA, along with the G4 (comprising India, Brazil, South Africa, and China) and the G20, has been instrumental in an effort to develop a 'middle ground' on trade negotiations in the WTO. In short, IBSA stands for South-South cooperation and IBSA presses for issues of poor states' development in WTO and

UN debates. At the same time, India, Brazil and South Africa, attempt to help each other in building their own economies by sharing technology and developmental experiences. The trade among the three countries increased from US$ 3.9 million in 2003-2006 to approximately US$ 10.4 billion in the year 2007-2008. [33] Over the years, Brazil has emerged as India's biggest partner in the Latin America and Caribbean region with bilateral trade crossing the 3 billion mark in 2007. Bilateral trade increased to US$ 3.12 billion in 2007 from merely US$ 488 million in 2000. [34]

Notwithstanding these positive trends, there is no official mechanism such as a Secretariat in place, to monitor and operationalize the ties among the three countries of IBSA on a regular basis. However, the alliance is strengthened through Annual Summits of Heads of States and Governments that began in 2006, in Brasilia. Since then there have been summits in each country, with the last one held in New Delhi in 2009. There is a Trilateral Joint Commission in place though it meets annually. Another notable event is that, in 2004, IBSA created a Trust Fund, managed by the UNDP. It is a relevant innovation, considering the circle of traditional donors. The IBSA Fund aims at supporting viable and replicable projects based on the capabilities available in the IBSA countries and on their internal best practises, which could contribute to the national priorities of other developing countries. [35]

**Concluding Remarks**

To sum up, India's foreign policy has had to accommodate the changed scenario at the global level following the disintegration of the Soviet Union and the subsequent victory of capitalism. India redefined its traditional foreign policy goals like Non-alignment so as to acquire more technology and foreign direct investment from different states. All these processes have to be understood in the larger framework of hegemony at the international level represented by capitalist forces. In fact, states such as India have been weaving counter-hegemonic strategies to nullify the adverse impact of uneven global economy by restructuring their relations with states from the western bloc and reinvigorating their traditional ties with other states, such as post-Soviet Russia, in the case of India, while restructuring their domestic economies. Besides, India is slowly building closer ties with middle-level powers such as South Africa and Brazil as well as tying up with them in regional and trans-regional integrationist initiatives such as the IOR-ARC, India-SADC Forum, IBSA and so on. Such regional and trans-regional arrangements, though enunciated in the wake of globalisation in the 1990s, have now begun to take shape and are likely to emerge as major forces in the future. While serving economic benefits, regional and trans-regional alliances are considered as counter-hegemonic strategies against hegemonic trade and technology transfer practises of the developed world, especially by states like India. In brief, attaining economic strength through robust and enduring alliances and linkages so as to wield power in the arena of international relations has become one of the new mantras of India's foreign policy since the 1990s.

### Notes

1. Stephen Gill and David Law. 1993. "Global Hegemony and the Structural Power of Capital'' in Stephen Gill (Ed) *Gramsci: Historical Materialism and International Relations*, Cambridge: Cambridge University Press. p. 94.
2. Stephen Gill. 1993. pp. 101-103.
3. Rajen Harshe. 1997. *Twentieth Century Imperialism*. New Delhi: Sage Publication. pp. 163.
4. Ibid.: p. 162.
5. There are mainly three approaches in understanding foreign policy in the counter-hegemonic tradition: the Instrumentalist Approach, the World System Approach and the Neo-Gramscian Approach.
6. Stephen Gill. 2000. "Towards a post modern Prince? The battle in Seattle as a Moment in the New Politics of Globalisation", *Millennium*, 29 (1): 131-140.
7. C. Raja Mohan. 2003. *Crossing the Rubicon: The Shaping of India's New Foreign Policy*. New Delhi: Viking India.
8. Ibid.
9. C. Raja Mohan. 2003. p. 56.
10. C. Raja Mohan. 2004. "India and China: a shifting paradigm", *The Hindu*, July 29.
11. Information in the website of China's Consulate General Office in Kolkota, http://kolkata.china-consulate.org (Accessed on 11 November 2009)
12. Ibid.
13. India established its mission in Israel in 1994,and Israel in India in 1995. Indian Prime Minister Atal Behari Vajpayee visited Israel in 1999. Israel Prime Minister Ariel Sharon visited India in 2003. Indian Home Minister L.K. Advani visited Israel in 2003.
14. Rahul Sen, Mukul G. Asher and Ramakrishna Rajan. 2004. "ASEAN-India Economic Relations: Current Status and Future Prospectus", *Economic and Political Weekly*, 39(29): 3297-3308.
15. Documents, The First Indo-European Union Summit in Lisbon, June, 2000 in *World Affairs*, 4(3): 141-146.
16. Jerry Matsila's argument quoted in Saxena, S.C. 1997. "India and Southern Africa: The Emerging Relationship", *Africa Quarterly*, 37 (3-4): 1-26.
17. Government of India. 2003. *Annual Report 2002-2003*. New Delhi: Policy Planning and Research Division. Ministry of External Affairs. p. 100.
18. Government of India. 2003. *Annual Report 2002-2003*. New Delhi: Policy Planning and Research Division. Ministry of External Affairs. p. 105.
19. S. Sunandana. 1999 : 27-34.
20. Government of India. 2002. *Annual Report 2001-2002*. New Delhi: Policy Planning and Research Division. Ministry of External Affairs. p. 100.
21. Government of India. 2004. *Annual Report 2003-2004*. New Delhi: Policy Planning and Research Division. Ministry of External Affairs. p. 122.

22. Government of India. 1998. *Annual Report 1997-1998*. New Delhi: Policy Planning and Research Division. Ministry of External Affairs. p. 63.
23. Government of India. 2004. *Annual Report 2003-2004*. New Delhi: Policy Planning and Research Division. Ministry of External Affairs. p. 70.
24. Data gathered from the website of EXIM Bank of India, http://www.eximbankindia.com. (Accessed May 25, 2006).
25. Ibid.
26. Mahendra Gaur. 2005. *Foreign Policy Annual 2004: Events, Part I*. New Delhi: Kalpaz Publications. p. 211.
27. Thabo Mbeki. 2003. Speech Delivered by Mbeki Thabo, President of South Africa at the Indian Council of World Affairs, New Delhi. October 16. *Africa Quarterly*, 43(3): 83-90.
28. Thabo Mbeki. 2003. Joint Declaration by India and South Africa on the Occasion of the State Visit to India By Thabo Mbeki, President of South Africa. *Africa Quarterly*, 43(3):102-106.
29. Rajen Harshe and KM Seethi, eds. 2005. *Engaging with the World: Critical Reflections on India's Foreign Policy*. New Delhi: Orient Longman. p. 456.
30. Soumyen Sikdar. 2003. *Contemporary Issues in Globalisation: An Introduction to Theory and Policy in India*, New Delhi: Oxford University Press. p. 180.
31. Ibid.
32. Data gathered from the website of Consulate of Indian in Johannesburg, South Africa, http://www.indconjoburg.co.za (accessed on May 25, 2006).
33. Woodrow Wilson International Centre for Scholars (2009) *Emerging Powers: India, Brazil and South Africa: The Future of South-South Cooperation*, Special report, August, Washington. D.C, p. 5.
34. Data gathered from the website of Directory on Indian Industry, *http://www.indianindustry.com* (Accessed on 15 November, 2009).
35. Woodrow Wilson International Centre for Scholars (2009), p. 11.

# 3

# Managing Indian Economic Diplomacy in the Era of Globalization

M. Basheer Ahmed Khan

## Introduction

Since the cessation of international hostilities following the demise of the Soviet Union, the world witnessed a new found enthusiasm among nations of to cooperate amongst themselves for mutual benefit. This cooperation took the shape of economic relations among the states. With the collapse of the Second World it became easier for world economies to move closer despite political distances. What emerged as the triple concepts of 'Liberalization, Privatization and Globalization', offered more opportunities for world economies to find their own partners in development and co-creation of growth. Every country was very much aware of the 'open' world and the opportunities that were thrown up, notwithstanding the embedded challenges and threats. It is here that the concept of economic diplomacy sprung up as a decent practice for economies to show their 'economic state craft', besides statesmanship. In fact, economic diplomacy allowed nations to 'go deep into domestic decision making' too. A world of economic competition is as much or even more dangerous than political competition. The Harvard concepts of 'Red Ocean strategies' and 'Blue Ocean Strategies' remind us of war and peace. To gain access to foreign resources, to promote exports, to invite foreign investments are matters of great economic interest to nations and one nation's gain can be another nation's loss unless a win-win strategy is played through diplomatic mechanisms. It is here that nations have to manage their economic diplomacy and India is no exception in the era of globalization. There are considerable suggestions, initiatives and efforts to manage Indian Economic Diplomacy in an era of globalization.

## Economic Diplomacy

According to S.K. Dutta (2007), the term 'economic diplomacy' is of a very recent origin. It originated in the late 1960s. Earlier economic diplomacy was known as trade diplomacy. Although everyone has a general idea about economic diplomacy, there exists no exact definition of it. In a general sense it would mean exchange and promotion of ideas and issues on the exchange of goods, services, labour and investments to other countries.

In a more focused way, it would refer to the diplomatic service activities focused on increasing export, attracting foreign investments and participating in the work of international economic organizations, i.e. the activities generally focused on the affirmation of economic interests of a country at the international level. Rana (2007) defines economic diplomacy as 'the process through which countries tackle the outside world, to maximize their national gain in all fields of activities including trade, investment and other forms of economically beneficial exchanges, wherein they enjoy comparative advantage; it has bilateral, regional and multilateral dimensions, each of which is important'.

Berridge and James (2003) state that 'economic diplomacy is concerned with economic policy questions, including the work of delegations to conferences sponsored by bodies such as the WTO,' and include 'diplomacy which employs economic resources, either as rewards or sanctions, in pursuit of a particular foreign policy objective,' also as a part of the definition. The definition is even widened when said that it covers 'policies relating to production, movement or exchange of goods, services, instruments (including official development assistance), money information and their regulation' (Bayne and Woolcock (eds.) 2007). Further, economic diplomacy is not only played by governments, but also other non-state actors like NGOs (ibid.). As we can observe here, economic diplomacy has a broader spectrum in terms of decision-making, policy-making and the advocacy of the business interests of the states. As such, it requires meticulous planning, organizing, finding out the experts and putting them in place, giving them appropriate inputs from time to time and monitoring. It also has to be provided with appropriate budgets to ensure that the goals of economic diplomacy are obtained by the nations who enter into it.

Hence, economic diplomacy requires sound management to achieve its desired goals. Application of technical expertise that analyzes the effects of a country's economic situation on its political climate and economic interests through diplomacy is a major issue in managing economic diplomacy. The states involved in economic diplomacy, foreign business experts and business leaders, government decision makers all need to work together to address various issues of interest in foreign policy like technology development and cooperation, environmental concerns, health concerns along with trade and finance. Execution of economic diplomacy will be successful only when it is knitted with flexibility, versatility, strong business skills and sound judgment of the situation. With the advent of globalization, the situation- both political and economic-has become more complex for nations around the world. The avowed openness on the one hand and the need for retaining political and national ideologies on the other leads to greater fragility of the situation and the nations have to maintain their economic interests through carefully considered economic diplomacy for which more attention needs to be paid. The Indian situation is very precarious under these conditions. There is a pertinent need for building up economic diplomacy for India with opportunities abounding and economic needs compelling.

**India's Efforts at Managing Economic Diplomacy**

"India's 'economic diplomacy' has become more important now to protect and promote our commercial interests in an era of globalization and to face the challenges and exploit opportunities thrown up by a fast integrating world" (M.P. Gavai, 2009). This and similar statements from several people in offices that matter, clearly send a message that there is a national awareness about the need to orient our foreign policy in a way which would provide the right course of action for economic diplomacy as well. According to S. Dutta (2007), "India has begun sharpening its economic diplomatic wits in a bid to protect and promote economic and commercial interests in an era of globalization. Economic diplomacy is being pursued at different levels to achieve objectives of projection of India as a major economic power, multilateral trade and economic negotiations, regional and bilateral trade agreements, access to foreign resources, promotion of exports and Indian businesses abroad, and promotion of foreign investments in India." He further adds "In an attempt to bring about a change in mindsets, the government has already started orienting and retraining existing diplomats. A proactive attitude is fast replacing yesterday's passive approach. Contours of this are gradually being felt in the direction of India's foreign policy in the last couple of years with the formation of several economic and strategic fora by India at the global level" (Dutta, 2007, ibid).

Economic Diplomacy in action has seen several trade groupings. For example, in 2003 the India-Brazil-South Africa (IBSA) was the result of the meeting of the Heads of these three nations. The emergence of SAFTA was the result of the SAARC grouping. According to the Pakistan Prime Minister Mr. Shaukat Aziz the SAFTA, "would make more effective market access through smooth implementation of trade liberalization programs". If the SAARC grouping can be engaged in economic cooperation, the possibility of political cooperation need not be brushed aside. India could also make its presence in such groupings like G8, ASEAN and Shanghai Cooperation through which India could have greater economic participation both domestically and internationally.

As a planned step towards promoting economic interests, India has been orienting its foreign policy with initiatives of economic diplomacy and has been engaging nations of South East Asia and East Asia. The concept of South-South cooperation has also been a part of this economic diplomacy. The Non-Aligned Movement in which India played a major role all through has also been a measure to safeguard its economic interest in the first place by maintaining equal distance from the western world and the erstwhile Soviet Bloc.

**Conclusion**

In short, in the emerging environment of globalization, opportunities are springing up that can be streamlined in the interest of nations. Economic development is the concern of all nations, besides political dominance. In the sphere of economic development, given the resource crunch, jostling and elbowing are natural. It is here that the role of economic diplomacy arises. Diplomatic efforts have to ensure adopting a win-win strategy for even politically competing nations to ensure peaceful coexistence so as to optimize economic benefits. This requires an unprecedented managerial skill among career diplomats and their political bosses. India has been in the forefront of economic diplomacy since its independence. However, efforts put in by the concerned have been far less than desired. One of the recent successes has been that of the civil nuclear deal with the US, besides other nations like France. Yet there still is a long way to go to manage the economic diplomacy of India in the era of globalization with equations rapidly changing. Today, there are cooperative efforts among the US, Russia, China, Italy, Japan, Germany etc., which were warring against each other once upon a time. It is generally believed that in a liberalized and globally networked environment, much more needs to be done by India. Its current approach is deemed to be obsolete and traditional.

If economic diplomacy is to be managed professionally, it should be built into the foreign policy of the country serving the overall strategic interest of India. Such issues like dealing with neighbours, preparing defence requirements and mechanisms, ensuring energy security and attaining the political position to be a part of UN bodies including the membership of the UNSC.

Economic Diplomacy should aim at addressing the growing concerns of Indian business and exporting groups including that of achieving a strong position in multilateral trade forums. It should strive to get the best possible terms in our preferential trade agreements.

India should be able to achieve that position so that it attracts its share of foreign investment vis-à-vis other countries of Asia. It should reach investing groups abroad such that India can make available its large pool of technical and other resources to their advantage by enhancing competitive efficiency.

India's strength in terms of business outsourcing and the geographical potential for different business opportunities must be communicated effectively.

The current abilities of Indian corporate houses and their efforts to make overseas investments must be facilitated. The diplomatic missions can do a lot for information gathering, facilitation and providing assistance in terms of operations and safety.

Indian corporates will also be able to make strategic investments in infrastructure and technology build-up if appropriate support is made available through Indian diplomatic channels.

It is here that economic diplomacy efforts have to be modern, scientific, professional and informed. A commitment to make economic diplomacy the front arm of the country, training career diplomats in various intrinsic nuances, building up a large data pool, monitoring efforts appropriately, re-designing the diplomatic agenda and assigning a decent budget, are some professional requirements that would go to ensure that India remains a forerunner amongst nations who gain from economic diplomacy. Managing economic diplomacy in the era of globalization has to be based on these issues.

# 4

# India's Energy Security: Challenges and Opportunities

A. Subramanyam Raju

---

## Introduction

Energy availability is one of the foremost requirements of any country to grow economically and to prosper. It is being considered as central to the next revolutionary technological change, transforming our lives. [1] Thus energy security [2] has become an important concern to most of the countries in the world. India in its 2006 Integrated Energy Policy report defines energy security as, "The country is energy secure when we can supply lifeline energy to all our citizens as well as meet their effective demand for safe and convenient energy to satisfy various needs at affordable costs at all times with a prescribed confidence level considering shock and disruptions that can be reasonably expected." [3]

Economic reforms, population growth, urbanization, demographic transformation and a growing transport sector in India are resulting in a rapid demand for more and more energy. India has low levels of energy production and per capita consumption. Many people in India still lack access to electricity for their basic needs. The demand for energy consumption is likely to increase in future. India is largely dependent on energy imports. Energy security is linked up with both growth and poverty. On one hand India has to provide enough commercial energy for growth and on the other hand it has to minimize the inequality between urban and rural people's consumption levels of energy. [4] India has been projected to be the third largest economy by 2020 and is trying to transcend its role beyond South Asia to the rest of the world. It realized the need for coherent and enduring foreign energy security policy to secure energy imports at affordable prices and without any disturbance. Its energy policy is linked to both-the political and the security domains. It has been exploring various options to meet its demands through investments abroad and through bilateral/multilateral cooperation in the energy sector.

The paper analyzes the existing energy situation in India and its investments abroad. This paper further analyzes the problems and prospects of bilateral and multilateral cooperation with neighbouring countries in the energy sector.

In most of the rural areas of India, people use non-commercial energy for their consumption. Though non-commercial energy causes air pollution leading to respiratory, heart and lung problems [5], it reduces imports of oil and gas. There are about 600 million Indians, who do not have access to electricity and over 700 million people are using traditional biomass as the primary fuel for most of their basic needs. [6] There are about 80,000 villages, which are yet to be electrified. Out of these 18,000 villages can be electrified by using renewable resources. Apart from the inability of the government, rural people are often not in a position to pay electricity bills and instead they use sources like firewood, cow dung, agricultural residue and kerosene.

**India's Energy Security Scenario**

The Indian government had set up a group on *India's Hydrocarbon Vision 2025* in February 1999. The recommendations put forth by the group are: 100 percent exploration coverage of Indian sedimentary basins by 2025; exploration in frontier and deep water areas; offering of attractive fiscal terms; investment abroad in exploration of oil and gas resources; self-sufficiency in Petroleum refining and Storage of oil in various locations.

**Table 4.1.: India's Position in Global Energy Production and Trade, 2004**

| | Crude Oil (Mt) | Coal (Mt) | Natural Gas (BCM) | Petroleum Products (Mt) |
|---|---|---|---|---|
| Global Production | 3,923 | 5,878 | 28,721 | 3,719 |
| Indian Production* | 34 (0.87) | 430 (7.32) | 32 (0.11) | 108 (2.9) |
| Indian Consumption* | 130 (3.31) | 454 (7.72) | 32 (0.11) | 107 (2.9) |
| Global Trade* | 2235 (56.97) | 778 (13.24 ) | 838 (29.18 ) | 825 (22.18 ) |
| Indian Imports** | 96 (4.30) | 37 (4.76) | 6.9 | 9.75 (1.18 ) |
| Indian Imports Dependence | 73.85 | 8.15 | --- | --- |

*Figures in parentheses are percentage of global production; **Figures in parentheses are percentage of global trade

Source: EIA, *International Energy Outlook* 2006, Washington DC: US Energy Information Administration, 2006, cited in Nitya Nanda, "Trading in the World Energy", in Logia Noronha and Anant Sudarshan (ed), *India's Energy Security*, London: Routledge, 2009, p. 52.

India's energy production and its trade are given in Table 4.1. The table reveals that India is depending more on importing oil than on importing other resources. It is the sixth largest importer with a share of 4.3 percent. Though India produces a large amount of coal but it has become the sixth largest importer of coal. India's trade in natural gas is not as significant because of infrastructural constraints and liquefied natural gas imports started only in 2004.

The future energy requirements of India are given in Table 4.2. The energy demands from 1990-2020 are going to increase rapidly. For instance, the demand for oil and coal would almost quadruple by 2020. India, by 2020, would require seven times more gas than what it consumed in 1990 and, it would require five times greater hydropower, than it consumed in 1990. It is interesting to note that demand for nuclear energy, crop residue, fuel wood and animal waste would not increase by 2020. It is clear that India has to depend on import of oil, gas and hydroelectricity from other countries.

**Table 4.2: Energy Supply: Future Projection for India**

| Fuel | 1990 | 2000 | 2010 | 2020 |
|---|---|---|---|---|
| Coal: | 3,850 | 7,145 | 10,508 | 15,516 |
| Indigenous | 3,850 | 7,145 | 10,508 | 15,167 |
| Imports | ------ | ------ | ------- | 349 |
| Oil: | 2,416 | 4,245 | 7,553 | 10,723 |
| Indigenous | 1,410 | 1,592 | 1,774 | 1,955 |
| Imports | 1,006 | 2,653 | 5,759 | 8,768 |
| Gas: | 480 | 1,002 | 1,909 | 3,478 |
| Indigenous | 480 | 1,000 | 667 | 533 |
| Imports | ----- | 2 | 1,242 | 2,945 |
| Hydro | 249 | 324 | 625 | 917 |
| Nuclear | 24 | 31 | 25 | 12 |
| Total Commercial energy | 7,019 | 12,747 | 20,600 | 30,646 |
| Crop residue | 763 | 763 | 763 | 763 |
| Fuel wood | 3,134 | 3,134 | 3,134 | 3,134 |
| Animal waste | 1,314 | 1,227 | 1,113 | 939 |
| Total traditional energy | 5,211 | 5,124 | 5,010 | 4,836 |

Source: http:www.teriin.org/energy/security.htm

In 2002, India spent Rs. 84,000 crore to obtain oil to meet sixty nine percent of its oil fuel needs. [7] Its crude oil requirement is seen as growing to 364 mtpa by 2025 from 100 mtpa of now. India's economy is growing since the economic reforms were undertaken. If it has to grow at the rate of eight percent as per projection there should be uninterrupted supply of oil. Most of its oil comes from the Middle East. This may make India vulnerable to any event that may cause instability in that region. Any disruption in the oil supplies from the region or any price hike by the oil producers of the region could affect India's economy.

**Nuclear Energy**

India is presently able to produce about three percent (4000 Mw) nuclear energy. In 2002, the installed electricity capacity was about 139 Giga Watts. During 2002-2003 electricity production was about 639 Terra Watt hours (Twh), where 67 percent from coal-based stations, 20 percent from oil and gas, 10 percent from hydro and 3 percent from nuclear. India's requirements of energy by 2052 indicate that the total installed capacity will have to be about 1,350 Giga Watts and the total generation about 8,000 Twh. Of this, the coal and hydrocarbon (oil and gas) contributions would have gone down to 47 and 16 percent and hydro to 8 percent. The nuclear component is required to go up to 26 percent. [8]

Realizing its energy needs, India has recently signed an agreement with the US on peaceful nuclear energy cooperation. Through this agreement India is expected to produce about 20,000 Mw by 2020 and double this by 2030. The Nuclear Supplier Group (NSG), which treated India in the past three decades as a pariah, has agreed to a nuclear commerce with the latter. India's main focus on nuclear energy is not only to meet the demands but also to reduce its green house emission. It is one of the main countries in the world, which is concerned to reduce Carbon dioxide ($CO_2$) emission. It wants to reduce its dependency on other countries for its energy needs, particularly for oil from the Middle East. The global estimated oil reserves were estimated to be 1,188 billion barrels (one barrel is equal to 160 litres) and proven gas reserves were estimated to be 6,400 TCF (one TCF is equal to 100 million barrels of liquid fuel) as per the 2004 figures. [9] It is expected that oil will be available for about forty to sixty years, whereas gas for 100 years. If this is going to be the reality, then India, which is depending heavily on imports, should explore alternatives to secure its energy needs viz. nuclear energy.

**India's Investments Abroad**

One of the recommendations put forth by the group in its vision 2025, was to explore the resources abroad through investments to secure its imports. The Oil & Natural Gas Corporation (ONGC), ONGC Videsh Ltd. (OVL), Gas Authority of India Limited (GAIL) and private companies like Reliance Company have entered into a production-sharing contract. Negotiations are going on for oil explorations in other countries. Table 4.3 shows India's investments in oil and gas reserves in different parts of the world.

Having discussed the energy sector in India, in the following section an attempt has been made to focus on the cooperation between India and its neighbouring countries.

**Table 4.3: Indian Companies' Investment Abroad**

| Country | Companies | Estimated oil resources |
|---|---|---|
| Libya (Ghadames Basin) | OVL: 49 percent<br>IPR (US): 51 percent | Estimated oil reserves of 645 million barrels |
| Sudan (Greater Nile) | OVL:25 percent<br>China National Petroleum:40 percent<br>Petronas:30 percent<br>Sudan National Oil Company: 5 percent | Estimated oil reserves of 1 billion barrels |
| Syria | OVL:60 percent<br>IPR (US): 40 percent | Reserves yet to be estimated |
| Iraq (Block 8 Western Desert) | OVL: 100 percent | Reserves yet to be estimated |
| Iran (Farsi Offshore) | OVL: 40 percent<br>Indian Oil: 40 percent<br>Oil India:20 percent | Estimated oil reserves of 540 million barrels |
| Yemen | Reliance: 30 percent<br>ONGC:40 percent<br>BP:30 percent | Reserves yet to be estimated |
| Myanmar (A 1 block off Rakline Coast) | OVL:20 percent<br>GAIL:10 percent<br>Daewoo:60 percent<br>Kogas:10 percent | Estimated reserves 14-16 tcf of gas |
| Vietnam (Nam Conson Basin) | OVL:45 percent<br>PetroVietnam:5 percent<br>BP:50 percent | Estimated reserves of 2.04 tcf of gas |
| Indonesia (Coal fields)<br>South Sumatra | Tata Power Corporation: 30 percent<br>Reliance Company | ------- |
| Russia (Sakhalin-I) | OVL:20 percent<br>Exxon-N:30 percent<br>Sodeco:30 percent<br>SMNG-S:11.5 percent<br>RN Astra:8.5 percent | Estimated reserves of 1.15 billion tones of oil and 20 tcf of gas. |
| Venezuela (San Cristobal oil field) | OVL<br>PDVSA (Petroleos De Venezuela S.A.) | |

## India's Energy Cooperation with its Neighbouring Countries

India has realized the fact that it is necessary to have bilateral/multilateral cooperation to meet its energy needs. In one of the recent SAARC meetings, the member states identified energy as one of the important issues for growth. On 7 August 1998 at the Dhaka Workshop on *Improving the Availability of Power in South Asia: Search for Optimal Technology Options*, the participants agreed that South Asia would prosper by sharing energy resources. [10] The workshop realized the importance of setting up a Regional Power Grid, which would ensure quality power supply in the region. South Asia can promote South Asian Development Triangle [11] comprising North-eastern parts of India, Bangladesh and Nepal; Southern Grid connecting South India with Sri Lanka and the Western grid, connecting North India, especially Punjab with Pakistan's Punjab. It also can have growth quadrangle cooperation among Bangladesh, Bhutan, Nepal and North-eastern parts of India. Since energy is one of the determinants in the new millennium, the South Asian states should take initiatives in sharing energy resources.

Through cooperation, they could minimize the costs of research and improve efficiency. South Asia needs an integrated energy policy incorporating hydel power, oil, and natural gas, nuclear and renewable sources of energy. For instance, a proposal for a SAARC Power Grid is to connect the national power grids of all the countries in South Asia. This would help transmitting power from one country to any other country. Synergy among the neighbouring countries should be developed so as to explore these resources.

Apart from the initiatives for bilateral cooperation with South Asian countries, India is trying to have agreements with other countries such as Myanmar, Iran and Turkmenistan. There are a few initiatives at the multilateral level to have energy cooperation between India and others but they are yet to materialize.

### Bilateral Cooperation

**India and Bangladesh:** Bangladesh contains natural gas reserves of around 16.3 trillion cubic feet (Tcf). Further, it is estimated an additional 32.1 Tcf lies in undiscovered reserves. If these figures are proved to be correct, then Bangladesh could certainly become a major gas producer. Many people in Bangladesh want gas resources to be used for domestic purposes and oppose exporting gas to other countries particularly to India.

Bangladesh will benefit if it exports gas to India. An analyst rightly pointed out, "Dhaka's inclusive, and perhaps increasingly irrelevant debate on gas exports reflects the tragic sub continental tradition of wallowing in isolation and poverty rather than creating shared wealth." [12]

**India and Pakistan:** India's relationship with Pakistan is very important because any gas pipeline to India from the Middle East/Central Asia would require Pakistan's involvement and partnership. There was a positive step in the SAARC summit in Islamabad. Abdullah Yusuf, Secretary for Petroleum and natural resources, stated, "Pakistan may start buying up to 5 million tons of diesel from India instead of Kuwait because it makes 'better economic sense', that is, would prove cheaper." [13] Yaswanth Sinha, India's External Affairs Minister, addressing the SAARC Chambers of Commerce and Industry in Islamabad on 2 January 2004, expressed, "If Pakistan can find within itself the strength and wisdom to change its current approach towards India, there are immense benefits that it can derive as a transit route for the movement of energy, goods and people." [14] If this turns real, then both countries can benefit mutually. Thus economic interdependence will make it easier for the two countries to resolve their political problems.

Pakistan has a 500 KW primary transmission system extending from Jumshoro in the south to Tarbela and Peshawar in the north. All the lines are close to India's borders and may not require very complex transmission extensions. Pakistan's Power Minister stated, "There is a complete network on our side of course, on their (India) side as well. What we need are the connections, which would take a couple of weeks." [15] If Pakistan exports its surplus of 200 MW, it will get US$ 1.2 billion a year over a period of 20 years. [16] Also it can help the power plants to use their power at 80 percent capacity than the present 60 percent. If the plants run at 80 percent capacity utilization, the tariff would decrease to 3.5-4 cents. However, Pakistan is demanding Rs.3.00 (7 cents) per unit, whereas India is willing to pay Rs. 1.26 (3 cents) per unit. It wants to sell power in cents and not in rupees. This will require setting up of foreign exchange reserves. India gets power at Rs. 1.30-1.50 per unit from National Thermal Power Corporation (NTPC), whereas the Pakistani government is paying Rs.3.60 per unit to the Independent Power Producers (IPPs). It has to balance both-the internal and the external prices. India cannot buy power if it goes beyond Rs.1.50 per unit. There has been an asymmetry in the power tariff between these two countries. They have to sort out their differences and if so done, both will benefit from the power deal.

**India and Bhutan:** India and Bhutan had an agreement related to hydroelectric power supply. Under this agreement Bhutan is supplying power to India from Chukha Hydro Electric Project (336 MW). There is another project-Tala Hydro Electric Project (1020 MW), which is under construction and the surplus power from this project will be supplied to India. Bunakha (180 MW) and

Wang Chu (900 MW) projects are being planned and the Sankosh project (4060 MW) is under process. Bhutan is exporting 80 percent of its energy generation to India, which accounts for 30 percent of its GDP. Through Chukha Project, Bhutan earned Nu 1,454 million as profit in 1998-1999 from its power export to India. As a result it is in a position to increase revenues through the supply of power to India and to its own industries in the country. India provided technical and financial support to this project. It share was Rs.2.45 billion with 60 percent grant and 40 percent loan. Bhutan was able to redeem the entire cost of the project in five years. India is able to supply power to West Bengal, Orissa and North-eastern parts of India. However, India has to upgrade its transmission lines to increase its access to Bhutanese power.

**India and Nepal:** Nepal possesses the largest hydropower potential (83,290 MW) in South Asia. However, due to various reasons, Nepal is not able to tap its hydropower resources. It has been able to install only 283 MW capacities. There are proposals between India and Nepal for hydroelectric cooperation. Projects like Pancheswar Project, which has the capacity of about 6000 MW, needs special institutional and financial assistance. The other project West Sati (750 MW) is also proposed to be developed to export power to India. Due to factors such as technical, production and supply constraints and political differences, cooperation between the two countries could not be reached.

**India and Other Countries in Southeast Asia:** Economic relations with the ASEAN will certainly help India's quest for energy security. Presently India imports crude oil from Malaysia and Brunei and it is about 5.4 percent of its total imports from the world. It also imports 3.5 percent LPG from Malaysia. Since the ASEAN countries- Indonesia, Malaysia and Vietnam have about one percent of world's proven oil reserves and three percent of the world's proven gas reserves [17], India can work towards enhancing its energy trade with them. [18]

### Multilateral Cooperation

**India-Pakistan-Iran Gas Pipeline:** India and Pakistan had signed a Memorandum of Understanding in July 1993 regarding the exploration of the prospects of a natural gas pipeline from Iran to India via Pakistan. In 1995, Pakistan and Iran had signed an agreement to construct a pipeline from South Pars gas field in Iran to Karachi in Pakistan and with an extension to India. However, due to various factors it has not materialized. Pakistan insists on an onshore gas pipeline, whereas India prefers an offshore pipeline project.

It was estimated that a 2700 km overland gas pipeline through Pakistan would cost about US$ 3.1 billion. Out of this amount, India has to bear about US$ 1 billion and the rest by Pakistan and Iran. It is only later that BHP Billiton revised the cost to about US$ 7 billion. If it is materialized then Pakistan will get US$ 700 million as transit charges from India every year. [19] India has reservations about the onshore pipeline project on the following grounds: (a) India is keen on full-fledged economic relations with Pakistan. It would be possible only if Pakistan gives MFN to India. India has already granted MFN to Pakistan in 1995; (b) India has doubts about the safety and security of the gas line in the light of the ongoing tensions between the two countries; (c) India has to live at the mercy of Pakistan; and (d) there may be threats from the fundamentalists and terrorists of Pakistan to the pipeline.

In spite of these reservations on the part of India, the proposed project can still be pursued on grounds of it being mutually beneficial to both. For instance, the Indus Water Treaty between the two countries was successful. Even if the fundamentalists and disruptive elements obstruct the proposed line, the governments can take steps to prevent those activities. It is to be noted that the project is not a trilateral Government-to-Government project but it would be owned by an international consortium made up of national companies from the three countries, together with other international partners (may be companies from China, Russia and Australia). [20] Hence, it would not be possible for Pakistan to disrupt the supply of gas to India. It is to be noted that Pakistan owned gas lines from the Sui gas field were being blown up by insurgents (in Baluchistan) and India's own crude oil pipelines are being blown up in Assam regularly but the respective governments are able to manage the situation. [21] Hence India should not be bother about the threat from militancy.

India is keen on an offshore pipeline to bring gas from Iran to the Indian west coast. It is ready to construct a 2900 km offshore pipeline. In such a case, India does not need to pay any transit charges to Pakistan. Though initially it needs more investment, in the long run the cost would be marginal. It will require the definition of the continental shelf of Iran, Pakistan and India. However, Iran and Pakistan are keen on the onshore option, which is considered to be cheaper. The best option for India is to import gas through pipelines, because it reduces 35 percent of the cost compared to Liquefied Natural Gas (LNG) import through sea tankers. [22] Iran is also planning to export gas to China, via India. If this materializes, India will benefit by a transit fee from China. If India does not show interest, China may get gas from Iran via Pakistan.

Meanwhile, India has signed an LNG deal with Iran and some companies such as Tata and Essar are interested in investing in the latter. However, this deal is yet to be materialized because it is to be approved by Iran's Supreme Economic Council. This may be because India cast its vote against Iran in the IAEA on the nuclear issue and also because gas prices have gone up.

**Turkmenistan-Afghanistan-Pakistan-India (TAPI):** The US, which opposed the Iran-Pakistan-India gas pipeline deal, is encouraging India and Pakistan to import gas from Turkmenistan. The 1,680 km pipeline from Turkmenistan will transport 100 million standard cubic meters per day (mscmd) of gas from the Dauletabad gas field and India will have a share of 60 Mscmd. [23] The Turkmenistan-Afghanistan-Pakistan-India (TAPI) line will run from the Dauletabad gas field to Afghanistan. It will be constructed up to Kandahar and then through Quetta and Multan in Pakistan. The final destination of the pipeline will be the Indian town of Fazilka, near the border with Pakistan.

The pipeline will be 1420 mm in diameter with a capacity of 3.3 billion cubic meters (bcm) of natural gas annually. The cost of the project was estimated at US$ 3.5 billion in 2005. However the cost has now been estimated at about US$ 7 billion.

**Myanmar-Bangladesh–India Pipeline:** Myanmar possesses significant energy reserves: gas in Yadana field and another deposit in the Bay of Bengal. Two Indian energy firms, OVL and GAIL own twenty and ten percent stakes respectively in the Burmese fields, A-1 and in the adjacent A-3 block. The 290 kms pipeline passes through Arakan state in Myanmar and the Indian states of Mizoram and Tripura crossing through Bangladesh and Kolkata. GAIL conducted feasibility studies for a 550 to 600 kms long offshore pipeline to connect India through Bangladesh. In case of Bangladesh's continued refusal to permit gas to be supplied to India, an alternative route of the pipeline will have to go under the sea in the Bay of Bengal, where pipes may have to be laid as deep as 6,560 ft. under water. This would also be highly expensive. The pipeline may cost more than US$ 2 billion even if an economical route is followed.

Before signing an agreement with India, Myanmar signed a MoU with the Chinese company PetroChina in early 2006 to supply gas to China from the A-1 field over a thirty year period. China gave a soft loan of US$ 84-million to Myanmar for laying a 2380-km pipeline connecting the gas site at Kyaukphyu (Myanmar) to Ruili (Yunnan province of China). China also agreed to pay US$ 150 million annually for thirty years as a transit fee for the 990 km stretch through Myanmar. However, in the case of supplying gas to India, Bangladesh wants the pipeline to be laid along its existing roads and highways and the project to be managed jointly by both. All the problems to be discussed such as allowing Bangladesh a free trade corridor to Nepal, removing the existing trade barriers between the two countries should be included in a package deal. It is very unfortunate that Dhaka refuses to allow the supply of gas through its soil when it will also benefit from the pipeline in the form of US$ 100 million per annum as transit fee.

## Conclusion

India's energy security is linked up with both growth and poverty. The demand for energy consumption is likely to increase manifold. India is largely dependent on coal to meet its energy needs, which produces more carbon dioxide ($Co_2$). India is the fourth largest emitter of green house gases (GHG) in the world. Economic growth is the major cause of rising emissions. There has to be a major reorientation of its energy strategy if India has to reduce its carbon emissions, i.e. it has to shift from its current coal-based system to some other energy system. India needs to explore alternatives to secure its energy needs viz. renewable energy (wind energy, solar energy, hydroelectric power, etc.) and nuclear energy.

Through cooperation the South Asian countries can benefit more. For instance, hydropower potential in India, Pakistan, Nepal and Bhutan and gas resources in Bangladesh and coal in India are in abundance. This can not only improve their efficiency but also can minimize oil imports, which lead to reduced dependency on foreign currency. These countries should understand the benefits that could be available through regional cooperation. To realize this, there should be mutual trust and cooperation among these countries.

### Notes

1. Vijay L. Kelkar, "Long-Term Energy Security for India", *University News*, Vol. 41, No. 33, 18-24 August 2003, p. 17.
2. Energy security is defined as the "availability of energy at all times in various forms, in sufficient quantities, and at affordable prices." See United Nations Programme, *World Energy Assessment* (New York: UNDP, 2000), cited in Philip Andres-Speed, Xuanli Liao and Roland Dannreuther, *The Strategic Implications of China's Energy Needs* (New York: Oxford University Press Inc, 2002), p.13. Energy security can be defined "in terms of the physical availability of the supplies to satisfy demand at a given price." See Anant V. Naik, Sajal Ghosh and V. Raghuraman, *Energy Security Issues and India*, July 2003, see www.acus.org/energy.
3. Planning Commission, *Integrated Energy Policy: Report of the Expert Committee*, New Delhi: Government of India, 2006.
4. For details see Anant Sudarshan and Logia Noronha, "Contextualizing India's Energy Security", in Logia Noronha and Anant Sudarshan (ed), *India's Energy Security*, London: Routledge, 2009, p. 3.
5. For instance, according to Indian government report estimated that 0.59 million Indians die each year due to polluting traditional fuel.
6. Surya Sethi, "India's Energy Challenges and Choices", in Noronha and Sudarshan (ed), n.4, p. 19.
7. Anup Jayaram & Rajeev Dubey, "India's Oil Hunt", *Business World*, Vol.23, No.7, 8-14 July 2003, p. 31.
8. M.R. Srinivasan, "New Opportunities for Nuclear Energy", *The Hindu*, 2 August 2005, p.10.
9. *The Hindu*, 19 February 2008.
10. *Financial Express*, 8 August 1998.

11. ASEAN states have Growth Triangle like Southern Growth Triangle-Indonesia, Malaysia and Thailand, Northern Growth Triangle-Sumatra, Malaysia and Thailand and East Asian Growth Area-Philippines, Indonesian Islands, Malaysia and Brunei.
12. *The Hindu*, 12 November 2002.
13. Prem Shankar Jha, "Big Gulps of the Peace Pipe", *Outlook*, Vol. 44, No. 3, 26 January 2004, p. 10.
14. *The Hindu*, 3 January 2004.
15. *The Hindustan Times*, 16 January 1999.
16. Mahendra P. Lama, "Economic Reforms and the Energy Sector in South Asia: Scope for Cross-Border Power Trade", *South Asian Survey,* Vol. 7, No.1, January-June 2000, p.18.
17. Partha Pratim Pal & Mitali Dasgupta, "Does A Free Trade Agreement with ASEAN Make Sense?", *Economic & Political Weekly*, Vol. 43, No. 46, 15 November 2008.
18. For more details see A. Subramanyam Raju, "India-Southeast Asia Energy Cooperation", in T. Nirmala Devi & A. Subramanyam Raju (ed), *India and Southeast Asia: Strategic Convergence in the 21st Century* (forthcoming)
19. G. Pathasarathy, "The Quest for Energy Security", see http://www.rediff.com/news/2001/jul/106gp.htm.
20. Talmiz Ahmad, "Geopolitics of West Asian and Central Asian Oil and Gas", in Noronha and Sudarshan (ed), n. 4, p. 74.
21. Ravi Kumar Batra, "Natural Gas Pipelines: Geopolitics, Affordability, Security Dimensions", in Noronha and Sudarshan (ed), n.4, pp. 88-90.
22. Om Prakash, "The Oman-Indian Gas Pipeline Project: Need to Resurrect Again", see ipcs.o…/print Militray.jsp?action=show views+K value=503&military=1010&states.
23. See *The Hindu*, 23 April 2008.

# 5

# India and the Present Global Order: A Security Perspective

Suresh. R

## Introduction

The foreign policy of a country is determined by the internal as well as external factors. Shifts in international power structures from bipolar to multipolar or 'non-polar' and domestic settings determine the foreign policy of a country. The two major developments that have taken place in the global system in recent times are the disintegration of former Soviet Union and the accelerated pace of globalization. The collapse of Soviet Union resulted in the end of clashes of ideology which prevailed for nearly four and a half decades at the global level. This provided developing nations an opportunity to freely formulate their foreign policy. The intensity of regional conflicts in the context of super power rivalry has also been reduced.

Security perceptions of nations have also undergone a radical change in the post-Cold War period. Economic security appears to be the foremost concern of all nations-both developed and developing. Though the traditional security perception has not been abandoned outright it has lost much of its significance. The emergence of new forms of threats from transnational terrorist groups has added a new dimension to the security of nations. The operations of these groups have demonstrated that the traditional approach to security has become redundant. No nation howsoever powerful, can single-handedly tackle the threats posed to them. This again demands multilateralism in international relations to meet the challenges posed by transnational and non-state actors.

The globalization process which has spread to every nook and corner of the world has brought all nations to a common platform. The globalization process has not only brought nations together at but has also strengthened regional cooperation. The growth of powerful transnational and multinational corporations as a result of globalization appears to pose a threat to even the Westphalia state system. Some of these corporations are more powerful than nation states in terms of their area of operations and possession of resources.

The growth and development of non-state actors in international relations is a new phenomenon emerging in the post-Cold War period. Due to this development, international civil society organizations are gaining strength as players in intra-national and international levels. The existence of these international and national civil society organizations to protect and promote human rights and the environment have also accelerated the pace of the democratization process. The interaction among people as a result of the information revolution has further strengthened the bonds of universal brotherhood and understanding among people. A better understanding of basic problems transcending artificial boundaries would further weaken the role of the state as a player in international relations.

Today the strength of a nation appears to be not solely based on the possession of destructive weapons but on many other non-traditional factors including the strength of its economy, democratic institutions and human security. The security of the people living in a nation is as important as the security of the nation. In the post-Cold War period, human security is gaining significance in international relations. This new dimension of security has also been driven by globalization. It would be interesting to examine how India, one of the founder members of the Non-Aligned movement is adapting its foreign policy to the changing international context. This paper is an attempt to examine India's major security concerns and strategies in South Asia, Indian Ocean and at the global level.

**India in the Shadow of Cold War**

The post Second World War bipolar international power structure, the underdeveloped nature of the Indian economy as well as India's past, appear to have compelled Indian decision makers to adopt a Non-Aligned policy. In the Cold War period the options before newly independent nations were limited and interactions among nations were solely based on affiliation to either of the two blocs, led by two diverging ideologies.

Independent India conducted the experiment of an independent foreign policy to protect and promote its national interests. Consequently, India played a major role in the formation of the Non-Aligned movement along with Egypt and the former Yugoslavia. India also played a crucial role along with China in the initiation of the Panchsheel, [1] the five principles to govern bilateral and multilateral relations between and among nations. However, the flaws in this idealist approach in international relations were visible when China attacked India in 1962. Just one year after the first Non-Aligned summit held in Belgrade. When India was confronted with a real politic situation, neither the Non-Aligned movement, nor the UN emerged effective in curbing aggression under the collective security system.

Though India claimed that its foreign policy was Non-Aligned, [2] the Indo-Soviet Peace and Friendship treaty of 1971 clearly demonstrated India's 'Aligned' policies. [3] The Soviet invasion of Afghanistan in 1979 and India's meaningful silence on it, once again showed its special relations with the Soviet Union. [4] This pro-Soviet element in India's foreign policy helped the country to face external security threat and also gain wholehearted support from Russia in its nation-building process. Thus India's 'Non-Aligned' policy was only a label to actively pursue its foreign policy objectives.

In the Cold War period, nation states were deprived of wide foreign policy options. None of the developing countries were free from the impact of the ideology-based-superpower-game. Any kind of interaction with one bloc was viewed as a strategy to destabilize the other bloc and vice versa. In such a suspicious situation neither stable peace nor prosperity was possible. Regional conflicts emerged from the context of superpower rivalry. The end of the Cold War has helped nations to come out of the shadow and pursue an independent foreign policy. In the post-Cold War period, the balance of power appears to have been replaced by the balance of interests.

## India in the Post-Cold War Period and the Quest for Security

**India's Security Concerns:** India's traditional security concerns revolve around threats emanating from Pakistan and China. However, in the post-Cold War period a major threat from Pakistan has only a remote chance because of two major developments in the region. Pakistan's decision makers-both military and civilian are well aware of the fact that they may not get any support which they received in 1971 from their Cold War defence ally, the US. Secondly since Pakistan also is a nuclear weapon power, no major player at the international level or the UN would allow the outbreak of a nuclear war in South Asia. With regards to the threat from China, though there is an unresolved border problem, China may not initiate a 1962 type war with nuclear India due to nuclear deterrence. Here again global players and the UN would not allow a nuclear war in Asia. Thus, in the post-Cold War period India's traditional security concerns have undergone a marked change, though defence establishments pay least attention to these developments.

In the Cold War period, another major security concern for India was mainly the presence of external powers in the Indian Ocean region. It was this fear which prompted India to support Sri Lanka's proposal for declaring the Indian Ocean as a Zone of Peace by the UN in 1971. During the Cold War period, India strongly supported the elimination of great power presence in the Indian Ocean region, especially US presence. It was the movement of the US Seventh Fleet into the Bay of Bengal during the India-Pakistan war of 1971 to intimidate India, [5] which posed a major threat to India's security interests. Such a threat from the US in the present global scenario is totally eliminated from India's security concerns in the context of its decision to initiate defence collaboration with the US and the joint security monitoring in the Indian Ocean region.

In the post-Cold War period the major security concern for India emanates from cross border terrorism. All other traditional security concerns have been overtaken by economic issues. The challenges posed by international terrorism, global economic meltdown and environmental degradation including climate change are also grave. On the domestic front, India faces many challenges like poverty, illiteracy, social and economic inequality, communalism, regional imbalances and development based displacement etc. Thus, challenges to human security are more in number as well as grave in nature.

**India's Quest for Security:** India's quest for security has incorporated the new dimension of security, human security into the traditional concept of security. India placed equal importance upon the security of the people along with the security of the nation. In the Cold War period, there was a competition among nations to accumulate more and more weapons. Though the competition continues in the post-Cold War period, it has lost much of its vigour and popular support. This appears to be the reason for the shift in focus from military security to economic and environmental security. The plea for a human security approach is also a post-Cold War development. [6] The positive as well as negative impacts of globalization process have accelerated the momentum for a human security approach. On the positive side globalization has helped in the growth of civil society organizations at the national and the international levels. These organizations make democratic systems more participatory and people friendly. With regards to the negative impact of the globalization process, one may speak about the withdrawal of the state from welfare activities leading to a worsening of the position of the poor and marginalized sections of the society. [7]

In order to strengthen its economic and military power, India has taken strong policy decisions towards achieving a growth rate of 8 percent by focusing on agriculture, infrastructure development along with its quest for modernization of defence forces. Again India's reluctance to compromise on the nuclear weapons option, its strategic interaction with the US and the strengthening of its naval forces to the level of a Blue Water Force are part of this strategy. These steps also appear to be based on a new security perception rooted in a realist approach.

**Favourable Internal and External Climate for Realist Approach:** The international and domestic situations have been favourable to India to initiate the new security strategy. Post-Cold War international power structures based on multipolarity along with US initiatives to curb international terrorism through actions against states sponsoring terrorism, suite India's foreign policy objectives. The emergence of two major political fronts at the federal level has accelerated competition in the Indian polity. Each front, when in power, tries to formulate domestic and external policies to gain maximum popular support. This trend again prompts each front to pursue a realist foreign policy. India's decision to break the shell and declare itself as a nuclear weapon power and sign the Indo-US Civilian Nuclear Agreement and a number of policy decisions in the domestic and external fields mark this change. In the recent federal election the strong popular support for the ruling front to form a stable government without the conditional support from minor ideology based political parties, reflects popular support to the realist approach of decision makers.

**Indo-US Relations:** India's relation with the United States has acquired remarkable maturity and dynamism in the post-Cold war period. A number of independent developments have created the climate for this transformation, including the end of the Cold War, India's emergence as a dynamic economic force and an objective assessment of the strategic implications of a world dominated by knowledge-driven societies. At present India-US relations are moving beyond a bilateral partnership towards a global partnership, which is anchored not only on common values but also common interests. The strategic dimension of India's relationship with the US underlines the common interest in combating terrorism, proliferation of Weapons of Mass Destruction and enhancing global peace. There has been a convergence of views on strategic and security issues. There exists scope for India-US cooperation in the fields of defence, science and technology, health, trade, space, energy and environment. There is also a growing US recognition of India's central and enhanced role in international institutions and processes. US economic and political stakes in the growth of the Indian economy and its integration with the global market have provided an impetus to India-US cooperation in a way that meaningfully addresses constraints on India's growth, including the deficits of energy and infrastructure. [8] India's relations with the US are not at the cost of hostility to any other nation. This attitude of India is visible in its interaction with other nations including China and also in its involvement in regional groups.

**India and Regional and Multilateral Groups:** India has developed a friendly and cordial relation not only by bilateral exchanges with nation states but also strengthened bilateral cooperation through interactions in regional and multilateral organizations, such as ASEAN, EAS, SCO, BRIC, ASEM, IBSA, APTA, and IOR ARC. India is vigorously pursuing the objective of becoming a developed nation by 2020. This requires the Indian economy to maintain an annual average growth rate of 8 percent. India has framed the 'Look East' policy in pursuit of this objective. Now this 'Look East' policy is a vital part of India's foreign policy. [9] More than an external economic policy or a political slogan, the 'Look East' policy was a strategic shift in India's vision of the world and its place in the evolving global economy. It was also a manifestation of India's belief that developments in East Asia are of direct consequence to its security and development. Therefore India actively engaged in creating a bond of friendship and cooperation with East Asia; and this had a strong economic foundation and a cooperative paradigm of positive inter-connectedness of security interests. [10] India became a member of the ARF in 1996 and considers it as an experiment in fashioning a pluralistic, cooperative security order reflective of the diversity of the Asia Pacific region. India has also successfully clinched a free trade agreement with the ASEAN which comes into force from January 1, 2010. This would further enhance the Indo-ASEAN trade from the present US$ 30 billion to US$ 50 billion by 2010. India is also a member of the East Asia Summit (EAS) which includes the ASEAN members and China, Japan, Republic of Korea, Australia, and New Zealand. It focuses on energy, environment, climate change, and sustainable development. The 'Look East' policy of India included not only vigorous interaction with ASEAN but also improved relation with China. The ultimate objective was to evolve an Asian Economic Community on the lines of the EU.

Another major initiative of India towards multilateral interaction is the membership in the four nation grouping called BRIC (Brazil, Russia, India and China) to strengthen bilateral relationship that will help to be more effective collectively. This four nation group has several peculiar features. It represents 40 percent of world population and covers 25.5 percent of total geographic area and 40 percent of global Gross Domestic Product (GDP). It becomes bigger than the G 7, collectively by 2035. This grouping's political interaction could help to alter the shape of the international financial system and the global economy. One of the objectives of the grouping is democratization of international financial institutions. The joint declaration at the first summit meeting held in Russia focused on global food security. The BRIC countries supported the adoption of a wide range of mid-to long-term measures in order to provide for a solution to the issue of food security. [11] This clearly reflects the commitment of BRIC to resolve one of the basic problems before the international community, i.e. food security.

India is also a member of the three nation economic group known as IBSA (India Brazil and South Africa) which targets intra-IBSA trade to US$ 15 billion by 2010. Though India is not a member of the SCO (Shanghai Cooperation Organization) it had actively participated in the Summit meeting as an observer. It comprises of six nations viz., China, Russia, Kazakhstan, Kyrgyzstan, Tajikistan, and Uzbekistan. India's interests in participating in SCO activities are mainly in the area of energy, economic development, countering terrorism and countering drug trafficking. [12] India is an active member of the Bay of Bengal Initiative for Multi-Sectoral Technical and Economic Cooperation (BIMSTEC), another economic group that acts as a bridge between South Asia and South East Asia; comprising of Bangladesh, Bhutan, Myanmar, Nepal, India, Sri Lanka and Thailand. The IOR-ARC (an eighteen member group), aims at promoting economic and technical cooperation including expansion of trade and investment. The members are Australia, Bangladesh India, Indonesia, Iran, Kenya, Mauritius, Madagascar, Malaysia, Mozambique, Oman, Singapore, South Africa, Sri Lanka, Tanzania Thailand, United Arab Emirates and Yemen.

India is one of the five outreach countries in the G 8 along with Brazil, China, Mexico and South Africa. India is a member of the G 20 along with Argentina, Australia, Brazil, Canada, China, France, Germany, Indonesia, Italy, Japan, Mexico, Russia, Saudi Arabia, South Africa, South Korea, Turkey, UK and USA. India had also taken part in the Asia Europe Meeting (ASEM). [13] Thus, in the post-Cold War period, India adopted a pragmatic approach to promote its national interest and actively participated in all regional and multilateral forums.

**India and the Human Security:** With the end of the Cold War, the concept of security has increasingly come under the scrutiny of scholars of international relations. In the classical formulation, security is about how states use force to manage threats to their territorial integrity, their autonomy and their domestic political order, primarily from other states. To this, some critique of classical formulation of security opined that the protection and welfare of the individual citizen or human being is central. The conception of security that is cantered above all on the sanctity of the individual may be called Human Security. [14]

Though the idea of Human Security in its rudimentary form may be traced to the 1960s, it was the Independent Commission on International Development Issues in its North-South Report of 1980 that highlighted the changing thinking on development and security. The chairman of the commission Willy Brandt observed, "Our Report is based on what appears to be the simplest common interest that mankind wants to survive, and one might even add has the moral obligation to survive. This not only raises traditional questions of peace and war, but also how to overcome world hunger, mass misery and alarming disparities between the living conditions of the rich and poor." [15]

Another notable development in the idea of Human Security was the

Common Security Report of the Independent Commission on Disarmament and Security Issues chaired by Olof Palme. It acknowledges that Third world security was also threatened by poverty and deprivation by economic inequality. The report noted 'common security requires that people live in dignity and peace, that they have enough to eat and are able to find work and live in a world without poverty and destitution.' [16]

With the end of superpower rivalry the call for new thinking in security matters gained momentum. In 1991 the Stockholm Institute on Global Security and Governance issued a call for 'Common Responsibility in the 1990s, which maintained a 'wider concept of security', which dealt with threats that stemmed from failures in development, environmental degradation, excessive population growth and movement and lack of progress towards democracy.' Again in 1995, the Commission on Global Governance's report, Our *Global Neighbourhood*, stated, "The concept of global security must be broadened from the traditional focus on the security of states to include the security of people and the security of the planet." [17]

The aforementioned commission reports may be considered as precursors to Human Security thinking. However, a Human Security perspective was developed by the UNDP (United Nations Development Program) in the Human Development Report of 1994.This report contains a section on *Redefining Security: The Human Dimension*. [18] It proposes an alternative to traditional security and a necessary supplement to human development.

The report discussed in detail the question of 'security for whom' with reference to the traditional notion of security. These were concerned with security of territory from external aggression, or as protection of national interest in foreign policy or as global security from the threat of nuclear holocaust. It related more to nation states than to people. What this conception overlooked was the 'legitimate concern of ordinary people who sought security in their daily lives'. [19] Human Security is people-cantered.

The Human Development Report maintains that Human security means protecting the vital freedom of the individuals. It means protecting people from critical and pervasive threats and situations, building on their strengths and aspirations. It also means creating systems that give people the building blocks to survival, dignity and livelihood. Human Security connects different types of freedoms- freedom from fear, freedom to take action on one's own behalf and so on. To do this, it offers two general strategies: protection and empowerment. Protection shields people from dangers. It requires concerted efforts towards development of norms, processes and institutions that systematically address insecurities. Empowerment enables people to develop their potential to become full participants in decision-making. Protection and empowerment are mutually reinforcing, and both are required in most situations. Human Security complements state security, furthers human development and enhances human rights. It complements state security by being people-cantered and addressing insecurities that have not been considered as state security threats. By looking at 'downside risks', it broadens the focus of human development beyond 'growth with equity'. Respecting human rights are at the core of protecting Human Security. [20]

In the age of globalization, protection to the vulnerable groups in the society, who are affected by development based displacement or by a loss of job and income, assumes great significance. India had taken several steps to ensure Human Security or the security of its people. Being the largest democratic system in the world, it has a strong democratic structure to implement Human Security measures at the national level. Though the political foundations of India are strongly based on a parliamentary system, in the economic and social fields it is confronted with many challenges. These include poverty, unemployment, illiteracy, social inequality communalism, casteism and the economic disparity between haves and have-nots. All these factors have an implication on human security.

India had initiated several programs for providing security to the people. It includes measures which are aimed both at protection and empowerment of the vulnerable sections of the society. The major programs initiated are the National Rural Employment Guarantee Program (NREGP), right to education act, right to food, programs for the improvement of slums, National Rural Health Mission, Right to Information Act etc. [21]

**Conclusion**

The shift in the international power structure from bipolar to multi polar or 'non polar' after the disintegration of the former Soviet Union had posed many challenges to the erstwhile Non-aligned nations. In the Cold War period, nation states were deprived of a wider foreign policy option to promote their national interests. Thus the end of the Cold War marked the end of the strict international discipline imposed by superpower rivalry on nation states. Today there exist 'de-hyphenated relations' between nations and they are free to engage or disengage with anyone. With the passage of time, security concerns were overtaken by economic issues. The globalization process and challenges posed by international terrorism, the global economic meltdown and environmental degradation inclusive of climatic change have placed 'collective actions' and multilateralism at the forefront of international relations.

The protection and promotion of national interests, namely, peace, security and prosperity, is the foremost concern of any nation, though they adopt different means to achieve these objectives. The changes that took place at the international setting placed India in a new security environment and compelled it to adapt its foreign policy to changing needs. India appears to have adopted a two-pronged strategy to meet new security concerns. India has consolidated and projected its power and also initiated engagement with global powers and regional groupings, hitherto considered a taboo broadly falling under the spectrum of its 'enlightened national interests'.

The century old wisdom exposed in Kautiliya's Arthashastra (third century BC) called for a realist approach from decision makers. The present global order demands a pragmatic rather than an idealist approach so as to protect and promote national interests. When options to pursue national interests are limited, a common perception would evolve regarding areas of security. This happens mainly because of fundamental changes taking place at the domestic and the external levels and also due to the blurring of boundaries between Human Security and National Security on the one hand, and National Security and International Security on the other.

**Notes**

1. The five principles are-Mutual Respect for each other's territorial integrity and sovereignty, Mutual Non-Aggression, Mutual Non-Interference in each other's internal affairs, Equality and Mutual Benefit, Peaceful Co-Existence.
2. India has defined non-aligned policy as an independent foreign policy. It is not neutrality.
3. Indo Soviet Peace and Friendship Treaty of 1971, though not a defence treaty some of its provisions are termed as components of a defence treaty. For details see Suresh R, Indian Ocean as a Zone of Peace: A Comparative Study of the Responses of India and Pakistan from 1970 to 1989, Ph. D thesis, Pondicherry University, Pondicherry, 1994. pp. 75-87.
4. Ibid. pp. 227-230.
5. Ibid. p. 101.
6. Suresh R, Human Security: A Canadian Perspective, Holistic Thought, Vol. V, No.1 and 2, January- December 2006. pp. 103-113.
7. Suresh R, Foreign Policy and Human Rights - An Indian Perspective, Madhav Books, Gurgaon, 2009. pp. 42 – 49.
8. Ministry of External Affairs, Government of India, Annual Report 2008-2009. pp. 93-98.
9. India's Foreign Policy Today, Speech delivered by External Affairs Minister, Mr. Parnab Mukherjee, at Peking University on 6 June 2008.
10. Annual Report Ministry of External Affairs, no. 2.
11. The measures suggested include: (a) rendering additional resources and assistance to the agricultural sector through the channels of respective national budgets and international development institutions, mainly to household agriculture, which is the main source for food production; (b) joint technological innovations and international cooperation to introduce advanced technologies in the agricultural sector of developing countries to significantly

increase agricultural productivity. Intellectual property rights in the agricultural domain should strike a balance between the common good of humankind and incentives to innovation; (c) upgrading agricultural infrastructure, including irrigation, transportation, supply, storage and distribution systems and promoting technical assistance, access to credit and crop insurance policies. In this context public-private partnerships could play a significant role; (d) improving the exchange of knowledge and commercialisation of sustainable bio-fuels; (e) ensuring wider access to food at the national and international level through appropriate policies and well functioning distribution systems especially for the poor and most vulnerable people in developing countries; (f) sharing of best practices of operating successful public distribution programmes; and (g) equipping developing countries with financial and technological means to fully implement adaptation measures to minimize the adverse impacts of climate change on food security. See for details www.indianembassy.ru 16/08/2009.

12. Annual report, Ministry of External Affairs, no. 2.
13. Ibid.
14. Suresh R, no. 4.
15. The Independent Commission on International Development Issues, North-South: A Programme for Survival, Cambridge, 1980. p. 9.
16. The Independent Commission on Disarmament and Security Issues, Common Security: A Blueprint for Survival, 1982.
17. The Commission on Global Governance, Our Global Neighbourhood, Oxford University Press, New York, 1995, p. 306.
18. UNDP Report 1994, Oxford University Press, New York, 1994.
19. Ibid.
20. Ibid.
21. See for details India 2008, Publication Division, Government. of India, 2008.

# 6

# Indian Foreign Policy through Case Studies

Jigar Patel and Hardik Mehta

---

## Introduction

Observers of Indian foreign policy are often puzzled by its inchoate combination of idealist rhetoric on international issues, post-modern nitpicking in negotiations and isolationist behaviour when it comes to matters of national interest. 'What does India want?' they ask in frustration, "Do you want to be a major power, or do you just want to score points?"

The question is difficult to answer. When India achieved independence in 1947, the country's founding fathers assumed that it would be a leading international player, expanding rules for normative behaviour in relation to goals as well as means. But though India's founding fathers produced grand policy visions, such as the 1946 Asian Relations Conference for an institutional structure to buffer Asia against the Cold War, they were unable to translate their sweeping goals into action. The Asian Relations Conference ended with minor agreements on educational cooperation (Gonsalves, 1991).

Sixty years later, India's new policy-makers define India as 'a rising power' that is today beginning to match global goals and means in order to achieve the most favourable results for its citizens, and at the same time expanding normative principles for inter-state and transnational behaviour. India's steady 8-9 percent growth over the past decade, and the Indian government's proactive diplomacy in the same period, allowed Indian policy-makers to bring context and substance to the normative principles that their predecessors advocated-a development that one leading Indian analyst describes as 'crossing the Rubicon' from idealism to pragmatism (Mohan, 2003), and another as 'India Unbound' (Das, 2002); both phrases indicate what a large leap it is. Indian policy-makers used to advocate principles divorced from political realities, to use Morgenthau's definition (Morgenthau, 1982), but today they seek to combine normative principles with national interest. The transition is not easy to make, and as so often happens in the early phases of policy change, the conceptual shift in approach outpaces the implementers-most of them desk officers and/or their superiors who make policies through a case-by-case practice. Morgenthau was ill-placed to derive the consequent point that flows from his distinction-the transition from principles that are divorced from political realities to normative principles based on national interests is one of the most complicated transitions to make, especially in postcolonial countries. As other papers in this series have pointed out, categories of what is normative vary from culture to culture, and are hotly debated across cultures (Tocci, 2007, pp. 2-3).

However, Indian foreign policy is curious in this regard-traditional views of what is normative are very similar to European and US principles, but the colonial and Cold War experience led Indian policy-makers to be sceptical of European and US claims to normative behaviour on the one hand, and on the other to distrust their own normative heritage. Prior to the new policy-making described above, Indian positions on normative behaviour in international fora often appeared schizophrenic-Indian representatives claimed idealist positions, but often defended reprehensible regimes on grounds of state sovereignty even when there was no clear national interest involved. While India's new policy-makers have jettisoned abstract normative positions of their Cold War predecessors, elements of old decision-making remain, especially amongst Indian policy implementers.

Part of the problem is that Indian policy-making is shaped by two major strands that have never been synthesised to create a doctrine that takes into account the national interest; one is that of traditional principles drawn from the Gita and the Mahabharata and most heavily from the doctrine of statecraft framed by the 4th century BC scholar-statesman, Kautilya (also known as Chanakya); and two, modernist principles that uneasily combine Enlightenment values with a passive, sometimes dependent Realpolitic, instilled by the experience of British colonialism of the 19th to mid-20th centuries. Most Indians perceive the two strands as internally conflicting, especially when it comes to issues of normative behaviour.

Secondly, the most effective means of delivering these goals were normative means such as international alliances, trade, infrastructure development and free movement across national borders (Kautilya, Book VI, Chapters 1 and 2; and Book VII, Chapter 1).

Thirdly, the behaviour of a state was to be assessed by the transparency of its actions. Before a government act or agreement could be implemented, group of judges and ministers that administered the law would have to decide whether the government's acts and agreements were valid or void. The criterion for valid agreements was that they would have to be transparent (Kautilya, Book III, Chapter 1). [1] Incidentally, transparency was also underlined by the US President Woodrow Wilson in his Fourteen Points Plan and held it to be the turning point, after which, quiet diplomacy was increasingly supplanted by public diplomacy. [2]

Had the traditional strand remained dominant in Indian foreign policy doctrine; it would have been easy to classify India as a normative (although not necessarily naively idealist) international player. But British colonialism added a new element to Indian foreign policy-that of dependency. Whereas previous empires had been rooted in India and adopted foreign policies that served Indian state interests, Britain was a remote country and India's foreign policy was adapted to suit British interests. Thus what I term 'Unrealpolitic' international action (because it subordinates national interests to that of other countries) entered into Indian foreign policy. UnRealpolitic behaviour gained strength through the education policy framed by T.B. Macaulay in 1835, who argued that the Indian education system would have to generate contempt for native traditions and respect the superiority of European values and practices. [3] This led successive generations of Indian policy-makers and analysts to doubt their own ability to frame national interest.

How do these views affect India's behaviour as a foreign policy actor? During the Cold War, India's positions in the international arena were mostly normative but divorced from political reality (Morgenthau, 1982) and were directed to exclusively 'milieu goals' (Wolfers, 1962, pp. 67-80). From 1920, when the Indian National Congress leader M.K. Gandhi sent a delegation to the Paris Peace Conference to demand that the territories of the former Ottoman Empire be granted the same rights to self-determination as those granted to the territories of the former Austro-Hungarian Empire-qualified in this case, as the right to Muslim rule (Ghose, 1991, pp.128-129)-India's foreign policy focus was on decolonisation and multilateral constraints over Great Power domination. Furthermore, Indian leaders sought consensus rather than the usage of economic, political or military pressure to influence world affairs, an approach that lasted well into the 1990s.

Under Prime Minister Nehru (1946-64), India actively aided state and nation building in newly decolonised countries, especially in Africa, where the Indian Army and civil service helped countries such as Kenya, Egypt, Tanzania and Zimbabwe to build administrative and/or defence institutions, and spearheaded UN action against South Africa's apartheid (Reddy, 1985). Nehru's efforts were less successful in Asia. His hope that Asia's countries might set up a cooperative network that could prevent Great Power conflict shifting to the Asian theatre in the aftermath of the WWII proved to be unrealistic (Gonsalves, 1991). The Chinese revolution, followed by the Korean, Vietnamese and Cambodian wars, brought the Cold War to the heart of Asia.

Nevertheless, from the 1940s to the 1960s, India achieved considerable soft power across Africa and Asia (especially in the latter through its film industry, Bollywood) and wielded quiet diplomacy to effect an agreement between the US and China during the Korean War (1951) and protect dissidents in Hungary (1956). [4] In the early years of the Cold War, India founded the Non-Aligned Movement (NAM) along with Indonesia, Yugoslavia and Egypt at the Bandung Conference of 1955. Even if the NAM was treated as a mosquito-like irritant by the US and the UK during much of its existence, it did keep the idea of an alternative to the Cold War alive in Asia (Gonsalves, 1991).

Following the 1962 war with China-which was largely Tibet-driven and in which India suffered a crushing defeat-and Nehru's death in 1964, Indian foreign policy veered back to UnRealpolitic, which in this case put the interests of the USSR above its own. UnRealpolitic reached its zenith under Indian Prime Minister Indira Gandhi (1966-75 and 1978-84), during which period India aligned itself firmly with the USSR and its economy became dependent on the Soviet military-industrial complex. Although Indian foreign policy retained a normative element in its bilateral relations, in multilateral forums it adopted normative policies only rarely, such as sanctions against the apartheid in South Africa and support for a Palestinian state-not in the least because both of these positions were also supported by the USSR.

With the end of the Cold War, India experienced what some called an opportunity to combine normative and Realpolitic goals (Kumar, 2006), and others defined this as a conflict between the two (Mohan, 2003). But Indian policy-makers were slow to take advantage of this new opening. After the long winter of the Cold War, when India was estranged from the US and to a lesser extent from Western Europe, the end of the Cold War caught India unprepared and Indian diplomats withdrew into a lengthy introspection from which the country emerged at the turn of the century having lost most of its policy edge in East and Central Europe. The rise of Hindu nationalism during the Bharatiya Janata Party's (BJP) years in government (1998-2003) further shattered India's relatively strong relations in the Gulf and in North Africa. It was only in the early years of the 21st century that Indian policy-makers made a concerted effort to re-engage with the world and this time it was the Kautilyan strand in Indian foreign policy that came to the fore.

In contrast to India's Cold War leaders, the country's new policy-makers came to the conclusion that if India was to pull its weight internationally it would have to become an economic and regional power (Dasgupta, 2003, pp. 92-111; Schiff, 2006). This was a view that had been cogently put by Kautilya and kept alive during most of the Mughal Empire because its rulers became natives of India, something that was not done by the colonial rulers.

After the first wave of economic liberalisation in 1990-91, when many bureaucratic constraints on industrial growth were lifted, wave two of economic liberalisation prioritized resource and infrastructure development. New policy-makers believed that neither could be achieved without integrating into the global economy as was shown in the past decade by the spectacular rise of Indian information technology (Das, 2002). So they swung into an active diplomatic campaign to improve relations with the major powers, identifying them as the US, EU, Russia, Japan and China (Dasgupta, 2003) and implemented a 'Look East' policy in the wider Asian neighbourhood, especially towards the ASEAN countries where the Indian 'footprint' had a long reach (Saran, 2003, p. 115).

India, which had eschewed membership of multilateral forums under Indira Gandhi, joined a slew of regional trade and security organisations in the short span of a decade, such as ASEAN, the Shanghai Cooperation Organisation, the Asian Regional Forum, the Asia-Europe Meeting process and the East Asia Summit. Finally, India's new policy-makers also recognised that India would fail as a regional power until it could turn its South Asian neighbours around. As a result, the Indian government launched several new peacemaking initiatives with Pakistan, Afghanistan, Bangladesh, China, Nepal, and Sri Lanka, hoping that these would help pull South Asia out of the slough of hostility and poverty it had slipped into, following its independence from the British.

Former Indian Foreign Secretary Shyam Saran (2003, p. 115) put India's renewed focus on its neighbourhood as follows:

*Proximity is the most difficult and testing among diplomatic challenges a country faces. We have, therefore, committed ourselves to giving the highest priority to closer political, economic and other ties with our neighbours in South Asia...We regard the concept of neighbourhood as one of widening concentric circles around a central axis of historical and cultural commonalities... pursuing a cooperative architecture of pan-Asian regionalism is a key area of focus of our foreign policy. Geography imparts a unique position to India in the geo-politics of the Asian continent, with our footprint reaching well beyond South Asia and our interests straddling across different sub-categories of Asia – be it East Asia, West Asia, Central Asia, South Asia or South-East Asia.*

The new diplomacy had mixed results. On the whole it yielded rich dividends for improved relations with the major powers and East Asia; but South Asia proved to be an uphill climb. Turmoil in Afghanistan, Pakistan and Bangladesh put peace initiatives with India on the backburner; the Sri Lanka conflict re-escalated; Nepal underwent a revolution and Myanmar another wave of authoritarian crackdowns.

How did India respond to the troubles in its neighbourhood? This paper looks at various case studies of India's foreign relations-with China, Japan, the US, and the EU-to examine what kind of foreign policy actor India is, accounting for varied purposes and power. Do India's current foreign policy actions conform to its founding fathers' vision? If they are different, can they still be called normative? Have Indian views on what constitutes normative foreign policy changed? What can other countries expect from India?

**Case Studies**

The eight cases discussed below reflect different aspects of India's relations with its neighbourhood. One was a neighbouring country (Sikkim), three are neighbouring countries (Pakistan, Nepal and Myanmar), two are part of the wider neighbourhood and are closely involved in South Asia (China more than Japan), and two are not neighbours but are deeply engaged in South Asia (the US and the EU) and discuss their South Asia policies with India. The methodology used is adapted from Tocci (2007). The figure below indicates how the selected case studies reflect the different stylizations of foreign policy. Most of the examples are drawn from the current period, but one—Sikkim—is historical, although we analyse the current impact of an Indian action undertaken 20 years ago.

**Figure: Indian Foreign Policy - Selected Case Studies**

| Type of Actor | Normative | | *Realpolitik* | | Imperial | | Status Quo | |
|---|---|---|---|---|---|---|---|---|
| | Intended | Unintended | Intended | Unintended | Intended | Unintended | Intended | Unintended |
| Goals | Peace & regional integra-tion | Cooperation & coexistence | Commer-cial | Economic & political support | Stable border | Stable relations | *Realpolitik* with normative strand | Maintain bilateral relations |
| Means | CBMs talks trade | Trade border talks | Naval exercises | Military cooperation Govt. to Govt. Diaspora | Annexa-tion | Political pressure/ open borders | Political/ aid pressure | Strong bilateral/ wary EC/EP |
| Result | Moving to normative | *Realpolitik* | Mixed | Norm changing | Integra-tion | Greater acceptance | Status Quo | Moving to normative |
| Case Study | Pakistan | China | Japan | US | Sikkim | Nepal | Myanmar | EU |

The Indian cases do not fit entirely into Tocci's framework. For example, India's goals and means with Pakistan were normative, but the results were mixed normative and status quo; with a hesitant foray into Realpolitic, India-Japan relations are relapsing into a cross between status quo and Realpolitic. Similarly, India's merger of Sikkim was imperial but the results are beginning to be normative. India's goals as well as means with Myanmar had strong normative elements, but the results so far have been status quo. India's goals vis-à-vis the EU were also initially status quo, and the means had a minor normative strand, but the results have been normative.

Nevertheless, the categories serve to sharpen contrasts of detail which add to our understanding of India as a foreign policy actor.

**Normative Unintended: 'Chindia', 2005-07**

**Normative Goals:** The economist-politician Jairam Ramesh (2005), currently Minister of State for Commerce, wrote a book on the potential impact that India-China relations could have on the world if the two countries worked together as 'Chindia'. Chindia rapidly became a concept that defined India's new policy towards China which included a boost to bilateral trade and evolving common strategies in the global marketplace along with the settling of border disputes and developing cooperative mechanisms in Asia. A third goal emerged as a result of India's growing economic and strategic ties with East and South-East Asia avoiding being, or being seen, as a counterweight to China. India has been careful to deal with China within normative frameworks and this the Chinese leadership agrees to (Puri, 2005 and 2006; Varadarajan, 2007a and b).

In April 2005, the two countries signed a Strategic Partnership and set up high level talks to resolve their border disputes. In January 2006 they agreed on a Memorandum for Enhancing Cooperation in the Field of Oil and Natural Gas that permits joint bids on energy assets in third countries. In May 2006 India and China signed a Memorandum of Understanding for joint military exchanges and exercises, collaboration in counter-terrorism, anti-piracy and search-and-rescue efforts. In December 2007 they held their first joint military training exercise and in January 2008 announced they would formulate a joint global economic strategy, including common action in the World Trade Organisation and on regional climate change and agreed on civil nuclear energy cooperation.

These are normative goals and policies insofar as they are grounded in cooperation and international agreements without being directed against third parties. For India, however, pursuit of the normative goal of cooperation has also entailed subordinating other normative objectives, such as support for Tibetan Buddhists. India continues to offer shelter to the Dalai Lama, but has recently traded recognition of Tibet as part of China for Chinese acceptance of Sikkim as part of India (BBC, 2003), a classic Realpolitic action. More significantly, India's energy cooperation with China has led India to ignore normative requirements in both Sudan and Myanmar until 2007, when a course correction began.

**Normative Means:** Bilateral negotiations between India and China are supposedly governed by the normative 'Panchsheel' or five principles of peace-respect for each other's territorial integrity and sovereignty, non-aggression, non-interference in each other's internal affairs, equality and mutual benefit and peaceful coexistence-which are also applied to border settlement negotiations. [5] In policy practice, these normative means have been essentially respected as far as trade, climate change and border negotiations are concerned. In 2003 China and India agreed to reopen the Nathu La pass between Sikkim and Tibet, combining a soft border policy with recognition of each other's claims. Though there are complaints that China has violated the Panchsheel principles over 100 times in the past year by patrolling the Indian side of the border in Arunachal Pradesh, the Indian government has downplayed these violations, saying they are dealt with through the joint border cooperation mechanism (Singh, 2006; Muckerjee, 2008).

Both countries at first ignored a fresh wave of human rights violations in Sudan and Myanmar, where they have high energy (and in the latter, security) stakes at play; yet China has now used its good offices in Sudan and India is attempting to do so in Myanmar. [6]

However, China has shown a disconcerting readiness to drop normative means for Realpolitic ones. For example, under the Panchsheel principles the two countries agreed to exchange maps in order to facilitate border negotiations, and have exchanged maps where the less contentious middle sector is concerned. But the talks have moved to the more contentious northern and eastern sectors, and the Chinese are now refusing to exchange maps (Raman, 2008). China has also used norm-challenging means, such as nuclear and arms aid to Pakistan. Though this declined during the late 1980s and early 1990s, it grew sharply following India's tests in 1998, and was again raised following the India-US civil nuclear energy pact. China recently aided Pakistan's building of the Chashma II and unsafeguarded Khushab reactors with the promise of more reactors to come; supplied plutonium and provided components for ballistic missiles (Paul, 2003; Parthasarathy, 2007). In fact, the bulk of Chinese arms sales are to India's neighbours (Malik, 2001). Indeed, China sometimes seems to make hay from India's normative actions in its neighbourhood-for example, when India suspended arms sales to Nepal in 2005 to put pressure on the King to restore democracy, China stepped in place, though only briefly. [7]

**Non-Normative Results:** The results thus far have not been normative. Chindia has worked where the two countries' national interests have coincided, chiefly in the areas of trade and the pursuit of energy. It has not worked when it came to security issues-though the boundary talks may yet reach normative results based on soft borders and freedom of movement. China has in fact continued to pursue a mixed and partly non-normative approach towards India.

China's support for India's observer status at the Shanghai Cooperation Organization and the pacts signed in 2005-06, especially for joint energy acquisition when China previously outbid India, imply that normative policies have been pursued only when they have coincided with Chinese national interests (lower energy prices). Yet China's policy goal following the 1962 war, according to the secret talks between Nixon and Zhou Enlai, [8] was the containment of India by arming Pakistan and wooing the US, and from the late 1970s China has helped Pakistan develop a nuclear weapons programme. This policy appears to linger on in current Chinese policy (Johnston, 1998, p. 63; Griffin, 2006).

China's 'string of pearls' naval bases in the Indian Ocean stretching from Myanmar in the Bay of Bengal to Gwadar in Pakistan, may be primarily directed at economic expansion, but nevertheless encircle India (Prakash, 2007). While signing several strategic pacts with India, the Chinese government has denounced the growing India-US and India-Japan relations as attempts to contain China, initiate strategic competition in East and South-East Asia and wreck the non-proliferation regime (Jacob, 2006; Rediff News, 2007; People's Daily, 2006 and 2007).

The 2008 declarations made during Prime Minister Manmohan Singh's first visit to China, suggest that some of these irritants are becoming less salient. Chinese opposition to the India-US nuclear energy agreement is down to mild from vociferous (Chandrasekar & Raghavendra, 2008). More significantly, China discussed Pakistan for the first time with India and the 'Vision Statement' issued by Singh and Jiabao indicate Chinese acceptance of India's growing role in Asia:

*The (two countries) will explore together and with other countries a new architecture for closer regional cooperation in Asia and make joint efforts for further regional integration of Asia...The two countries will strengthen their coordination under the framework of Asia- Europe meeting and are committed to strengthening and deepening Asia-Europe comprehensive partnership. [9]*

In other words, in bilateral policy areas China's goals appear to be Realpolitic; but in multilateral areas of engagement, including South and East Asia, India and China are progressing towards normative cooperation. However, it should be noted that China sought to engage with India only after the US did so, which implies Realpolitic goals. And in the 'Vision Statement' of 2008 China has wangled an extraordinary Indian commitment to 'oppose any activity that is against the One-China principle,' [10] without an evident quid pro quo.

Indian suspicions, roused by China's non-normative actions, have led to irrational Indian responses at times. Though the two countries agreed to reopen Nathu La in 2003, it was eventually opened only in 2006 because Indian security analysts feared that infrastructure development on the Chinese side of the pass could bring Chinese arms and troops to the Indian border in hours, and therefore resisted improvement of roads on the Indian side. While China- India trade has risen rapidly, doubling to $38 billion in 2005-07, the trade deficit, which was in India's favour in 2005, has grown to US$ 9 billion, a result that unfavourably impacts upon the quest for normative relations as far as India is concerned.

**Conditioning Factors**

External factors have clearly played a role in explaining India's non-normative results in its relations with China. China's deep engagement in South Asia often leads it to pursue actions that could be inimical to Indian interests. China's infrastructure development, including military infrastructure in Tibet, has heightened Indian fears that China is gaining an unassailable military edge (Rakshak, 2008). India's growing ties with the US, Japan and South-East Asia could challenge China's domination in East and South-East Asia. The two countries are engaged in maritime rivalry in the Indian Ocean.

Yet non-normative results are also explained by internal factors. The two countries have a tendency to overreact to each other's actions, due to their prior history of mistrust and misperception. As sinologist John Garver (2000, p. 311) commented, '[w]hat exists in the Indian Ocean is a classic security dilemma in naval guise. Each side acts to defend itself, but in doing so, threatens the other'.

**Realpolitic Intended: India-Japan Maritime Cooperation, 2006-07**

**Realpolitic Goals:** India-Japan Maritime Cooperation is primarily directed towards protecting commercial sea lanes in the Indian Ocean and East Asian straits, through which over 60 percent of the two countries' energy imports travel, through a subsidiary interest is joint disaster management. The Indian and Japanese navies first worked together in a relief mission for the Tsunami-affected in 2004, along with the US and Australian navies. In 2006, the two countries announced they would boost military cooperation in counter-terrorism and safety of regional maritime traffic and international cooperation for disaster management (Suryanarayana, 2006). In 2007 they held joint exercises with Singapore in the Malacca Strait; with the US off the Japanese coast and in the Bay of Bengal with the US, Singapore and Australia. They also held a quadrilateral meeting on the sidelines of the East Asia Summit.

These goals could be classified as normative, were it not for the US and China factors. China had blocked initial Japanese efforts to join multilateral patrols in the Malacca Straits, opposed the Japanese and Indian bids for seats in the UN Security Council and was reluctant to have India at the East Asian Summit. Both India and Japan, therefore, have a common interest in 'multipolarity' in East and South-East Asia, against dominance by a single country or a bipolar US-China divide (Saran, 2003). To this however, Japanese Prime Minister Abe added in 2007 the proposal of India joining Japan to create an 'Arc of Freedom and Prosperity' constituting democracies in Asia, [11] which would by definition exclude China, prompting Chinese accusations of a policy of containment. [12] The proposal did not take off because the Indian government did not respond and it was shelved when Prime Minister Fukuda replaced Mr. Abe.

At present India-Japan maritime cooperation can be considered Realpolitic with a normative strand, as it conforms to international law and is not directed against any other country.

**Attempted Realpolitic Means:** The term Realpolitic does not apply to Japan-India maritime cooperation in itself. Japan briefly attempted Realpolitic means when Prime Minister Abe proposed the Arc of Freedom and Prosperity, which would have antagonistically challenged growing Chinese domination in Asia, but the idea has been indefinitely shelved. A secondary point is that although maritime cooperation is now an established mechanism between the two countries, more normative cooperation, such as working together for the Sri Lankan peace process, is on the backburner.

This indicates that the two countries are still more comfortable cooperating in traditional areas of national interest convergence and not moving beyond these into more normative terrain.

**Realpolitic Results:** The impact of India-Japan maritime cooperation has been to exacerbate Chinese suspicions of Japan and its opposition to any US-Japan-India alliance (Zhaokui, 2007). Although the US, as a partner in Japan-India maritime exercises, made clear that the joint exercises were not part of an effort to contain China (Armitage & Nye, 2007), as did the Indian and Japanese leaders (Abe, 2007; Varadarajan, 2007), China's relations with Japan plummeted since Prime Minister Koizumi's adoption of a 'normalisation' policy that entailed overturning Japan's post WWII ban on military missions overseas (although he authorised solely civil-military missions) and saw him visiting war memorials that also housed the graves of accused war criminals from the Japan-China war (Calder, 2006, pp. 4-7). Moderating these Realpolitic results however is the fact that China will not allow its suspicions to compromise its relations with India and Japan and China is slowly mending fences.

## Conditioning Factors

External factors set the context for India's Realpolitic approach towards Japan. China had reached an equilibrium with the US under the Nixon administration in the late 1970s and had grown in dominance in East and South-East Asia during the 1990s, when the Clinton administration was focused on European integration and the wars in former Yugoslavia. But Japan's new military exercises and the revival of traditional suspicions regarding the 'normalisation' policy have reignited Chinese fears of an alliance to contain it, fears that some US analysts fanned by advocating a US-India alliance as a counterweight to China (Carpenter, 2001; Weiss, 1999; Hill & Associates, 2005).

Yet, as far as internal determinants are concerned, what diminishes the degree of Realpolitic in India-Japan relations is the fact that India is not prepared to join in a policy expressly aimed at containing China. Both Japan and India have strong economic ties with China. At the same time, analysts in both countries perceive Chinese statements of mistrust as an attempt to restrict their expanding international and Asian roles (Chellaney, 2007).

**Realpolitic Unintended: US-India Civil Nuclear Energy Agreement, 2005-07**

**Realpolitic Goals with a Normative Strand:** The US-India civil nuclear energy agreement was negotiated for Realpolitic goals, to allow India to free itself from the 'nuclear apartheid' as former Foreign Minister Jaswant Singh put it (1998, pp. 41-52) and gain access to civil nuclear energy technology and supplies while continuing to be an unrecognised nuclear weapons-possessing state. The US goal was to acquire a stable ally in an increasingly and dangerously unstable South Asia post-9/11. Though the agreement was based on India's normative conduct-India had not exported nuclear technology or material to other countries and had not threatened the use of nuclear weapons in war-the fact that the two 'estranged democracies' (Kux, 1994) only came together post-9/11 suggests Realpolitic intent and behaviour. The end of the Cold War provided an opportunity for India and the US to develop a common cause, but the 1998 Indian nuclear tests propelled the two into dialogue and brought US pressure on India to join the Non-Proliferation Treaty (NPT). After 9/11, US policy underwent a drastic revision-following the 9/11 attacks the US and India worked together in forwarding military-military and against counter-terrorism. For the first time the two countries began to 'cooperate for their greater security' (Gaffney, 2003).

**Realpolitic and Normative Means:** The means that India and the US used to push through the agreement were primarily normative: negotiations, diaspora support including lobbying, trade, international backing (Russia, France, Mr El Baradei of the International Atomic Energy Agency IAEA). However the agreement itself did both-broke established norms and set new ones. It bypassed the existing regulations of the Non-Proliferation Treaty and set the new norm of exception for a responsible democracy. The Indian government was itself unsure of whether the agreement was Realpolitic or normative-in other words, whether the agreement intended to project India's power abroad or whether it contributed to improve and diversify India's civilian energy supplies-and it did not promote the civil nuclear energy agreement as being about either weapons or energy. Thus, although the agreement was one of several advantages, including collaboration in space research and agricultural development, the visible markers of US-India relations in 2005-07 were accelerated military-military ties, comprising naval and air exercises, mountain warfare training, counter-terrorism and border monitoring practices.

**Un-Realpolitic Results**

In some ways, the Realpolitic goals of the two countries were illusory. In the US, the thrust of improved relations with India had always had a strong normative strand, summed up in the phrase launched during President Clinton's visit to India in 2000 but which has become common currency since then, 'the world's largest and oldest democracies' (Albright, 2000; Ros-Lehtinen, 2005; Thain, 2004). Yet in India there was an opposing normative push, the governing UPA coalition, in power with the Indian communist parties that were antagonistic to the US, always had a hard time selling the importance of a significantly closer relationship with the US to its partners.

Indian domestic opposition to the civil-nuclear energy agreement appears to have revived the Unrealpolitic strand in Indian foreign policy. From the BJP's accusations of compromising India's nuclear weapons programme [13] to the arguments of compromising the independence of India's foreign policy made by communist parties', [14] neither influential political group is prepared to recognise that the agreement is a testimonial of confidence in Indian democracy. While the BJP sought and failed to negotiate a similar agreement during its tenure, according to former Deputy Secretary of State, Strobe Talbot (2004), the Communists' argument that the US-India civil nuclear deal makes supplies conditional on Indian support for or participation in US foreign policy 'adventures', suggests that the Indian government is liable to subordinate its national interest to that of another country. The example they use is of Iran which points to the contrary. The Indian government's position on Iran's nuclear programme is somewhere between the Russian and Chinese positions and the European one. India is opposed to Iran acquiring nuclear weapons but advocates negotiations rather than coercive instruments to resolve the impasse (Sivaswamy, 2005).

The factors blocking an agreement that is clearly in India's national interest are solely internal and reflect the domestic politics in India. The Communist parties see the US as an imperialist hegemony with whom India should not have strong relations; the BJP is not willing to let the agreement go through under Congress' watch. Hence, opposition by these parties has put the agreement in jeopardy. The Communist parties delayed negotiations with the IAEA until January 2008, which represents the next step for getting the Nuclear Suppliers Group on board. Meanwhile, as the US begins the race for Presidential nominations, time is running out for Congress to ratify the agreement.

**Status Quo Unintended: The EU-India Strategic Partnership, 2004-07**

**Status Quo to Normative Goals:** Despite the fact that India entered into a 'Strategic Partnership' with the EU in 2004, which was followed by the launch of a Joint Action Plan in 2005, India's goals are to replicate at the EU institutional level the country's strong bilateral relations with several EU member states. EU's goals in the strategic partnership have stressed upon India as a rising power, citing its newly warm relations with the US, India's growing relations with China and its Look East policy as reasons for multilateral cooperation with India, especially for peace and stability in South Asia (European Commission, 2004). Indian analysts concluded that the EU's failure to achieve a Common Security and Foreign Policy made a substantive policy partnership unlikely (Dasgupta, 2003). Moreover, many of them argued, with reference to the civil nuclear energy agreement, that the EU is 'not willing to take political risks' with India (unlike the US), it will not put the EU-India partnership at the same level as that with China's, and it tends to hyphenate India with Pakistan, though this impression is now fading (Jain, 2005, pp. 6-7). In essence, EU's relationship with India is that of a status quo power, in contrast to the US relationship which is that of a revisionist power, rewriting the rules in India's favour (Mohan, 2006). European analysts had a more positive view of the relationship, but this too was in terms of its potential rather than practice (Cameron, et al., 2005). Up until 2006, progress was chiefly in space cooperation and to some extent in trade. Although on paper, both sides reiterated that their cooperation goals were normative-shared values of democracy and pluralism, commitment to multilateralism, mutual areas of interest in South and West Asia (Government of India, 2004)-in practice there was little coordination on any of these goals.

In 2006 this situation began to change, with the EU gradually coordinating its policy towards Nepal along with India. By 2007, the partnership had developed to the point that the Joint Statement issued at the November 2007 EU-India Summit said that India and the EU 'would preserve and promote peaceful uses of technology through forward looking approaches among countries committed to disarmament and non-proliferation', rather coyly implying EU acceptance of the civil nuclear energy agreement. The Joint Statement emphasised an EU-India commitment to stabilisation and reconstruction in Afghanistan, an area of cooperation that the Indian government had suggested in 2004 in its 'Response' to the EU proposal for a strategic partnership (Government of India, 2004) but got little purchase due to troop-contributing countries' fears of a hostile Pakistani reaction. The Joint Statement also expressed shared views on the conflicts and/or peace processes in Nepal, Sri Lanka, Pakistan and Bangladesh. Each region welcomed the other's inclusion in multilateral structures of which it was part, such as the Asia-Europe Meeting process and the SAARC. And the two announced a slew of new collaborations to deal with climate change that included research and development of alternative energy sources such as bio-fuels and solar energy. [15]

In other words, the goals of the partnership are moving from status quo to normative; a trend that was predicted given the normative self-perception of both regions, but also carries potential for collision between differing perceptions of normative versus 'intrusive' behaviour (Abhyankar, 2003).

**Status Quo Means**

The means that the EU and India used to develop their strategic partnership were chiefly governmental-from ministerial summits to diplomatic and administrative negotiations. Although parliamentary exchanges gathered some steam in 2006 and in March 2007, the European Parliament set up a Delegation for Relations with India, [16] a partner group still has to be set up by the Indian Parliament. Of the implementing groups set up under the Joint Action Plan, the ones that have worked, in terms of moving to the next step, are in science and technology, alternative energy, bio-fuels, aviation, maritime matters and trade. The soft-power elements of the partnership-civil society and cultural exchanges and think tank round tables-have become marginal. The Civil Society Roundtable set up under the partnership is described in the Summit Statement of November 2007 as 'a useful forum'. [17] Cultural exchanges consist of a small film festival and the think tank roundtables that were envisaged at the 2002 Summit met twice between 2003 and 2004 but were then dropped for unspecified reasons. Hard-power elements were even more marginal; an India-EU security dialogue was set up only in 2006 though it was announced in 2005, and meets only once a year; the second dialogue was described as 'a fruitful discussion on global and regional security issues, disarmament and non-proliferation', in other words nothing concrete. Consultations on terrorism are scheduled to resume in 2008 after a gap of three years, [18] although they were the first priority in the 2005 Summit Statement. [19]

By contrast the political statements on South Asia have grown more concrete-while generalised desire for peace and stability in the subcontinent was expressed in all the summit statements, it was only in the 2006 statement that India and the EU spelt out priority steps country by country, and the 2007 statement was even more concrete. On Myanmar, the 2007 Joint Statement called for dialogue with Aung San Suu Kyi and the ethnic groups, and support for UN efforts, including the human rights Rapporteur; on Nepal and Bangladesh it urged early elections; on Sri Lanka it stressed on a 'credible' devolution package and reiterated that there was no military solution; and on Pakistan briefly expressed the hope that stability and democracy would soon return. Despite this apparent policy convergence, joint action was only discussed in relation to Afghanistan 'to continue cooperating and coordinating their efforts to impart greater strength to... a coherent and united international commitment'. [20]

However, the EU has used normative means to expand the partnership through its funding programmes, targeting universities, media and think tank exchanges. The initiative has by and large been one-way as the Indian government has not targeted European universities, the media or think tanks; some Indian analysts view EU development assistance as a projection of its soft power (Abhyankar, 2003).

**Status Quo Results**

The partnership has yielded some soft-power benefits which will aid research and development, especially scientific and technological, in both regions. EU-India trade grew from €40 billion to €47 billion from 2005-06; the EU is one of India's largest trading partner along with China. However, India is the EU's ninth largest trading partner, [21] and accounts for only 1.4 percent of EU outflows. [22]

The two are converging in their political approaches to conflict and/or instability in South Asia, but whether this will result in joint policies and coordinated actions is an open question. As of now it appears likely that each will take independent policy actions. Nevertheless, the EU and India are building institutional ties at a number of different levels, which will strengthen the normative elements of the partnership over time. The problem is, 'how much time?' Meetings are still relatively infrequent and interactions between the EU and Indian officials are around one-twentieth of those with China (Jain, 2005). Despite their efforts, the EU is relatively unknown in India and India is known only in those member states with which it already had strong bilateral relations. In sum, EU-India relations will grow steadily but at a low profile; it would be possible to replace both-hard and soft-power elements of the strategic partnership by research and development goals.

**Conditioning Factors**

The EU-India strategic partnership is overshadowed by the India-US and India-China partnerships, both of which deal with issues of immediate and overweening interest for India. By contrast, although the EU is engaged in South Asia, India has little to gain from EU support, as the EU still has limited leverage in South Asia. It was the American and Chinese attention to India that influenced the EU to seek a strategic partnership with India in the first place, and in the near future these Realpolitic factors may influence EU relations with India more than what the normative factors of pluralist democracy that both regions cite as shared characteristics will. India's approach is to use the EU's competitive reaction to the US in its favour-Indian priorities being to gain scientific collaboration and ensure some freedom of labour movement.

Internally India has yet to come to grips with the EU as an umbrella institution for European countries. Within India, EU member countries are more active diplomatically than the EU is. The EU erroneously sees this as a 'visibility' problem to be solved through better communication and people-to-people contact, but most Europeans view themselves and are viewed as citizens of a particular European country rather than an overarching European Union. Until some balance is achieved between the EU and the member states, the EU will be seen more as a funding and trading organisation than as a strategic policy-maker.

**Conclusion**

What kind of a foreign policy actor is India? From the cases above, a mixed picture emerges, but certain general conclusions can be derived nevertheless. The most important of these is that Indian policy-makers and a large proportion of its middle class of almost 250 million, perceive the country as a rising power. Moreover, this perception is shared by important international players, especially the US, EU and the South East Asian countries. For the first time since it became an independent country, India's leaders describe their new international weight as being based on growing economic clout rather than moral precepts or history (decolonisation). For the first time too, they seek to marry normative goals and behaviour to policies furthering their national interest, broadly defined as extending from traditional to human security for its citizens. Speaking at a think tank in 2007, Foreign Secretary Shiv Shankar Menon identified three key goals for India's foreign policy, 'Firstly, ensuring a peaceful periphery; secondly, relations with the major powers; and, thirdly, issues of the future, namely food security, water, energy and environment'. [23]

The means that he listed to pursue each goal were different. To build peace in the neighbourhood, India looks to create social partnerships, offer economic benefits such as zero tariffs for the poorer South Asian countries, support cross-border infrastructure and development projects, stress upon 'civilisational linkages' that grew from the flow of people and ideas since ancient times and work for intra-regional trade through the SAARC, ASEAN and the East Asia Summit. Significantly, Menon described the neighbourhood, as Saran did, in the same terms as Kautilya, 'expanding circles of engagement, starting with the immediate neighbourhood, West Asia, Central Asia, South-east Asia and the Indian Ocean region'.

Looking at the cases discussed in this paper, there is a clear distinction between India's policies in South Asia and India's policies in East Asia. In South Asia, India has increasingly engaged in peace-making both with its neighbours (Pakistan) and between warring factions within its neighbours (Nepal). India has not been so proactive with the one South-East Asian country with which it shares a land border, Myanmar and is proceeding gingerly in peace-making with its most powerful neighbour, China. Indian policy-makers, therefore, perceive a greater threat to the country's security from instabilities within the South Asian neighbours, an assessment that both-the US and the EU share. They also act with more confidence in seeking to resolve the threat, perhaps because South Asian countries share a common regional forum, the SAARC (even though SAARC's mandate is restricted to economic cooperation). It is significant that Menon's speech was remarkably silent when it came to the peace initiatives that India launched in the late 20th and early 21st centuries, indicating that the country's policy-makers are unwilling to 'talk up' their peacemaking capabilities, or include these in their doctrine of international relations. Whether this means that Indian policy-makers continue to have reservations about the scope of normative actions in international relations, as they did during the Cold War, is an open question.

India's reservations during the Cold War were related to upholding state sovereignty. Hence, while India was one of the UN's largest troop- contributors, it sent troops only under the UN mantle. The only exception was the Indian peacekeeping mission to Sri Lanka in the 1980s, which resulted in a stalemate and withdrawal. As a result, the initiative did not result in expanding India's peacekeeping tenets. Today, the situation is different. India's sovereignty is not under question and India's non-normative behaviour in Sikkim is unlikely to be repeated. India's peace initiatives with Pakistan and in Nepal have been sufficiently sustained to indicate that India is being proactively normative in its behaviour with its neighbours. With India having joined the UN Peace-Building Commission, the inclusion of peacemaking capabilities in its foreign policy doctrine is likely to occur in the coming decade. Turning to the broader Asian neighbourhood, the first striking point is that India's Look East policy indicates a new departure for India- a focus on maritime interests. India has found it easier to develop strong relations with its neighbours at sea than with its land neighbours, and these successes have entered the Indian doctrine. Today Indian policy-makers see India 'at the confluence of two seas'-to use the words of the 17th century Indian ruler, Dara Shikoh. Furthermore, the Indian Navy is involved in an increasing number of multilateral exercises to improve maritime security. [24]

India's Look East policy has clearly been the primary impetus to India's recent economic growth and has deepened strategic relations with the major powers, whom Menon listed as the US, EU, Japan, Russia and China (in that order). India-US strategic cooperation was founded on maritime security in South-East Asia and the Indian Ocean, as was India-Japan strategic cooperation, and the former was accompanied by a rapid rise in trade. Till 2005, the US was India's largest trading partner, with a trade volume of US$ 32 billon that year. The US has now been outstripped as a trading partner by the EU and China, but arguably it was the India-US strategic partnership that prompted the India-EU and India-China partnerships, both of which gained substance only after they took off. Menon tellingly commented that the India-US partnership had a 'positive effect… on our dealings with the rest of the world' (Menon, 2007). That said, India's goals of partnering with the Great Powers were quite different from India's goals as regards Asia; they were, in Menon's words, "access to markets, high technology and resources crucial to our future economic growth and development". While Indian goals thus mix Realpolitic and normative elements, the means that India has used are by and large within the normative framework of international law (the EU-India and India-Japan strategic partnerships).

But they have also on occasion sought to alter or expand international law (the US-India civil nuclear energy agreement). At the same time, India is developing institutional partnerships, for example in space, technology, defence and with agricultural agencies (the EU and the US), as well as through membership of regional forums (the ASEAN Regional Forum and the East Asia Summit).

If these points indicate that India is beginning to expand as a normative foreign policy actor and has been able to bring some depth to its normative behaviour as a rising power, it is also worth noting that Indian policy-makers have encountered a surprising obstacle to achieving some of their goals, in particular the civil nuclear energy agreement in the form of domestic political opposition. This casts doubts on whether there is internal consensus or even clarity on what constitutes national interest. Similarly, India's China policy appears to be timid to the point of subordinating one strand of national interest-of settling border disputes on normative principles and retaining the right to deal normatively with regional issues (Tibet and Taiwan), to another strand of national interest, trade and relations in South-East and East Asia, where China dominates.

These factors indicate that India might remain a rising power for a longer time if the country's political parties have no overarching and non-partisan conception of national interest. This is unlikely to affect India's behaviour as a normative foreign policy actor, although it may dent policy-maker confidence and could mean that India's ability to be effective in its actions will be curtailed. Much depends on how well the India-EU and India-US partnerships develop on the one hand, and how steadily India's Look East policy progresses on the other hand. The potential is good-each set of relationships is based on a strong foundation of goodwill, little strategic competition and diaspora ties. The India-China relationship is more complicated and lacks the foundation that the other three have, but it too could improve as the others progress. In short, India is steadily becoming a more influential as well as a normative foreign policy actor, despite domestic confusion, and this trend is set to grow over the coming decade.

**Notes**

1. Agreements reached in secret were automatically void—although if negotiated by government representatives, the motives of the negotiator and the costs and benefits of the secret agreement would have to be weighed before declaring it void (Kautilya, Book III, Chapter 1).
2. "...open covenants of peace, openly arrived at, after which there shall be no private international understandings of any kind but diplomacy shall proceed always frankly and in the public view" as quoted in Rai (2003).
3. "I have read translations of the most celebrated Arabic and Sanskrit works. I have conversed, both here and at home, with men distinguished by their proficiency in the Eastern tongues... I have never found one among them who could deny that a single shelf of a good European library was worth the whole native literature of India and Arabia... We must at present do our best to form a class who may be interpreters between us and the millions whom we govern, a class of persons Indian in blood and colour, but English in tastes, in opinions, in morals and in intellect. To that class we may leave it to refine the vernacular dialects of the country, to enrich those dialects with terms of science borrowed from the Western nomenclature, and to render them by degrees fit vehicles for conveying knowledge to the great mass of the population" (Macaulay, 1835).
4. See Nehru's speech in the Lok Sabha (House of Commons) on November 19, 1956, (available on the website of the Embassy of India in Budapest: http://209.85.175.104/search?q=cache:ihyjhZG0FHgJ: www.indianembassybudapest.org/html/TnCMinister/Press percent2520Release percent2520-

percent252024percent2520oct.htm
+India+on+Hungary+in+1956&hl=en&ct=clnk&cd=1&gl=in).

5. Agreement on Trade and Intercourse between the Tibet Region of China and India, signed on 29 April 1954 and expanded two months later to cover all bilateral relations between India and China, reiterated in the 1993 Agreement on the Maintenance of Peace and Tranquillity on the Line of Actual Control in the India-China Border Areas (http://mea.gov.in/celdemo/panchsheel.pdf).
6. See Myanmar section below.
7. China asserted that the dismissal of parliament was 'Nepal's internal matter', and supplied the King with arms while other countries cut off military aid (Asian Centre for Human Rights, 2005). China revised its policy following pressure from the US, UK, EU and UN.
8. Record of Historic Richard Nixon-Zhou Enlai Talks in February 1972, George Washington University, Document 3, p. 7. (http://www.gwu.edu/~nsarchiv/nsa/publications/DOC_readers/kissinger/nixzhou/1307.htm)
9. For the full text of China-India joint document, see China View (http://news.xinhuanet.com/english/ 2008-01/14/content_7422097_3.htm).
10. Ibid.
11. The concept of an Arc of Freedom and Prosperity had been outlined by the Japanese Minister for Foreign Affairs, Taro Aso, at the Japan Institute of International Affairs on 30 November 2006 (www.mofa.go.jp/announce/fm/aso/speech0611.html).
12. See www.expressindia.com/fullstory.php?newsid=91247.
13. "Indo-US nuclear deal: Unacceptable, BJP will renegotiate", Organiser, 9 December 2007.
14. "N-deal will erode India's independent foreign policy: Karat", Rediff News, 8 November 2007.
15. India-EU Joint Statement, November 30, 2007. (http://www.delind.ec.europa.eu/en/political_dialogue/summits/eighth/8_joint_statement.pdf)
16. "European Parliament keen on Lok Sabha ties", Nerve News, June 13, 2007 (http://www.nerve.in/news:25350053868).
17. See India-EU Joint Action Plan – Implementation Report, presented at the 8th EU-India Summit, 30 November 2007. (http://www.delind.ec.europa.eu/en/political_dialogue/summits/eighth/8_jap_imp-rep.pdf).
18. ibid
19. "Political Declaration on the India-EU Strategic Partnership", 7 September 2005 (http://www.delind.ec.europa.eu/en/political_dialogue/summits/sixth/political_declaration.pdf).
20. India-EU Joint Statement, November 30, 2007, op. cit. p. 4.
21. "EU-India Trade in Facts and Figures", Brussels, November 29, 2007 (http://trade.ec.europa.eu/doclib/docs/2007/november/tradoc_136935.pdf).
22. "EU-India Trade in Facts and Figures", Helsinki, 12 October 2006 (http://trade.ec.europa.eu/doclib/docs/2006/october/tradoc_130593.pdf).
23. Shri Shiv Shankar Menon, "The Challenges Ahead for India's Foreign Policy", Speech by the Indian Foreign Secretary at the Observer Research Foundation, New Delhi, 10 April 2007 (http://meaindia.nic.in/cgi-bin/db2www/meaxpsite/coverpage.d2w/coverpg?sec=ss&filename=speech/2007/04/11ss01.htm).
24. Cited by Shinzo Abe (http://www.mofa.go.jp/region/asia-paci/pmv0708/speech-2.html).

# PART II

# INDIA AND CHINA

# 7

# Challenges Across the Himalayas: Need for a Firm/Pragmatic Foreign Policy towards China

Sudhir Jacob George

India is confronted with several challenges from across the Himalayas-in short, from China. The long standing unresolved border issues; China's occupation since 1962 of a large territory in the western sector; its stance and designs in the north-east and its activities in Tibet, are a threat to the environment and water resources of the Indian subcontinent.

Environment and its conservation have metamorphosed into one of the most important aspects of Non-Traditional Security. Today, nations of the world are beset with several environmental problems and issues that cut across regions and nations. Water is going to be the most serious challenge that nations will have to contend with, in the 21st century. In South Asia, international rivers constitute as significant proportion of the region's water supply, however water resource management problems arise in the region mainly due to the transnational nature of the sources of water and their uneven geographical distribution. These problems can be divided into the scientific and non-scientific or public/political issues) and stem from a combination of four scenarios:

1. Growing awareness of global and regional disparities in water resource availability engendering increased expectations that bring about a change in water demand.
2. Maintenance of existing levels of water resource availability and their utilization is becoming difficult on the same resource base.
3. Abuse or disregard by one nation, during resource utilization is potentially dangerous for others, usually downstream riparian states.
4. Environmental threats coupled with human displacement caused by imprudent interventions in utility spheres.

In South Asia most of the rivers shared by the riparian states i.e. Nepal, India and Bangladesh, besides Pakistan are now confronted with China emerging as a potential threat with its interventionist polices in Tibet to satisfy its increasing demand for food and water-which is the source of most of the major rivers flowing through South Asian states of the subcontinent.

The Brahmaputra, the lifeline of Assam, flows from Southwest Tibet where it is know as the Tsangpo, through Assam into Bangladesh where it empties into the Bay of Bengal. With over thirty five tributaries, viz, the Subansiri, Bharalu and Dhansiri, flowing through the states of Arunachal Pradesh, Nagaland and Meghalaya, the Brahmaputra runs through some of the most picturesque places in this part of the world. Although this magnificent river flows almost 1,450 km of its course in Tibet and is an important river dividing the whole of Bangladesh into two equal parts, in India, the Brahmaputra mainly meanders through Assam. Here the river has witnessed several civilizational upheavals. The valley is an alluvial land and these rapidly flowing snow fed rivers of the Himalayas find little resistance from its friable soil. Thus they are constantly carving out new channels simultaneously eroding their banks.

The regulation of this mighty river by evolving well coordinated (with Nepal and Bangladesh being involved) scientific methods of flood control, utilizing the excess water by interlinking of rivers and harnessing hydro power can bring about a radical transformation in the life and economy of not only the North East but the entire country as also the other riparian states. The very fact that this has been ignored has given an opportunity to separatist tendencies in the region, to raise the bogey of neglect of the region and its people by the Indian state. It has resulted in the demand for separation form the country, which to an extent has the support of the masses of the region. This has given some neighbouring countries, including China, an opportunity to fish in troubled waters.

However one of the serious problems that looms large on the people of the North East and Bangladesh is, China and its search for water to meet the country's needs in the coming decades. The Tibetan plateau is the principal watershed in Asia and the source of ten major rivers including the Brahmaputra (the Yarlung Tsangpo in Tibet), the Sutlej and the Indus. About 90 percent of Tibetan run-offs flow downstream to China, India, Bangladesh, Nepal, Pakistan, Thailand, Myanmar, Laos, Cambodia and Vietnam. The Chinese scheme to divert water form the south to the north has three segments, the eastern, central and the western routes. The third one should make India and Bangladesh nervous and concerned. The southern part of the western route envisages the diversion of the Yarlung Tsangpo, which will have an immense bearing on the lives of millions in the subcontinent. Originating from a glacier near Mount Kailash, it is the largest river on the Tibetan plateau and the highest in the world. It runs though Tibet before flowing into India, where it becomes the Bharamaputra. One of its interesting features is the sharp U-Turn (known as the Great Bend) that it takes near the Indian border.

It has been discovered recently, that the river's gorge forms the longest and the deepest canyon in the world. It is on this Great Bend that China is planning one of its most important projects-the water diversion scheme. The scheme has two parts; one is the construction of the world's largest hydro-electric power plant on the Great Bend, dwarfing all other similar projects. It is expected to generate 40,000 mega watts, more than twice the electricity produced by the Three Gorges Dam. The second is the diversion of the waters of the Tsangpo which will be pumped northwards across hundreds of kilometres of mountainous region to China's North-Western provinces of Xinjiang and Gansu (http://formus.opendemocracy.net/node/4700, 16.8.09). For South Asia and its people and more particularly India, the enormity of the scheme and its closeness to the Indian border cannot be ignored. It is not only the sheer size of the project, which has to be reckoned with but also the fact that if accomplished, it will have disastrous consequences for millions of people, downstream. Thus, perhaps the next World War would be over water. 'China's green light for the project could indeed be considered a declaration of war by South Asia'.

The project was first reported in the Scientific American over a decade back (June 1996). The article giving credence to the Chinese plan stated, "recently some Chinese engineers proposed diverting water into this arid area (Gobi Desert) from the mighty Tsangpo /Brahmaputra River which skirts China's southern border before dipping into India and Bangladesh. Such a feat would be impossible conventionally but could be accomplished with nuclear explosives. One of the reasons for China refusing to ratify the CTBT could perhaps be the desire to keep open the option of experimenting with peaceful nuclear Explosions".

The Chinese plan, as publicized by the chief planner of Yarlung Tsangpo project is to drill a 15 km tunnel through the Himalayas to divert the water before the U-turn and direct it to the other end of the bend. It was emphasized that its hydropower potential could be used to pump water to North-West China over 800 kms away. In recent years, the Chinese have been discreet abut the project though a few reports have continued to percolate. A news report from Beijing in October 2000 stated, "Chinese leaders are drawing up plans to use nuclear explosions, in breach of the international test ban treaty, to blast a tunnel through the Himalayas for the world's biggest hydro-electric plant".

The construction of this multi-billion project is tentatively reported to begin in 2009. The consequences of a huge storage on the Yarlung Tsangpo and the diversion of the waters to north western China are multiple and far reaching for Tibet, India and Bangladesh. More importantly this project threatens the human rights of the people living downstream. Can one state wilfully violate the human rights of people of neighbouring countries to selfishly uphold the needs and 'rights' of its own people? (http://forums.opendemocracy.net/node.47020, 16.8.2009).

**Consequences of the Chinese Plan**

If the project pulls through, India as well as Bangladesh would be at the mercy of China for adequate release of water during the dry season, and for protection from floods, during the rainy season. The unprecedented floods in Arunachal Pradesh in 2000 and the overflowing of the Parichu Lake and the lingering threat to Himachal Pradesh in 2005-06 are ominous signs. India is aware from its domestic experience of the difficulties in securing a resolution to water disputes. Thus when it comes to a trans-boundary question (where the boundary is not even accepted and demarcated), it seems an uphill task to find a workable understanding.

Precipitation in Northern and North-eastern India, including in Assam and Bangladesh, is very high-80 percent during the four monsoon months (June to September) and low (2 percent) during the remaining eight months. China, for her own interests could withhold water for power generation and irrigation during the dry season and release water during the flood season with catastrophic consequences for eastern South Asia. Further an event in June 2000 could be a warning to what may occur on a larger scale, if the Tsangpo project is completed. At that time, the breach of a natural dam in Tibet, led to severe floods that resulted in hundreds of deaths in the hilly state of Arunachal Pradesh. Obviously areas downstream, in Arunachal and Assam are extremely vulnerable to what takes place upstream in Tibet.

The massive diversion of the river to China's North-West would have even more devastating consequences. North-East India and Bangladesh would be starved of their lifeline. Nutrient rich sediments that enrich the soil of these regions would be held back in reservoirs instead of reaching the river's delta. Millions would be affected. A water war could ensue.

One aspect that merits consideration is that once a project is on the drawing board, China reckons it as prestigious and thus, it would ensure its implementation whatever be the consequences, as the leaders in Beijing do not like to lose face. There is also the competition angle. Beijing is aware of the Indian plan to link most of the Indian rivers. The Chinese would not like to be seen as lagging behind India in grandiose schemes. If the Tsangpo project is implemented, large parts of the scheme of linking the rivers in India would be redundant.

Lastly and this aspect bears serious consequences: the Great Bend is located in a highly earthquake prone area. A huge reservoir and a few Nuclear Power projects could provoke new earthquakes, even more devastating than the August 1950 tremor or that hit the North-East, when thousands lost their lives. Will men be wise to learn from the past and comprehend natures limit and reactions before wanting to alter her? Has man learnt to heed to past experiences? (http://forums.opendemocracy.net/node.4702, 16.8.2009).

Besides the Tsangpo diversion project, China's hyper-development activity in and around Tibet with the introduction of the Rail network into Tibet and massive Road construction projects are major hazards to the eco-system of the Himalayan belt. The Qinghai-Tibet rail line, of which 1,110 kms have been laid, passes though the Himalayan mountain terrain and runs from Golmud to Lhasa in Tibet. With this rail line, having been operationalized since the July 1, 2006, Beijing has been connected to Lhasa by rail, the rail line traversing a total distance of 4,064 km. The Golmud-Lhasa section of the Beijing-Lhasa Rail, climbs over a pass of 5,072 meters-16,737 feet above the mean sea level, making it the highest rail network in the world. It is contended that the new rail line has pushed the Himalayan regions (Tibet's) economic growth to 13.2 percent (2006 figures), a ten year high. The rail to Lhasa has carried more than 1.5 million passengers to the roof of the world, since 2006. The Chinese authorities view the rail line as an important toll in modernizing Tibet that has been a part of China since its occupation by Chinese troops in the 1950's. Further, besides the extension of the rail network into Tibet, the new roads that have been built in the Himalayan region viz., the Sichuan-Tibet highway, as also the China Nepal Highway have led to the flooding of Tibet by the Han Chinese majority. This indeed is a major threat to Tibet's indigenous population. The sudden surge in the population of Tibet together with the construction activity has led to the acceleration of environmental degradation in the pristine Himalayan region with long term consequences for the neighbouring countries viz., Nepal, India and Bangladesh besides Tibet. (http://www/phayul.com/news/article).

The unresolved boundary between Indian and China is another major challenge that India is confronted with, for over five decades now. The essence of the border dispute is over China's refusal to accept the McMohan Line as the border between the two countries. In the 1950s soon after occupying Tibet, China occupied a large tract (approx 38,000) sq km of Aksai Chin in Ladakh, in Jammu and Kashmir, bordering Pakistan and built a highway (NH 219) through it connecting it with the Chinese province of Xinjiang. India regards this as an illegal occupation. In 1963, almost 5,180 km in Pakistan occupied Kashmir was ceded to Beijing by Islamabad under a Sino-Pak boundary agreement. Indian reckons this too as an illegal occupation.

(http://www.rediff.com/news/2006/nov/16sld.htm)

In the middle sector or southern Tibet, China asserts that the border dividing Tibet and Sikkim and U.P are disputed. In the eastern sector, it lays claim upon the entire state of Arunachal Pradesh. While China officially stakes claim upon the entire Indian state of Arunachal, it is the small district of Tawang in Arunachal Pradesh that borders Tibet and Bhutan, that it is eyeing the most. Tawang is famous for its monastery built in 1681 in honour of the fifth Dalai Lama, Nagwang Lobsang Gyatso. It is also the birth place of the present Dalai Lama, living in exile in India. China cites the monastery as evidence that the district once belonged into Tibet and it is seeking its return, in order to settle the row between the countries. The Chinese in this connection state, "we do not recognize the entire Arunachal Pradesh state as being part of India and Tawang is particularly special. It has long standing historic links with Tibet and it is important for us to be able to settle the problems". This statement is indeed ironic since Arunachal is principally a Buddhist region historically and Tawang and its monastery which is a special place for the people of Arunachal Pradesh, which is an integral part of India. It is indeed strange that the Chinese very often rake up the issue of Tawang and Arunachal.

Recently on August 7, 2009, on the day of the 13th round of negotiations between India and China on the border issue, the official Chinese news agency raked up these issues stating, "China did not accept the illegal McMohan Line. In Chinese thinking Arunachal Pradesh is southern Tibet and that's that". Earlier the Chinese radio launched a scathing attack on India for proposing to place an Army mountain division and an Air Force Squadron in Arunachal. It is indeed ironic that since 1989 when Deng Xiaoping signalled to Rajiv Gandhi that the two countries defreeze their relations, Beijing has engaged in a massive exercise to establish 'multi-dimensional' relations with all countries of South Asia-the military facet being the most prominent. Adhering to its String of Pearls Policy, it has acquired deep sea ports in Gwader (Baluchistan and Sri Lanka (Hambonthota) and Myanmar, with which an incipient nuclear relationship is thought to be in the offing. However, though this does not amount to encircling India but it is bound to undermine India's diplomatic and cultural space in the Indian Ocean Region (I.O.R) (*The Deccan Chronicle*, 11 August, 2009).

Further, compounding the aforementioned Chinese moves, a recent article written by a Chinese analyst under a pseudonym lays bare the sincerity of the Chinese towards normalizing ties with India. The August 8, 2009 article which coincided with the recently concluded 13th round of Sino-Indian border talks was captioned 'If China takes a little action the so called great Indian Federation can be broken up'. In this article the analyst states that China should back aspirations of Nagas, Assamese, Kashmiris and Tamils for their independent states, as in

Europe. The premise being with the exception of the Hindi heartland, India did not exist as a Nation in history. The article titled 'Zhan Lue' (Strategy) also argued for encouraging Bangladesh to strive for the independence of West Bengal and wresting the 90,000 sq. km of Indian territory in 'Southern Tibet' i.e. Arunachal Pradesh. Although this article may not reflect the views of the Chinese government the fact that a prominent Chinese think tank published it indicates some official sanction. Another article published a few months ago visualized a partial war with India. The analyst said, "the best for China would be to dismember India and to make her spit what she has swallowed"(see the comments of the Director, China Studies, Chennai's comments in a Report of *The Deccan Chronicle*, 11 August 2009).

Despite the intransigence of China over the border issue and its activities in Tibet and in the neighbourhood, India has consistently followed the policy of normalization of ties with its neighbour lying across the Himalayas. In this direction India has accepted the Autonomous Region of Tibet as part of China and has reigned in Tibetan exiles living in India from indulging in anti-China activities from its soil. India has also enabled the Beijing Olympic torch relay run through New Delhi without any blemish. Notwithstanding these gestures, China has not made its position clear and categorical as regards Sikkim and continues to make provocative statements about Arunachal Pradesh. Besides, it was totally opposed to India's nuclear tests and the de facto nuclear power status it gained consequent to it. China was also opposed to India's civil nuclear arrangement with the United States. However adhering to a pragmatic policy vis-à-vis China, India has augmented its economic and trading ties with it, and it is proving to be beneficial to both the countries. Keeping aside the irritants India has gone ahead and entered into a Ten-Point Strategy in November 2006 with China, to strengthen ties. This Ten Point Strategy inter alia also includes concluding the bilateral Investment Promotion and Protection Agreement.

On the trade front, both the countries signed a historic agreement to resume border trade through the strategic Nathu La pass. Trade between the two countries via the Nathu La commenced form the 6th of July 2006, after 44 years of closure. The re-opening of trade through Nathu La is contended to boost the local economies of the land locked mountainous regions of the two Asian giants. In this direction the Commerce Ministry of the Government of India has liberalized trade with China through the Nathu La in Sikkim, enhancing the limit on the value of a single consignment to rupees one lakh from just twenty five thousand rupees. The liberalized rules notified by the Directorate General of Foreign Trade, meets the long pending demand of the Sikkim based, India-China Trade Association. Though, India and China commenced trading through Nathu

La in June 2006, only a limited basket of items were permitted both-for exports and imports. As per the present terms Indian can export only twenty items, while China can sell only fifteen commodities to India. Due to heavy restrictions, trade through Nathu La has stagnated at rupees nineteen lakh. These are insignificant in volume as compared to the total two way trade figures between the two countries which is valued at fifty billion dollars!

The pragmatism shown by Indian leadership in its efforts to normalize ties by increasing/strengthening bilateral economic and trade links, is commendable. However India's trust deficit with China can never be liquidated, unless the thorny issues, in particular the boundary issue, is resolved. To this end, India has to adhere to a firm line vis-à-vis China particularly in respect of the impending threats from the other side, to its river water sources, territories and its standing in the region.

To grapple with this harsh reality vis-à-vis China, India will have to adhere to the following principles:

1. It will have to have to strive towards a settlement of the border issues with out, at any point, compromising on its territorial integrity in the western, middle and eastern Sectors. On the border issue, protecting India's national interest to the hilt should be the only mantra.
2. As regards Chinese efforts to tinker with the water sources of the subcontinent in particular the Tsangpo/Brahmaputra, India's policy should be clear and firm. It should adhere steadfastly to the principle that no international waterway should be tampered with, as all the riparian states are stake holders of the water emanating form a single source, in this case the Tibetan Himalayan watershed. If China at some point ignores this fact and goes ahead with its river diversion plan in the Himalayas, India will have to internationalize the issue and compel China to adhere to international legal norms as regards the sharing of international river water(s).
3. On the trading front India must force China to stop its clandestine trade across the Eastern and North-Eastern regions of India and trade only through the established legal channels between the two countries and adhere to set inter-state trading norms. The flooding of Chinese goods into the east and the North-East has wreaked havoc for the local domestic consumer industry and this malaise is spreading rapidly to other parts of India. To counter this, India will have to launch a vigorous-quality and cost controlled-consumer goods drive to edge out the Chinese goods now present all over the country, particularly in the eastern and the North-eastern states.
4. Though the Chinese may be having an edge in military terms it is imperative for India to be vigilant vis-à-vis China all the time. In this direction, it is

imperative to strengthen our borders and enhance the fire power of our armed forces by equipping all the three wings with superior weapons and technology.

5. Finally and the most important step that India has to initiate is to enhance and extract the support and loyalty of our people living in the strife torn frontier state/states. This is indispensable because when people are united and loyal to their motherland/ Nations State, no outside entity can cast an evil eye upon it or indulge in any misadventure against it. To attain this, all the pending problems of the border people will have to be addressed as soon as possible, so that our citizens living on the nation's frontiers can be the bulwark of our defence and the country's fortress on the frontier(s).

**References**

http://forums.opendemocracy.net/node/47020 dt.16.8.2009.

http://www.rediff.come/nesw/2006/nov/16sld.htm

http://www/phayul.com/news/article

McDonld Bernadette. Whose Water Is It? The Unquenchable Thirst of Water Hungry World. National Geographic Society Press, Washington D.C. 2003.

Pearce, Fed When The Rivers Run Dry: Water - the Defining Crisis of the 21st Century. Beasonc Press, Boston. M.A., 2006.

Shiva, Vandana. Water Wars: Privatizations, Pollution, And Profit South end Press, Cambridge, M.A. 2002.

The Deccan Chronicle (Hyderabad) 11.8.2009.

The Deccan Chronicle (Hyderabad) 12.8.2009.

Zaman M.Q. 'Rivers of Life: Living with Floods in Bangladesh" Asian Survey, Vol. .33. No October, 10 1993, pp. 986-996.

# 8

# Maritime Dimensions of India-China Relations

R.S. Vasan

It was way back, during the Ming dynasty that the Chinese Admiral, Zheng He undertook seven voyages around the world. During these voyages he visited East Africa, Persia as well as other littorals in the Indian Ocean Region.

Chinese interest in its maritime neighbours can be traced to ancient times and this has included not just the South China Sea but also the distant corners of both the Pacific as well as the Indian Ocean. If that was the case with the ancient sea farers from China six centuries ago, closer home, the kingdoms of Southern India established their sway over large parts of Southeast Asia. Not only them, western India also housed the great Admiral Kanhoji Angre, who successfully kept all offenders, including later day colonial masters at bay due to his naval prowess.

Thus, it is evident that both India and China understood the importance of the seas and made determined attempts to conquer them and exercise control in distant areas since times immemorial. Though both nations were characterized by a reduced interest in maritime affairs for some time, a sustained GDP growth and a robust economy have revived this interest in these two Asian giants, in this modern era.

As it stands today, the modernization of the PLA Navy has caused a lot of consternation not just in its neighbourhood but also in distant corners of the world. China's maritime prowess is growing in strength with sustained economic positives. The Chinese have a well orchestrated policy to increase their maritime clout particularly in the Indian Ocean. The maritime interests of the Chinese today mainly stem from:

- **Requirement of Strategic Nuclear Deterrence:** The Chinese are indeed worried about the Taiwan factor and the possible intervention of the West led by the US. It has therefore heavily invested in military modernization and also building up a credible nuclear force. Nuclear submarines (SLBMs) number over ten and more would be built with the capability to strike targets in US. While no official figures are available, the military spending has been estimated to be from about 70 to 200 million dollars. With the political leadership not willing to take any chances with adversaries both in the immediate neighbourhood and the extended neighbourhood, China has taken every precaution on land, over water, in the air and in cyber space.

- **Energy Dependence:** The acute dependence of China on energy products from around the world is yet another factor that has compelled the Chinese to start stepping out of the confines of the Malacca Straits. Over 80 percent of the energy flow into China is through the Malacca Straits. China's economy is dependent on the ability of the Chinese Government to maintain sustained energy supplies through the seas. That large quantities of oil and gas need to be imported bring in the factor of energy chain vulnerability that obviously engages the attention of the political and military planners of energy dependent countries. It is a challenge indeed to be able to operate in far off areas and wield influence by using the maritime forces as instruments of national policy. China is addressing these challenges in a well calibrated strategy along with a foreign policy that aims to bring the Indian Ocean Region nations under its influence one way or the other. The most popular handle used is the investment in the target country and a dedicated effort to build linkages that could serve as leverages in the hour of need.

Also instead of putting all its eggs in one basket, it is also exploring the possibilities of finding alternate viable routes for the transhipment of oil and gas. Thus, it is seriously contemplating cutting across the Kra Isthmus to bring down the dependence on Malacca Straits. However, even the Kra Isthmus would be under the surveillance of India and this thought would be discomforting as it bears a factor of vulnerability in the Indian Ocean due to the strategic positional advantage enjoyed by India.

1. **India's Emergence as a Regional Power Centre:** Indian Navy's growth in the region has been quite impressive and there is no one within the immediate neighbourhood who could match the might of the Navy. At the time when the Indian Navy was growing at a rapid pace, China went to the extent of publicly declaring that Indian Ocean is not India's ocean clearly indicating that it would challenge the maritime supremacy of India in its backyard. China which is dependent on the critical Sea Lines of Communication (SLOCs) would want to address issues of vulnerability of SLOCs that criss-cross under the watchful eyes of Indian surveillance architecture. With the predominant presence and power of the Indian Navy the Chief of the Naval Staff has identified the Indian Ocean as a 'weak area' for the Chinese.
2. **Policy of Encirclement:** China has been assiduously building spheres of influence in India's neighbourhood to further its national objectives. Pakistan has remained a strong ally for over five decades and there is convergence of ideas and thoughts about containing India. In a calculated move, China has

invested heavily or is planning to build deep water ports not only in Pakistan but also in Sri Lanka and Myanmar. It is also looking at Bangladesh as a friend who would perhaps open up its ports for use by the Chinese in need. These have been described as dependency ports by the outgoing Navy Chief Admiral Suresh Mehta who maintained, "They are not happy and are concerned with our presence in the Indian Ocean. And therefore they have to do this, i.e., build dependency. That is their strategy and they are doing it to come over here and be present in the Indian Ocean in larger numbers."

3. **Fears of Strategic Alliance of Those Perceived as Inimical to Growth of China:** China has always viewed with suspicion the US led initiatives in the Indian Ocean/Bay of Bengal for coordinated naval exercises. The combined exercise conducted in 2007 among US, Japan, Australia, UK, Singapore and India was seen as grouping of those who wanted to convey a message to China about the coming together of democracies against what was perceived as an undemocratic Government that ignored human rights. The declaration that promotion of democracy is a goal, also was not very comforting to China which saw the declaration as a scheme to belittle the progress of China by highlighting human rights abuses.
4. **Requirement of Tackling Maritime Terrorism and Piracy:** Though the number of piracy attacks in the Malacca straits has come down drastically, the increasing incidents of piracy particularly in the Somalian waters is a matter of serious concern for all maritime nations including China. While many nations did send their men of war to patrol the waters off Somalia, India sent a strong message to the pirates by assertive action by sinking a commandeered vessel that was being used for hijacking ships. China did not want to be left behind as the opportunity presented China to test out for itself its own capability to operate in distant waters and also to send a strong message to observers around the world not just about the capabilities of PLA-Navy but also its intentions. After its successful and sustained operations in the Gulf of Aden since December 2008, China has flexed its muscle and declared that it is here to stay as an Indian Ocean power whenever the circumstances so demand.
5. **Peaceful Development:** The Chinese have publicly adopted a strategy of peaceful development for growth. However under the garb of peaceful development, China is spending a lot of money towards military modernization with a view to be able to possess the military might that would provide the essentially powerful tool of foreign policy. The main adversary is US with its known displeasure with China on many counts including the human rights record. However, both China and US have dependent

economies and there are limits to posturing. That would remain within a certain sphere of actions that would not go out of hand. Depending on the situation, definitive amount of sabre rattling would be witnessed with self imposed restraint on both sides to see that the situation does not go out of hand. Peaceful development as a strategy appears to be paying rich dividends to China as it knows that it has put its adversaries at ease with these proclamations which only provide some additional time to refine their strategies. Indian Ocean therefore forms part of this peaceful development in which China would continue to invest in the Indian neighbourhood economically, politically and also in other spheres of mutual interest. The response of India and other nations would depend on how they view military modernization and economic growth-as threats or as opportunities for mutual cooperation.

6. **Ship Building and Mercantile Trade:** China is way ahead in terms of its ship building capacity and in terms of its mercantile trade. The ports serve the import export needs of the country not merely for energy but also for receiving raw materials and exporting finished products which have captive markets in the west and also in many other parts of the globe. Unlike India, China's shipping is completely state owned and is fully supported in its expansion plans. Chinese are competing with the best ship yards for ship production. It may be recalled that in a global tender, China was kept out of a port only on security considerations.

When a similar examination in the case of India is undertaken, it would reveal somewhat similar patterns in the perception of the Indian planners. Indian Navy started growing only after the successful attacks on Karachi during the liberation of Bangladesh. Additional funding support and some sound planning enabled the Indian Navy to grow into a potent force to be recognized as such. India has also started reaching out to other corners of the world in a show of strength with its visits for power projection and cooperation with the navies of the world, including China.

Mercantile trade growth has not been very impressive despite the large dependence on the seas for export and import of various products. Slowly the face of ship building and refit industries are also changing and there is lot of promise for the future as more and more operators have shown interest in maritime related industry, in the country. India's maritime industry's growth was stagnant for a long time. The long gestation period for infrastructure and lack of funds prevented the growth in this sector at the desired pace. However, there are more and more private operators who are now interested in ports, ships, off-shore installations and infrastructure.

A study of India's stated/perceived foreign policies in the Indian Ocean region would be necessary in order to understand the power play in the region in which both India and China have serious strategic interests.

**India's Maritime Foreign Policy in the Indian Ocean Region**

Many analysts seem to think that 'China has an edge in the IOR region. However, a dispassionate analysis clearly illustrates a slightly different point of view. A closer examination of the maritime relations in the IOR would reveal facts which may actually place India in a slightly better place.

**Sri Lanka:** Both due to historical and cultural relations that have existed for centuries, the relations between the two neighbours have been good. There were of course phases of strained relations due to the Tamil factor. However, this remained a factor only till the assassination of the former Prime Minister of India, Rajiv Gandhi. Successive Governments including coalition governments at the Centre have not given any quarter to the supporters of the LTTE. India provided material and moral support to the fight against the LTTE despite some resistance by some regional parties who continued to support the LTTE with full knowledge of its track record of violence, extortion, child recruitment, illegal trade and drug peddling.

While the development of Hambanthota in southern Sri Lanka has been claimed as a win for the Chinese in the power play in the IOR, the facts are that India did not capitalize on the opportunity to develop this port that was offered to it in the first place. India cooperated actively during the tactical phase of its sea battle with the LTTE and the intelligence inputs provided by Indian surveillance proved crucial in neutralizing the logistical ships of the LTTE which were carrying military hardware that was difficult to get across to the LTTE controlled areas. The Chinese also provided essential military hardware. During the entire phase of the war, the Indian Coast Guard and the Indian Navy were in constant dialogue with their counter parts to sort out issues as and when they developed. The Chinese had no such interaction when it came to maritime military cooperation. Even after the development of Hambanthota, it is unlikely that it would be offered for military use by the Chinese while the intention of the Chinese would indeed be to use this facility as a dependency port in times of crisis.

Sri Lanka has gained from its friendly relations with India, Pakistan and China in its war against the LTTE. However, as asserted every now and then by the leaders on both sides, India does enjoy special relations and it is unlikely that Sri Lanka would want to break this mutually beneficial association. Sri Lanka however cannot be blamed for using the China/Pakistan card as leverages for getting a little more from its bigger neighbour.

There is another dimension to the relation between the two countries and that relates to Fishing in the Palk Strait. The fertile fishing grounds around the Kachchativu Island which was ceded by India about 35 years ago has remained an Island of contention for fishermen from Tamil Nadu and Sri Lanka. However, this is localized and is unlikely to involve China in the immediate neighbourhood in any perceivable manner.

**Bangladesh:** If Gwadar in the Arabian Sea is the port of origin in the scheme of things for the Chinese, ports in Bangladesh are on the radar scan of China for developing 'dependency' ports. There is a talk of accessing some of the ports of Bangladesh through the network of roads and rivers from China. Depending on the Government in power in Bangladesh, relations with India go through a cycle of ups and downs. The Chinese would have plans for engaging Bangladesh in investments and also by supplying essential military hardware including ships. Bangladesh also has maritime border disputes with both India and Myanmar. With the criticality of energy products, and the expectations of such finds in the EEZ, there would be territorial disputes over sea areas. Bangladesh would be looking for support and also would be in the process of equipping itself with a decent sized navy that could intervene should it be necessary. It is not that the Bangladesh Navy would be in a position to take on the might of the Indian Navy, but she would like to have a minimum deterrence vis-à-vis its maritime neighbours. It is here that the Chinese initiatives are of importance in the Bay of Bengal.

**Myanmar:** India distanced itself from the Military Junta for a long time as it felt that democratic processes were suppressed and human rights were constantly abused. The Chinese had no great respect for human rights and found it easy to engage with the military rulers of Myanmar. The supply of arms and ammunition and the excellent relations that China enjoyed with Myanmar was not comforting for India. Overriding its stand on Myanmar, India was compelled to engage with the military Junta to prevent total control of the Myanmar Government by the Chinese who were looking for a foot hold in the Bay of Bengal. The Chinese had already leased the Coco Islands for setting up their listening posts much to the discomfiture of Indian strategists. It appears that not much can be built on the Coco Island, yet, it is significant that this Island bears the first foot prints of China in the BoB.

**Pakistan:** China and Pakistan have enjoyed excellent strategic and military cooperation for many decades due to India being identified as a common enemy. The opportunity for getting a foot hold close to the Strait of Hormuz came the Chinese way when Pakistan was looking at developing another Port along the

Makaran coast. The devastating attacks by the Indian Navy in 1971 had clearly brought out that having just one port was counterproductive as the blockade of such a port could be easy for a determined Navy supported by its Air force. China readily jumped at the opportunity and invested heavily in the port development. Unlike Sri Lanka, Pakistan has no qualms about providing all facilities to China who has stood by Pakistan in its hour of need through all the sixty two years of Pakistan's existence.

However, the deployment of the Chinese units from Gwadar would not escape monitoring by the US led task forces close to the Strait of Hormuz. With the increased strategic realignment with India, it is quite likely that US would provide the necessary intelligence on the actions of the Chinese.

**West Asia:** Many analysts have felt that the western neighbours were ignored in the quest for gaining diplomatic and political ground in the east with the look east policy. This can be analyzed by the predominant presence of US led forces who have been in and around the Strait of Hormuz for monitoring the activities in Iran and Iraq and also for intervening as and when required.

**Singapore:** The relations between the two countries have been very good and there has been regular interaction between the maritime forces of the two countries. Singapore has consistently attempted to have good relations with both India and China and has by and large succeeded in balancing the relations. The trade relations are growing and many Singapore based marine companies are using Indian sea farers and their skills for even managing their maritime enterprise. Singapore has also been actively participating with Malaysia, Indonesia and Thailand in combating piracy in the Malacca Straits.

**Other South East Asian Countries:** There is good interaction at both the working and the top level in terms of extending the spheres of cooperation mainly in the areas of Search, Rescue and Disaster Management. The positive and timely assistance provided by the Indian maritime forces post Tsunami to the affected countries has bolstered the image of India as a capable country which has the wherewithal to manage large scale disasters simultaneously in different theatres.

**Vietnam:** While there have been historical differences and wars between China and Vietnam, presently there is a climate of economic cooperation. Vietnam has a decent maritime force and also is a claimant to many of the disputed areas of the Spratley Islands.

**Indonesia:** The past legacy of Sri Vijaya Empire has visible influences even today. This is another country that could be developed as an independent power centre along with Vietnam to provide the counter balance in the region to China's growth.

**Thailand:** Thailand has also had its differences with China on ownership issues in the Spratley Islands. However, the peaceful development concept adopted by China has reduced tensions in the areas of conflict. Due to historical reasons, Thailand has good relations with India. It is the only country in the region besides India that operates an aircraft carrier and has shown a keen interest in developing its maritime potential.

**Spratley Islands**: Different islands of over 4, 00,000 Square kilometres of area have been a bone of contention between the Littoral states in the China. China seems to have differences with all the states in the region on the ownership. However, in 2002 all the claimants agreed to defer resolving of the disputes to a later date. Despite such understanding, China has in the past shown its aggressive intent by dispatching its patrol vessels much to the consternation of other nations in the region who view such acts as provocative and without reason.

**Maldives:** For military and strategic analysts particularly in India who have been apprehensive of the recent Chinese overtures in the Indian Ocean, the news of the impending defence/security pact between India and Maldives likely to be concluded by the end of August by the Defence Minister Mr. Antony would provide a certain degree of assurance that China cannot have a cake walk in our maritime neighbourhood.

The Chinese have been wooing Maldives too by providing aid and investing in that country. There was talk about the likely use of Marao one of the largest atolls, by the Chinese to promote their commercial and military interests. However, due to historical and cultural relations with the Maldives and the active role played by India in thwarting an attempted coup by launching 'Operation Cactus' in the Maldives in November 1988 the ties between the two countries have remained strong. During the Presidency of Gayoom, India gave a lot of importance to the improvement of relations with the Maldives. The relations with the new president Mohammed Nasheed, popularly called Anni, have also been extremely productive. In addition to this, the intention of the new Government to cooperate in the security realm with India is indicative of the continued importance that both countries have attached to the strategic dimensions in the Arabian Sea. The perceptions of both the Governments also appear to converge when it comes to tackling terrorist attacks sponsored by radicals.

India also readily reached out to its neighbours including the Maldives immediately after the Tsunami on December 26, 2004. The humanitarian aid and relief was provided under 'Operation Castor'. With low lying atolls, the threat of inundation due to Tsunamis is quite high and there lies a need to provide quick relief to the victims in the event of such an eventuality. The fear of getting submerged with the rising sea due to global warming haze prompted the Government of Maldives to seriously scout for real estate for its citizens in other parts of the world. India obviously enjoys the positional advantage and has the wherewithal and material advantage to provide help and succour in the event of a natural calamity or manmade disaster in the Islands.

In more specific terms, India would be transferring two helicopters to the Maldives for surveillance and would also install an integrated radar network with linkages to naval command centres on the West coast of India. As per reports, the first Helicopter would be handed over by the Defence Minister during his visit from 20-22$^{nd}$ August. The second from the Navy would be transferred at a later date. It is evident that these helicopters would also be used for disaster mitigation related tasks.

From the point of view of Indian security, in a post 26/11 scenario, this is an important development as India augments its Maritime Domain Awareness (MDA) potential in the Arabian Sea by the expanded surveillance/response capability. The strategic location of the Maldives that straddles the Sea Lines of Communication (SLOCs) would enable the combined surveillance mechanism to detect, identify, track and prosecute targets on establishing the threat potential. India gifted INS Tillanchang a Fast Patrol Vessel (named after one of the Islands in the A&N group of Islands) in April 2006 to the Maldives National Security Service (NSS). The vessel is now named Huravee after a hero and a freedom fighter and would be an effective component of the response mechanism in Maldivian waters.

The air elements of the Indian Navy and the Indian Coast Guard have been undertaking reconnaissance sorties in the EEZ and would now be in a position to augment the surveillance efforts of the Maldivian security forces. There has been active and positive cooperation between the security forces of the two countries and many security personnel from Maldives are being trained in India. It has also been reported that the team of experts from Maldives would be visiting Andaman and Nicobar group of Islands to be exposed to means, methods and the manner in which security of over 524 Islands is being coordinated by the tri services Commander.

While it is always not necessary to look at all these developments in the Indian Ocean through the Chinese prism, this development in the Arabian Sea has enormous significance for India's maritime posturing vis-à-vis China whether intended or not.

It may appear that China has encircled India. In reality, forward posturing despite the friendly bases would be a challenging task given the long distances from Chinese waters and the long vulnerable supply chains. In the long run, the PLA-Navy would be looking at Gwadar, Hambanthota and similar ports in Myanmar and Bangladesh as forward posts that could help in extending logistical support. The Chinese recently did operate for extended periods off the Somalian coast on anti piracy patrols demonstrating the capabilities of a blue water navy. Since having left Hainan for the first time on the $26^{th}$ of December 2008, for the anti piracy task in the Gulf of Aden, the Chinese fleet has maintained an active patrol in the Gulf of Aden by rotating its units every 2-3 months. It is also interesting to note that one of the Chinese guided missile destroyers Shenzhen (DDG 167) called at the port of Kochi on its return passage last week (August 10, 2009) and exchanged notes with the Indian naval counter parts. There exist no doubts that the Chinese have fine tuned their procedures for such extended operations and their confidence in such operations has gone up tremendously.

**Extra Regional Powers:** Despite some efforts in the past to declare Indian Ocean as a zone of peace in reality there is nothing to suggest that any one was serious about this declaration of the few. During the Cold War, both the western led NATO and the Soviet Union led WARSAW forces moved around in the Indian Ocean guarding their assets and stalking each other to prevent a nuclear war. With the near unipolar world of today, it is the US writ that largely runs in the IOR. The Combined Task Force 150 has been active in the Strait of Hormuz and the Task Force 151 has come into being to tackle the piracy menace off Somalia. After the break-up of the Soviet Union, Russia is slowly trying to be a force to reckon with and some of the old prejudices appear to be suggesting a return to restarting the Cold War.

There are no doubts that the Indian Ocean would continue to be a centre of gravity in the present century and no one would like to miss a party here as Asia leverages its economy and the power of its people in the Asian Century.

To conclude, it appears that both China and India would continue to compete to extend the military and economic spheres of influence amongst the littorals in the Indian Ocean Region. The fact that China and India would be in the top three slots by 2020 in economic terms does not necessarily mean that there would be total estrangement between the two countries. The vexed border issue would remain a thorn in the relations between the two countries. However, there is space for both the countries to prosper together without seriously undermining their economic growths.

It is safe to assume that both the countries would avoid confrontation as long as possible to consolidate their respective positions. The keen sense of competition would prevail as was witnessed in the efforts of both the countries to scout and acquire energy fields in many parts of the world. China would increase its efforts to prevail in the maritime neighbourhood of India. It has succeeded in Pakistan in a big way. It would continue to build spheres of influence in Bangladesh, Myanmar and even Sri Lanka. The Maldives would be a difficult proposition for China due to the historical relations with India and the recent security pact that was signed by the two governments.

From the Indian view point, the counters should also include better relations with the Littoral states in the South China Sea and active engagement with the navies and the Coast Guards. The Indian Navy and the Indian Coast Guard have been visiting countries in this area and are engaging the maritime forces in joint exercises. Good relations with these countries would serve a twofold objective of keeping our options open in the South China Sea and also in bringing about a sense of balance in the smaller navies in the region, who do not exactly endorse all the moves made by China in the region.

India has also done well in initiating a forum called 'Milan' which has been active for over a decade now and has brought together the navies from the region and allowed them to interact on professional, social and cultural platforms provided at Port Blair in the Andaman and Nicobar group of Islands. Also, the offer of India for conducting training in combating terrorism has been well received and the Indian Coast Guard has been regularly conducting the necessary training for participants from several countries identified in the ASEAN Regional Forum (ARF). From the point of maritime strategy, whatever moves are initiated by China in the Indian Ocean, all need to be countered not only in our backyard but should also be complemented by our proactive but non-offensive actions in China's backyard.

# 9

# India's Policy towards Rising China

G. Supriya and Mohanan B. Pillai

## Introduction

The entire world considers the rise of China, in the age of globalization, as both-an opportunity as well as a threat and ponders over a wide range of economic, strategic and political actions that could help the world community at large to engage China in the new context of world politics. Due to shifts in global political economy and because of the financial meltdown in the United States, the world is keen and interested in a better understanding of China's emergence. In international relations, as Kenneth Waltz puts it, "a drive for hegemony by any one state may be successful despite the resistance of other states, or for some reason the other states may not resist; but under certain conditions that have often existed in international politics systems of balance do develop". Therefore the perception of intent or threat is more important than the intent or the threat itself in the balance of power. Keeping this in mind, we shall analyze the rise of China from both-the liberal and the realist perspectives with a view to assess India's China policy. Although there are merits in the power-structure analysis about the 'China threat', some obvious and common limitations can be noticed when scrutinized against the background of a changing international system that has been affected by the historical trend of globalization. China's engagements with the world market and multilateral international economic organizations are accompanied by its involvement in international and regional security institutions and all of these actions make anyone very cautious while arguing about the threat of China in the new century. Although the structure of the international system compels states to maximize their relative power positions, such power maximization often proves to be dysfunctional as it triggers a counterbalancing coalition of states, especially in the globalized world. Therefore, the authors in this paper try to analyze 'the rise of China, a threat' perception and India's policy options towards China in its regional and global context'.

The attempt here is not to explicate India-China relations in all its details. Rather it is an attempt to examine the reasons for the lack of a long-term strategic vision in India's policy towards China. This paper argues that this lack of a strategic approach has to do with domestic political constraints that have made it difficult for India to carve out a coherent foreign policy vis-à-vis China. While China has displayed a remarkable consistency in its dealings with India, India seems to be satisfied in muddling along from one high-level visit to another and anxious to keep China pleased. The absence of a guiding strategic framework in India's China policy can have grave implications for India's national security interests as well as for its emergence as a global player.

**Arguments of Emerging China as a *Threat***

Most Western scholars who have argued that China will be a threat to the security of Asia, particularly the eastern region in the new century, choose to use the power-structure transformation analysis to support their point. The power structure perspective is one of the hallmarks of the neo-realist paradigm. According to this paradigm, when any state becomes wealthier and more powerful, it will inevitably seek greater regional and global political influence, which will lead to a change in the power-structure in the region and in the world at large. The change in the power-structure caused by the burgeoning of a newly rising regional and world power usually poses a long-term danger for the security of the region and even for the stability of the world. While a rising power's total strength aggregates and expands, it will be more capable of furthering and expanding its national interests in the region and in the world, which will cause those established powers that want to maintain the status quo to react fiercely. Under such circumstances the newly rising power will wage large-scale wars to revise or overthrow the established order in the region and even in the world. Needless to say, China has been rising in the East Asian region and to some extent in the world since the closing years of the last century.

According to the power structure analysis and as per the 'established power versus rising power' pattern, China is a threat to the security of East Asia region and to the United States and its main ally in East Asia-Japan. Based on this analysis, some Western International Relations scholars have predicted with pessimism that Asia is likely to see more international conflicts in the near future (Brown 1996:3) According to these scholars, the history of international relations also strongly supports this argument. In the late 19$^{th}$ century and in the period between the two World Wars, Germany turned out to be the threat to the security of the East Atlantic region as an emerging and rising power. It was Germany's aspiration for expansion that caused the two World Wars. Just like Germany, Japan was a rising power before the Second World War and its expansion in the Pacific region in the 1930s and 1940s eventually led to the instability in the Pacific. It is said that history is the great laboratory within which international action occurs (Kaplan 1976:3). The historical pattern is that a rising power dissatisfied with secondary status might try to enhance its power position by confronting the dominant but declining power.

According to one realist study in the West, war is most likely when the power of a rising, dissatisfied country becomes equal to that of a dominant state. Then 'power parity provides the opportunity to act for those who are committed to changing the status quo' (Lemke, Warner 1996 40:235-260). The logic has been applied to China as a rising power which is seeking to change the status quo in the East Asian region. Some Western scholars even argue that besides the fact of China being a rising power, Chinese assertiveness is also caused by its history and its domestic affairs, which makes China a threat to its neighbours and even to the United States. For example, Michael D. Swaine and Ashley J. Tellis point out, "China's historical memory of past greatness and the desire to restore previous eminence; its determination to erase the painful legacy of a century of national humiliation; its desire to recreate the traditional Sino-centric world order as a means of regulating political and economic structures of super-ordination and subordination; its belief that China's external security in the past was primarily assured by a strong state able to dominate or at the very least neutralize the strategic periphery; and so on"(Ashley, Swaine 2000:198). At the same time the domestic situation in China is also cited as an argument about Chinese threat. The domestic political conditions are such that the competitors for leadership in China usually adopt aggressive foreign policies that would garner popular support with nationalist sentiments on the one hand and elite support from the institutional remnants of authoritarian rule, especially the military, on the other.

According to *Avery Goldstein's* stimulating analysis, the power-transition theory and the institutionalist theory, offer sharply contrasting views about the implications of China's rise. Power-transition theory expects this rise to be dangerous because it poses a challenge to the international order underpinned by American power. Institutionalist theory interprets China's rise as an opportunity for building cooperation, rather than intensifying conflict. Goldstein explains the logic of these two theoretical perspectives in the context of China rise and sets forth their different implications for three flashpoints in East Asia (the South China Sea, Korea, and the Taiwan Strait). These expectations are then compared with the still skimpy empirical records from the post-Cold War era. Events in the South China Sea and Korea mainly lend credence to the expectations of the institutionalist theory, though the evidence is arguably not conclusive. In the Taiwan Strait, however, the evidence follows expectations from the power-transition theory. Goldstein's analysis clearly indicates that there are persuasive theoretical alternatives to John Mearsheimer's offensive realism. In fact, careful analysis reveals that offensive realism has only limited insights to offer on the challenges presented by the rise of China. Therefore we should pay close attention to contending perspectives.

**Liberal Perspectives on the Issue of *China Threat***

Although the arguments cited above are seemingly meritorious, there are some obvious and common limitations to them when scrutinized against the backdrop of a changing international system as mentioned before. When western neo-realist International Relations scholars try to apply the power-structure theory to analyze the 'China threat', they seem to neglect the fundamental structural changes in the international system. It is quite clear that the power structure theory emphasizes the strength of the states and treats the states as the dominant actors in the international system. But for all the strength of states as the principal actor in the international system, the dominance of states as the focus of political authority is declining with the impact of globalization on the international system since the end of the Cold War. For example now any state is not only unable to decide the exchange rate of its own currency but also unable to decide to go to war as was previously the case with political power. Although what will fill this power vacuum is still the issue, we can argue that the behaviours of states, be it an established power or be it a rising power, have changed in the changing international system.

Using the power-structure analysis, without noticing or mentioning the fundamental changes in the structure and in the actors in the current international system, the arguments about the threat from China as a rising power appear less persuasive. Actually it is against the background of the systemic changes in the international relations influenced by the quickening pace of globalization since the end of the Cold War that China's economic and to some extent its military power is growing. In other words, Chinese economic power has been increasing almost simultaneously with the rapid development of globalization from the late 20th century. Just as Thomas L. Friedman described, "a new international system has now clearly replaced the Cold War: globalization. That's right, globalization- the integration of markets, finance, and technologies in a way that is shrinking the world from a size medium to a size small and enabling each of us to reach around the world farther, faster, and cheaper than ever before. It's not just an economic trend, and it's not just some fad.

Like all previous international systems, the present system is also directly or indirectly shaping domestic politics, economic policies, and foreign relations of virtually every country (Friedman, Ramonet 1999:110-127). Friedman's description of globalization may exaggerate the case to some degree, but most people would agree that globalization has directly or indirectly reshaped the foreign relations of almost every country, big or small, including the United States, an established power, and China, a rising power. No doubt, globalization has led to the integration and the interdependence of all the actors in the international system to an unprecedented degree and the cooperative attitude of states-still the main actors in the international system. Most importantly, China as a rising power seems to be orienting itself much more than the established powers towards cooperation, because it perceives that political authority of states in the contemporary international system is declining. For example, the Chinese premier, Zhu Rongji went to Washington to discuss China's admission into the World Trade Organization in April 1999 when the NATO led by the United States was conducting air strikes against Yugoslavia, which China did not support and during which the Chinese Embassy was hit by U.S. missiles. Obviously, the Chinese premier's visit reflected the tremendous changes in Chinese attitude towards the international system.

Unlike Germany in the late 19th and early 20th century or Japan in the period between the two World Wars, China as a rising power prefers to merge into international cooperative regimes like the WTO and tries its best to cooperate with the established powers and follow international norms and rules. The behavioural change of the rising power is caused by the changes in the international system. In the traditional international system dominated by power politics, the level of integration and interdependence was very low because there were no international institutions such as the WTO, the IMF or the World Bank. While in the contemporary international system pushed by the forces of globalization, both established powers and rising powers are willing to cooperate with each other. (Jiang 2005:5).With the guidance of such a new ideology that moved away from orthodox Marxism, China has adjusted its attitude toward the world economic system from self-reliance to cooperation. China has already become a member of the IMF, the World Bank, and other international economic institutions and has been very active in those institutions that it once condemned as tools of capitalist imperialism.

In December 2001, the Chinese government proudly declared to the world that China had become the member of the WTO after long negotiations with the United States and the European Union. All these actions exhibit clearly the willingness of the Chinese government to integrate China into the world market system and catch up with the quick pace of globalization. This is in sharp contrast with the actions of Germany and Japan in the period between the two World Wars. Germany and Japan carried out autarchic economic policies in the 1930s, which led them to leave the world market and caused them to confront established powers like Great Britain and the United States. In contrast, China has not only shifted in its attitude towards the world market from self-reliance to cooperation but also has been playing a more active role in these international economic regimes. One of the main reasons for why China as a rising power has not followed the examples of Germany and Japan in the 1930s is the change that has come to strike the international system. All states-the main international actors-operate in the international social-economic-political geographic environment and these specific characteristics of the international system help determine the pattern of the behaviours and intentions of the states.

In the traditional international system, existing till before the Second World War, there were few international cooperation regimes to regulate the behaviour of states and the space for rising powers to grow was so narrow that the main manner for them to further their national interests was either to concur or to conflict with existing powers. While, under globalization, international cooperation regimes are playing more and more important roles in the contemporary international system, it has become more difficult for the rising power to further its national interests without cooperation with other powers within those regimes. The past few years have also seen the increasing interest and willingness on the part of China to embrace multilateral security mechanisms. This includes its engagement with the ASEAN Regional Forum (ARF). The ARF was initially established as a partial response to existing territorial disputes (South China Sea) with China and the concern regarding US military readjustment in East Asia after the Cold War. China's engagement with the ARF, the regional multilateral security institution, has been widely recognized as a significant contributing element to encouraging the development of features of a more inclusive nature of multilateralism. China's participation in security institutions (Johnston, Ross 1999:238) shows that in the globalized international system, self-interested actors prefer to construct institutions to enhance cooperation on security issues. Perhaps the adjustment of China's behaviour came from its anticipation of other states' preferences for cooperation within international security institutions, or from the institutions' monitoring and sanctioning provisions. But the fact remains that China is experiencing a kind of socialization under these international security institutions.

### India's Policy Towards China

A rising China has caused strong reactions from around the globe. As the sole superpower the US is concerned about the policies that are to be followed towards the East Asian Giant; so is the case with India-its closest neighbour. One of the most important foreign policy priorities for India, since its Independence, has been to secure a global environment that is conducive, and if possible supportive, of Indian aspirations. Improving the well-being of the Indian people and modernizing India's economy were our highest national policy priorities. Jawaharlal Nehru told the Constituent Assembly in December 1947, "Talking about foreign policies, the House must remember that these are not just empty struggles on a chessboard. Behind them lie all manners of things. Ultimately, foreign policy is the outcome of economic policy. Hence, the key challenge and priority will be to build relationships around the world with big and small countries that enable us to push our development process and sustain a higher rate of economic growth in turbulent and difficult times" (Art 1980:1-14).

The Indian political establishment is fond of arguing that there is a distinct continuity that defines Indian foreign policy. One can relate this easily to Kenneth Waltz's structural-realist theory of international politics, according to which states fashion their foreign policies in response to the systemic constraints imposed by the international system where domestic politics is not an important variable in the process. In a certain sense, this holds true for Indian foreign policy in general. There have been a few dramatic shifts in Indian foreign policy over the years and these shifts have been engendered by events such as the end of the Cold War and the disappearance of the Soviet Union.

In so far as India's China policy is concerned, there is visible continuity in the official position of India. There is a consensus across the Indian political spectrum for improving bilateral ties with China and for resolving Sino-Indian differences through dialogue. However, this official policy hides a broader debate in India about how to deal with China. It has been pointed out that there are three broad views in India on how to deal with China and they have been classified as the pragmatists, the hyperrealists and the appeasers. (Malik: 2003) The pragmatists view China as a long-term threat and as a competitor but argue that this competition can be managed by engaging China economically and balancing against China by emerging as a major power in the international system. The hyperrealists view China as a clear and present danger and would like India to contain China by forging alliances around China's periphery and by strengthening its military capabilities. The appeasers view China as a friendly and benevolent neighbour and would like India to engage with it whole-heartedly since China, in their opinion, is not a threat to India in any way.

Along similar lines, Steven Hoffman has also delineated Indian perceptual positions on China. (Frankel, Harding 2004:33-69) He has outlined three ideal types which he classifies as the Mainstream position, China-Is-Not-Hostile position and the China-Is-Hostile position. These ideal types closely correlate with the pragmatists, the appeasers, and the hyperrealists of the above-mentioned typology (Pant 2006). The Mainstream Indian perspective on China, according to

Hoffman, views China as a potential threat to Indian security but hopes that effective Indian diplomacy can avert major problems in future. The China-Is-Not-Hostile perspective holds that China is a rational and peace-loving state that does not have malevolent intentions vis-à-vis India. In marked contrast, the China-Is-Hostile position views China as a short and long-term strategic rival of India and calls for Indian diplomatic assertiveness vis-à-vis China.

The Communists caution against an alliance with any power which limits India's ability to foster mutual trust and forge amicable relations with its neighbours, while the Congress has drawn attention to the emergence of a global market and a globalizing polity that makes a policy of universal global engagement most appropriate.

Though the multiplicity of views reflects Indian democracy at its best, in many ways it also impedes the formulation of a long-term strategy. The consequence is that the Indian government, realizing that there is a plethora of views on China, takes the path of least resistance, a policy that keeps most groups satisfied, if not happy, even though it is a policy only in name. (Pant 2006).

However, the inherent nature of the relationship between China and India is one of tension, whether in the economic, energy, nuclear, strategic or security realm. Without the continued careful attention by both parties to mitigate them, these pressures are likely to increase as both India and China take up leadership roles in Asia. As already mentioned, China was stymied by India joining the East Asia Summit at the request of some of the smaller members who did not want China to overwhelm the group. China's 'string of pearls' policy that focuses on areas of strategic importance to India, such as Burma and Pakistan, will ensure that India remains wary of China and tries to build its avenues of leverage within the region. Pressure is also likely to rise as both nations expand economically, increasingly competing for foreign investment and supremacy in services and manufacturing industries. Given these inherent pressures and yet the importance to both countries of a stable and secure environment in which to grow, the two nations will continue to maintain a dual policy of 'hedging and engaging' (similar to that of the U.S. with China) in order to walk the narrow path between remaining friendly but protecting against the eventuality if the other does not.

**Concluding Remarks**

In relation to the analysis presented above we could conclude by saying that China's rise has created daunting theoretical and policy challenges for India. Although the structure of the international system compels states to maximize their relative power positions, neighbouring countries try to maintain peace and stability in the region. India and China are the two major powers in Asia with global aspirations and some significant conflicting interests. As a result, some amount of friction in their bilateral relationship is inevitable. The geopolitical reality of Asia makes sure that it will be extremely difficult, if not impossible, for Hindi-Chini to be bhai-bhai (brothers) in the foreseeable future. If India and China continue to rise in the next few years, a security competition between the two regional giants will also be inevitable. If India is serious about its desire to emerge as a major global power, then it will have to tackle the challenge posed by China's rise. A rising China will not tolerate a rising India as its competitor. Even if a rising India does not have any intention of becoming a regional hegemonic, China will try its best to constrain India as it has already done to a large extent; and it is that containment that India has to guard against.

This reality should be accepted by Indian policy-makers who should initiate a serious attempt to manage these frictions by expanding the zone of cooperation with China even as they try to steadfastly pursue their national interests. They need to display the confidence to craft a foreign policy that best serves their national interests. Again, India can learn a lot by examining how China has managed its relationship with the US in the last two decades.

The joint vision of the leaderships in India and China could ensure a global order in which simultaneous development will have a positive impact upon their own peoples and economies, as also on the rest of the world.

**References**

Ansari, Hamid. *Emerging China: Prospects for Partnership in Asia?* Conference organised by the Indian Council of World Affairs and Association of Asian Scholars on 21 November 2009. New Delhi.

Ashley J Tellis, "*A Grand Chessboard,*" Foreign Policy, January/February 2005.

China's Independent Foreign Policy of Peace" from 9. Alastair Iain Johnston and Robert S. Ross ed., *Engaging China-The management of an emerging power* (Routledge London and New York 1999) p. 238.

Douglas Lemke and Suzanne Warner, "Power Parity, Commitment to Change, and War." *International Studies Quarterly*, 40: 235-260, 1996.

Gerald Segal, *Defending China,* Oxford University Press, 1990.

Gerald Segal, *Foreign Policy Affairs*, September-October1999.

James Brook, *"Japan's Ties to China: Strong Trade, Shaky Politics,"* New York Times, February 22, 2005.

Jiang Y.E, Ritsumeikan Annual Review of International Studies, 2002. Vol.1, pp. 55-68.

Michael D. Swaine and Ashley J. Tellis, *Interpreting China's Grand Strategy: Past, Present and Future,* (Rand6. Michael D. Swaine and Ashley J. Tellis, *Interpreting China's Grand Strategy: Past, Present and Future,* (Rand 2000) p. 198.

Michael E. Brown, et al, eds., *East Asia Security*, (MIT Press, 1966), Robert Ross, et al, eds., *East Asia in Transition-Towards New Regional Order*, (M.E. Shape. Inc. 1995), Mutiah Alagapa, *Asia Security Practice: Material and Ideational Influences* (Stanford Univ. Press, 1998),

Michael D. Swaine and Ashley J. Tellis, *Interpreting China's Grand Strategy: Past, Present and Future* (Rand 2000) etc.

Minxin Pei, "China's Governance Crisis", *Foreign Affairs*, Sep/Oct, 2002 pp. 96-109, p. 104.

Minxin Pei, *"China's Governance Crisis"*, Foreign Affairs, Sep/Oct, 2002 pp. 96-109, p. 97.

Morton A. Kaplan, *System and Process in International Politics* (New York: Krieger, 1976).

Nicholas R. Lardy, *Foreign Trade and Economic Reform in China, 1978-1990* (Cambridge University Press, 1992).

Quansheng Zhao, Guoli Liu, *The Challenges of a Rising China,* The Journal of Strategic Studies, August-October 2007, Vol. .30, No. 4-5, pp. 585-608.

Robert J. Art, "To What Ends Military Power?" International Security, 4 (4), Spring 1980, pp. 4-14.

Shintaro Ishihara, "Chinese Threat is Axis around Which U.S-Japan Relations Will Turn in the Future" 2001, Global Viewpoint. Distributed by Los Angeles Times Syndicate International, a division of Tribune Media Services.

Soong-Bum Ahn, "China as Number One" *Current History*, September 2001, pp.250-256. p 251.

Soong-Bum Ahn, "China as Number One" *Current History*, September 2001, pp.250-256. p 252.

Steven A. Hoffman, *"Perception and China Policy in India,"* in Frankel and Harding (eds), no. 10, pp. 33-68.

Susan L. Shirk, "One-Sided Rivalry: *China's Perceptions and Policies Toward India*," in Frankel and Harding (eds), no. 10, pp. 93-94.

The statement has been borrowed from S. Menon, India's Foreign policy, Delhi University, New Delhi, 19 January 2009, at www.du.ac.in/du/Indias percent20Foreign percent20Policy.pdf

Thomas L. Friedman and Ignacio Ramonet, "Dueling Globalizations: A Debate between Thomas L. Friedman and Ignacio Ramonet" *Foreign Policy*, Fall 1999, pp110-127.

**Websites Referred**

http://chineseembassy.org.uk/diplomacy/foreign.accessed on 31.12.2009

http://www.chineseembassy.org.uk/economy/generaleconomy/mainindicators.htm. accessed on 31.12.2009

http://search.peopledaily.com.in. accessed on 31.12.2009

http://English.peopledaily.com.cn/200203/01/eng20020301_91199.shtm.accessed on 31.12.2009

http://www.cia.gov/library/publication/the-world-factbook/geos/ch.html#econ accessed on 31.12.2009

http://casi.ssc.upenn.edu/iit/baru. accessed on 31.12.2009

See Harsh pa ant http://www.idsa.in/strategicanalysis/IndianForeignPolicyand China_hvpant_1006 accessed on 31.12.2009. accessed on 31.12.2009

http://www.futurecasts.com/book percent20review percent204-05.htm accessed on 31.12.2009

Pant V Harsh on India's foreign policy and China at http://www.idsa.in/system/ files/strategicnalysis_hvpant_1206.pdf accessed on 31.12.2009

Prime minister's speech at the India Today Conclave is also available at http://www.pmindia.nic.in/speeches.htm accessed on 31.12.2009

# 10

# India's Look East Policy: An Empirical Study

Amal Sarkar

## Section 1: Introduction

In the 1990s, India decided to aggressively increase trade and strategic relations with the Southeast Asian countries as part of its 'Look East' policy. The aim was to build upon its historical and cultural ties to expand markets, counter Chinese influence in the region and improve India's standing as a regional power. Security concerns related to insurgency in India's north-eastern states were also a factor in improving relations with its eastern neighbours, including Myanmar's Military Junta. The 'Look-East' policy is an opportunity for India to grow economically and strategically. *The partnership should energize the process of getting us closer to our shared goal of making this truly the 'Asian Century'*. In a fruitful culmination of six-year-long negotiations, on the August 14, 2009, India and the ten nations of the Southeast Asian bloc, ASEAN signed a Free Trade Agreement (FTA) in Bangkok which the Indian industry has called a 'win-win' situation for both the parties. The deal was signed at a meeting of economic ministers of the Association of South East Asian Nations, comprising of Brunei, Burma, Cambodia, Indonesia, Laos, Malaysia, the Philippines, Singapore, Thailand and Vietnam. The Accord, India's first with a trade bloc, will cover 11 countries with a combined Gross Domestic Product of over US$ 2 trillion. The combined population is of the order of 1.6 billion. However, the FTA is now limited to trade in goods only. After signing the FTA, the two regions have now started negotiations to include investments and services also. With services contributing to 55 percent of its economy, India is quite keen on tapping the growing services market in Southeast Asia.

In the 7th ASEAN-India Summit held in October 2009, India was positive towards a healthy trade between India and ASEAN and confirmed to support ASEAN in many aspects of its operation. ASEAN leaders welcomed the signing of the agreement on trade in goods and expressed the hope that it would come into effect by January 2010. The Leaders touched on cooperation in various areas-ranging from trade and investment, infrastructure connectivity, tourism, science and technology, food security, agriculture and forestry, education, HRD, health care and traditional medicine, disaster management and climate change, to political and security cooperation, including combating terrorism (exchange of information and security of the Sea Lanes). They entrusted officials to work further on the areas of services and investments. India has contributed USD 50 million under the ASEAN-India Cooperation Fund and ASEAN Development Fund. It has also proposed to host the ASEAN-India Summit in India in 2012 and set up a task force to prepare a Vision Statement for ASEAN-India relations leading up to 2020. Noting that ASEAN-India trade had grown at a healthy rate despite the economic slowdown, they agreed to set a higher target of USD 70 billion trade value, to be achieved in two years. They also noted that the ASEAN-India Business Council would be reactivated.

**Section 2: A Literature Survey**

Jagdish Bhagwati believes that India should be considering the regional option as a serious complementary effort to securing further liberalization at home and abroad. India has recently signalled its willingness to depart from an exclusive reliance on the multilateral approach by announcing its desire to negotiate a Free Trade Agreement with ASEAN countries. According to him, India has already fired the regional salvo. Perhaps the curious choice of ASEAN as India's preferred regional trade partner is justified under the current circumstances. There exist a lot of studies on Indo-ASEAN economic relations (Ambatkar 2000, Asher et.al. 2005, Baru 2001, Kumar et.al.2006). According to Paul Bowles and Brian MacLean (1996), the process of the formation of the ASEAN Free Trade Area (AFTA) in 1991 is an indication of a significant change in attitudes towards preferential trading arrangements in Asia. The study outlines the change in policy and concludes that mainstream economic approaches are not sufficient to provide satisfactory explanations for the formation of the AFTA.

Kumar, Sen and Asher (2004) have provided a roadmap for the India-ASEAN partnership. Their study focuses on the ways in which the emerging partnership between India and ASEAN can be taken forward for mutual benefit. It discusses the issues concerning trade liberalization in both regional and multilateral contexts. Further, it analyses the prospects of investment flows and trade in financial services and information and communication technology. Asher, Sen and Rajan (2004) outline the future of India-ASEAN economic relations. The study has made an overview of economic relations including a discussion of the India-ASEAN FTA and various aspects of trade flows between ASEAN and India. It further says that mutual trust is a vital component for sustaining the dynamics of this emerging economic relationship. The study concludes that the significant complementarities that exist between ASEAN and India can only be realized if all ideological and informational hurdles are removed.

Razeen Sally and Rahul Sen (2005) discuss the trade policies in Southeast Asian countries in their wider Asian and global contexts. The study compares and contrasts trade policies in individual Southeast Asian countries. It also analyses these policies in the context of regional and global economic integration, and the emergence of two other major Asian economies, China and India. In another study made by Karmakar (2005), the economic scenario in the Asia-Pacific region has been analyzed. This study discusses the overview of the potential of an agreement on trade in services between India and ASEAN countries. She analyses the trade creation potential of an agreement on trade in the service sector between the members of ASEAN and India.

The relations between India and ASEAN have been marked by several phases; a rather distant relationship based on strategic links with individual countries (Dong Zhang 2006). It is an urgent need for India to be incorporated in the 'New Asia', instead of staying at its periphery, as it has in the past. One important study (Sudsawasd and Mongsawad 2007) focuses on the unexplored trade potentials and economic impacts of bilateral Free trade Agreements between ASEAN-5 member countries and the seven-candidate FTA partners using the Gravity Model and the Computable General Equilibrium (CGE) model. The finding from the study recommends ASEAN nations as strategic partners for India. Laurence Henry (2007) remarks that FTA should be rooted in the larger process of economic and diplomatic exchanges in Asia. He says that regional agreements are not a new phenomenon but their success has been more or less conclusive. Further, ASEAN nations are very interested in balancing Chinese power through India, in the region.

In a recent study (Aekapol Chongvilaivan's 2008), it has been remarked that India's effort towards the FTA with ASEAN countries is motivated mainly by its fears that it might 'miss the boat of globalization' and that it has to catch up with China's ties with ASEAN. It further questions whether the India-ASEAN FTA is beneficial to both parties or not. According to him, free trade may not always be beneficial to all members. He remarks that India-ASEAN FTA is likely to provide an economic opportunity for companies in ASEAN countries to strengthen their competitiveness in the global market. In another study (Chanda and Sasidaran's 2008), the reasons behind India's growing interest in framing various kinds of regional and bilateral agreements with Asian economies have been discussed. It discusses the various possible explanations for India's 'Look East' policy. The possible explanations have been examined both from Indian as well as ASEAN viewpoints. It concludes the extent to which India has been able to realize its interests under these agreements and the hurdles that have been come up in this negotiating process.

Satu Limaye (2008) discusses the Indo-ASEAN trade in goods Agreement in details. He remarks that India is falling steadily behind China. Asher and Palit (2008) focus on India's 'Look East' Policy, initiated in 1992, which is all set to enter a new phase with the signing of the India-ASEAN FTA. They say that the rising volume of India-ASEAN trade has coincided with the rapid expansion of the Indian economy. A very recent study (Parashar 2009) concludes that there is ample scope for expanding regional economic cooperation. The author has identified the area of investment cooperation involving export of Indian technology, consultancy and management and banking services as most fruitful areas for regional economic cooperation.

**Section 3: Basic Economic Features of India and ASEAN**

There was a similar process of historical evolution experienced by the countries of the ASEAN region. The region accounts for about 7.5 percent of the world's population and a rapidly growing share of world output. These countries have plural socio-cultural and ethnic identities and similarities of race, religion, language, and customs and so on. In view of the poor economic growth of many developing countries in the 1970s and 1980s, it is important to note the relatively strong economic growth of the ASEAN-5 countries, except Philippines (Table 10.1).

**Table 10.1: Annual Growth Rate in Real GDP in ASEAN-5 Countries (Average Percent)**

| Period | 1971-79 | 1980-89 | 1990-96 |
|---|---|---|---|
| Indonesia | 7.8 | 5.3 | 8.0 |
| Malaysia | 8.1 | 5.8 | 8.7 |
| Philippines | 6.3 | 2.0 | 2.7 |
| Singapore | 9.1 | 7.3 | 8.3 |
| Thailand | 7.1 | 7.4 | 8.8 |

Source: Asian Development Bank, different issues.

The five ASEAN countries namely Indonesia, Malaysia, Philippines, Singapore and Thailand stand at the centre of the most dynamic economic region of the world, and their performance has been part of the Asian 'miracle' that has been well studied by economists and policymakers the world over. The main causes behind it are the relatively stable political climate, high levels of both public and private investment, efficient use of advanced technology, either home-grown (as with Malaysia's rubber and palm-oil research) or imported, and improving human-resource endowments (Brookfield and Byron 1993). The role of the relatively egalitarian income distribution in ASEAN countries was also one important factor behind it. Among other things, this may have fostered the development of education, an important factor in improving the stock of human capital. Another major influence on rates of development is undoubtedly the degree of outward orientation in trade policy.

**Table 10.2: Economic Indicators of ASEAN and India**

| | Gross Domestic Product at PPP (million US$), 2008 | Rate of Growth in Real GDP (%), 2008 | GDP per capita at PPP (US$), 2008 | Inflation Rate (% change in consumer price index), 2008 | Growth rates of money supply (M2), (%), 2008 |
|---|---|---|---|---|---|
| India | 3361295 | 6.7 | 2923 | 10.7 | 18.4 |
| Brunei Darussalam | 20076 | 0.4 | 50442 | 2.7 | 0.3 |
| Cambodia | 28421 | 6.7 | 2030 | 19.7 | 4.8 |
| Indonesia | 908368 | 6.1 | 3975 | 9.8 | 14.6 |
| Lao PDR | 14324 | 7.2 | 2387 | 7.5 | 18.3 |
| Malaysia | 383116 | 4.6 | 13816 | 5.4 | 13.4 |
| Myanmar* | 49207* | 13.6* | 888* | 26.8 | 24.1* |
| Philippines | 317258 | 3.8 | 3507 | 9.3 | 15.4 |
| Singapore | 244177 | 1.1 | 50456 | 6.5 | 12.0 |
| Thailand | 546420 | 2.6 | 8216 | 5.4 | 9.2 |
| Viet Nam | 240390 | 6.2 | 2788 | 25.6 | 20.3 |

Source: Asian Development Bank (2009): Key Indicators for Asia and the Pacific, 40th Edition, August, Manila, Philippines. Note: * for the year 2005.

Singapore is the richest country in the ASEAN region (Table 10.2). According to per capita income, Brunei has become the second richest country in the region; mainly because of her rich oil-reserves and low-population density. The four out of ASEAN-10 belong to Least Developed countries. They are Cambodia, Laos PDR, Myanmar and Vietnam. It should be mentioned here that these countries have became the members of ASEAN at a later stage (early 1990s). Their per capita incomes were comparable with those of India in 2008. In the ASEAN, Myanmar is the least developed nation of the group. On the other hand, Singapore can be treated as an industrially developed one. On the basis of per capita income and the openness of the economy, Indonesia, Malaysia, Philippines and Thailand have now become semi-developed nations. They are integrated into the global economy more than India.

**Table 10.3: Structural Shifts in ASEAN 5 between mid 1960s and 1970s (percent in output)**

| | Agriculture | | Industry | | Service | |
|---|---|---|---|---|---|---|
| Country | 1965 | 1987 | 1965 | 1987 | 1965 | 1987 |
| Indonesia | 56 | 26 | 13 | 33 | 31 | 41 |
| Malaysia | 28 | 22 | 25 | 38 | 47 | 40 |
| Philippines | 26 | 24 | 28 | 33 | 46 | 43 |
| Singapore | 3 | 1 | 24 | 38 | 73 | 62 |
| Thailand | 32 | 16 | 23 | 35 | 45 | 49 |

Source: Asian Development Bank (1989).

The economies of the ASEAN region are characterised by a wide diversity of experiences in growth and structural changes. As mentioned above, the relatively more developed nations in the region are Indonesia, Malaysia, Philippines, Singapore and Thailand. Let us look at an important indicator of the development process i.e. change in the composition of the GDP during 1960-1980. During the period, the region witnessed a significant structural change in production (Table 10.3). Throughout ASEAN, the growth of manufacturing production exceeded that of either services or agriculture over 1965-80. The contribution of the agricultural sector in the GDP had declined significantly while those of the industrial and service sectors increased significantly, particularly the industrial sector. Singapore had experienced structural change in the economy long before the other members. The other four members registered their structural shifts towards industrial and service sectors between mid 1960s and 1970s. The speed of the shifts and the sectors which have benefited vary between countries. This is undoubtedly due to the initial big differences in industrial structures in those countries, and also to different policies and experiences over the period. But the share of industry increased in all ASEAN countries (but only slightly in the Philippines), partly due to the adoption of deliberate diversification strategies focused on industrialization.

However, India is lagging behind. The structural change in the Indian economy took place between 1980s and 1990s (Table 10.4). The period prior to the eighties has been one of sluggish growth and slow pace of structural changes. The nineties seem to have injected a new economic dynamism in the economy. That is because the country has initiated economic reforms characterized by liberalization, privatization and globalization. It was during this period that it started the process of rationalizing its policy regimes. The nature of such changes in India and ASEAN is quite different. In the case of the former, the change was more towards the service sector whereas in the case of latter, the change was more towards the industrial sector; particularly manufacturing.

**Table 10.4: Structural Shift in Indian Economy between mid 1980s and 1990s (Percent in GDP)**

| Sector | Agriculture | | Industry | | Services | |
|---|---|---|---|---|---|---|
| Year | 1980 | 1997 | 1980 | 1997 | 1980 | 1997 |
| India | 38 | 27 | 26 | 30 | 36 | 43 |

Source: World Development Report, 1998-99, World Bank.

**Section 4: Trade Policies of India and ASEAN**

The experiences of ASEAN countries have eradicated the export pessimism that engulfed many developing countries in the 1960s and 1970s and generated optimism for a better future for poor countries (Asian Development Outlook, 1999). These countries, which had few indigenous resources to depend on pursued liberal economic policies, and within two decades, radically changed their economic structures. They have demonstrated that poor societies can substantially transform their economies and alter their prospects (Krueger 1989). They have also demonstrated that rapid growth can be consistent with rapidly rising living standards for the poorest segments. Their experience shows that an export-oriented industrialization induces structural changes that occur as productivity and real wages rise, shifting comparative advantage from labour-intensive to skill and technology-intensive industries (Adams and Davis 1991). Some ASEAN countries like Indonesia, Malaysia, the Philippines, and Thailand became 'semi-industrialized economies' in the early 1990s. Many economists believe that there has been a 'flying geese' pattern of industrial development in ASEAN, with Singapore leading the way followed by other ASEAN countries. They are strongly integrated into the global economy (Table 10.5). An outstanding feature of ASEAN's economic success has been exceptionally high saving and investment rates that have shown increasing disparity with the rest of the world. The strong and rising saving performance has been reflected in contributions from both the private and the public sector. In addition, these countries have been able to tap successfully additional foreign savings to complement their already formidable domestic asset.

**Table 10.5: Global Economic Linkages of ASEAN and India**

| | Exports of goods and services (% of GDP), 2008 | Imports of goods and services (% of GDP), 2008 | Trade in goods (% of GDP), 2006 | Net FDI (million US$), 2007 | Exchange Rate (local currency units per US$, period averages), 2007. | Ratio of International Reserve to Import (months), 2006 |
|---|---|---|---|---|---|---|
| India | 22.7 | 28.0 | 37.4 | 34982.0 | 41.35 | 11 |
| Brunei Darussalam | 67.7@ | 27.8@ | 81.1 | 88.2^ | 1.51 | 4 |
| Cambodia | 52.7 | 75.7 | 116.1 | 867.6 | 4056.17 | 4 |
| Indonesia | 29.8 | 28.6 | 44.4 | 6928.2 | 9141.00 | 7 |
| Lao PDR | -- | ----- | 54.8 | 323.5 | 9603.16 | 4 |
| Malaysia | 103.6 | 80.5 | 186.2 | 8455.5 | 3.44 | 8 |
| Myanmar* | 0.2* | 0.1* | 0.3 | 427.7 | 5.56 | 6 |
| Philippines | 36.9 | 38.7 | 86.3 | 2916.0 | 46.15 | 5 |
| Singapore | 234.9 | 215.3 | 366.5 | 24137.1 | 1.51 | 7 |
| Thailand | 76.4 | 73.7 | 126.0 | 11232.8 | 34.52 | 6 |
| Vietnam | 78.2 | 94.7 | 139.1 | 6700.0 | 16105.10 | 4 |

Source: Asian Development Bank (2009): Key Indicators for Asia and the Pacific, 40th Edition, August, Manila, Philippines. Note: ^ 2006, @ 2007, *2006.

Although countries varied considerably with respect to starting conditions, natural endowments, and individual experiences, there is a broad acceptance of the key policy settings that have contributed to the region's strong economic fundamentals. Economic performance of the outward-oriented economies has been superior in almost all respects to that of the inward-oriented economies. Outward orientation encourages efficient firms and discourages inefficient ones. By creating a more competitive environment for both the private and public sectors, it also promotes higher productivity and, hence, faster economic growth. The economic achievements of the countries in this region over the past quarter century hardly have a parallel. As a result of strong, sustained economic growth since 1970, Singapore has now joined the ranks of the rich industrial countries. On the other hand, India belonged to the low-income group during the same period. Till now, the economy is significantly dependent on agricultural sector, and suffers from basic socio-economic problems like vast population, huge unemployment rates, high rate of inflation and acute adverse balance of payment situations and so on.

After Independence, India chose an import substitution policy at a time when the world economy was growing rapidly. However, the import substituting industrialization strategy did not work as it was anticipated. This created uncompetitive and inefficient industries. Another adverse effect of the import substitution strategy was the slowing down of exports, which created persistent balance of payment difficulties. Since the early 1990's India has put emphasis on trade liberalization programs. She has begun to open up her economy so as to promote competitive efficiency in production and to achieve neutralizing in the incentive structure between production for exports and import substitutes. Besides lowering import tariff, one major area of trade policy reform has been the adoption of managed floating exchange rate systems. The Indian Rupee has also been made convertible on the current account since the Government of India initiated reforms in 1991. The country has recognized the inter-relationship between trade policy regimes and the exchange rate policies.

Table 10.6 shows that during the 1990's India significantly depreciated her currency against the US dollar.

**Table 10.6: Exchange rates to the Dollar in India (Annual Average)**

| Currency | 1993 | 1994 | 1995 | 1996 | 1997 | 1998 |
|---|---|---|---|---|---|---|
| Rupee | 30.5 | 31.4 | 32.4 | 35.4 | 36.3 | 41.3 |

Source: Asian Development Outlook-1999, ADB.

Following liberalization, import of a number of products has now been permitted which had been banned earlier. The tariff structure is being rationalised by distinguishing their trade, revenue and protective objectives. Although in many respects import policies continue to be restrictive and tariff rates remain high, the move towards outward-looking policies is very encouraging. Another noticeable feature of the present trade liberalization process is that the incidence of non-tariff barriers has significantly come down (Sarkar 2006). From 1990s onwards, India has also taken some measures such as concession on international capital financial flows. It has opened up its economy and integrated more with the world. Resultantly, India's net FDI inflow has significantly increased.

## Section 5: Nature of Commodities in India's Export Basket to ASEAN

India's major exports to ASEAN include oil meals, gems and jewellery, meat and meat preparations, cotton yarn, fabrics made-ups, engineering goods, transport equipment, machinery and instruments, electronic goods, marine products, fruits and vegetables, rice, drugs and pharmaceuticals, dyes and intermediates; primary and semi-finished iron & steel and fine chemicals. Service transactions, investments, project executions, and manpower flows, too, have added significantly to the economic interaction between the two sides. Thus, the export basket is diversified, with manufacturing goods playing an important role. The share of gems and jewellery has occupied the top position in the export basket. It has remained at over 10 percent, the next important item being machinery and instruments (Table 10.7).

**Table 10.7: Top-ten Commodities in India's Exports to ASEAN (Percent in total exports to ASEAN)**

| | 2004-05 |
|---|---|
| Gems & Jewellery | 10.91 |
| Machinery & instruments | 5.19 |
| Dyes, intermediates etc. | 4.96 |
| Primary & semi-finished iron & steel | 4.41 |
| Oil meal | 3.82 |
| Drugs, pharm.& fine chemicals | 3.48 |
| Transport equipment | 3.27 |
| Electronic goods | 3.17 |
| Inorganic/organic/agro.chemicals | 2.99 |
| Manufactures of metals | 2.48 |

Source: Author's calculation from CMIE's *Foreign Trade & Balance of Payments* (July, 2005), Mumbai.

The growth rates have been shown in Table 10.8. To estimate the exponential growth rate of India's different products to ASEAN, I have used the semi-log linear function of the following form: $\text{Log } Xjt = a + b*t$; where, Xjt is India's exports to jth ASEAN country in million US dollars, 't' is trend variable and 'a' is the intercept term. The annual growth rate has been computed as b*100. Among the top ten products under study, the products which have registered impressive growth rates are gems and jewellery, machinery and instruments, dyes and intermediates and transport equipments (Table 10.8).

Under the agreement, India has been allowed to continue protecting its farm sector, and has excluded 489 products from the FTA. Computer software and information technology are also exempted. A smaller list of products, described as 'highly sensitive', such as palm oil and coffee, will see tariffs reduced over about 10 years, but only modestly. Palm oil, tea, coffee and pepper are on the 'highly sensitive list', meaning import duties on them will be lowered by around 40-45 percent only by 2019. On the other hand, tariffs on electronics, chemicals, machinery and textiles will be reduced and eventually eliminated. The pact will eliminate duties on 4,000 items by 2016, covering 80 percent of India's imports from the Southeast Asian nations. Refined petroleum products, organic chemicals, pharmaceuticals, gems and jewellery, metal scraps, which are among India's major exports to ASEAN, are likely to be the gainers. Auto components, several items of agriculture, textile and chemicals have been put on the negative list, which means there will be no tariff reduction.

**Table 10.8: Annual Growth Rate in India's Exports to ASEAN (Percent)**

| | 1998-2005 |
|---|---|
| All | 25.61 |
| Gems & Jewellery | 20.51 |
| Machinery & Instruments | 19.38 |
| Dyes, Intermediates etc. | 35.19 |
| Primary & Semi-finished Iron & Steel | 34.85 |
| Oil meal | 7.82 |
| Drugs, Pharm.& Fine Chemicals | 10.98 |
| Transport Equipment | 36.88 |
| Electronic Goods | 14.02 |
| Inorganic/Organic/Agro.chemicals | 19.61 |
| Manufactures of Metals | 15.17 |

Source: Author's calculation from CMIE's database, Mumbai.

**Section 6: Prospects of the FTA**

Traditionally a supporter of multilateral trade negotiations, India has finally woken up to the importance of being in an influential trade bloc. The government of India's 'Look East' policy is welcome, as India's entry (one of the fastest growing economies in Asia) into the ASEAN would make the region one of the strongest and most influential in world trade. India's participation at the ASEAN Summit was essentially a part of its 'Look-East' policy, which began with a 'sectoral dialogue' partnership in 1992. It was subsequently upgraded to a full dialogue partnership in 1995 and membership of the ASEAN Regional Forum in 1996. The first ASEAN Summit with India as a member took place in Cambodia in 2002. The India-ASEAN FTA, to come into effect in 2011, has the basic objective of enhancing trade relations, but this would entail significant liberalization by India. The framework FTA has a built in 'early harvest program' which was started from November 1, 2004. In the third India-ASEAN Summit in Laos held in November, 2004, India and ASEAN set a target to more than double their two-way trade to 30 billion USD by 2007. India's trade and economic interaction with the ten-nation ASEAN has been growing significantly. As a result, India's trade volume with ASEAN has expanded rapidly since the early 1990s (Sarkar, 2009). The agreement opens up tremendous potential for increasing trade and investment on both sides.

The rule of origin is a vital component in any FTA as it determines the country of origin of products to be traded. If a product does not satisfy the ROO criteria then it is deemed as originating from a third country and cannot be traded under the FTA. The two criteria being followed by India are the value addition method and change in tariff heading (CTH). The ASEAN countries use the value addition method which specifies a minimum percentage of value addition to be achieved with domestic inputs to make a product eligible for concessional treatment under the FTA. The rules of origin (ROO) are a safeguard to prevent third countries from taking advantage of the FTA between two other countries. The Inconsistency in ROOs increase administrative costs, add regulatory complexity, and ultimately becomes a non-tariff barrier to trade. In such a scenario both India and ASEAN may fail to tap benefits from further tariff reductions. The agreement on rules of origin (ROO) is one of the most lenient that India has negotiated with her preferential trade partners. The value-addition requirement has been agreed at 35 percent, with provisions for regional cumulation and requirement for a change in the 6-digit tariff sub-headings only. The two partners have also agreed to whittle down the negative list of products on which there would be no tariff reduction. For both, the FTA offers a significant improvement over their current tariff bindings and market access offers in the WTO. However, ASEAN has rejected India's twin criteria of determining ROO which it generally uses in its various FTAs with other countries.

India has 489 tariff lines under the negative list which includes 302 agricultural items, 81 items from textiles and clothing, 52 items from machinery and auto, and 32 items from chemicals and plastics. The agricultural items are copra, coconut oil, coconut, rice, rubber, some fish types like mathi, chemmeen, crab, milk and milk products, honey, cashew, banana, pineapple, mangoes, orange, vanilla, jathi, coriander, jeera, ginger, turmeric, tapioca etc. In addition, there are 22 other items from various other sectors. For products that are not on the negative list, duties will be reduced in a phased manner and it will be brought down to zero by 2019. Five items-tea, coffee, pepper, crude palm oil and refined palm oil-are on the 'highly sensitive' list and will undergo a partial duty cut. The tariffs for the products in the 'highly sensitive' list will be reduced step by step but even after 10 years it will not be reduced to zero. The protection will continue. For example, for palm oil it is currently 80 percent and in 2019 will only be reduced to 37.5 percent, for coffee and tea its now 100 percent and it will come down to 45 percent, for pepper from 70 percent to 50 percent.

The first phase of implementation is supposed to be over by 1 January 2010. The crucial trade pact is expected to break duty barriers in the 1.7 billion consumer market in the region. ASEAN is an important market for Indian industry and the FTA would give an access to a trillion dollar economy. There are several reasons why India is interested in closer relations with ASEAN. Per capita income of ASEAN is twice that of India's, providing market opportunities. India also perceives opportunities through integrating into the value chain of MNCs located in ASEAN. Finally, some ASEAN countries such as Singapore and Malaysia could potentially become important sources of investments, particularly in infrastructural projects and venture capital. On the security front, India's 1600 km long border with Myanmar and maritime security involving the Indian Ocean and the Malacca Strait provide additional impetus for engagement with the ASEAN.

**Table 10.9: India Trade with Major Trading Partners in ASEAN* in 2007-08 (US$ million)**

| Country | Exports (X) | Imports (M) | Total Trade (X+M) | Trade Deficit (M-X) |
|---|---|---|---|---|
| Indonesia | 2,058 | 4,823 | 6881 (19.95 %) | 2,765 |
| Malaysia | 2,524 | 6,005 | 8529 (24.73 %) | 3,481 |
| Singapore | 6,852 | 8,111 | 14963 (43.39 %) | 1,259 |
| Thailand | 1,807 | 2,301 | 4108 (11.91 %) | 429 |
| India's Total | 13,241 | 21,240 | 21,240 | 7,999 |

*Note: Other ASEAN members are not so much important as these four members for India's exports.

Source: Author's calculation from RBI's Handbook of Indian Economy 2008-09.

According to market size, Singapore occupies the top position for India's exports in the region, followed by Malaysia (Table 10.9). It should be noted here that one feature of Indo-ASEAN trade is that India suffers huge trade deficits vis-à-vis this region. It stands at 8 billion USD as in 2007-08. One objective to sign the FTA was to raise the volume of exports to that region. But, it seems to have very little hope in the near future. Because, India's tariff wall is very much higher than that of ASEAN (Table 10.10). In other words, India imposes higher tariff rates on her imports from the ASEAN region. Therefore, there is not much scope for further tariff reduction on ASEAN's imports from India under the FTA. On the contrary, as the present level of tariff rate is high, there is much scope for further tariff reduction on India's imports from the region. It can be expected that the rate of growth in India's imports would be much higher than that of ASEAN from India under the FTA. For example, no tariff rate is imposed by Singapore on India's exports to that country. On the contrary, India imposes a high (24.7 percent) tariff on imports from Singapore. Therefore, by the FTA, India has to bring down the high rate of import duty towards zero. Assuming the elasticity of bilateral import demand to remain constant in future, it can be said that India's trade deficit would widen significantly under the FTA regime.

**Table 10.10: Simple Average Tariff Rates in 1998 (Percent)**

| Country | Tariff Rates of India's Imports from ASEAN | Tariff Rates of ASEAN Imports from India |
|---|---|---|
| Brunei | 22.4 | 5 |
| Indonesia | 23.3 | 8.9 |
| Malaysia | 29.6 | 10.3 |
| Philippines | 25.4 | 12.8 |
| Singapore | 24.7 | 0 |
| Thailand | 23.7 | 21.1 |

Source: Arif and Cheen (2006), p.75.

**Conclusions**

The proposed agreement will however, benefit India. It is a window of opportunity for the Indian economy, especially at a time when the global economy is facing a slowdown. Economists are divided over the benefits of FTAs. One view is that FTAs encourage high-cost producers in contracting countries. Goods of low-cost producers in other countries/regions might suffer higher duty before they enter the contracting countries. In the process, the consumers may not benefit and the governments lose out on revenue. There are over 350 trade agreements in the world. Advocates of FTAs say that in the context of failed multilateral trade talks at the World Trade Organization, FTAs offer best options to increase trade. It is expected that the Indo-ASEAN FTA would improve India's position in the region in the light of the preferential access extended to China by ASEAN. India would get greater market access with better terms of trade and hope to compete successfully with goods from other countries in the region. Further, the FTA would set the field towards moving on to freer trade in commercial services between India and ASEAN.

It is further expected that this FTA will create stronger economic linkages with ASEAN in order to ensure its support as a crucial ally, given China's rising competitiveness in the global economy. It would bring India in a position to secure its economic and strategic interests in the region. It carries special importance in the light of the recent failure of the WTO talks. The FTA certainly is a crucial first step in this direction. It is important therefore for both partners to recognize that incremental convergence and economic diplomacy works best in countries whose socio-political systems until recently were fraught with non-economic considerations. The limited expected gains from the India-ASEAN FTA in goods should not be a cause for despondency. The services sector from India will benefit the most as ASEAN is the net importer of the services sector, in which India has already established a cutting edge.

## References


Adams, F.G. and I.M. Davis. (1994): "The Role of Policy in Economic Development of the East and Southeast Asian and Latin American Experience", *Asian-Pacific Economic Literature*, Vol. 8, pp. 8-26.

Ambatkar, Sanjay (2000): "The Quest for Looking East: Case Study of Indo-ASEAN Economic Linkages", *Foreign Trade Review*, Vol. XXXV, July-December, No. 2 & 3, pp. 22-39.

Arif, Mohamed and Lim Chze Chen (2006): "ASEAN-India FTA: Issues and Prospects", in Kumar, N., Sen, R. and M. Asher (ed.), *India-ASEAN Economic Relations: Meeting the Challenges of Globalization*, ISEAS (Institute of Southeast Asian Studies, Singapore, pp. 69-92.

Asher, G. Mukul and Rahul Sen (2005): "India-East Asia Integration: A Win-Win for Asia", *Economic and Political Weekly*, September 3, pp. 3932-3940.

Baru, S. (2001): *India and ASEAN: The Emerging Economic Relationship towards a Bay of Bengal Community*, Working Paper No. 61, Indian Council for Research on International Economic Relations, New Delhi.

Bhagwati, Jagdish:"*India's Trade Strategy Today*", web: http:// www.jstor.org/ stable/4412960.

Brookfield, Harold and Yvonne Byron (1993): *South-East Asia's Environmental Future: The Search for Sustainability*, Oxford University Press, Singapore, chapter 10.

Chongvilaivan Aekapol (2008): "India's Ties to ASEAN Must Look beyond Trade in Goods," *The Nation,* 4 November.

Dong Zhang (2006): "Development of Trade and Economic Relations between India and ASEAN", *AUSAID Working Paper*, September.

Karmakar, Suparna (2005): India–ASEAN Cooperation in Services – An Overview, ICRIER Working Paper No. 176, 2005.

Krueger, A. O. (1980): "Trade Policy as an Input to Development", *American Economic Review*, Vol. 70, pp. 288-292.

Kumar, Nagesh (2005): "A Broader Asian Community and a Possible Roadmap", Economic and

Political Weekly, September 3, pp. 3926-3931.

Kumar, Nagesh, Rahul Sen and Mukul Asher eds. (2006): *India-ASEAN Economic Relations: Meeting the Challenges of Globalization*, RIS (Research and Information System for Non-aligned and Other Developing Countries), New Delhi.

Laurence, Henry (2007): "Trade and Economic Arrangements between India and Southeast Asia in the Context of Regional Construction and Globalization", *CSH Occasional Paper*, June.

Mukul G Asher and Amitendu Palit (2008): "Trading Across the Bay of Bengal," *ISEAS Paper,* no. 32.

Nagesh Kumar, Rahul Sen and Mukul Asher (2004): "India-ASEAN Economic Relation — Meeting the Challenges of Globalization," *ISEAS Working Paper,* no. 23.

Parashar Pradnya (2009): "India-ASEAN Economic Relations," *IIMA Working Papers*, No. 35.

Paul Bowles and Brian MacLean (1996): "*Understanding Trade Bloc Formation: The Case of the ASEAN Free Trade Area*", http://www.jstor.org/stable/4177188.

Rahul Sen*, Mukul G. Asher and Ramkishen S. Rajan (2004): "ASEAN-India Economic Relation: Current Status and Future Prospects," *ISEAS Working Paper*, No. 59.

Razeen Sally and Rahul Sen (2005): *"Whither Trade Policies in Southeast Asia? The Wider Asian and Global Context,"* ASEAN, Economic Bulletin 22, No. 1, (April):92-115.

Rupa Chanda and Sasidaran G (2008): "Understanding India's Regional Initiatives within Asia," *ISAS Working Papers*, no. 373.

Sarkar, Amal (2009): "India's Trade Linkage With ASEAN: An Econometric Study", *Foreign Trade Review*, Vol. XLIV, No.1, April-June, Indian Institute of Foreign Trade, New Delhi, pp. 26-43.

Sasatra Sudsawasd and Prasopchoke Mongsawad (2007): "Go with the Gang, ASEAN!" *ASEAN Economic Bulletin,* ISEAS 24, no.3, pp. 339-356.

Satu Limaye (2008): "India-Asia Pacific Relations: Consolidating Friendships and Nuclear Legitimacy," *Comparative Connections,* January.

# PART III

# INDIA, PAKISTAN AND WEST ASIA

# 11

# Changing Threat Perception from West Asia: India's Options

A.K. Pasha

Jawaharlal Nehru's bold initiative to organize the first Asian Relations Conference in Delhi at the Indian Council of World Affairs, Sapru House in March 1947 signalled his determination to make India a major global player. In the inaugural speech, he fervently pleaded for Asian unity, cooperation, solidarity and identity. Nehru said, "We stand at the end of an era and on the threshold of a new period of history… we can look back on our long past, and look forward to the future that is taking shape before our eyes…Asia …has suddenly become important again in world affairs…the time has come for us, peoples of Asia, to meet together, to hold together and to advance together. It was not only a vague desire, but a compulsion…" With considerable clarity, he pinpointed the strategic role of Asia in global politics in, what he called, the 'atomic age', "In this atomic age Asia will have to function effectively…Indeed, there can be no peace unless Asia plays her part. There is today conflict in many countries, and all of us in Asia are full of our own problems. Nevertheless, the emergence of Asia in world affairs could be a powerful influence for world peace". Nehru, therefore, pleaded for a 'close union of countries bordering on the Indian Ocean, both for defence and trade purposes', a system of defence, stretching from the West to Southeast Asia in which 'India because of her intrinsic importance and her strategic position was to play a significant role'.

For Nehru, India was 'the natural centre and focal point of the many forces at work in Asia. Because of this, the history of India is a long history of her relations with other countries of Asia'. He foresaw that 'the coordination of various countries in Middle East, India and the Southeast Asia is not only possible, but undoubtedly certain in the future.' He rejected the idea of a pan-Islamic bloc and said, "Some people, living in a world of their own creation, imagine that there is a pan-Islamic block which may threaten India. This is pure fancy. Every one of the Islamic countries is developing on intensely national lines and there is absolutely no room in them for an external policy based on religion. Indeed even their domestic policy has little to do with religious dogmas. The interests of these countries are and will continue to be our interests". He also indicated that the question of 'Asiatic Federation' was necessary, both for defence and trade purposes. The gathering of such large number of Asian leaders in Delhi and the conference call for Asian unity 'announced the arrival of Asia on the world stage'. Later Nehru declared, "...the world is something bigger than Europe... Asia counts in World Affairs. Tomorrow it will count much more than today." Thus, the underpinnings of India's foreign policy were laid during the freedom struggle as also anti-colonial struggle and in the initial decades of nation building. All of this gave rise to non-alignment. [1]

**Cold War Backdrop**

Nehru's opposition to western backed military alliance systems—Middle East Command, Middle East Defence Organization, Baghdad Pact, CENTO, SEATO, and NATO as also bilateral military alliances was due to his fear that the cold war would reach India's doorsteps. He was particularly opposed to US military assistance to Pakistan, Iran, Turkey and Dulles's strategy of Collective Security through military pacts. He proposed non-aligned policy and the concept of collective peace and enlisted the support of Egypt's Nasser and others. He proposed the Panchshila or five principles of peaceful coexistence. The Afro-Asian conference held at Bandung, in 1955 was a reaffirmation of the concept of area of peace articulated by Nehru. The foreign policy of India was articulated as a belief in a just global order, commitment to decolonization and universal disarmament. His approach to secure peace through regional cooperation [Panchshila], the Non-Aligned policy and so on, received a rude shock when the UK-US intervened in Iran in 1952-53 to overthrow Dr. Mohammed Mossadeq over the issue of nationalization of the Iranian oil companies. He was also particularly shocked at the violent turn of events when Israel attacked Egypt over the Suez Canal.

Subsequently Anglo-French forces intervened in Egypt in 1956 with the clear purpose of overthrowing the Nasser regime. Nehru wrote to Dulles, "I cannot imagine a worse case of aggression. If this aggression continues and succeeds, all faith in international commitments and the UN will fade away and the old spectre of colonialism will haunt us again...The whole future of the relations between Europe and Asia hangs in the balance. There can be no peace; howsoever it might be imposed if it means conquest by force of arms". Nehru publicly branded Israeli action as a case of 'clear, naked aggression'. Regarding the Anglo-French intervention, he remarked, "After fairly considerable experience in foreign affairs, I cannot think of a grosser case of naked aggression than what England and France are attempting to do..." He further said, "In the middle of the $20^{th}$

century, we are going back to the predatory method of the $18^{th}$ and $19^{th}$ centuries. But there are self-respecting, independent nations in Asia and Africa which are not going to tolerate this kind of incursion by the colonial powers." Towards Britain he remained 'not unfriendly and expressed his views more in sorrow than in anger', but he did not conceal the strength of his feelings and his deep regret that Britain, with her record of liberal policies, should now have become again the symbol of colonialism. "Unless these wrong courses are halted the future appears to me to be dark indeed..."

Although Nasser emerged victorious diplomatically from the Suez Crisis, US attempts to push the Eisenhower Doctrine rekindled Western attempts to dominate the area. In the aftermath there were two fiercely competing security systems working in the region-an Arab security system led by Egypt and supported from outside by USSR, China and India. The other was the Western backed security system supported by Turkey, Iraq, Iran, Pakistan, US and Britain. This was indirectly supported by Israel, Saudi Arabia, Jordan and others. The formation of the UAR-bringing Egypt and Syria together in February 1958, overthrow of the monarchy of Iraq in July 1958 and the Egyptian 1962 military intervention in Yemen to support the republican regime led to a virtual alliance between the US and Israel. This and the King's or Islamic alliance between US allies in the Gulf region led to the defeat of Egypt, Syria and Jordan in the Israeli invasion of these Arab countries in 1967. Since then the conservative countries led by Saudi Arabia dominated (all US allies) the region. Nasser's death in 1970 also reduced Egypt's primacy in Arab affairs. US interests came to be identified as support to Israel and Arab allies, safeguarding its oil and other commercial interests and also to contain Soviet and Communist influence in the West Asian/Gulf region. Meanwhile British withdrawal from the East of Suez led to the independence of Gulf monarchies. After its withdrawal, Britain was looking forward to the 'recession of the wave of anti-colonialism in the hope that disillusioned Asian statesmen would then be willing to cooperate with the West'. Not only the Gulf Arab rulers/families were beholden to the British, now after independence they were more than willing to cooperate with the West.

## New Directions in India-West Asia Relations

The Bangladesh crisis and the Indo-Pak war in 1971 had a major impact on India's ties with West Asia, as Pakistan sought to get closer to the Arab States. With great skill India managed to convince the Saudi and other Arab [Muslim] leaders about its desire to live in peace with Pakistan and respect its territorial integrity. The 1972 Shimla agreement and the release of Pakistani POW's helped the atmosphere as Saudi Arabia's concern for Pakistan's integrity had become a major issue in India's bilateral ties. Moreover the new Egyptian President Anwar Sadat's preoccupation with the liberation of Sinai from Israeli occupation and his growing friendship with Riyadh, as also mounting differences with Moscow, constrained him to follow a policy of 'neutrality' and 'passive posture' towards India on the issue. Egypt's posture during the 1971 crisis in the sub continent brought home to India the harsh reality of little to choose between the so called progressive and conservative Arabs in their stand towards such a crucial issue affecting Indian security. In the light of new regional developments, India had to reorient its policy from one of heavy reliance on Cairo to other power centres, which had emerged in the region particularly Iraq, Algeria, Libya, Iran and the Arab Gulf monarchies. Iran continued to give diplomatic and political support to Pakistan after the latter's defeat and division in the Indo-Pak war of 1971.

The dismemberment of Pakistan was perceived by the Shah as part of a larger conspiracy aimed at Iran. Israel's refusal to withdraw from occupied Arab lands compelled Egypt and Syria to launch a surprise military attack on Israel on October 6, 1973 which came as a rude shock to the US. Coupled with this was the oil embargo by OAPEC members on US and its allies who supported Israel. India due to its consistent support to the Arab causes managed to get assured oil supply. Moreover the above policy also opened significant possibilities for Indian exports. It also soon led to a large presence of Indian workers in the Gulf area. So far India's economic interaction was mainly concentrated with Egypt, Iran, Iraq and Sudan and at a low key with other Arab countries. But after the 1973 War, India's economic and political contacts widened especially with the oil rich Gulf States. Soon after the 1979 Iranian revolution, the outbreak of war between two major NAM members Iran-Iraq (in September 1980) was a cause for deep concern to India.

Of particular significance to India was the fact that both were New Delhi's major suppliers of crude oil supplying about 75 percent of Indian oil imports. In addition many Indians were working in several projects sending remittances. Indian policy makers feared major powers involvement in yet another conflict in the Gulf area where developments related to security and instability had a direct bearing on India's security. India as the Chairman of the NAM did try hard to find a solution to the Iran-Iraq war but without success. Non-involvement in internal or intra-regional disputes has been an integral part of India's Arab policy and it applied to Iran-Iraq as well, though in fact both sought India's support against the adversary which India found hard to provide.

On surface, India was strictly neutral but friendly ties with Iraq gave a certain tilt towards Baghdad. India's inability to mediate in the war exposed the inadequacy of Indian diplomacy in the region. Much to the dismay of India, towards the end of the Gulf War, great power naval presence substantially increased in the Gulf area and in seas surrounding India which assumed large dimensions in the wake of the 1990-91 Iraq-Kuwait crisis. The Soviet withdrawal from Afghanistan and the disintegration of the USSR together with the end of the Cold War and the emergence of Pax-Americana in the region initiated a gradual but necessary change in India's policy, while at the same time continuing its basic policy. It can be said that it is now much more realistic as well as practical in terms of its objectives. In the wake of the 1990-91 Kuwait crisis and the Madrid Peace Conference which was held in October 1991, India decided to establish diplomatic ties with Israel on the January 29, 1992. Things changed dramatically after 1991 when both the Arabs and Israelis decided to sit down and negotiate their problems.

With this new development India was encouraged to break the ice with Israel and the Jewish state was no more a pariah as before. The major post-Cold War shift in India's foreign policy towards West Asia and the North African region was the establishment of diplomatic ties. After the Madrid peace conference, growing rapprochement between the Arabs and Israeli's propelled India to attend West Asia peace talks. Defence cooperation and war on terrorism was also cited. Procuring spare parts for Soviet built arms acquired priority and Israel soon emerged as a major supplier of arms. Apparently Egypt wanted India to postpone its establishment of diplomatic ties with Israel until a reasonable settlement was concluded between Israel and the Palestinians. PLO leader Arafat also stressed that he would have preferred India establishing ties 'slowly' to enable the PLO to attain its objectives in Arab-Israeli peace talks, He pointed out that many Arab states were involved in the peace process that had no diplomatic ties.

### Arab-Israeli Peace Process

After Egypt signed its peace treaty with Israel in 1979, Jordan became the second Arab country to sign a peace treaty with Israel in 1994. Soon after, many Arab countries like Qatar, Oman, Tunisia, Morocco and Mauritania came to have lower level contacts with Israel and offices there. But the Arab Israeli Peace Process suffered due to the assassination of the Israeli Prime Minister, Yitzhak Rabin and the emergence of Likud under Netanyahu and Ariel Sharon who undermined the Oslo peace accords. US President Clinton tried to salvage the situation at the Camp David Summit in July 2000 but failed. The result was the second Intifada and more violence. Israel's refusal to withdraw from occupied Arab lands as per UN Security Council Resolutions 242 and 338 and the non-resolution of the Arab-Israeli Conflict [AIC], and Israel's opposition to the establishment of an independent Palestinian state in West Bank and Gaza are not in India's interest as it has and will fuel terrorism which is leading to wider regional instability. This has undoubtedly allowed Islamic groups especially Hamas, Hezbollah, Islamic Jihad and others to grow and is also leading to these groups to use the Israeli-Palestinian issue to resort to violence and terrorism. There were also major changes as far as the PLO was concerned.

After the PLO leader Yasser Arafat appeared before the UN in 1974 and the PLO was recognized by Arab states at Rabat, the PLO went on a peace offensive under Egyptian influence after it moved to Tunis in 1982-3 when Israel invaded Lebanon. In 1988 Arafat accepted UNSCR 242 and renounced violence and recognized Israel. After the 1991 Madrid conference and the Oslo Peace accords of September 1993 many expected Israel to withdraw from Arab lands leading to final peace between Israel and its neighbours and the formation of a Palestinian state. But the assassination of Israeli Prime Minister, Rabin on November 4, 1995 and the emergence of Likud leaders like Benjamin Netanyahu and Ariel Sharon led to the collapse of peace. Many have accused Arafat of rejecting Israeli peace offers in Camp David (July 2000) talks with US President Clinton and Israeli PM Ehud Barak. Although Arafat was willing to concede 77 percent of historic Palestine and wanted Israel to withdraw from the 23 percent of Palestine i.e. Gaza, West Bank and East Jerusalem, Israel was willing to offer only Gaza and parts of West Bank, and flatly refused to remove Jewish settlements. Rejecting the right to of the Palestinian refugees return and reiterating its stand that Jerusalem would remain the eternal and undivided capital of Israel, it continued the building of its apartheid security wall in West Bank and said that its control over water resources in West Bank will remain absolute. Meanwhile Ariel Sharon reoccupied Palestinian lands in March 2002, carried out indiscriminate arrests, killings, curfew, house demolitions, humiliating check points and so on. The result has been that deprivation, destruction and death rained on Palestinians. Palestinian suicide bombings against Israelis and the Jewish states's excessive use of force have continued unabated. Arafat was seen as an obstacle to peace and Israel painted him in the darkest colours since September 2000.

The result was US President Bush and his neo-conservative dominated team refusing to meet and deal with Arafat whom they described as an obstacle to peace. If Arafat had accepted US-Israeli proposals at Camp David he would have perhaps become an international hero eligible for another Nobel Prize. But Arafat avoided a violent end to his life by rejecting the proposals and remained largely popular among the Palestinians. Soon Sharon projected Arafat as a terrorist. Under these circumstances the US and UK were telling others that the road to peace in Palestine ran through Baghdad. Iraqi WMD's and the toppling of Saddam's regime became a priority for Bush. The result was US invasion of Iraq in March 2003. Israel had bombed Iraqi nuclear reactors in May 1981 and since then Israeli policy had been to destroy Baathist Iraq which was perceived as a threat to Israeli security. Soon after the US invasion and occupation of Iraq the Quartet—the US, EU, UN and Russia announced the Road Map for Peace between Israel and Palestine calling for a 'Viable and Independent Palestine'. Sharon raised objections to the plan and the US insisted on political reforms in the Palestinian Authority.

Arafat appointed Mahmoud Abbas and subsequently Ahmed Qoreai as PM but Israel continued its policy of relentless killings of Palestinians in Gaza and West Bank, demolition of houses, confiscation of land and construction of Jewish settlements on Palestinian land. Hamas and Islamic Jihad and young Palestinians took to violence after the display of such an Israeli attitude. The death of Arafat in November 2004 and the election of Mahmoud Abbas as PA President on the January 9, 2005, together with heavy resistance in Iraq to US occupation, growing anti-Americanism sweeping the Arab-Muslim world, made the US put pressure on Sharon to implement the Road Map for peace. The Sharam-el-Sheikh summit in Egypt involving Mahmoud Abbas, Sharon, Mubarak and King Abdullah of Jordan found all making commitment towards a Palestinian state. But Israel refused to make a commitment for full withdrawal from West Bank and remained adamant on the issue of the return of Palestinian refugees. These are definitely negative developments.

Israel's refusal to withdraw from occupied Arab lands as per UN Security Council Resolutions 242 and 338, the non-resolution of the Arab-Israeli Conflict [AIC] and Israel's opposition to the establishment of an independent Palestinian state in West Bank and Gaza are not in India's interest as it has and will continue to fuel terrorism which is leading to wider regional instability. The time has come for India to vigorously support the creation of an independent sovereign state of Palestine at the earliest and strongly impress on Israel to implement the innumerable UN Resolutions and Peace Accords signed in this connection. Recently the Saudi foreign minister Saud-al-Faisal described the Israeli-Palestinian conflict as the region's 'core problem on whose settlement the resolution of other disputes in the region depended. It is the hope that the US will restart the peace process and lead the region to peace and stability.' US allies in the region like Egypt, Jordan and the GCC states and others have made similar appeals to the US and demanded action on the AIC. But it appears that the US has lost interest in resolving old conflicts like the AIC.

Former Saudi Ambassador to the US, Prince Turki-al-Faisal was more categorical when he said that US efforts to solve the Palestinian question must now get results and 'talking is not enough. We have talked about procedures for fifty years, now we have to talk about how to tackle the hard issues of the Palestinian problem. This is what we are looking for from the US. We think that this may be a time for the US to put its foot forward'. Prince Turki's remarks came as moderate Arab states showed growing impatience with US policies in the region especially in the context of staunch US support for Israel in its invasion of Lebanon against Hezbollah in July-August 2006 and what they saw as US inaction on the Israeli-Palestinian peace track. Continued denial of their basic rights in the face of universal support and growing concern for the sad plight of the Palestinian people, is an issue, which India has to address on a top priority basis.

If this issue is resolved to the mutual satisfaction of both the parties one of the root causes for the growth and spread of violence and terrorism in West Asia would have been addressed. It has also become obvious that both Israel and the Palestinians are incapable of reaching a solution to their conflict, which very often threatens peace and security in the region. Moreover other regional problems and contentious issues are getting interlinked with this core problem thereby posing greater danger of terrorism acquiring a much larger regional dimension, and perhaps transnational dimensions as well. Since India has come to establish good relations with the US and Israel, it has become imperative to find an external solution to the vexed AIC. The consensus which exists among all the major powers towards the establishment of a Palestine state could be the starting point. To begin with, India must not only impress on the Israeli government to halt its brutal and oppressive policy towards the Palestinians but also mobilize global support in this direction.

In this effort, the focus obviously has to be on the US which is the backbone of support to Israel giving over US$ 3 billion a year, besides providing diplomatic and political support to Israel. Many in the region and elsewhere are of the view that if the US wants it can apply pressure on Israel [like in 1956 by US President Eisenhower over Israeli occupation of Sinai] to withdraw from occupied Arab lands. Any delay in the resolution of the Arab-Israeli conflict has the potential to adversely affect peace, security and stability in the region with consequent implications for India. The Road Map for Peace in West Asia has failed to take off. Much of the onus for this failure lies on the Israeli side but the US cannot be merely an onlooker. The release of few hundred Palestinian prisoners, which were first of all illegal arrests, was seen as a major Israeli concession but this gesture did not impress either the Palestinians or world public opinion. Palestinians are facing enormous hardships and feel humiliated in their own homeland.

The whole situation is caught in the midst of US inaction, desire of the

Palestinians to go through the peace process and the negative approach of the Israeli authorities to genuinely implement the Road Map. Palestinians need India's support [and other states as well] to get justice for their long sufferings. The Palestine issue has become one of the most important flash points, leading to repeated conflicts. The escalating violence can and should be contained. India should speak out in favour of the Palestinians and condemn Israeli atrocities which are taking monstrous proportion. This is essential not only to repair our ties with the Palestinians but also to strengthen ties with the GCC states. But can India expect anything from an Israel which has become the second-largest supplier of arms for India after Russia and has close closer militarily and in sharing intelligence and security cooperation. [2]

**Turmoil in the Gulf Region: The Iran-Iraq factor**

The Iranian revolution of 1979 led by Ayatollah Khomeini and the mobilization of the people on the basis of Islam was a major blow to US influence in the Gulf Region. The US since then has been consistently devising strategies to regain its influence in Iran. Meanwhile, the House of Saud was shaken by the Mecca Mosque take over in November 1979. After the Iranian revolution there was fear that it may affect a section of India's minority population especially after inflammatory speeches were made by Iranian leaders, and their support to Kashmiri militants but since there was no repetition of the Iranian revolution elsewhere in the region except for minor events like the Kaaba [Saudi Arabia] Mosque takeover in 1979 and the *coup* attempt in Bahrain [1981], and as the Sunni Arab governments took effective steps to check Iran, the impact on India was marginal. But there was no doubt that the growing challenge from Khomeini's Iran and the Iran-Iraq War among other issues posed serious challenges to the House of Saud. These events coupled with the ongoing Arab-Israeli conflict especially Israeli invasions of Lebanon and with the Soviets fully entrenched in Afghanistan; the Saudis gradually realized that their close ties with Pakistan need not come in the way of establishing good ties with India. Under these circumstances King Fahd invited Mrs. Indira Gandhi to Saudi Arabia in 1982. In an interesting development in early April 1981 Mr. Eric Gonsalves, Secretary in the Indian Ministry of External Affairs in an interview published in *The Washington Post* said among other things that the sale of US arms to Saudi Arabia and other Gulf States could provide these states with a false sense of security that could lead to their royal families being toppled as the Shah of Iran. He gave the interview on the eve of Saudi Foreign Minister's visit to India. This created a ripple in India's ties with Arab Gulf monarchies. [3]

The US in Saddam Hussein found an ally to invade Iran and was also gradually supported by the GCC states. The US dual containment policy led to the Iran-Iraq war to continue for eight years from September 1980. In the midst of this war Israel bombed the Iraqi nuclear reactor at Osirak in June 1981 near Baghdad. This pushed Iraq to seek WMD's. But the US tried to win over Saddam Hussein to its side as the Iraqi ruler had his own independent ideas. Although the Iran-Iraq war came to an end in July 1988, Saddam's concerns multiplied due to a fall in oil prices in view of over production by some GCC states. Iraqi domestic position had become precarious and with no funds coming from the GCC or elsewhere, Saddam invaded Kuwait in August 1990. For the US, Saddam Hussein's blunder came as a big gift. The US administration mobilized over thirty countries for a grand coalition of countries to expel Iraq from Kuwait. UN economic sanctions were imposed on Iraq and coalition forces led by the US launched an attack on Iraq and expelled the Iraqi forces and Kuwait was liberated by the end of February 1991. It must be mentioned here that the US undermined all peaceful efforts by Arab League, OIC, UN and others to get Iraq out peacefully from Kuwait. From the very beginning the US was determined to destroy Iraq's military which would lead to the overthrow of Saddam Hussein. The Indian government partly shared the fear of the West, in particular the US, that Saddam Hussein would control thirty percent of the world's oil reserves, if he were not pushed out of Kuwait. No wonder India allowed (initially) the refuelling of US military planes and went along with the sole superpower (US) at the UN. [4]

**Post-Cold War Context**

Around this time it was clear that the Cold War was coming to an end with the disintegration and the collapse of the USSR. Earlier after suffering heavy losses, Moscow had decided to withdraw from Afghanistan. Although Iraq was a close ally of Moscow, the new Russian leaders had no inclination to come to the rescue of Iraq as they needed western support to tide over their own economic problems. Despite the Iraqi expulsion from Kuwait, defeat at the hands of the US and the acceptance of UNSC Resolutions on WMD's, and acceptance of its border with Kuwait, UN sanctions on Iraq were maintained mainly at the behest of Kuwait. The civil war in South of Iraq involving the Shias and the Kurds in northern Iraq provided the US-UK combine to impose no fly zones on much of Iraqi territory. Under the pretext of protecting the Kurds and Shias, both the countries resorted to (almost) daily bombing of Iraqi facilities both military and civilian which had already been devastated in the 1991 war. In the post-cold war era all Indian governments worked to establish close ties with the US and also with Israel. [5]

**Primacy of the Gulf**

The 70's and 80's saw India's ties growing with Gulf states as India began to import its oil from them and growing remittances came to India from Indian workers, as also exports and investments became important. All these issues brought India and the GCC States closer. For India, the Gulf region in particular is important for a number of reasons. First, over 70 percent of India's oil [increasingly gas as well] is imported and a bulk of it comes from the Gulf region and the demand for oil is growing at an estimated 6-8 percent annually with domestic oil production gradually declining. India annually imports oil and oil products to the tune of over Rupees one lakh crore. Any disruption of oil supplies or increase in oil prices due to uncertain situations in the Gulf region has and will adversely affect Indian economy both in the short and long terms. Secondly, nearly 50 lakh Indians are gainfully employed in the GCC states that send over US$ 28 billion as remittances annually. Not only is this foreign exchange significant, but also is the safety and security of the workers of prime importance to India. Thirdly, the region is important in terms of trade especially exports (about 16 percent of India's total) which fetch us valuable foreign exchange. Besides these factors, investments from the region both official and private are significant for the Indian economy. Numerous Indian companies [public and increasingly private] are engaged in lucrative joint ventures and in building various projects and are making huge profits. Finally, security and stability in the region is also significant. Revolutions, invasions, sanctions and wars, foreign military interventions including naval bases and huge naval flotillas, and civil wars together with acquisition of large-scale sophisticated arms and foreign military advisors will surely impact on India's security and defence preparedness

India's geographical proximity to the Gulf region and especially the location of Muslim countries on its borders (East-West) compels New Delhi to view its security in encouraging secular governments in the area which incidentally are under mounting pressure from a growing number of Islamic groups. It must also be noted that US-Israeli policies in the region are principally responsible for creating instability and opposition groups-secular and religious are increasingly using violence and terror groups are growing. US domination of the area through its military and naval presence as also control of oil resources and blind support to Israel's aggressive policies is being opposed by most Arabs. In all GCC states, pro-US policies are encouraging religious extremism and many groups and people are embracing violence. Such groups may resort to greater violence and terror in future not only against the US-West and Israel but also against US friends in the area. Since bulk of the Indians live and work in GCC states, some Indian's are likely to be influenced due to mounting extremism preached by

Islamic groups.

The large scale purchase of arms by Gulf states would not only lead to pressure on India's defence budget but also may lead to presence of foreign military advisers especially from Pakistan in these states and probable transfer of weapons to states hostile to India. According to a recent US report there has been a shift of focus for terrorism from West Asia to South Asia. The 2001, September 11 events in the US have strengthened the hands of Israel under the garb of combating international terrorism as it has become clear that the US has almost given a free hand to Israel to do what it wishes in Palestine especially the military occupation of West Bank and use of IDF including US weapons to suppress Palestinians. Most secular Arab regimes are on the defensive due to internal challenges and India has been supporting the GCC conservative Arab regimes lately than the former. For New Delhi, in the fight against terrorism in Kashmir and other parts of India and in the larger context of South Asia, it needs cooperation from the Gulf States especially UAE, Saudi Arabia and Oman.

In this connection India has signed extradition treaties with the GCC States. One can argue that India cannot make much of a difference so far as the Arab-Israeli Peace equation is concerned but upgrading of ties with Israel since 1992 has undoubtedly led to greater Indo-Israeli military and political cooperation and especially under the enthusiastic support of the BJP led NDA. Muslim and other groups and parties in the region have adversely reacted to this development especially since India has traditionally maintained close ties with the Arab states. Both privately until recently and now publicly, growing number of political leaders in the Arab/Islamic World have also expressed concern and growing apprehensions about the direction of New Delhi's domestic and foreign policies: increasing-religious extremism at home and closer identification with Israel-and undue emphasis on the fight against global terrorism [clearly the US-Israeli agenda].

The BJP's [with the help of others like Shiv Sena and the Sangh Parivar] communally biased policies against the Muslims [pogroms, whipping up anti-Muslim hatred and inciting violence against Muslims as in Gujarat, Maharashtra and elsewhere] have led to internal turmoil and economic disruption which has, by and large affected the entire country. This is having an impact on India's interaction with the Gulf States as political contacts, with some exceptions [Saudi Arabia's King Abdullah and Kuwaiti Amir visited India recently] are declining and may isolate it further. Moreover Pakistan continues to paint India in dark colours at international forums particularly the UN and the OIC on violation of human rights and killings in Kashmir, treatment of Indian Muslims and of India being hegemonic in South Asian affairs. The NDA government in New Delhi and its support to the BJP government in Gujarat and their short sighted policy towards minorities especially the killings of Muslims and Christians (elsewhere as well) has provided a handle for outsiders to meddle in India's internal affairs. Only sound secular domestic policy and vigorous support to secular forces in the Gulf region and opposition to mounting outside military interventions may prevent the spread of terrorism in India. It has also become clear that placing undue emphasis on Israeli collaboration for fighting terrorism in India is unwise, as it would send a wrong message domestically as well as regionally. [6]

US-Israeli policies in West Asia are undermining peace, security and stability leading to periodic threats of military intervention or wars or to propping up threatened fragile regimes against their own populations who are demanding political participation. Another issue which is impacting India's foreign policy in the region is the US invasion and occupation of Iraq and instability [also the fear of split] in many parts of Iraq, in addition to US accusations of Iranian interference in Iraqi affairs which is used by the US to put pressure on Iran to cease 'its ideas and programs'. This has also put pressure on Indo-Iranian ties. US attempts to reshape Afghan affairs to increase its influence [as also that of Pakistan] has also strained Indo-Iranian ties. US determination to stay in Iraq and its attempts to put pressure on Iran for regime change is partly linked to help project its power to Central Asia, [and then ultimately to contain China] due to the oil and gas reserves there. The fact that the US has continued to keep it full forces in Iraq is mind boggling.

The daily killings of innocent Iraqis by the US and other forces and the destruction of holy places are fuelling Iraqi resistance. The Iraqi resistance to US occupation has not only intensified but the US has confirmed that from being sporadic attacks by the old Baathist elements, a full scale guerrilla war and now a well organized sophisticated resistance is going on against US forces. India did a wise thing by not sending troops to Iraq at US request. The anti-US sentiments sweeping the Islamic world are likely to intensify in the coming years due to USA's war against some Muslim states and groups. US-Israeli policies are spreading hatred and extremism and this is the prime reason for spreading of violence and terrorism. India with the GCC states and Iraq and other like-minded states in West Asia should work for speedy a end to US occupation of Iraq which will put an end to the atrocities committed by US occupation forces. Needless to add US invasion of Iraq has resulted in the death of over one million Iraqis and two million have become refugees mostly in neighbouring states and more than two million have become refugees within Iraq. [7]

From the Indian perspective increasing bilateral ties with Gulf States is not only important due to trade, oil and gas, but also due to the unique proximity of these states to events in the wider West Asian region. The common political and strategic concerns of India and these Gulf states will reinforce and strengthen mutual cooperation. Given the close GCC-US relations as also growing Indo-US ties, if India in cooperation with the US and others vitally interested in Gulf security, works out a harmonious approach which reassures the Gulf states of the need to work for peace, security and stability in the region, outside interference could be contained, which many perceive to be the root cause of much of the problems which India and the GCC states face. 1990s saw the reassertion of regional identities in the face of external interference. The critical space is widening and it is in this context that India and GCC can create opportunities for mutual benefit and jointly prepare to meet emerging domestic and external challenges in the Gulf region. [8]

Instability in the Gulf region poses a greater threat than ever before, as India's reliance on Gulf oil is growing. Although the issue of terrorism is important and imported arms from Israel are vital for India's security, [given very strict US conditions and reluctance to sell arms directly to India] at the same time there is no need for India to place undue emphasis on bilateral relations between India and Israel as the NDA did. The United Progressive Alliance [UPA] government's common minimum program stated that 'it will maintain the independence of India's foreign policy stance on all regional and global issues even as it pursues closer strategic and economic engagement with the US'. But the reality is that in the context of the Gulf, US policy is actually affecting India. Pax-Americana in the Gulf has serious implications for India. US influence over Gulf oil may in the future affect India's quest for energy security. All of this calls on India for new initiatives, dynamism and recognition of the traditionally close historical relationship with the Gulf States. India's economic ties are unlikely to suffer with these states in the immediate future, but one needs to be cautious in developing closer ties with Israel until the process of reconciliation gets under way between the Arabs, especially Palestinians and Israelis. The UPA coalition should attempt to balance the traditionally close ties with the GCC states with Israel. Security and stability in the region is linked with early resolution of the Iraq crisis, (withdrawal of US forces) end to Palestinian sufferings and early establishment of a viable Palestinian state and encouraging political reforms and genuine democratization in the wider Arab world which alone can contain the growing slide towards religious resurgence, violence and terrorism leading to instability in the region. [9]

### US and the War on Terror

By early 2001 West Asia in general and the Gulf region in particular had come to see violence on a large scale not only due to the Intifada but also as a fallout of Afghanistan's Taliban and other groups opposed to the US, Israel and its Arab allies. Even countries like Saudi Arabia had come to witness greater violence within its territory. All of this had led to the 9/11 events in the US, which linked global violence/terrorism to the region. The new Bush administration propounded a new National Security Strategy (of the US) whose main feature was pre-emptive strikes and offensive counter-proliferation strategies. Under this plan, the US wanted to restore nuclear weapons to the centre stage of national security policy. All these led to the undermining of multilateralism especially in the UNO. Soon after 9/11, the Doctrine of the War on Terror was proclaimed by President Bush. This unlimited war on terror was based on the twin doctrines of hegemony and pre-emption. Soon the US invaded Afghanistan and overthrew the Taliban government. Then the US Nuclear Policy Review identified seven countries against which nuclear weapons may be used in forwarding US national interest in certain cases. These are all Asian countries-China, Iran, Syria, Iraq and North Korea. Russia a Eurasian power is the sixth. The doctrine of the war on terror is primarily focused on Asia-from West Asia-the Gulf region to East Asia-which is seen as the 'theatre of war'. After Afghanistan, Iraq became the next target of the US. It was invaded in March 2003 and its leader Saddam Hussein was toppled under the pretext of WMD's, human rights violations and support to terrorism. The real reason for US invasion was Iraqi oil. All of it was in violation of the UN and the International law.

The US invasion and occupation of Iraq and Afghanistan has boosted Islamic groups resorting to violence. Shia-Sunni- Kurdish sectarianism has led to civil war in Iraq with fear of its disintegration. The US has also threatened Syria via Lebanon and Iran on the nuclear issue. Regime change which was applied in Afghanistan and Iraq was being threatened in Iran and Syria as well. This had led to greater violence in Iraq as both Syria and Iran support the Iraqi resistance which is fighting US occupation. Religious groups from Hamas, Hezbollah, Islamic Jihad, Al Qaeda and many more have emerged which preach violence to counter US – Israeli hegemony in the West Asian region. [10]

Unable to capture Osama bin Laden, George Bush diverged his attention to Iraq and to overthrow Saddam Hussein with or without UN support. The UN resolutions 678, 687, and 1441 were being used to invade Iraq and control its oil, despite opposition from UNSC members Russia, France China, Germany and others like Syria. US-UK leaders were unable to secure a UNSC resolution on the use of force against Iraq and went ahead and attacked Iraq on March 20, 2003 after the US gave 48 hours ultimatum to Saddam Hussein to step down from power. The US did not want to give the UN arms inspectors more time as demanded by UNSC members. Operation Iraqi Freedom was unleashed and hoped that the Iraqis would greet the US liberating forces from the tyrannical regime of Saddam Hussein. Massive air attacks with stealth bombers B-52 and other bombers with satellite guided precision bombing on command and control centres with decapitation attacks, shock and awe policy were expected to put an end to Saddam and his regime. After three weeks of carpet bombing, more than a lakh US soldiers including hundreds of special operation forces and CIA agents met the Iraqi resistance in some places but Iraqi forces simply melted into the civilian crowd. There were massive civilian causalities on the Iraqi side during and after the war.

The US occupied Baghdad on April 9, 2003 and since then there have been daily demonstrations and fierce resistance by the Iraqis' demanding the withdrawal of US forces from Iraq. US inability to restore basic services in most of the Iraqi cities has fuelled protests throughout the country but it was most intense in the so-called Sunni triangle especially in places like Fallujah, Sammarra, Ramadi, Baaquba, Al-Anbar province, Mosul and Baghdad. The US began to play the sectarian card. They used Shia national guards to suppress Sunnis and also Peshmergas or the Kurdish guards to kill Sunnis and silence them. The US could find neither WMD's nor Saddam Hussein's links with Al Qaeda and with mounting Iraqi resistance especially in places like Baghdad, Tikhrit and Fallujah (where the US had used chemicals cluster bombs and phosphorus bombs)along with mounting criticism of US brutality against Iraqis-the Abu Ghuraib abuses-the US could not control and subjugate the Iraqis through its representative Paul Bremer who handed over power to an interim Iraqi government led by Prime Minister Ayad Allawi in June 2004 with the primary duty of holding elections. Elections were held on January 30, 2005 amidst mounting violence and boycott by Sunni Arabs. The Shias and Kurds who have been favoured by the US since 1991 voted in large numbers and under the proportional representation system have gained a majority of seats in the National Assembly. The subsequent elections have only widened the differences between the Shias, Sunnis and Kurds which has led to more violence, and may perhaps lead to a wider civil war and an ultimate break up of Iraq.

### Iran and the Region

After US invasion of Iraq, Iran has been one of the beneficiaries of the rapid changes in Iraq. The Shias have gained power and dominate (with Kurds) the Iraqi political scene. This has also boosted the morale of the Shies in Bahrain who are in a majority but have been denied power by the ruling Sunni Al-Khalifas. The Shias in Saudi Arabia have also remained largely outside the political process which is dominated by the House of Saud. The Shias who constitute a majority in the Eastern Saudi oil rich region of Al-Hassa especially around Dammam, Qatif, Dhahran and Ras Tanura are virtually excluded from the oil industry. But since the Iranian Revolution which has greatly influenced them, they have become bold and assertive. Although the Shias have not posed any serious challenge to the Saudi regime despite having organized themselves into the Islamic Revolutionary Party, they are likely to challenge the Saudi monopoly of power. The Shias feel victimized by the Saudi-Wahhabi combination because the *Sharia* courts do not recognize them as genuine Muslims and the anti-Shia *fatwa's* of the senior *ulema* Sheikh Abdul Aziz Ibn Baz are clear and too well-documented. Majority of the Saudi Shias who dislike the Saudi ruling family have been greatly influenced by the Iranian revolution whose spiritual appeal is still quite considerable. But they realize that their destiny is in Saudi Arabia and not outside.

Even though isolated acts of sabotage are alleged to have been committed by the Shias since 1979 and even during the Gulf war over Kuwait, they are closely watched by the Saudi security forces and their movements are severely restricted. The other areas of concern in the Gulf region have been the status of three islands in the Gulf claimed by the UAE but under Iranian occupation since 1971, the security of ships passing through the Strait of Hormuz at the mouth of the Gulf, several border problems involving some GCC states, Iran's nuclear program, role, status and future of huge migrant workers in GCC states; safety and security of oil pipelines and installations; and also the anti-normalization groups which have sprung up in all the GCC states opposed to the US and any normalization with Israel. As far as the three islands under Iranian control but claimed by the UAE is concerned the US has been trying hard to persuade UAE to take the issue to the UNSC through which sanctions could be imposed on Iran, and then it could be used for regime change in Tehran. But not only is the UAE opposed to this, Saudi pressure on Abu Dhabi also seem to be working so as to prevent an escalation of conflict between the GCC and Iran. Oil and gas have been found near the islands but Iran remains adamant on this issue and in future the islands issue could become a flash point in the Gulf region. [11]

Gulf region has 63 percent of oil and 39 percent of gas reserves globally. 45 percent of OECD oil comes from the Gulf and the USA imports 60 percent from the Gulf. In 2003 oil exports from Gulf were 705 million tones. Oil production/reserves outside the Gulf are declining. At current rates of production, Gulf oil is likely to last at least for the next 150 years. Besides the Gulf region, the entire West Asia and North Africa also have substantial oil and gas resources. Due to this, the region has become the focus of attention especially of the USA.

As the Gulf region has more than two thirds of the proven world's oil reserves and produces over 20 million barrels of oil per day which is largely exported by ships to the US, Europe, Asia and elsewhere, the area through which this oil is transported in huge super tankers is the international choke point-Strait of Hormuz at the mouth of the Gulf where Oman and Iran are coastal countries.

Due to conflictual relations between the US and Iran, there is fear that if the US tries to bring about regime change in Iran, the Ayatollah regime may try to block the narrow waterway thereby affecting global oil supplies which may push oil prices still higher. In the recent past we have seen the attacks on USS Cole and French Oil tankers off the Yemeni Coast, the recent abortive attack on US naval ships in the Gulf of Aqaba from Jordan, attack by pirates on a luxury cruise liner off the Somalian coast, all of which highlight the need for cooperation on maritime security in the Gulf region, Red Sea near Bab-el-Mandeb and the Arabian coastal areas. The breakdown of the state system in Somalia and the networking among militant groups remind us of the need for utmost vigilance of extremist groups. [12]

**India and Iran**

Iranian President Ahmadinejad's views on Israel, holocaust and nuclear energy all indicate the growing pressure from the US on Iran for regime change. Since India's policy is 'No more nuclear weapons states', especially in its neighbourhood, India voted twice against Iran at the IAEA on September 24, 2005 and February 4, 2006. But to contain the damage the Indian PM said, "our relations with Iran, we relish a great deal. We have civilizational links. We are in the same region as Iran. And our concern with regard to Iran is that Iran is a signatory to the NPT. Iran must, therefore, have all the rights-which go with its being a member of the NPT. But it has also certain obligations, which it has voluntarily taken". [13]. Despite this negative Indian stand, Iranian President Mahmoud Ahmadinejad's brief visit to India on April 29, 2008 was a positive development. Among the bilateral issues discussed were the IPI gas pipeline and the LNG contract. What the National Security Advisor, M.K. Narayanan said is most interesting. He said, "There is a great deal happening between India and Iran which is not in the public realm: what we have avoided is getting involved in any conflict diplomacy. We believe that we understand Iran better. India and Iran have civilizational and economic ties. Iran is a big country and you need to deal with them diplomatically and with erudition. Any mishandling will impact negatively on us. We have capabilities and capacities." Of course, he was referring to India's own sizeable Shia population [about 25 million] which gave a certain vantage point to engage with Iran as our immediate neighbour with a large

Shia population.

India's Ex-Foreign Secretary Shiv Shankar Menon meanwhile criticized the idea that the US and its allies could find a solution to the Iran issue without talking to Tehran. He said, "Ultimately, you need to have in place a system in which Iran is a party to whatever you agree on her own program. Otherwise, whatever you do, any of the alternatives or the other options-sanctions, military action-none of them is a lasting solution. In fact, it is only likely to exacerbate the problem." Meanwhile, the former US Ambassador to India, Robert Blackwell, acknowledged that Iran had the potential to be a divisive issue in Indo-US relations especially over its nuclear energy program. He said, "It is my impression that although India very much wants Iran not to acquire nuclear weapons, if it faces a binary choice of either that or an American attack on Iran it would choose to try to deal with a nuclear Iran, without the attack. But [that] is not the view that is now dominant in Washington". [14]

Under the circumstances should India watch the unfolding of events in Iran like it did when the US invaded Iraq in 2003, which led to the overthrow of a secular regime? As things are today in Iraq, it has become a hotbed of religious fanaticism much worse than Afghanistan, with violence and terrorism spreading to the neighbouring areas fast. Will India remains immune from all this? Will Indian workers be safe in the GCC states? Is India's oil and gas supply from the Gulf region secure? The time has come for the Indian government to play an active role to defend its national interests as also to restrain the US from repeating in Iran what it did in Iraq. Can we prevent another tragedy in our neighbourhood? From Palestine to Iraq to Afghanistan and now to Iran the fire is getting closer to India. Not only has the US role brought uncertainties to the gas pipeline from Iran to India but has also jeopardized the future of India's energy security. After US President Barack Obama's offer of talks to Iran, there is growing realization in Delhi about the need to mend fences with Iran. There is talk of PM Manmohan Singh's visit to Iran in early 2010. [15]

There are nearly ten million migrant workers from over 100 countries in the GCC states alone in the Gulf region. More than six million are from India alone residing in these countries. The safety and security of these workers is a matter of utmost concern to several governments. More over due to growing anti-Americanism in the region in the wake of Afghan, Iraqi and other developments, religious groups have become very active. This is also due to the absence of democratic structures and authoritarian rule by family based GCC political systems. In future the migrant workers may be targeted by these groups leading to problems of security and stability in the entire Gulf region. Related to this is the growing concern over the safety of oil installations especially the security of oil pipelines which criss-cross the entire Gulf region and the innumerable oil terminals all of which are high value targets for extremist groups. We have seen how resistance groups in Iraq have been blowing up oil pipelines and terminals with huge success thereby affecting Iraqi oil exports and pushing up world oil prices. In future such groups could target oil and gas installations in the GCC states where there is growing resentment against local rulers for their pro-US policies in the region. This could not only affect oil production but will push oil prices higher than what they are today thereby affecting the economies of many countries. There could also be attacks [some have already taken place] on western installations and facilities in the Gulf region by extremist groups. US pressure on the Gulf rulers to normalize ties with Israel is also under attack by anti-normalization groups in most of the GCC states.

The US for its strategic objective to defeat the USSR supported Osama bin Laden who created the Al Qaeda which is held responsible for the 9/11 attacks on the US. Israel which saw PLO as a threat supported the creation of Hamas. But for the Israeli invasion of Lebanon in 1982 and its occupation of Southern Lebanon until 2000, there would have been no Hezbollah. Similarly US invasion and occupation of Iraq has led to the growth of several extremist groups not only in Iraq but with links throughout the West Asian/Gulf region. In order to ensure its place as the sole superpower and to secure for itself energy security, the US invaded Iraq defying the UN, world public opinion and in breach of international law. It has now become very clear that the US intends to stay longer in Iraq than many had thought otherwise. With unlimited access to Iraqi oil, it's easier to undermine the OPEC and with US energy security nearly complete the US policy makers are getting ready to put pressure on Iran and Syria and then to reorder the map in the Gulf region. Iraqi resistance to US occupation has intensified. Since the fall of the Iraqi capital Baghdad to US forces on the 9th of April, 2003, the US occupation-induced anarchy, lawlessness, looting, insecurity, growing violence and total chaos has led to a massive loss of life and growing anti-Americanism in Iraq. There has also been mounting Iraqi resistance to US occupation.

Initially it was a hit-and-run tactic against US troops. Hundreds of US soldiers were killed and injured by this. The Iraqi resistance 'was beginning to show signs of greater professionalism, deploying organized reconnaissance to attack with maximum efficiency and minimum loss of life'. Many US-UK planes and helicopters were also downed. The resistance has only intensified leading to increasing loss of US lives [over 3000 killed and over 75,000 injured till June 2009]. Car bombs and suicide attacks are still taking place almost on a daily basis throughout Iraq. The violence is increasingly taking a sectarian turn with attacks on Sunnis by Shias and vice versa. The US is clearly following a divide and rule policy-with loyal Kurds on their side and with a policy of appeasement towards the Shias. The Sunnis are seen as trouble makers and behind the resistance in the so-called Sunni triangle. The Sunnis fear Kurdish and Shia domination and the long-term oppression as practiced during Saddam Hussein's regime. The resistance has been striking with impunity not only in Baghdad and Mosul but all over Iraq. In future clashes between Arabs and Kurds could intensify in Iraq.

**The Iraqi Quagmire**

Despite Iraqi elections, the sectarian divide in Iraq will further widen in line with the US policy of divide and rule with religious groups and parties gaining ground thereby undermining secularism which was the basis of the Iraqi political system under the Baathist rule. In the new dispensation, the Shias will dominate Iraq and the Kurds would try to achieve maximum autonomy. The US has found political sectarianism very useful to control Iraq. The Sunnis will continue to be killed and suppressed by the US in future just like the British who killed and suppressed Shais (using Indian soldiers) during and after the First World War. The US forces for the foreseeable future will remain in Iraq to provide security to the puppet Iraqi governments which will be manipulated and the 10 or 12 military US bases will form a permanent feature of US military presence in Iraq. From Iraq the US will try to implement its regional strategy towards Iran, Syria, Saudi Arabia and others. This will only make Iraq the magnet and training ground for Islamists from all over the world. It might become a more dangerous place than Afghanistan and Somalia. Since Iraqi oil is going to last at least for 150 years, with growing US demand for oil, Iraqi oil is indispensable for the US. So far the US used to get its job done in the Arab world through Israel, now both Israel and the US will work in tandem to rearrange the whole Arab world according to their strategic needs. What Lord Curzon said of states dominating the Arab world being in a position to influence India, is coming true. Pax-Americana and Israeli domination of the region should be a wakeup call for India to devise new policies to prevent fragmentation, violence, wars, instability and terrorism which is spreading fast in the Arab world and whose impact will be surely felt in India and broadly in South Asia as well. Instead what we see is the ambition of India's elites to achieve 'great-power status' riding on the coat-tails of the US-West. This is being pursued with great enthusiasm and vigour by the Prime Minister Manmohan Singh led UPA-Congress government. [16]

Notwithstanding the arrest of Saddam Hussein and his key advisers and their being killed, the Iraqi people have not buckled to US dictates and it is unlikely that they will meekly surrender to the US led occupation of their country. The US invasion and occupation of Iraq seen as illegal, unjust and unnecessary is fuelling deeper anti-US feelings not only in the Gulf region but also worldwide and this would lead to wider complications for the US. Also, since the US does nothing to restrain Israel's monstrous policies towards Palestinians and since people worldwide know that only the US could apply effective pressure on Israel, the Pax-Americana established by force and suffering of the people will be increasingly challenged and no amount of talk about terrorism and WMD's will work in future. As long as it remains in Iraq and manipulates Iraqi governments, the spill over is likely to be felt in the entire Gulf region, where violence by extremist groups could lead to instability and insecurity. As former US Ambassador in India Robert D. Blackwell said, 'Asia's century is now underway... because Asia is poised to become the strategic centre of gravity in international politics... Although the US will not face an Asian peer competitor in the foreseeable future, regional powers are developing sufficient capabilities to threaten American vital national interests, and those of its friends and allies'. [17]

In the name of political and ideological restructuring, political reforms, war on terror, and democratic deficit, the US has been spreading its physical control over the entire oil rich Gulf region. All the GCC states have US military bases where huge forces are based, together with massive naval presence in the Gulf region and around it, and the US is using its influence to forge still more strategic alliances thereby establishing ever more military bases. The ultimate goal of the USA is to contain China, Russia and possibly India. But the Indian government has been working to establish closer ties with the US in this backdrop. As seen before, India has core interests in the Gulf region. Security and stability in the Gulf region is of utmost concern to India. The challenge from terrorism and religious and ethnic extremism from the Gulf region is growing. India has been striving to maintain good ties with the GCC states and it is in this connection one has to see Indo-Iranian ties including the visit of Iran's President Md. Khatami as the Republic Day Guest in 2003 and King Abdullah of Saudi Arabia to be the Chief Guest at the Republic Day celebrations in 2006. In a situation where powerful countries like China, Russia and even France and Germany cannot oppose the US, India has quietly decided to work with the sole superpower, including in the Gulf region. Although many in India are aware of US policies leading to periodic upheavals and turmoil in the Gulf region, India is compelled to work with the US given its close ties with Pakistan, the Kashmir issue, and the nuclear issue and so on. However, India at the same time tries to maintain its autonomy as showcased by its refusal to send troops to Iraq and its determination to maintain the viability of the oil pipeline with Iran, despite overt US objections and pressures. USA's short-sighted policies are undoubtedly generating tremendous tensions in the Gulf region but our diplomatic efforts should engage the US, Arabs, Iranians, Israeli's as well as the Turks and Kurds.

## Conclusion

Until 1973 India's policy towards West Asia was mostly Cairo-centric and it was premised on the support to Arab nationalism, Palestinian cause, and support to the Arab secular regimes, need to contain Pakistan's attempt to isolate India in the region as also Western attempts to enlist Arab states in a western sponsored military alliance. Since the 1979 Iranian revolution, India became cautious of Islamic fundamentalism, especially because of the fallout in Afghanistan and growing Saudi-Pakistani cooperation. The prolonged Iran-Iraq war, accumulation of sophisticated weapons and rise in oil prices were areas of concern in the 1980's. The 1990 Kuwait crisis and growing US military especially naval presence in the Gulf region became a matter of concern for India. The emergence of the US as the pre-eminent power after the end of the Cold War and the disintegration of the USSR and India's own domestic economic and political problems during the period 1990-1991, made India vulnerable to US pressure. Thus, 1991 was a turning point in India's foreign policy. The result was India's decision to establish diplomatic ties with Israel [early 1992] and also establish close political, strategic and military ties with the US.

All Indian governments since then have striven to establish close relations with the US. It is now virtually taken for granted that the US and India are natural allies. Pakistan-supported Kashmir militancy, the Babri Masjid demolition, Mumbai bombings and the killing of Muslims in communal riots, all added to complications in Indo-West Asian relations. After the Pokhran nuclear tests in 1998, although India's image improved in the region, it soon came to be balanced by Pakistani tests as Muslims felt 'more secure from any Israeli threats under the Pakistani nuclear umbrella'. The 9/11 events brought home the issue of global terrorism and violence closer to India via Pakistan's support to Kashmiri militancy. India sought to invest through ONGC [VL] all over the world to ensure its energy security as dependency on Gulf oil and gas was seen as risky as also due to growing Indo-Israeli and Indo-US ties. Israel was also perceived as an important player to develop closer ties with the US.

Despite opposition to the US invasion of Iraq, India could hardly do anything to prevent this blatant aggression in clear violation of the UN Charter and international law and opinion. Due to massive opposition from the Indian public, the Left, the Congress and other parties, the BJP led NDA government was forced not to send Indian troops to Iraq at the behest of Israel and the US. India did achieve some 'strategic autonomy' by this bold decision. But there is no doubt of the fact that India's ties with the USA in military the field have improved rapidly. India has shown keen interest in buying US military equipment. This has long-term implications as world wide the US tends to strengthen ties with military structures ultimately leading to coups and military interventions and threats to democracy. The Indo-US 123 nuclear agreement and the EUMA arrangements are likely to restrict India's room for manoeuvre.

Many feel the space for independent foreign policy to suit the strategic interests of the country is shrinking. Apparently some of the decisions and promises [terms and conditions of the deal India has acceded to with the US] made are not disclosed and shared with the public for fear of being exposed. As Rajiv Sikri argued, "India's ruling elite and its supporters, who are ecstatic after the signing of the India-US nuclear deal, have failed to appreciate that a lasting strategic partnership cannot be crafted by stealth and subterfuge". He points out that it appears 'that there is more to the deal, perhaps even confidential agreements or understandings, than the Indian government is willing to admit'. Sikri argues that the real US policy goal is to ensure that India's foreign policy is 'congruent' with that of the US. We must keep in mind the fact that the US will never abandon Pakistan as a strategic ally in favour of India.

The US will consolidate its grip over Pakistan and would like to have India also as an additional strategic partner and also try to use India's huge military assets, especially naval facilities. These Indian facilities the US needs to contain China as also Russia. Indirectly India is likely to get sucked into the US strategic plans at least in Asia. Also India's ties with Iran have become hostage to US policies towards Iran as India [under US pressure] additionally has to confront the issue of Iranian quest for nuclear technology. But more than ever it has become imperative for India to keep our lines of communications wide open and follow a wise and judicious policy at home and strive to reduce the number of flash points in the broader West Asian and Gulf region, where accumulation of sophisticated arms, lack of democracy, growth of religious extremism and availability of oil/gas and enormous wealth has drawn global attention. Ever since India's decision to establish diplomatic ties with Israel, Indo-Israeli ties of course have improved quite rapidly, especially during the BJP led NDA when there was talk of a strategic alliance with the Jewish state. This has led to India and Israel closely cooperating on the war on terror.

India's increased dependence on Israel for 'defence supplies and advanced defence technologies' is obviously under US pressure. [18] The so-called war on terror and the policy of exporting democracy have led to unilateral military action by the US to fulfil its global ambitions and to keep the world unipolar. But there is no doubt that the Palestine issue remains fairly popular in India with overwhelming support from all sections of Indians for an early end to the misery and sufferings of the Palestinians. Many Indians see the continuing Israeli violence in Palestine mainly due to inflexible Israeli policies. Although India is keen to join the Arab-Israeli peace process, it has become imperative to coordinate its efforts with Russia, China and the regional states like Egypt, Turkey, Saudi Arabia and others. This calls for strengthening efforts towards a multipolar world, making the UN and other multilateral structures and the Non-Aligned movement truly effective. But with India taking a 'less strident position against Israel in the UN much to the chagrin of the Palestinians' and having 'made considerable attempts to moderate anti-Israeli resolutions' at NAM meetings, it is obvious that the expectations of many, especially in the West Asian region that the Congress-led UPA government would restore the balance it had pursued in its policy towards West Asia earlier, remains largely elusive. Any contention that Israel is a major arms supplier to India and hence the government should soft pedal any firm stand against Israel will obviously affect India's credibility in the West Asian region [and also the wider Islamic world] where bulk of India's interests lie. India must continue to support wholeheartedly the Palestine cause and ensure justice is given to the Palestinians and other Arabs struggling for freedom. Suicide bombings, lack of democracy, dependency syndrome, the growing clout of religious groups and especially non-state actors, narco-terrorism, maritime security, WMD's, arms race and mounting outside military interventions are matters of growing concern to India as threats from all of these factors are bound to increase in future from West Asia.

**Notes**

1. Uma Iyenger ed., The Oxford India Nehru, [New Delhi: Oxford University Press, 2007] pp. 471 and 511; AK Pasha, "India and Israel: Growing Cooperation", World Focus, vol.14, no. 8, August 1993, pp. 19-2; See also AK Pasha, "Gulf-Asia Historical Relations: An Overview", World Focus, Vol. XXX No.5 [353] May 2009, pp. 183-196; RR Sharma, Ed, India and Emerging Asia [New Delhi: Sage Publications, 2005] pp.12-79; See also Mahavir Singh, Ed, Building a New Asia [New Delhi; Shipra, 2005]; Hari Sharan Chhabra, Nehru and Resurgent Africa (New Delhi: Africa Publications, 1989); AK Pasha, "Asian Security: Flash Points in the Gulf Region", World Focus, Vol. 26, nos. 10-12, October-December, 2005, pp. 25-33; AK Pasha, "India and West Asia", World Focus, vol. 25, October-December 2004, pp. 41-46; MS Agwani, "India and the Arab World", in BR Nanda, Ed, Indian Foreign Policy : The Nehru Years (New Delhi : 1976), pp.72-73; AK Pasha, "Tipu's Sultan's Diplomacy in the Gulf Region", Gulf Studies Program, Working Paper No. 10, February 1997, CWAAS, SIS, JNU, New Delhi; AK Pasha, "South India and the Gulf: Trade and Diplomacy during the late 18th Century", in NN Vohra edited: History, Culture and Society in India and West Asia, (New Delhi: Shipra, 11C, 2003) pp. 237-49; AK Pasha, "India's Cultural Diplomacy in West Asia", in MH Ilias and PJ Vincent ed., India-West Asia Relations: Understanding Cultural Interplays [New Delhi: New Century Publications, 2007] pp.39-58; AK Pasha,

"Nehru and the Crises in West Asia", Détente, [New Delhi], Vol. 9, no.1, May-June, 1990, pp. 4-9; AK Pasha, "Indo-Egyptian Ties: Retrospect and Prospects", Third World Impact , vol.2, no. 20/23, November 1991, pp. 23-27; AK Pasha, "Tipu's Relations with the Ottoman Empire", Détente, Vol. 10, nos. 4-5, January-April 1992, pp. 6-11; AK Pasha, "Tipu and the Ottoman Empire", in B Sheik Ali, ed., Tipu Sultan: A Great Martyr [Bangalore University: Prasaranga, 1993] pp. 219-32.

2. P R Mudiam, India and the Middle East, [London: British Academic Press, 1994), p. 56; K R Singh, "India and WANA", in Bimal Prasad, Ed; India's Foreign Policy: Studies in Continuity and Change (New Delhi: Vikas, 1978] pp. 247-59; AK Pasha, Arab-Israeli Peace Process: An Indian Perspective [New Delhi: Manas, Publications, 2000]; JN Dixit says: "There was even an extraordinary unrealistic assessment from our mission in Baghdad that Saddam Hussein should be treated with kid gloves because he was not likely to be defeated by the combined forces of the international community under the UN umbrella led by the US", JN Dixit, India's Foreign Policy, 1947-2003, [New Delhi: Picus Books, 2003] p. 213; The Hindu, 14-04-2008.
3. AK Pasha, "India and West Asia: Continuity and Change," in, Nalini Kant Jha, edited, India's Foreign Policy in a Changing World: Essays in Honour of Professor Bimal Prasad (New Delhi: South Asian Publishers, 2000) pp. 240-69; The Hindu, 6 December 2005; Marc Lynch, "Iraq and the Arab Street: Iraq and the Arab Public Sphere", Politics and Society, vol.31, no.1, March 2003, pp. 55-91; Naveed S. Sheikh, The New Politics of Islam : Pan–Islamic Foreign Polity in a World of States (London: Routledge Curzon, 2003), p. 60, p. 8. In May 2004 the Lancet report found that about 100,000 additional Iraqi deaths had taken place since the US invasion in March 2003. A team from Johns Hopkins University identified more than 12,000 family members and tracked those who had died since the invasion- an estimated 650,000 additional Iraqi civilian casualties. Most of these deaths have been of men aged 15-44.
4. Richard Horton, "The death toll in Iraq", The Hindu, October 13, 2006; Amin Saikal, Islam and the West: Conflict or Cooperation (London: Palgrave, Macmillan, 2003) p. 130; AK Pasha, "The US Invasion of Iraq and the Muslim World", in VD Chopra, ed., Genesis and Fall out of US-UK Military Action in Iraq (Delhi: Kalpaz, 2004) pp. 207-226; see also AK Pasha, "India's changing threat perception from West Asia", in Journal of Strategic Studies [ Bahrain] Vol. 5, no.16, Autumn 2009, pp. 9-52.
5. See also AK Pasha, "Arafat, Palestinians and the Future", Mainstream, vol. XLII no.50, December 4, 2004, pp. 7-10; Zafar Imam, Iraq-2003: The Return of Imperialism [New Delhi: Aakar Books, 2004]; AK Pasha, "Significance of Indo-Russian Strategic Partnership: Its Impact on Arab World", in VD Chopra, ed., Global Significance of Indo-Russian Strategic Partnership [Delhi: Kalpaz Publications, 2005] pp. 135- 172.
6. The Hindu, 23 June 2005; See also Toby Dodge, Iraq's Future: The Aftermath of Regime Change. Adelphi Paper 372, (London: Routledge, 2005); see also Toby Dodge and S. Simon, eds., Iraq at the Cross Roads: State and Society in the Shadow of Regime Change, Adelphi Paper 354, IISS (Oxford: OUP, 2003) pp. 77-92; Seymour M. Hersh, Chain of Command: The Road from 9/11 to Abu Ghraib, [New York; Harper Collins, 2004]; Frontline, August 25, 2006, pp. 18-22. According to JN Dixit on 31-1-1998 IK Gujral made a statement that GOI will not "tolerate" any military action against Iraq and that India had cautioned the US by means of a letter to President Clinton. IK Gujral stressed that India's concern was that such an attack would result in regional tension and create danger for Indians in GCC states. Dixit,

n.2, p. 376.

7. Richard J. Kozicki, "India and the Arab World after Indira Gandhi: Continuity in Foreign Policy", Arab-American Affairs, Fall, 1985, no. 14, pp.1-17; AK Pasha, Ed, India, Bahrain and Qatar: Political, Economic and Strategic Dimensions (Delhi: Gyan Sagar, 1999); See also AK Pasha, Ed, India and Oman: History, State, Economy and Foreign Policy (Delhi: Gyan Sagar, 1999); see also Harish Kapur, Foreign Policies of India's Prime Ministers, [New Delhi: Lancer, 2009] pp. 315.
8. AK Pasha, "India and the Gulf States: Challenges and Opportunities", Rajen Harshe and KM Seethi Ed: Engaging with the World: Critical Reflections on India's Foreign Policy (New Delhi: Orient Longmans, 2005) p.389-424; AK Pasha, "Pax Americana in the Gulf Region: Implications for India's Quest for Energy Security", in SN Malakar, edited: India's Energy Security and the Gulf (Delhi: Academic Excellence, 2006) pp.116-122; AK Pasha, "Post-Arafat Palestine", World Focus, vol. 26, no. 5, (305) May 2005, pp. 7-10.
9. Boutros Ghali, Egypt's Road to Jerusalem : A Diplomat's Story of the Struggle for Peace in the Middle East (New York, Random House, 1997), pp. 80-81; 120, 214, 257, 278; Salim, Mohd. El Sayed; Ed; Egypt and India in the Post-Cold War World : Comparative Paradigms (Cairo : CAS, Cairo University, 1996); AK Pasha, "India's Policy towards the Arab World in the 21st Century" in V D Chopra, ed., India's Foreign Policy in the 21st Century, [Delhi: Kalpaz Publications, 2006] pp. 215-250; Bansidhar Pradhan, Changing Dynamics of India's West Asia Policy", International Studies, vol. 41, no.1, 2004, p.51; Why the US promotes India's great power ambitions, Analytical Monthly Review, Vol. 3, no. 12, March 2006, pp. 15-30; A K Pasha, "Egypt's Search for food security", Détente, vol. 7, no. 5, January 1989, pp. 10-15; A K Pasha, Egypt in a Changing World (New Delhi : National Publishing House, 2003) pp. 242-260; P R K Swamy, "Mubarak in busy, please mail the Nehru award", Asian Tribune, 7-7-2007.
10. AK Pasha, "India's Cultural Diplomacy in West Asia and North Africa", in Anwar Alam ed., India and West Asia in an Era of Globalization.[New Delhi: New Century Publications, 2008]; During 2007-08 India paid almost US$50 billion for oil and products imports; AK Pasha, "Rediscovering Old Bond with Egypt", The Pioneer, 23 December 1991; AK Pasha, "A Great Leap Forward Taken by India and Israel", India Abroad [New York], 17 January 1997, pp. 2-3; AK Pasha, "India-Saudi Relations: Past and Emerging Challenges", in G Dietl, G. Pant, AK Pasha and PC Jain Ed; Contemporary Saudi Arabia and the Emerging Indo-Saudi Relations (New Delhi: Manak Publications, 2007) pp. 143-166; AK Pasha, "Safety and Security Aspects of Hajj", The Pioneer, May 24, 1997; AK Pasha, "India's Cultural Diplomacy in West Asia", in AK Sinha and AK Singh eds., New Horizons in History, Classics and Inter-Cultural Studies, [Delhi: Anamika Publications, 2007] pp. 295-310.
11. Mustafa Alani, Dhafer Al Ani and Mahmood Sariolghalam, "Developments in Iraq and Iran", in Gulf Research Center, Year Book, 2004, [Dubai], pp. 249- 272; AK Pasha, "India's West Asia Policy: Continuity and Change", Strategic Analysis, vol. XVI, no.6, September 1992, pp. 783-804; AK Pasha, "India and West Asia: Past and Future", in NS Sisodia and Ashok K Behuria, eds., West Asia in Turmoil: Implications for Global Security, [New Delhi: Academic Foundation, 2007] pp.441-470; AK Pasha, "Yemen-Saudi Security Relations: Implications for India", Third Concept, vol. 8, no.87, May 1994, pp.33-36; Dilip Hiro, Blood of the Earth: The Battle for the World's Vanishing Oil Resources, [New Delhi: Penguin Books, 2008]; AK Pasha, "Indo-OIC Relations: Perspective and Trends", Journal of Peace Studies, vol. 1, no.3-4, March-June 1994, pp. 22-50; AK Pasha, "The Recent Gulf Crisis:

India's Options", Strategic Analysis, vol. XVII, no.10, January 1995, pp. 127-86; Mustafa Alani, "The Curse of oil and the disintegration of Iraq," Gulf Monitor, GRC, Vol. no. 4, June 2007, p. 8-9.

12. Christian Koch, "Iran, the National Intelligence Estimate and the Gulf Security", Gulf Monitor, GRC, Vol. 2, no.1, January 2008, pp.4-7. See also AK Pasha, "India, Iran and the GCC States: Common Political and Strategic Concerns", Encounter, March, April 1998, pp.66-74; AK Pasha, "India and the GCC States: Challenges and Opportunities", World Focus, vol. 24, no. 2, (278) February 2003 pp. 9-15; See also Meena Singh Roy ed., International and Regional Security Dynamics: Indian and Iranian Perspectives, [New Delhi: IDSA, 2009]
13. AK Pasha, "Why is the Islamic World Important for India? Hard news, vol.1, Issue, 7, June 2004, pp. 56-57; AK Pasha, "India-Saudi Ties", Bahrain Tribune, 20 January 2006.[With N Janardhan]; See also AK Pasha, "Communal Revivalism in India: Its impact on ties with West Asia and North Africa", in Muchkund Dubey, edited, Communal Revivalism in India: A Study of External Implications (New Delhi: Har Anand, 1994), pp. 54-88.
14. Musa Hamad al Qallab, "Analyzing the Military Posture of US and Iranian troops in the Gulf Region", Gulf Monitor, GRC, Vol.1, no. 4, June, 2007, pp. 10-12. See also AK Pasha, "India, Iran and its Regional Influence", World Focus, vol. 26, no. 8, (308) August 2005, pp. 3-8; AK Pasha, "The Iraq Crisis: An Overview", World Focus, Vol.25, no.1, January 2004, pp.3-6; see also AK pasha, "Democracy in the GCC States", in Area Studies- A Journal of International Studies and Analyses, Vol. 2, no. 2, July-December 2008, pp. .33-51.
15. Talmiz Ahmed, "The Iran-Pakistan-India gas pipeline", Seminar, no.584, April 2008, pp. 48-51; AK Pasha, "India's Cultural Diplomacy with the Arab World", Arab League Special Issue [New Delhi], 60th Anniversary 2006, pp. 42-45; AK Pasha, "50 Years of India's Ties with West Asia", The Pioneer, 19 August 1997; Mohammed Abdel Salam, "Civilian Nuclear Program in Arab Countries", Security and Terrorism, Research Bulletin, Nuclearization of the Gulf, Gulf Research Center, Issue, no.7, December 2007, pp. 28-30. The Hindu, 21 April, 2008; Anna Rulska and David Jackson. "At the Crossroads of Foreign Policy Decisions: India and the Middle East", in Jack Covarrubias and Tom Lansford Ed, Strategic Interests in the Middle East: Opposition and Support for US Foreign Policy, [Burlington: Ashgate, 2007] pp.109-120; see also AK Pasha, "India and West Asia: Challenges and Opportunities", in Anjali Ghosh, Tridib Chakraborti et al, ed., India's Foreign Policy, [New Delhi: Pearson, 2009] pp. 301-356.
16. The Hindu, 21 April, 2008; AK Pasha, "India-Saudi Ties Ready for a New Dawn", GCC-India Research Bulletin [Dubai: UAE] Issue no.1, January 2006, pp. 6-7; AK Pasha, "Relations to a New Dawn", Arab News [Jeddah], 26 January 2006.[with N Janardhan]; AK Pasha, "Indo-Saudi Arabian Summit is long over due", The Pioneer, 3, August, 1992; K Natwar Singh, "Whither Foreign Policy and Diplomacy", Seminar, no.584, April 2008, pp. 70-71; AK Pasha, "India-Oman: Emerging Security Partnership", GCC-India Research Bulletin, Issue no. 2, June 2006, pp. 10-11; AK Pasha, "India and Persian Gulf: An Overview", World Focus, Issue on New Dynamics in Persian Gulf, Vol. XXVIII, no.2, [326], February, 2007, pp. 39-45; The Hindu, 23 February 2008.
17. Anoushiravan Ehteshami, "The Year of Crisis in Iran" [2005],in Gulf Research Center, Year Book, 2005-06 [ Dubai], pp. 349- 355; AK Pasha, "Indian Perceptions on Persian Gulf ", World Focus, Vol. XXVIII, Nos.11-12, Nov-Dec, 2007, pp. 446-457; AK Pasha, "Recent Developments in the Gulf Region: An Overview", World Focus issue on Persian Gulf, Vol.

39, no.2 [338]. February 2008, pp. 43-47.

18. Rajesh Kumar Mishra, "Nuclear Proliferation Challenges and India's response", Strategic Analysis, Vol. 31, no. 5, Sept. 2007, pp. 791-814; See also AK Pasha, "Iraq and its Future: An Overview", World Focus, Vol. 26, no. 2 [302], February 2005, Issue on Iraq and its Future: Doubts and Fears, pp. 3-6; AK Pasha, "Iran and Iraq: Are they Becoming Friends?" South Asia Politics, Vol. 4, no. 5, September 2005, pp. 29-34; see also Rajiv Sikri, Challenge and Strategy: Rethinking India's Foreign Policy [New Delhi: Sage, 2009] pp. 176-183.

# 12

## Indo-Pak Relations: New Trends

Sudhir Singh

---

Since the assassination of Benazir Bhutto in December 2007, the contours of the Indo-Pakistan relationship have changed a lot. The demise of Benazir coincides with the restoration of democracy and the ouster of the military dictatorship, which was ruling Pakistan since October 1999 after the removal of the democratically elected government of Nawaz Sharif. In February 2008, general elections took place after several years and in March 2008 under the leadership of Yusuf Raza Gillani, the PPP led government came into power. It was a democratic government after almost a decade. Significant about the formation of this government was that it started its innings with the philosophy of the 'era of consensus' under the name *Charter of Democracy* [1] agreed between the former Prime Minister Benazir Bhutto and Nawaz Sharif in 2006, when they were in exile. This charter talks about the strengthening of democracy. Although it is an open secret that both Benazir and Nawaz ruled two terms each but they never cooperated for the strengthening of democracy and exclusively they could not form a consensus to eliminate the Black Law [8th Amendment], which still hangs as a blot on elected governments. This infamous 8th amendment was inserted into the 1973 Bhutto constitution by the military dictator General Zia Ul Haq during his military rule [1977-1988]. General Zia was dedicated to weakening the roots of democracy and for that purpose he gave extraordinary rights to the President in the form of the power to both-central as well as provincial elected governments, without citing sufficient reasons. [2] It is significant here to mention that even Nawaz Sharif was partner to General Zia in countering the influence of Prime Minster Mohammad Khan Junejo, who got elected as the Prime Minister after the 1985 election. General Zia was anxious with the growing influence of Junejo and wanted to curtail his growing power. [3] Benazir Bhutto and her party on the other hand, were dedicated to the restoration of democratic rights in line with her late father Z.A. Bhutto who laid the foundations of the PPP in 1967, insisted on the empowerment of the poorest of the poor and gave the slogan of *Islamic Socialism*. [4]

It is also pertinent to mention here that whenever the military felt that democracy was strengthening its roots, it engineered hurdles for democratic governments. Benazir Bhutto came into power first in December 1988 after the general elections. Right from the next month of her coming into power the military engineered unrest in Kashmir and generated tension between India and Pakistan. It was the first occasion when Kashmir became violent and saw probably the first act of cross-border support by Pakistan to the unrest in Kashmir. Since then, whenever military felt that its stake was threatened it accelerated the pace of violence in Kashmir and in due course of time in the rest of India. In February 1997, Nawaz Sharif came into power with an unprecedented two-thirds majority and one of the most vital electoral promises he made was the normalcy of relationship with India. In May 1998 both India and Pakistan exploded their respective nuclear devices and after that Prime Minister Vajpayee agreed to visit Lahore. This visit took place and both the Prime Ministers declared the historic Lahore Declaration. Vajpayee visited the Minar-A-Pakistan and symbolically it was an approval of the formation of Pakistan. When Vajpayee and Nawaz Sharif were sketching the Lahore Declaration, the Army in the meanwhile was planning to capture Kargil and eliminate the generosity and mutual understanding created by the Lahore Declaration between India and Pakistan. After Kargil, there have been several attacks on India with the Mumbai-Attack being the latest.

To understand the entirety of Indo-Pakistan relations, one has to know the internal dynamics of civil-military relationship in Pakistan. Since its inception, Pakistani military has sustained its hold over the corridors of power and has not allowed even the democratically elected governments to intervene in their areas of self-interest. The negation of democratic governments is the best guarantee for the sustenance of military dominance. Pakistan has a good relationship with almost all its neighbours [Iran, Afghanistan and China] minus India. The self-interest of Pakistani military has accelerated the hostility with India and exploited this situation so as to forward their dominance. However, in some countries the military has played a positive role in the promotion and protection of democratic values. In Turkey for example, the military had strengthened democratic values and traditions. In contrast, the Pakistani military is known for its suppression of democratic values and aspirations of the common people. Because of this, resources for welfare have been diverted towards military preparedness. Former Secretary General of the United Nations, Boutros Boutros Ghali propounded in his famous study entitled *Militarism and Human Rights* that militarism was based on the negation of basic rights of common citizens and therefore cannot let the latter exist along with itself. Pakistan, Burma and some other authoritarian states fit such categorization. Pakistani authors Hasan Askari Rizvi and Ayesha Sidika have elaborated their views on Pakistani military in their respective works and concluded that the military has been the largest infringer of the rights of the poorest of the poor. One has to understand the civil-military relationship in Pakistan so as to understand Pakistan's relations with India.

Since the restoration of the PPP led government in March 2008, President Zardari in the capacity of the Chief of the PPP as well as the President of Pakistan aired his views in an extremely genuine manner, although, Zardari's own position is not secure given the volatility of the situation in contemporary Pakistan. But he dared to speak the truth along with the international community regarding Pakistan being the hot bed of international terrorism. In July 2009, communal riots erupted in the Chinese occupied Xingjiang province resulting in major casualties and China has started reveal to people that the Ughiour Muslims there took their training in Pakistan. China is an all-weather friend of Pakistan. Despite this reality, Pakistan has used terror as an instrument for the pursuance of its foreign policies and exploited everyone including foes like India and friends like China and the United States.

The two-nation theory was the basis Pakistan's existence and a logical corollary of this theory was that Muslim majority areas of the sub-continent be constituted to form one state, since they already constituted a nation. It was on this basis that the monolithic state structure of Pakistan was established. But the creation of Bangladesh proved that merely on the basis of a common religion, a nation could not be kept united. In the Presidential address of the Muslim League session of 1930, Iqbal had declared, "I would like to see the Punjab, the North West Frontier Province, Sind and Baluchistan amalgamated into a single state. Self- government within the British Empire or without the British Empire, the formation of a consolidated North-West Indian Muslim state appears to me to be the final destiny of Muslim at least of north-west India." [5] It was only later in his correspondence with Jinnah dated June 21, 1937, that the poet philosopher seems to have taken the cognizance of Bengal's demographic and therefore political importance as far as the Indian Muslim community was concerned. [6]

For the sustainability of a multi-cultural, multi ethnic nation, it is required that accommodation of peripheral forces into the mainstreaming process be part and parcel of the policy of the concerned country. Pakistan never realized this reality due to a gamut of reasons and even after partition, several ethnic conflicts erupted and dampened the nation building process. One of the most important factors behind this Pakistani policy is to maintain the hostile with India so as to prove the relevance of Pakistan's existence. The dominance of the military in Pakistan has even prevented democratically elected governments to build bridges with India. It is for this reason that Pakistan provided all-round support and became host to the Mujahideen forces during the Afghan war of 1979. One of the important tasks of Pakistan's Afghan policy was to score Strategic Depth in India. The same logic propelled Pakistan to nurture diverse streams of terrorism including the Taliban and the Al-Qaeda. What President Zardari said in July 2009 about the role of Pakistan in fomenting Jehadi forces is absolutely true but the billion dollar question is how successful would the democratically elected Zardari be in eliminating this menace? It is significant to mention here that within a few days of his famous confession address, the spokesperson of the Pakistani military asserted that Pakistan still had contact with the Taliban and the Al-Qaeda and proposed that it could bring the Taliban on the negotiation table, provided its core concern related to India be addressed properly.

Pakistan used the Kashmir card and declared to the world that Kashmir had become a nuclear flash point within South Asia after Pokhran II. However, this did not help much as the same U.S., which played a pro-Pakistan role during the Bangladesh liberation war, asked Pakistan blatantly to step down from Indian lands during the Kargil conflict [1999]. As rightly put by a noted scholar, there are no permanent friends or foes in foreign policy only convergences of interests that determine foreign policy. In the post-Cold War era, the U.S has felt India's emergence in a significant manner and has started engaging India in an unprecedented manner. A much debated conclusion to the 123 Nuclear Agreement between both the nations is ample proof of this argument. In July 2009, U.S Secretary of State, Hillary Clinton visited India but not Pakistan. This is significant because earlier the U.S. Administration held India and Pakistan together. China has also been allergic to the ongoing bonhomie between India and the U.S. China has been pursuing the policy of encircling India within South Asia. The boundary dispute and the issue of Tibet resulted into the 1962 war and despite many rounds of high-profile summits and regular meetings, these issues have seen no breakthrough. But despite these negative developments, the same logic of convergence of interests forced even China to reformulate its policies towards India.

During the Kargil Crisis, both-the Pakistan Prime-Minister and the Chief of Army Staff [COAS] visited Beijing to garner Chinese support. But not only did the Chinese decline to extend their support, they also advised Pakistan to settle the Kashmir issue with India at the bilateral level. Recently Pakistan and Afghanistan based Taliban and Al-Qaeda have been noted to pose a threat to the Xinjiang province of China. This province is the bridge between China and Central Asia and holds abundant natural gas, oil and other resources. The Chinese nuclear explosion site Lopa-a-Noor is also situated here. The growing tentacles of Islamic fundamentalism in Xingjiang with the collaboration of the Taliban and Al-Qaeda have pushed China to reconsider its South Asian policy. They have singled out terror as the common problem they share with India and despite a gamut of differences over other issues, they have agreed to collaborate with India. Although China has invested huge capital in Pakistani projects exclusively in the Gwadar harbour, the prevailing situation in Xingjiang has pushed the Chinese to reconsider their policies which has led to a reduction in the importance enjoyed by Pakistan.

Kashmir remains a discord between India and Pakistan. Pakistan covertly argued that incorporation of Kashmir into Pakistan was the natural process. Since 1988, terror has been used by Pakistan in Kashmir in particular. Despite all round efforts towards cross-border support, Pakistan has not been able to achieve its goal. Though some feel that parting with Kashmir by India would settle the issue once and for all, there are others of the opinion that such an act would be a confirmation of the Two-Nation Theory and at the same time a negation of the plural and multi-ethnic system of India. But what would be the guarantee of Pakistan settling just with Kashmir? It may certain areas and regions, the granting of which would become impossible. That may lead to endless violence and would be extremely dangerous form all points of view. Eminent Pakistani scholar, Ayesha Siddika is also of the opinion that incorporation of Kashmir into Pakistan would not restore normalcy between India and Pakistan. She argued in her famous book '*Military Inc*' that Pakistani military has developed into an oligarchy and that oligarchy has been responsible for all kinds of problems in Pakistan. [7] This oligarchy required this hostility so as to sustain the status quo.

Even after six decades since independence, Pakistan has not been able to establish a separate identity. U.K based Pakistani scholar, Farzana Sheikh has argued on this line in her recently published book. [8] She argues that Pakistan has not been able to establish its identity and is therefore trying to replicate India to no avail. India has undergone tremendous development. India has been rated as an emerging power in the 21st century. One can see this potential in India's growth not only within Asia but also at the international level. It is in the larger interest of Pakistan to allocate adequate attention towards its internal problems instead of being obsessed with India. The same logic is relevant for India. If India has to become an important global power in the 21st century then India has focus on all geographical areas of the world. Within South Asia, India must play the role of a responsible power and restrain itself despite provocative efforts. A strong Pakistan is what India should promote. But Pakistani rulers seem to underestimate this fact and ignore its progression towards development.

There are many reasons why Pakistan thinks that a growing Indian may disturb the traditional system. One of the important factors has been Afghanistan. Since the elimination of the Taliban and Al-Qaeda post 9/11 and the U.S attack on Afghanistan, India has been active in the reconstruction process in Afghanistan. The role of Pakistan in fomenting the Taliban and Al-Qaeda has been extremely important, although several harbingers of the global anti-terror movement including the U.S, the Western World, China, Iran and Saudi Arabia have also been responsible for the birth, promotion and protection of terror in South West Asia in pursuance of their policy of containment of communism against the USSR. India being one of the oldest victims of terror has been exclusively clear that terror in any form is dangerous for humanity and therefore needs to be eliminated. After the elimination of the Taliban and Al-Qaeda; under the banner of the Tokyo conference, India pledged to extend support to the reconstruction of Afghanistan. Pakistan took offence as a stable Afghanistan is potentially dangerous to Pakistan due to a variety of reasons, the most important among them being the negation of the recognition of the Durand Line by Afghanistan.

Afghanistan still remains as an important obsession with Pakistan. Afghanistan has slowly become Pakistan's backyard harbouring all sorts of jehadis-from Morocco to Mindanao. The Karzai government despite its fragility has become a bone of contention for Pakistani rulers.

China is another power in the South Asian matrix that is guiding Pakistani policies. China wants to emerge as a dominant power in Asia and at the same time wants a multi-polar world with itself as an important power. But this is precisely an anti-US agenda. The US agenda for world politics though does not coincide totally with India's, it converges on several counts including the shaping of Asian politics in the 21st century.

China had been a close ally of Pakistan and during the 1965 and 1971 wars, it threatened India not to cross its limits. Sino-Indian relations have always been fragile due to mutual distrust. But since 1988, when Prime Minister, Rajiv Gandhi visited Beijing followed by successive Indian Prime Minister's visits, it has improved significantly. Though China has not resolved quite a few issues with India, it has put them aside for increasing bilateral economic cooperation that has improved drastically in the past few years. And it is within this changed situation that China has modified its foreign policy to a détente with India while pressurizing Pakistan. This has also been so due to visible unrest in the Xingjiang province. For the past few years, Pakistan is caught up in a battle for survival against these home grown terrorists itself. This has further convinced China not to extend an all round support to Pakistan as was being done earlier.

**War against Terror and the US Role**

Today despite the installation of a democratically elected Gillani government after long innings of the military dictatorship, military hegemony in Pakistan continues. It is important to note that this dominance is three dimensional; the military has penetrated into the society, politics and economy. It has also grabbed the intellectual discourse and the imagination of the people. Even the political leadership has provided fodder for the dominance of the army. A classic example being the *Charter of Democracy,* announced by the leaders of two main opposition parties; the Pakistan People's Party [PPP] and the Pakistan Muslim League-Nawaz [PML-N]. [9] It is pertinent to mention here that the PPP is today ruling the country and the PML-N is in opposition. However their mutual agreed 2006 CoD emphasized the significance of the Kashmir dispute, an issue that in the long term is bound to keep the military's importance intact. The Military has pushed the Kashmir issue to the fore so as to settle its scores with the democratically elected Benazir Bhutto government. The Kashmir issue has not only kept bilateral relationships between India and Pakistan hostage but also has tremendously negated any possibility of the emergence of the SAARC as a viable platform for regional cooperation within South Asia-a region which has remained poor even at the outset of the 21st century. The military has sustained its power by basing itself on the exploitation of the common masses simply with an eye for a Himalayan share of the state budget for itself. According the eminent Pakistani journalist, Najam Sethi, "the military bends the rules and makes its own rules so that no one can call it corruption." [10]

Pakistan is fortunate in the sense that disturbances in the neighbourhood are quite regular which lead to a massive inflow of funds. This was the case in 1979, when the USSR intervened in Afghanistan and the US went on with their war of resistance and continues to be so in the light of the Obama Administration coming out with its *AfPak Policy*, nominating Richard Holbrook as the representative.

Recently in July 2009, Indian Prime Minister Manmohan Singh met his Pakistani counterpart during the NAM conference in Egypt. However, the bogey of Kashmir was raised here too. To this one may cite Robert Black, US Assistant Secretary of State for the South Asia, "on the question of Kashmir, obviously that is for the two countries for the resolve". [11] We are aware about the fact that Pakistan is not serious to bring those behind the Mumbai attack [November 2008] to justice. They are roaming freely in Pakistan. Pakistani President has however admitted candidly that terror had been promoted by the Pakistani state for the promotion and protection of their vested interests but now they were working against the Pakistani state itself. The terror network and Pakistani military are interdependent for their survival. Giving the example of Mehsud, senior Pakistani security analyst Dr. Ayesha Siddika says, "He [Baitullah Mehsud] was originally supported by the military and the ISI. But he had begun to bite the hands that fed him. His death was a powerful signal to them all." [12]

Baitullah had after all been an ISI 'asset'. Pakistan's military signed a landmark ceasefire agreement with him in 2005, which gave him the control of South Waziristan. The relation soured only after the military stormed Lal Masjid in July 2007 in which hundreds of terrorist were killed. Since its inception, Pakistani military has been using terror as a bargaining chip against India. This has compounded many folds after 1990 and in the foreseeable future too there is hardly any possibility of stoppage to cross-border terrorism. Despite these prevailing realities, India must engage Pakistan into a dialogue with a clear mandate that bilateral issues including Kashmir will be resolved only at a bilateral level as agreed in Shimla and in the Lahore Declaration. In the changing international scenario, India has to decentralize its attention from its neighbours, to the world-though it should bear in mind its security interests in the region. Pakistan and China are bound to propagate hostility against India due to the prevailing contours of the international system. At the outset of the 21st century, India has emerged as an important power within Asia, with the potential of becoming a major global power. India needs to reformulate its foreign policies according to this reality.

**Concluding Remarks**

In this situation, Pakistan is not very open. In the prevailing State of Nature within Pakistan how must India pursue its relationship with it? This has been one of the most complex puzzles of South Asia in particular and for the entire globe in general. I would like to state that India must adopt the line of tolerance despite all sorts of provocation from the Pakistani side either by state or non-state actors. Right now Pakistan is passing through one of the most turbulent times. Jehadi forces are of course extremely active in Pakistan and have emerged stronger and are trying to capture the reins of power from democratic forces. The Islamists have emerged as the second fiddle of the Jehadi forces and the military although seems to be acting at the behest of democratic forces and the US, it has interests entwined with the Jehadis. The only common agenda for these groups is promoting hostility with India. The democratic regimes right from Z.A. Bhutto till that of Gillani, have not been conducive to positive bilateral relationships with India. But despite these harsh experiences India has limited options. In the prevailing circumstances India must extend its support and also engage the democratic government in Pakistan. The strengthening of democratic forces could turn the balance towards an average situation. We must understand the fact that despite all recent projections by western media that the people of Pakistan have become anti-Indian or anti- west, the reality was reflected in the electoral outcome of February 2008. In this election Islamist forces lost their ground badly. They had their provincial governments in NWFP and Baluchistan and additionally they were a third force in the National Assembly. The February 2008 election not only removed them from power from NWFP and Baluchistan but eliminated them from national politics too.

It is extremely significant that the Islamist can now not claim that they enjoy the trust of the common people. It is vindicated with the fact that the people of Pakistan are in favour of a cordial relationship with India. This is the basic puzzle of the Pakistani system and India being one of the important outside actors within this system should contribute positively. Democracy and military rule are simultaneous in Pakistan. The full restoration of democratic government and the rebuilding of the Pakistani state is a future that would have to fall on the side of the possible rather than the likely. [13] Nevertheless, for a state that has been under military rule for more than half of its history and under corrupt or undemocratic civilian regimes for the rest, Pakistan has an astonishingly large number of citizens committed to democracy. [14]

These people are in favour of good relations with India. In 1997 the Nawaz Sharif led PML-N had declared in its manifesto that they would strengthen relations with India and the people of Pakistan gave him unprecedented majority. Similar promises were made by Asif Zardari before the 2008 election and the people of Pakistan gave the PPP the mandate to rule. This is a positive aspect and India must nurture this trend and at least for its own sake should do anything to sort out its hostility against Pakistan.

Outside actors are extremely important in the case of Pakistan. Even the Chinese have understood that they need to maintain a balance vis-à-vis Pakistan. Another important actor has been the United States. It has been argued by scholars that Pakistan is dominated by the AAA-Army, Allah and America. Since the inception of Pakistan, the US has supported it tremendously. But things have now changed dramatically. India has emerged as an important power in Asia and for the proper balance of power within Asia, the US wants India as a partner, more so in the face of a growing China. The new Obama administration has also not club India with Pakistan.

However, the US as an important country of the international system will sustain its relationship with Pakistan. The War against Terror is on and Pakistan is an important partner but the space and importance of Pakistan have reduced. Some understanding has crept into the Chinese leadership too. They know very well that if the US has to be neutralized in Asia, in particular and in global affairs in general, they have to engage India and needless to say that these calculations are being reflected in Chinese policies towards South Asia.

**Notes**

1. Under the Charter of Democracy, both principal political parties, the PPP and the PML-N had agreed to work for the strengthening of the democratic institutions. This was signed by Benazir Bhutto and Nawaz Sharif in December 2006, while they were in exile ousted by military dictator General Musharraf.
2. Siddika, Ayesha, Military *Inc*, Pluto Press, London, 2007, p. 89.
3. Ibid, p. 88.
4. Cohen, Stephen Philip, *The Idea of Pakistan*, Vanguard Books, Islamabad, 2005, p. 135.
5. *Indian Annual Register* [Calcutta] , July-December 1930, p. 337.
6. Ahmed, Kamruddin, *A Social History of Bengal*, Dacca, 1970, p. 31.
7. Op, Cit, No-2, p. 17.
8. Sheikh, Farzana, *Making Sense of Pakistan*, Hurst, London, 2009.
9. Op, Cit, No-7, p. 250.
10. Ibid, p. 249.
11. Subrahanium, Nirupama, U.S bid to ease India's Concern, *The Hindu,* New Delhi, August 16, 2009, p. 11.
12. G. Parasarhy, Mission Not Accomplished, *Times of India,* New Delhi, August 13, 2009, p. 13.
13. National Democratic Institute for International Affairs, *The State of Democracy in Pakistan: A Survey Mission Report,* June 4-14, 2002, Washington, 2002.
14. Op. cit, No-4, p. 277.

# 13

# Three Frontiers Theory and India's Troubled Relations with Pakistan and China

L. Premashekhara

During the past six decades of their existence as independent states India and Pakistan have fought three major wars and innumerable number of minor skirmishes all along their long border. Mutual distrust, deep animosity and rivalry in various fields ranging from nuclear science to sports have marred bilateral relations between these two South Asian nations. Several scholarly attempts have been made to explain the possible causes for the failure of these two nations to establish lasting friendship. The issue of religious divide has been accepted as the fundamental cause for deep-seated hostility between the two nations. The roles played by political parties and their leaders, men in uniforms, business houses, and prevailing regional and international political scenarios also have been cited as potential causes for the persisting problems between New Delhi and Islamabad.

The Sino-Indian frontier dispute erupted almost suddenly in mid-50s, led to acrimonious charges and counter-charges, eventually culminating into the war of October-November 1962 that wounded India's pride. With this war, China asserted its military supremacy in the Himalayan region and established firm control over Aksai Chin. Bilateral negotiations to end the border row began in 1980 and, during the past two decades, New Delhi and Beijing have concluded, apart from the significant 'Agreement on the Maintenance of Peace and Tranquillity Along the Line of Actual Control in the India-China Border' signed during the official visit of Prime Minister P. V. Narasimha Rao to the Chinese capital in September 1993, several agreements to maintain peace along this Line of Actual Control (LAC) and establish friendly relations. Although the border issue remains unresolved till date and raises its ugly head like a hydra once in a while as it is happening these days following alleged Chinese incursions into areas adjacent to the Kongka Pass in Ladakh and Beijing's protests against the Tibetan spiritual leader Dalai Lama's visit to Tawang monastery, it has not led these two Asian giants into war since the end of the war of October-November 1962 and any future war is also remote. Instead, these two Asian giants have taken their bilateral cooperation to significant levels in many fields, and interestingly, China has emerged as India's biggest trading partner.

In this context, this study makes an attempt to present a new hypothesis called the 'Three Frontiers Theory' that emphasizes the nature of the frontier and projects the same as the fundamental reason for, troubled relations between India and Pakistan on one hand, and gracious ties between India and China on the other. This paper contains four parts. The 'The Three Frontiers Theory' and the author's own classification of frontiers are explained in the first part. The second part makes an analysis of the historical background of the frontier between India and Pakistan. The third part contains the application of the 'Three Frontiers Theory' to analyse the Indo-Pakistan relations and the same is done in the case of Sino – Indian relations in the subsequent part. Conclusion forms the final part.

The Three Frontiers Theory classifies the frontiers between the states of the world into three categories: (i) Single-edged frontiers, (ii). Double-edged frontiers and (iii) Dull frontiers. A single-edged frontier is the one that gives strategic advantage to one of the two states say State A. A Double-edged frontier provides strategic advantage to both State A and State B. The Dull frontier does not give any strategic advantage to either.

The frontier that existed between Germany and France during 1871 to 1919 was a very good example of single-edged frontier. It provided considerable amount of strategic advantage to the newly unified Germany vis-à-vis France thereby acting as a single-edged frontier in Germany's favour. There are innumerable examples for double-edged frontiers and perhaps the most striking one is the Radcliffe Line that separates India and Pakistan. This Line provides strategic advantage to both countries thereby forcing the two to maintain constant vigil on each other's motives and moves. The present Line of Actual Control or the *de-facto* boundary between India and China is the best example of dull frontiers. It doesn't provide any kind of strategic advantage to either and has eliminated the usefulness of an armed conflict between the two neighbours ever since it was created as a result of the border war of 1962.

For the sake of convenience the State that enjoys strategic advantage in case of a single-edged frontier, is referred to as a *Ridge State,* and the one that is deprived of that advantage, as a *Valley State***.** This nomenclature has been coined on the basis of the general assumption that one who positions himself on a ridge tends to possess advantage vis-à-vis the one in the valley below. In the case of a double-edged frontier, the two states on its either side can be called *Plain States* since both of them are on an equal footing just like two contenders standing on an even surface enjoying relatively equal amount of advantage among themselves. Similarly, in the case of dull frontiers, the states that lie on either side of it can be called *Canyon States* since a canyon hardly allows the two adversaries on its either side to gain any advantage against the another. These nomenclatures will be used throughout this essay.

Let us now examine the possible impact of these frontiers on the bilateral relations between State A and State B. In the case of single-edged frontier in favour of State A: it being the Ridge State enjoys strategic advantage and its attempts are usually directed at maintaining the status quo as Germany did during 1871 to 1914. On the other hand, state B, the Valley State, possesses a sense of insecurity and nurtures a desire to convert the frontier advantages to it or in other words, single-edged in its favour. French attitude towards Germany during 1871 to 1914 is a good example of this scenario. The magnitude of State B's sense of insecurity depends upon the linguistic, religious, cultural, ethnic, and economic closeness or remoteness that exists between itself and State A. The intensity of its desire to convert the frontier is determined by its recent history, national power, pressure groups and the level of their capability to influence state policies, and the mindset of the leadership. Economic clout, diplomatic influence and the military might of its allies, if it has any, do also play significant roles in shaping State B's attitude towards the frontier and the State A that lies beyond. The level of its sense of insecurity and intensity of its desire to convert the frontier together generate hostilities between the two states. State A's effort to retain the strategic advantage it enjoys or in other words keeping the frontier single-edged in its own favour and remain as a Ridge State then shapes the further course of hostilities, and determines the path through which the hostilities lead to war. Depending upon the outcome of the war four different courses can be visualized in bilateral relations between the two states.

First, if state B fails in its attempt it will go back to square one, plan and prepare for one more attempt. In that case one more round of military showdown becomes a certainty.

Second, if State B succeeds in converting the single-edged frontier in its favour and becomes a Ridge State then State A will initiate its own preparations for annulling this outcome of the war. In this case also a show of strength will become the logical outcome.

Third, if the outcome of the war converts the frontier into a double-edged one providing advantages to both the states and making them Plain States, then begins an era of mutual distrust, suspicion of each other's motives, constant watchfulness and preparedness for war. War will break out as and when either of the two finds it convenient to beat the drum and the other responds with action. Fourth, if the war results in the creation of a dull frontier that provides advantages to neither of the states making them Canyon States then gradually begins an era of mutual trust, friendship, and cooperation. This may bring the two closer to each other and they may establish some sort of an economic union. If the success of that economic union is supported by ethnic, linguistic, religious and cultural closeness, it may even encourage them to consider the idea of a political union as well.

History is replete with countless examples of Valley States trying to become first, Ridge States; and if it is not possible, then one of the Canyon States. Let's now study some such attempts that have taken place in recent times.

The South American state, Chile's expansion into the north in the second half of the 19th Century is a classic example of a state's attempt to convert its frontiers into single-edged in its favour (Chile-Peruvian frontier) and also dull (Chile-Bolivian frontier). Before the Pacific War of 1879-81 the northern frontier of Chile was lying far below the Atacama Desert. Iquique and Arica that are now located in northern Chile were then parts of Peru. Bolivia, which is now a land-locked country, then enjoyed a strip of coastline with Antofagasta as its main harbour. Bolivia's presence in the north of Chile was a cause of concern for the rulers in Santiago because the former could threaten the northern plains of Chile anytime. Chile's woes would greatly increase if Bolivia and Peru joined hands. Such a development would not only put the security of northern Chile in jeopardy but also pose a serious challenge to Santiago's position in the Southern Pacific Ocean. In order to remove all these threats and make its northern areas safe, Chile initiated a successful campaign against its northern neighbours and when the war ended two years later Bolivia had been pushed beyond the Andes [1] and Peru the Atacama. The frontier that was established between Chile and Bolivia then was a dull one. The high Andes became natural frontier between the two countries and took away from Bolivia the strategic advantage it enjoyed earlier. As far as Peru was concerned, the dry and inhospitable Atacama Desert that became the newly accepted frontier made any future Peruvian campaign against Chile an impossible task. While providing Chile immunity from any Peruvian adventure the Atacama would permit Chile to threaten its northern neighbour at will. Thus Chile successfully converted its frontier with Bolivia from single-edged one against itself into a dull one and also created a single-edged frontier with Peru to its own favour. These changes denied Bolivia any opportunity to threaten northern Chile either singly or jointly with Peru.

The expansion of the United States of America in all directions except in the east, during the first century of its existence as an independent republic, is another interesting example for a nation's desire to establish dull frontiers. The thirteen states that formed the Union following the successful War of Independence didn't have natural frontiers except the Atlantic Ocean in the east.

The new nation was surrounded by three of the great powers-the British in the north, the French in the west, and the Spanish in the south. The Americans had plenty of reasons to be concerned about the security of their young republic. The British apathy towards the US was common knowledge. Though Washington didn't have any problems with Spain and France, the continuation of such trouble-free relationship for an indefinite period was not ensured because of the unpredictable nature of European power politics during that period of uncertainty. Any conflict in Europe involving Britain, France and Spain was likely to spill over into their North American possessions, and the danger of the US getting dragged into it was always lurking in the minds of American policy makers. This threat was reduced to a considerable extent when Napoleon's France was compelled to sell Louisiana to the US in order to meet its war expenditure in 1800. Washington also purchased Florida from Spain a couple of years later. These two purchases increased the geographical size of the US manifold and also opened up the possibilities of further expansions into the west. Within the next fifty years Washington annexed all the Indian territories through various means. [2] Following the merger of Texas into the Union and the Mexican War of 1846-48 the US frontiers extended up to two natural limits—the Pacific Ocean in the west, river Rio Grande [3] and the Nevada as well as Arizona deserts in the south and the southwest. Thus the US succeeded in adding two more dull frontiers to its west and to its south to the one already existing in the east.

Still Britain remained a source of concern. British capability to undermine the security of the US and hurt the national pride of the American nation was amply demonstrated during the war of 1812 when the invading English army entered the American capital and set the presidential palace on fire. However, no more hostilities were witnessed in US-British relations after the Treaty of Ghent of 1816, and the border has remained quiet since. The frontier between the US and Canada is indeed a double-edged one potent enough to be explosive. However, the linguistic, cultural and economic closeness between the people of the two countries and the resulting spirit of 'Anglo-America' have given it the colour of a dull frontier. Thus the US has successfully established dull frontiers on three sides and converted the double-edged frontier in the north into a dull one. As a result the US has not faced any threat from any of its neighbours since 1816 and enjoyed the freedom to concentrate on economic development, economic as well as geographical expansion outside the North American continent and also to develop political and military power to meet threats that may emanate from extra-regional powers.

The expansionist attitude the US demonstrated during the first hundred years of its existence encourages one to assume that the British presence in Canada discouraged the Americans from expanding towards the north. They would certainly have extended their northern frontiers up to the Arctic if Canada had been inhabited and controlled only by the Indians and Eskimos. The American leaders as well people were forced to be content with the existence of a double-edged turned dull frontier in the north. Although we don't have a crystal ball to look through, it can be safely assumed that it is highly unlikely that the people of the US and Canada would convert the present dull frontier into a double-edged one and initiate hostility. On the contrary, if the present economic closeness between the people of the two countries continues for some more time, they may take it to further heights and establish a stronger economic union among themselves. In that case, the economic union coupled with the existing linguistic and cultural closeness among the people of the two North American giants (probably excluding the French speaking Quebec) may pave the way for a political union as well sometimes in future.

Though the present frontier between India and Pakistan was created in 1947 its historical roots can be traced back to early 13$^{th}$ Century when the Delhi Sultanate, the first ever Muslim kingdom in India was established by Qutb-ud-Din Aibak in 1206 A. D. The western frontier of the newly established Delhi Sultanate in the Punjab region ran along Lahore, Dipalpur, Uch, Samana and Multan (referred to as *Lahore-Multan Line* hereafter) due to the repeated raids of the Mongols that left trans-Indus regions politically chaotic and outside Delhi's effective control most of the time. In other words, the political frontier of India in the northwest receded from the Hindukush to the banks of river Ravi in the north and to the lower course of river Indus in the south. This Lahore - Multan Line was not a defensible frontier at all since it ran almost in the middle of the Indus plain. The scientific boundary for the proper defence of north-western India was Kabul-Ghazni-Kandahar Line (referred to as *Hindukush Line* hereafter) that ran along the eastern slopes of the Hindukush Mountains. [4]

Indian history bears testimony to the fact that any invader from the Central Asian region who succeeded in crossing this Hindukush Line and entered the Khyber Pass found it relatively easy to establish his control over the Punjab plains. The Mauryans especially Emperor Ashoka realized this and extended his authority beyond Jalalabad in eastern Afghanistan in order to enable his army to effectively counter and prevent any invading army from crossing the Khyber Pass which acted as a gateway to the Punjab plains in particular and northern India in general. The Punjab was subjected to repeated raids by the Central Asian tribes and the Mongols whenever the narrow strip of land lying between the Hindukush Mountains and the Khyber Pass (referred to as *Hindukush–Khyber Corridor* hereafter) fell out of the control of any North Indian empire. Thus for millennia the Hindukush-Khyber Corridor played significant role in the defence of the Punjab plains. It is equally interesting to note that any power that controlled this piece of land extended its sway over the Punjab with considerable ease and the power that controlled the Punjab extended its domination over Northern India-Rajputana (present day the State of Rajasthan) and the vast Gangetic plain sooner of later. [5] Hence the successive rulers of northern India saw to it that the Hindukush-Khyber Corridor remained in their hand, and if that was not possible, they preferred it to be controlled by friendly powers that would act as buffers between themselves and their potential adversaries from Central Asia.

The importance of the Hindukush–Khyber Corridor was first realized, as mentioned earlier, by the Imperial Mauryas in the Third Century B.C. Emperor Ashoka had understood the danger the Empire would face in case this Corridor was to slip into the hands of the enemies when he was the governor of Taxila (located in the northern part of present the Pakistan). He further strengthened his mastery over this area when he became the emperor in 269 B.C., and the town of Jalalabad situated in present day eastern Afghanistan served as an important frontier outpost during his reign. Following the decline and fall of the Mauryan Empire during the Second Century B. C., however, this Hindukush-Khyber Corridor fell into and remained in the hands of local chieftains for almost a century. Under the early Kushans this Corridor was located right in the middle of the empire. [6] The post-Kushan empires of northern India somehow failed to realize the significance of this Corridor and consequently paid dearly for this gross negligence. The Mongols repeatedly raided north-western India and their menace became a regular feature till the advent of the Imperial Guptas. The Mongols continued to remain as a potential source of threat to the security of Northwest India until the Gupta emperor Chandragupta Vikramaditya repelled them in the 6th Century A.D.

The Mongol menace once again became serious in early 13th Century. Chengiz Khan crossed the Khyber and entered the Punjab plains in pursuit of the prince of Khwarizmian Empire, Jalal-ud-din Mangbarni [7] who had fled to India following the annihilation of his Empire by the Great Mongol. Chengiz Khan's army entered the city of Lahore in 1221 A.D. This was the most serious threat the young Sultanate of Delhi could ever face. The Sultanate, which was just fifteen years old, was still weak and surrounded by enemies on all sides except perhaps the North-west. In this situation had Chengiz Khan chosen to march towards Delhi, he would have sacked the infant Sultanate and that would have been the end of the first ever Muslim empire in India. Iltutmish, the Sultan of Delhi, however, was realistic and demonstrated exemplary diplomatic skill by declining support to the Khwarizmian king, and thereby avoided the Great Mongol's wrath

(Habibullah 1961: 95). Chengiz Khan left India satisfied with the plunder of Lahore. Though the Mongols continued to raid the north-western frontier regions of the country for another century, they ceased to be a serious threat to the foundation of the Delhi Sultanate that acquired tremendous political and military strength under the Khaljis. The Mongol menace ceased completely by early 14th Century A.D. when an invading Mongol army under Iqbalmand was decisively defeated in A.D. 1308. This was due to the rational measures undertaken by the rulers of Delhi especially Emperor Ala-ud-din Khalji, not only to fortify the trans-Indus region but also to extend Delhi's effective military control up to the Hindukush-Khyber Corridor thereby not allowing the enemy to set foot into the Khyber Pass. In fact, the new frontier army, created by Ala-ud-din Khalji, under the leadership of Ghazi Malik took the war to the Mongol territory in Afghanistan.

The Mughal rulers kept this area firmly under their control for nearly two centuries. Following the decline of the Mughals, however, Delhi lost its control over the Hindukush-Khyber Corridor to the Afghans resulting in the latter becoming capable of threatening Punjab. The Afghan ruler Ahmad Shah Abdali successfully raided Punjab and even defeated the Marathas in the third battle of Panipat in 1761 A.D.

The British who turned India into their colony during the later half of the 18$^{th}$ and early half of the 19th centuries realized the extent of danger from the northwest and took adequate measures to minimize the same. They did something no Indian ruler had done earlier. They demarcated the Indo-Afghan boundary and formalized the same with a written treaty in 1893. Though the British failed to extend India's north-western frontier up to the Hindukush Line, the scientific boundary line for the defence of northern India, they succeeded in delineating the India-Afghanistan border (the Durand Line) that firmly placed in their control the Khyber Pass that, for millennia, had been the gateway to the Indus plains from the northwest. The Durand Line followed the eastern limits of the Hindukush-Khyber Corridor. It was the activities of the Imperial Russian Army that prompted the British to go for delineating the Indo-Afghan border and to strengthen their positions there. The defence of the Punjab plains assumed importance in 1888 when the Imperial Russian army under the leadership of Captain Grombechevsky reached Hunza in northern Kashmir. The British apprehension and their threat perception vis-à-vis Imperial Russia were demonstrated by Durand, the experienced frontier expert, when he said, 'the game had begun.' (Woodman 1969: 72) The Russians were, if allowed, capable of threatening the security of the densely populated Punjab. The British administration overcame this menace by formally delineating Afghanistan's border first with India in 1893 and with Russia in the Pamirs two years later. The two European powers who were involved in the 'Great Game' in the northwest of India made significant moves towards 'peace' by signing a treaty on March 11, 1895.

Accordingly, a narrow corridor called 'Wakhan' was created between the Russian controlled Tazhik territories and the princely state of Jammu & Kashmir of the British Indian Empire, and the same was placed under the control of Kabul. Further, with the Anglo-Russian Convention of 1907, London succeeded in getting Moscow accept Afghanistan as a buffer between Russia and India and never to cross it. Not fully convinced of Russian sincerity, the British rulers took from the State of Jammu & Kashmir the Gilgit region [8] that shared common boundary with the Wakhan Corridor, and placed an Army unit there in order to monitor the movement of the Russian army across the Corridor and deter any possible Russian adventure.

Thus, right from the Imperial Mouryas to the British colonial rulers every major ruler of northern India realized the importance of the Hindukush-Khyber Corridor in the defence of north-western India. They took adequate measures to keep the enemies beyond the Hindukush Mountains or, if it was not possible, the Khyber Pass. Indian history bears testimony to the fact that those who neglected this golden rule paid heavy price, and alas, it happened again and again.

Though the Mongol threat disappeared by the early 14th Century A.D., it did irreparable damage to the cultural and religious unity of India. Repeated Mongol invasions limited the north-western frontier of the Delhi Sultanate to the Lahore-Multan Line. All the territories west of this line came under effective control of successive Muslim rulers that facilitated large scale religious conversion under state patronage. North-western India's socio-religious features changed permanently with it adopting Islam and most of the social values it stood for, and the rest of the country remaining predominantly Hindu both in religious and societal sense. Thus Northwest India developed a socio-religious character that differed distinctly from that of the rest of the country and, whereas, closer to that of Central and West Asia. It was in this part of India the Islamic state of Pakistan was established in 1947.

Despite the religious divide between the two parts of India that were separated by the Lahore-Multan Line, people on both sides of this Line remained united economically and culturally, and evolved common literature, music, dance, art and architecture. Military conflicts that occurred here were just campaigns of one contending political master against the other in the region and their respective armies. General populace was hardly a party to these conflicts. The protagonists of the Pakistan movement, however, ignored the cultural closeness and economic interdependence among the people on both sides of the Lahore-Multan Line and highlighted only the religious divide. The demand for a separate Muslim homeland got theoretical foundation when poet Mohammad Iqbal floated a radical assumption called the 'Two Nations Theory'. This *assumption* maintained that Hindus and Muslims were two different nations; consequently they shouldn't be under one state. Some of them even maintained that there existed identical socio-religious character in north-western India and its western and northern neighbours. Choudhury Rahmat Ali recognized the closeness among the people of north-western India, Afghanistan and Iran, and stressed upon the need for unity among them so that they could together 'survive and thrive in the world.' He emphasized this as the most important justification for the creation of a separate homeland for Indian Muslims.

In his famous monograph *Now or Never* [9] published in 1933, Ali argued for the separation of north-western India from the rest of the country and its merger with Iran, Afghanistan and Tokharistan to create Pakistan. (Pirzada 1963: 28-32). Though the word 'Pakistan' literally means 'Land of the Pure,' [10] it originally appeared in Ali's thinking as an acronym with each letter denoting a unit of the proposed state- P-Punjab, A-Afghania (NWFP or North-West Frontier Province) [11], K-Kashmir, I-Iran, S-Sindh, T-for Tukharistan or Tokharistan, A-Afghanistan and, finally, N-Baluchistan. [12] Though his idea of a union of Iran, Afghanistan, Tukharistan, and the Muslim areas of north-western India was far-fetched and politically untenable, he was the first protagonist of the Muslim homeland who underscored the socio-religious similarities among the Muslim population of these lands despite their astounding ethnic diversity. Moreover, Ali was the one who coined the name 'Pakistan' ending Muslim League's hitherto unsuccessful search for a suitable name for the Muslim homeland it was campaigning for. [13] Aitzaz Ahsan, a noted legal personality and a Pakistani politician today calls these lands together as 'Indus' and maintains that despite geographers and historians treating the Indian subcontinent as one single unit, "Indus and India have always been distinct and separate" (2000: 259).

The Indian National Congress, which was in the forefront of India's freedom struggle, rejected the Two Nations Theory. On the other hand, the Muslim League accepted it and used it to strengthen its demand for creation of a separate Muslim homeland. What the League failed to recognize was that the division of India on religious lines would create a *double-edged frontier* in the middle of the Indus plains; and the two nations would become *Plain States* living in the state of mutual distrust and constant angst.

The League, however, succeeded, with the active support from British colonial masters, in getting Pakistan created on August 15, 1947. [14] The partition was carried out in such a hurry that it led to unprecedented losses and human tragedy noted in Mankind's history (Wolpert 2006) [15] and the irony was that the Radcliffe Line that divided the Punjab between India and Pakistan did run almost in the middle of the Indus plain just like the centuries old Lahore-Multan Line. This Line, and the Line of Control in Kashmir (created as a consequence of the Kashmir War of 1947-48) together, according to the *Three Frontiers Theory*, is a *double-edged frontier* and the reason for the continued animosity between India and Pakistan.

The India-Pakistan borders, both *de jure* and *de facto*, can be divided into two distinct segments-the southern segment and the northern segment (referred to as the Southern Line and the Northern Line respectively hereafter). The Southern Line separates the Indian states of Gujarat and Rajasthan from the Pakistani provinces of Sindh and Punjab. The Northern Line separates the two parts of the divided Punjab and Kashmir. These two Lines have historical roots of markedly different lengths and credibilities. The Southern Line is in fact not only centuries old but also runs along natural barriers though minor ones. The *Runn of Kutch* [16] has been serving as a natural frontier between Sindh and the Kutch region of Gujarat from the dawn of history and forms the lower segment of the Southern Line. Though the upper segment of the Southern Line-the line that separates the Pakistani provinces of Sindh and Punjab on one hand and the Indian state of Rajasthan on the other is just a couple of centuries old, it is located almost in the western limits of the Thar Desert or the Great Indian Desert, a geographical barrier. It also has gained credibility as it served as an accepted boundary during the Raj between the British provinces of Sindh and the native states of Khairpur and Bahwalpur that became part of Pakistan on one hand, and the native kingdoms of Udaipur, Jaisalmer and Bikaner that formed part of the Indian state of Rajasthan on the other.

Consequently these boundary lines didn't cause any irritation or mutual suspicion on either side when they became international borders separating India and Pakistan in 1947. Nor did any major military campaigns occur along this Line during any of the India-Pakistan wars of 1965 and 1971 and it has remained totally trouble free for almost four decades. Islamabad's claim over part of the Runn of Kutch and Pakistan Army's subsequent incursions into the area in the spring of 1965 was nothing more than Ayub Khan administration's attempt to test the strength of its recently modernized army and air force and also India's retaliatory capabilities just before a major campaign in Kashmir (Chadha 2005: 89), which actually began clandestinely in July that year and assumed, during the last week of August, the proportion of an open attack on the Indian positions all along the Chicken's Neck-Chhamb Jaurian sector with a clear aim to severe

Jammu & Kashmir from India once and for all by destroying the Jammu-Akhoor road, the only road link between the Kashmir Valley and the rest of India during those days. Thus this Southern Line can be safely termed as a dull frontier.

On the other hand, the Northern Line that separates the divided Punjab and Kashmir is a double-edged frontier and is the primary reason for deep mutual distrust and persisting animosity between India and Pakistan. The Northern Line, like its southern counterpart, can also be divided into a southern segment-Radcliffe Line between the two Punjabs and a short international border between the Pakistani Punjab and the Indian controlled Kashmir, and the northern segment-Line of Control (LOC) between the two Kashmirs. Though their origins are markedly different, both, being double-edged frontiers, have been playing strikingly similar and significant roles in keeping India and Pakistan in the state of constant angst, with the defence forces of the two adversaries contesting fiercely all along this Line during the wars of 1965 and 1971. The double-edged nature of this Line along with the unprecedented violence that accompanied the partition [17] created from the very beginning mutual hatred and distrust amongst the people of these two states.

The impact of partition on Punjab was devastating as the 'operation was performed in Punjab...and it was performed without an unaesthetic.' (Jha 2003: x) The partition divided this huge province, which for centuries had remained as one linguistic, cultural and economic unit despite the religious difference. Two of its great cities-Lahore and Amritsar-located in the middle of the province became frontier cities overnight. On the irrationality of drawing an international border between these two cities, R. Coupland wrote way back in 1943 itself:

"Between these two cities there is no natural dividing line of any kind. Any boundary set between them would be wholly artificial, geographically, ethnographically and economically. *Inter alia* it would cut in two the system of canals on which the productive capacity of the whole area largely depends. It would also leave the capital city of each Province exposed and defenceless, right up to the frontier. Such an artificial line, despite its obvious disadvantages, might serve, if it were to be the boundary between two Provinces in a single federal state... But it is no mere Inter-Provincial boundary that is being contemplated. It is to be a regular international boundary between two separate independent National States" (Coupland 1943: Pt III: 86).

The large scale violence, abductions and rapes that accompanied the partition of the Punjab province affected the psyche of its people on both sides deeply and the resulting anger and hatred have become deep-seated. In such a situation defending a border from the feverishly hostile enemy right in the middle of the Indus plain became a cause of constant apprehension and worry for the two

Punjabs in particular and India and Pakistan in general.

Kashmir is another interesting case. The leaders of Muslim League firmly believed in this mountainous state's merger into and integration with Pakistan simply because of its overwhelming Muslim majority. The attitude of the Hindu ruler of this princely state, however, prompted the new government in Karachi to adopt initially coercive and subsequently military means to achieve Kashmir's merger with Pakistan and `complete' the `unfinished agenda of Partition' that in turn resulted in the former acceding to India and the initiation of both military and diplomatic confrontations between New Delhi and Karachi over the issue of sovereignty over this state. When the cease-fire came about after a fourteen month long fight, Kashmir lay divided between the two contenders and the dividing line or the Line of Control didn't follow any geographical barrier. In fact, it had moved to the east, away from the erstwhile dividing line of river Jhelum, a geographical barrier though a minor one, and thus extended the double-edged frontier from Punjab to Kashmir leading to increased anxiety and hatred among the people and governments of India and Pakistan.

Apart from religion, there is one more angle to the Kashmir question as far as Pakistan is concerned. All major rivers of Pakistan either originate in or flow through Kashmir. Thus Kashmir is the source of water for Pakistan and it's anybody's guess what will happen to that country if the whole of Kashmir falls into hostile hands. It is not known whether the Muslim League leaders were aware of this fact or not when they went all out against, first, Kashmir's independence and later, its merger with India. The Leagues' futile attempt to get merged into East Pakistan the whole of Assam despite its overwhelming Hindu majority in all districts except Sylhet may be a case worth mentioning here. Recognition of the future need for more land of the growing population of East Bengal was the only logical rationale they had in their designs for sparsely populated Assam. If they could recognize the future land requirements of East Pakistan before Partition, they, it can be safely assumed, must certainly have recognized the water requirements of West Pakistan as well. Though the Indus Water Treaty of 1960 allotted three western rivers of Indus river basin-Indus, Jhelum and Chenab-fully to Pakistan, [18] Islamabad's worries did not disappear. Pakistan has been visibly sensitive to any Indian plan to harness the waters of these three rivers for even the purpose of electricity generation which would not have hampered or reduced the flow of water into Pakistan in any manner.

So, religion is not the only factor that determines Pakistan's Kashmir policy. Like Bengal and Punjab, Kashmir too had clearly distinct and contiguous Muslim and non-Muslim majority areas. The British would certainly have divided Kashmir too between India and Pakistan on religious basis if it were a British province instead of being a princely state in 1947. The first Kashmir War of 1947-48 and the cease-fire of 1 January 1949 did give *Muslim Pakistan* control over almost all Muslim regions of Kashmir except the Valley. Still, Islamabad has not given up its claim for the whole state despite the non-Muslim population in Jammu region and Ladakh *as Kashmir as a whole is very vital for Pakistan's economic viability* and this very fact prompted successive rulers of Islamabad to work for getting Kashmir into their *Muslim Pakistan* even if this hilly state had non-Muslim majority in all its regions.

Another interesting dimension of the Kashmir dispute is that Pakistan's economic dependency on Kashmir has made the part of Kashmir under New Delhi's control as an *economic single-edged frontier* in India's favour. Pakistan's attempts to establish control over the whole of Kashmir is nothing but a Valley State's effort to convert the single-edged frontier in its own favour. India being the economic Ridge State in this case, has been working hard to keep the frontier as it is, or in other words, economically single-edged in its own favour. Thus, Kashmir is the *economic Alsace and Lorraine* of South Asia and this explains the protracted Kashmir imbroglio and India-Pakistan animosity. Given the economic and geopolitical issues involved, India and Pakistan would have demonstrated the same hatred towards each other even if their people followed a common religion.

The present India-Pakistan crisis can also be viewed in a different but positive way. This geographical landmass of South Asia is the home of ancient civilizations and it has witnessed the rise and fall of thousands of principalities, kingdoms and empires in its awfully long history. These developments were accompanied by countless wars and armed conflicts. Perhaps more armed conflicts have been fought in the Indian subcontinent than in any geographical area of a similar size anywhere in the world. Establishment of a European rule brought about a steep decline in the number of political masters which in turn gradually reduced the frequency and diversity in the armed conflicts in South Asia. Once the British became the undisputed masters of the subcontinent, armed conflicts in this land became a thing of the past. Not even a single armed conflict occurred for more than a century. Partition of the subcontinent and subsequent developments created two major political masters in the lands south of the Hindukush and the Himalayas. In contrast to previous centuries when scores or hundreds existed, now there are only two major political contenders left in the fray, and consequently the intensity and ferocity of hostilities too are high which is obvious as both are striving hard to make the present arrangement, with minor modifications, permanent in a land where no arrangement lasted for a period of decent length in the past.

It is an irony of history that the frontier separating Asia's two giants-China and India-was transformed from the one guarded by a few hundred club-wielding policemen into world's highly militarized one in a surprisingly short period in the latter half of the 1950s. The frontier erupted almost suddenly, led to acrimonious charges and counter-charges eventually culminating into the border war of October–November 1962 that wounded India's pride. Although several attempts were initiated by both governments in the form of bilateral talks and confidence building measures in the 1980s that led to several agreements initiating an era of mutual economic and scientific cooperation, the border issue remains unresolved.

What all happened in the realm of Sino-Indian relations during 1949-62 has become an inseparable and unforgettable chapter in the history of modern India. The plethora of material painstakingly researched and compiled by numerous scholars [19] conclusively establishes that there were two broad sets of reasons for the war of 1962. The Indian insistence on the legitimacy of one of the several lines that put the whole of Aksai Chin under its control and New Delhi's undue haste in getting it accepted by Beijing either through negotiations or through low-key military operations during 1959-62 described as 'Forward Policy' belong to the first set of reasons. On the other hand, frequent changes and shifts in China's claims and stances form the second set of reasons.

The Sino-Indian frontier saw military activities in a major scale in its eastern flank during the beginning of the second decade of the previous century. It was India that initiated those military activities and China did the same in the western flank forty years later. These military moves, first by India and followed by China later, together are, according to the 'Three Frontiers Theory', attempts on the part of New Delhi and Beijing to convert 'Single-edged Frontiers' against themselves into 'Dull Frontiers.'

There existed no linear boundary [20] between India and China before an attempt for creating one for the first time in history was initiated by India during 1911-14. In fact, no linear boundary existed between empires/kingdoms of Asia in the historical past. What separated one from the other was a broad stretch of land of varying width usually being a geographical landmark like a mountain, or a desert and the like. Interestingly, rivers which are closer to linear boundaries in nature hardly acted as lines that separated one empire from the other. Usually these frontiers (between two empires) were uninhabitable areas or areas with sparse tribal or nomadic population which was numerically a minority and militarily insignificant and consequently played no role in the regional politics of the time and thus, posed no threat to or undermined the interests of the empires which they separated. The reason for Asiatic states not attempting to establish linear boundaries was probably the frequent changes in the location of frontiers. The constant warfare between the states never allowed a particular stretch of land to remain as a frontier for a time span adequate enough for it to secure acceptance and legitimacy. Thus absence of permanent frontiers was the reason for absence of linear frontiers or at least attempts at establishing them. [21] It was so in the case of India and China too. Of course the mighty Himalayas were regarded as the traditional frontiers between the two civilizations. But the fact is that it was not so most of the time. Military activities involving the armies of Tibet, Nepal, Punjab (the Sikhs), Kangra, Jammu, Kashmir, Ladakh, Hunza, Baltistan and, occasionally, imperial China were common during the historical period causing constant shifts in frontiers. As a result, when 'the Republic of India and the People's Republic of China, after they came into existence had faced an unfinished task of converting their frontiers into legal boundaries' (Swamy, 2001: 39).

Before 1911 Tibetan suzerainty extended to areas south of the Himalayas in the eastern sector. [22] In other words the present north-eastern state of Arunachal Pradesh was not under the political and military control of British India. The traditional frontier between Tibetan territories and British India ran roughly along the northern edges of the Brahmaputra plains far below the mighty Himalayas which were traditionally believed to be an impassable wall providing absolute protection to India from any invading army from the north. [23] The British Indian troops in Assam would have been put under tremendous stress if Tibet became expansionist or it came under stricter Chinese control once again as was the case before the decline of the Beijing-based imperial authority. [24] In this way this line acted as a Single-edged Frontier in favour of Tibet of which China was the suzerain and thus India found itself in the unenviable position of a Valley State.

In order to eliminate any future threat from either Tibet or China or Russia a section of British Indian authorities conceived a plan of pushing the Indo-Tibetan frontier to the higher reaches of the Himalayas and also delineate it. Colonel Francis Younghusband led an expedition in 1911 into the Tibetan territories south of the Himalayas and successfully established Indian authority there. These territories which British India established a *de-facto* control over were christened 'North Eastern Frontier Agency (NEFA).' [25] An unsuccessful attempt to formalise Indian sovereignty over these newly acquired territories was made by the British Indian authorities during 1913-14. When the tripartite negotiations involving India, China and Tibet held in Shimla in 1913 failed to produce the desired result, Sir Henry McMahon, the then Foreign Secretary of the Indian government arranged bilateral talks with Tibet in New Delhi in March 1914. The boundary line he proposed and got accepted by the Tibetan representative in this meeting bore his name and ran almost right along the crest of the Himalayan

Mountains thus establishing a natural boundary between India and Tibet. The Tibetan authorities in Lhasa, however, soon repudiated their representative's action of accepting the McMahon Line. As a bigger blow to the Indian official's plan the Chinese government too declared that any agreement between Tibet and India would be 'illegitimate and null' (Ibid.: 42).

Sir Henry McMahon had a vision about the necessity of linear boundary for the security of India which, unfortunately, was not understood and shared by his superiors in New Delhi and London at that time. His efforts which were aimed at converting the Single-edged Frontier against India in the eastern sector into a Dull Frontier were met with opposition not only from the Chinese side but by the very government he represented. The then Viceroy, in his report to London, disowned McMahon's dealings with the Tibetan representative. The British government too expressed it's disapproval of McMahon's moves by transferring him from India to Egypt (Ibid.). Even the Survey of India did not include NEFA in India in its maps. Thus, Sir Henry McMahon became a tragic hero in the saga of India's quest for converting a Single-edged Frontier into a Dull Frontier in the eastern sector.

The British authorities finally accepted the relevance of McMahon Line in the 1930s and maintained that it was India's legal boundary with Tibet and the Survey of India too followed suit by publishing maps that showed NEFA as an Indian territory for the first time in 1938. After some initial hesitation the government of independent India too echoed this view when Prime Minister Jawaharlal Nehru asserted in the Parliament, "Our maps show McMahon Line is our boundary and that is our boundary-map or no map. The fact remains that we stand by that boundary, and we will not allow anybody to come across that boundary." (Maxwell, 1997: 75). This assertion by Nehru is a clear indication that the government of independent India accepted the perception of the erstwhile British colonial regimes regarding the necessity of McMahon Line for India's security. It demonstrated its resolve to continue the policy of converting Single-edged Frontiers against India into Dull Frontiers when it annexed in February 1952 Tawang which the British had left with the Tibetans despite it being located south of the Himalayas as well as the McMahon Line. China which had established politico-military control over Tibet year ago did not react to the Indian move at all. 'This puzzling silence can be construed as China's acquiescence in India's filling out in the McMahon Line' (Maxwell, 1997: 73). In the Sino-Indian war of October-November 1962 the Chinese People's Liberation Army (PLA) violated the McMahon Line, crossed the Himalayan Mountains occupied Tawang and made significant gains further south. [26]

The Chinese government, however, declared unilateral cease-fire after a month long campaign, vacated all the occupied areas including Tawang and withdrew its army to its own territory north of the McMahon Line. Though this action of Beijing has all elements of a typical Chinese riddle, it is not difficult to decipher it. Had the PLA remained in the areas south of the Himalayan Mountains for some more time it would have been cut off from China once the mountain passes got closed due to heavy snowing during winter which was about to set in. In such an eventuality the Chinese soldiers would have become sitting ducks for the Indian army and the impressive victory achieved by the PLA would have turned into a great fiasco for Beijing (Premashekhara, 2008:17). The Chinese realized the fact that it would be difficult or even impossible for them to keep NEFA (present Arunachal Pradesh) under their control during winter since the Indians enjoyed easy access to that territory throughout the year including winter months. The peculiarity or uniqueness of this region is that a Chinese controlled Arunachal Pradesh would act as a Single-edged Frontier in India's favour during winter and in China's favour during the rest of the year! It would, in a way, act as a Double-edged Frontier. It means this frontier would never be quiet. In order to avoid such a situation Chinese authorities realized the fact that it would be wise to regard the McMahon Line as boundary line since it was a Dull Frontier and did not provide strategic advantage to either of the powers and did nothing to disturb it except issuing statements staking their claim on the territories south of the McMahon Line. Thus the Sino-Indian frontier in the eastern sector was first converted by the British into a Dull Frontier during 1911-14 and was accepted by the Chinese as such later in 1962. [27]

The Sino-Indian frontier in the western sector is more complex in nature than its eastern counterpart. Here, it was China that converted a Single-edged Frontier in India's favour into a Dull Frontier. There existed no clearly delineated boundary between the Ladakh region of Jammu & Kashmir and Uyghur Xinjiang (formerly Sinkiang) and the British exhibited least interest in having one, ever since they came to possess Kashmir following their victory over Maharaja Ranjit Singh in the Fourth Sikh War in 1839. The governments in both London and Kolkata, [28] however, were alarmed when an Imperial Russian army led by Capt. Grombechevsky reached Hunza in northern Kashmir in 1888 after his successful campaigns in Central Asia.

A careful study of British India's frontier policy in the north shows that London and Kolkata always wanted 'friendly buffers' lying between densely populated regions of northern India on one hand and imperial Russia and China on the other. Their attitudes towards and dealings with Afghanistan, Swat and Tibet were all demonstrative of this policy.

With regards to the issue of delineating Kashmir's boundary with China in the Aksai Chin region, [29] the British contemplated three lines-Ardagh-Johnson Line, Macartney-MacDonald Line, and Trelawney Saunders Line. [30] While the Ardagh-Johnson Line, [31] running along the Kuen Lun Range in the north and northeast, placed the whole of Aksai Chin within the territory of Kashmir, the Macartney-MacDonald Line, [32] on the other hand, put much of Aksai Chin in Sinkiang. The earlier Trelawney Saunders Line [33] ran along the Karakoram Range and thus placed the whole of Aksai Chin in Sinkiang (Lamb, 1964: 86).

The British, however, did nothing serious to get any one of these lines accepted by Beijing as there appeared to be no consensus among various officials and bodies dealing with Indian affairs in London and Kolkata. Initially John Ardagh's views of placing the entire Aksai Chin in India gained acceptance in London when he argued that China's weakness made it useless as a buffer between the northern frontiers of British Indian Empire and the Russian Empire. Highlighting the eagerness with which Russia annexed the whole of Central Asia in less than forty years and advanced its borders towards India, Ardagh predicted that Moscow would eventually annex the western part of Sinkiang and pose serious threat to India's security in the Kashmir region and argued for extending Indian sovereignty right up to the Kuen Lun Range with the whole of Aksai Chin within Indian territory (Maxwell, 1997: 32). Although he conceded that in a general sense the Karakoram mountains formed a natural boundary, "easy to define, difficult to pass and fairly dividing the people on either side", he rejected this mountain range as a proper border as it's very 'physical condition' would deny the Indian army of proper information regarding the movement of the enemy on the other side (Ibid.). The officials in India, however, rejected Ardagh's views as 'impractical theorising of an armchair general' (Ibid.). The Viceroy Lord Elgin 'warned' London that any attempt to implement the Ardagh-Johnson Line and bring Aksai Chin under Indian control would 'entail a real risk of strained relations with China and furthermore might precipitate the very Russian advance which Ardagh wished to forestall'. [34] London accepted the Indian officials' point of view and approved the Macartney-MacDonald Line and the same was proposed to the Chinese on March 14, 1899 (Ibid.: 33). Thus, this Macartney-MacDonald Line was the only border line British India officially ever proposed to China. The Chinese, however, never replied to this proposal.

The British lost their interest in the issue once the Russian threat disappeared following the Anglo-Russian Convention of 1907 and China ceased to be a source of threat as it plunged into political instability following the revolution of 1911. These developments, and several other similar ones which the history of the British Empire, in Asia in particular and the world in general, is replete with, amply demonstrate that London's attitude towards India's borders with its neighbours was determined not by India's interests but the empire's interests vis-à-vis other empires. It were the two variables of Russia and China that shaped London's policy towards India's borders. In the words of Stephen A. Hoffmann:

"They [the British] had to be concerned with the political and strategic implications for the empire of any boundary agreement concluded with other powers bordering India. Such powers included Russia and China, and relations with them were seen from London as set by such matters as Anglo-Russian dealings in Europe and the Middle East and British interests on the mainland of China. Thus, London tended toward avoidance of forward claims and lines" (1990: 14).

Thus, the 'British approach towards the border was that of an imperial power and not one of defending the Indian nation state.' (Swamy, 2001:42). Despite these historical ambiguities and absence of any formal treaties the government of independent India unilaterally accepted a slightly modified Ardagh-Johnson Line as the international boundary between India and China insisting on New Delhi's sovereignty over the whole of Aksai Chin. This stand was not effectively challenged as long as civil war raged on in China and the Chinese frontier remained far away from India as Tibet enjoyed independence and Sinkiang experienced Russian influence. Once China achieved political stability under the communists following their victory in the civil war in 1949, Tibet lost its independence to the new central government in Beijing and Sinkiang reverted to Chinese rule and, consequently, China's frontier once again came closer to that of India. History repeated itself and Aksai Chin once again became a *disputed* territory.

The British maps had shown no marked boundary at all in the Sino-Indian frontiers from Nepal to Afghanistan. The Survey of India continued to reproduce the same maps for several years after independence. It, however, published maps in 1954 marking a definitive boundary between India and China in the western sector which placed the whole of Aksai Chin in India. India did insist time and again that Aksai Chin belonged to it but did nothing to establish its authority there. New Delhi became aware of Chinese presence in that region only when the Chinese media announced in 1957 that their frontier guards and about three thousand civilian builders had completed the construction of a road there. Although the Indian ambassador in Peking reported this matter to New Delhi in September 1957, the latter took ten full months to send a patrol team to Aksai Chin to find out whether the Chinese claim on road construction was true. [35]

Then onwards began a series of allegations, accusations, counter-accusations and failed negotiations with China firmly holding on to its claim. Beijing on its part changed its claims lines frequently pushing the same westward every time thus arousing Indian anxiety greatly (Woodman, 1969: 245-78). All these finally led to the border war of October-November 1962 which resulted in the Chinese occupation of all the areas right up to the Karakoram Mountains. Beijing's attitude here was markedly different from its policy in the eastern sector. Here, the PLA didn't withdraw from the region as it did in the east; instead, maintained that the Karakoram Mountains were the traditional frontier between Kashmir and Sinkiang and the same must be accepted as the international boundary between the two countries. Beijing was reasonable in thinking that the extension of Indian sway over areas beyond the Karakoram Mountains would make Aksai Chin a Single-edged Frontier in India's favour throughout the year except during the winter months and seriously undermine Chinese security in and control over Tibet. Hence, they wanted to limit Indian control up to the Karakoram Mountains only thus creating a natural and Dull Frontier between the two countries. [36]

Neither any government in London nor any British Administrator in India had ever attempted to extend India's control beyond the Karakoram Mountains although such an idea was contemplated whenever the Russian, and Chinese to a lesser extent, threat came closer to India's northern frontiers. At the same time they never accepted the presence of any hostile element on this side of the Mountains. In other words, they wanted mighty mountains ranges to form India's northern frontiers in both eastern and the western sectors. They extended Indian authority up to the Himalayas in the east during 1911-14 and maintained that Macartney-MacDonald Line which ran almost along the eastern slopes of the Karakoram Range which India's limit in the western sector. They were well aware of the dangers that the empire would have to face were it to cross the Karakoram, as the areas beyond that mountain ranges were indefensible from the Indian side. The government of independent India, however, lacked such wisdom and followed an ill-conceived and audacious policy and challenged Beijing's authority over Aksai Chin when China emerged with a fiercely nationalist government under the communists, which was stronger out of the decades of chaos and re-unification of all the regions under its strong central authority. The British had avoided such a daring policy during their heydays as global power and when China offered little resistance. The policy independent India followed towards China with regards to the border issue was geographically unscientific, strategically illogical, politically irresponsible and militarily suicidal. It was doomed to end in a disaster and humiliation, and that is what happened finally. The war of 1962 resulted in China successfully converting the border in the western sector into a Dull Frontier. Thus, the Sino-Indian frontier which was Single-edged in India's favour in the western sector and in China's favour in the east was converted into a Dull Frontier during the period between 1911 and 1962 and this is the reason for relative peace that prevails in the Himalayan region since then.

Although Beijing and New Delhi have not officially accepted the change, they have not done anything significant to disturb the status quo and alter the so-called 'Line of Actual Control' (LAC) since the end of the war of 1962 giving the indications of this feeling that there exist no border disputes between India and China. Of course, there have been minor incursions into each other's territories, the Somdorong Chu incident of June 1986 and the Kongka Pass incident of July-August 2009 being the major ones. Such incidents are bound to occur when borders are not defined in written agreements and delineated on land. Both countries handled these incidents in a positive manner and never allowed the situation on ground to deteriorate. The Indian government's handling of the situation in the present case is particularly remarkable. It did not give in to media outrage and remained calm maintaining that there were inbuilt mechanisms to handle these kinds of situations effectively. This is markedly different from New Delhi's attitudes during similar situations before the war of 1962. Reality being so, it is unlikely that India and China will go to war over the boundary issue again. Such a war will alter the Dull Frontier created over a period of half a century out of military moves and push India and China to situations similar to the ones existing before 1962 which is not going to serve the interests of either country.

During the past two decades New Delhi and Beijing have concluded, apart from the significant 'Agreement on the Maintenance of Peace and Tranquillity Along the Line of Actual Control in the India-China Border' signed during the official visit of Prime Minister P. V. Narasimha Rao to the Chinese capital in September 1993, [37] several agreements to maintain peace along this LAC. Therefore, it can be safely assumed that both New Delhi and Beijing have realized the fact that the present LAC is the scientific boundary between the two countries. Their hesitation to officially convert the LAC into official international border is understandable. Such a move will, especially in India, create strong public resentment. Such resentment is actually the result of a lack of understanding of history on the part of the Indian people. A careful analysis of historical documents and proper understanding of events in the past 120 years would demonstrate clearly enough that India has been the gainer in its border row with China. India now possesses Arunachal Pradesh, which was in fact not even a part of its territory before 1911. On the other hand Aksai Chin, which is under Chinese control now, was a part of the Indian territory only in maps as a result of British India's ambiguous policies and independent India's cartographic expansion in 1954. In reality India never controlled that region. [38] If the Indian public is properly educated on historical facts they may not oppose any move by their government to convert the Line of Actual Control into an international boundary.

In fact, the Chinese offered to convert the Line of Actual Control with minor modifications into an international border between the two countries in the fifth round of border talks held during 1983-84. This meant China was ready to recognize Indian sovereignty over Arunachal Pradesh provided India accepted Chinese sovereignty over Aksai Chin. The Indian government, however, rejected it (Sali, 1998: 113, Ganguly, 2009: 14). The Chinese offer was wise in more than one respect and Indian acceptance of the same would have solved the vexed border row, freed Indian armed forces from the tremendous burden it has been shouldering and radically overhauled Sino-Indian relations. It is difficult to gauge whether China still favours such a solution to the border problem. However, it is in the interest of the Indian people and the government to probe the matter and work for legitimizing the Line of Actual Control into an international border and formally establish 'Dull Frontiers' which will remove the threat of any armed conflict between the two Asian giants permanently. A Dull Frontier with China is very much in India's interest. It will free India from the tremendous tension along its northern borders and help New Delhi to deal with challenges and threats emanating from other sources and directions more effectively and decisively.

On the other hand, Indo-Pakistan borders have remained double-edged since the days of their creation. Sadly, it is virtually impossible for a dull frontier to appear in South Asia unless India pushes its western borders up to the Hindukush-Khyber corridor and Pakistan becomes the undisputed master of all areas lying between the great mountains in the north and the great seas in the south. Either of these solutions can never be achieved without seeing one of the two countries permanently disappearing from the world map, which is unacceptable to the people of either country. So, whatever both countries, mainly Pakistan, have been doing to alter the present arrangement, will never result in the creation of dull frontiers between the two.

In this regard, the question that arises is-how long will it take for the two present political masters of South Asia to accept the prevailing politico-military arrangements *as they are* and create permanent borders, recognize and respect them, and co-exist peacefully? The economic single-edged frontier in India's favour in Kashmir, and Pakistan's attempts to rise from the position of Valley State to the position of a Ridge State there, as well as the double-edged frontier in the Punjab region that makes them Plain States, and thus, the resulting distrust, hatred and animosity, are all realities of the past six decades. All these negative aspects collectively make the possibility of peaceful co-existence remote.

Positive changes depend largely on the mindsets of the people and the leadership. In this regard, there is a lot for them to learn from the European experience. Almost all the borders in Europe are either double-edged or single-edged in favour of one or the other. The European states, however, have now accepted these frontiers as fait accompli and learnt to live with them. It is true that this has happened after nearly two millennia of mutual distrust, animosity and countless armed conflicts including two horrendous world wars. The fact is that it has finally happened. It is for the people and the leader of India and Pakistan to decide how many more decades or centuries they need to accept the present frontiers and arrangements as they are and live peacefully with them, develop and prosper together, and stand proud among the family of nations in this era of globalization.

**Notes**

1. Bolivia thus became a land-locked country. It has made several unsuccessful attempts during the past 125 years to have a coastline once again initially through force and later through negotiations.
2. The "moral aspect" of these means is not elaborated here since it lies outside the subject matter of this study.
3. Though the river Rio Grande shifts its course once in while and causes some confusion among the two nations that lie on its either side, Washington and Mexico City have never allowed the same to assume crisis proportion.
4. Presently the Hindukush Mountains run from northeast to southwest in eastern Afghanistan. Pushthu speaking Pakthuns or Pathans who have been separated by the Durand Line from their fellow Pakthuns in the North West Frontier Province (NWFP) in the erstwhile British Indian Empire and in present Pakistan since the end of the Anglo-Afghan hostilities during the last quarter of the 19th Century populate the land on either side of the Mountain predominantly. Tazhiks are majority in northeast and Uzbeks in the west. Both Tajiks and Uzbeks have people of their ethnicity in neighbouring Tajikistan and Uzbekistan respectively. The ethnic closeness of the three major ethnic groups of Afghanistan to the people of neighbouring states prompted both the Moscow and London to ponder over the idea of dividing the country between the then Soviet Union and Pakistan in early 1950s. This plan was dropped later because it was thought that a neutral buffer of Afghanistan would serve the interests of both superpowers better during the heydays of Cold War.
5. Prior to the War of 1965 the then President of Pakistan Field Martial Ayub Khan declared that history was on his side. He also boasted of hoisting Pakistani flag atop the Red Fort in New Delhi within fifteen days. He said that it was a historical fact that one who controlled Punjab would control Delhi one day: and he was the one who controlled Punjab in 1965.
6. Though the Kushans were originally from Tibet, the empire they established in the First Century B. C. was actually had the distinction of being the first ever-Afghan empire worth naming. The three Kushan emperors viz. Kuzala Kadafissus, Vima Kadafissus and Kanishka controlled vast areas on both sides of the Hindukush-Khyber Corridor. The imperial capital of Purushapura (modern Peshawar) was actually located on the eastern side of the Corridor.
7. Following the annihilation of the Khwarizmian Empire by Chengiz Khan, its ruler Allauddin

Mangbarni fled to the Caspian region. His son Jalaluddin Mangbarni crossed over to India via Iran. He was closely followed on his heals by the Mongol army. Jalaluddin Mangbarni forged an alliance with the Khokars by marrying the daughter of their chief and disappeared into the deserts of Sind.

8. It was called "Gilgit Agency" during the British period and as "Northern Territories" under Pakistani rule and was under the direct rule of Islamabad till recently. However, these regions have been rechristened as "Gilgit–Baltistan" and political processes to create a legislative body with members elected by the people of the region are underway these days. Interestingly, this region was and is not a part of Azad Kashmir or Pakistan Occupied Kashmir or POK as it's known in India.
9. Rahmat Ali released *Now or Never*, as a monograph on 28 January 1933 in Cambridge. Interestingly Rahmat Ali felt disenchanted with not only the geography of Pakistan but also the politico-bureaucratic system the Muslim state came under when it was established and started a campaign against it. Consequently he earned the wrath of the establishment and was deported to England and died there in 1951. He lies buried in a cemetery in Cambridge, England, not in the country to which he gave its name.
10. The word "Pak" literally means "pure" in Arabic.
11. Ali called it Afghania because this region is inhabited mainly by the Pushtu speaking Pathans who were separated from Afghanistan by the Durand Line in the later part of 19th Century.
12. Interestingly, he chose the last letter of the name Baluchistan, not the first.
13. At one stage the leaders of Muslim League had even insisted on naming the proposed Muslim homeland as India.
14. It had been British policy to keep a smaller part of their possessions under their own control and give independence to the larger part. Northern Ireland and Kuwait are the best examples of this policy. Such a move, however, was not possible in the Indian subcontinent as the Indian freedom movement was firmly opposed to any British plan of retaining a small part of India in London's control and giving independence to the larger part. This opposition might have prompted the British to think of a different plan- divide India on religious ground, and support the smaller one so that it would remain indebted to London for a long time even after independence. This would enable London to maintain its presence and continue to influence the developments in this part of the world even after the end of its colonial empire.
15. The latest in the series of scholarly investigations into the British "role" in the partition of India and how they did it is: Wolpert, Stanley (2006) *Shameful Flight: The Last Years of the British Rule in India*, Oxford University Press, London.
16. The Great Runn of Kutch and the Little Runn of Kutch are filled with the waters of the Arabian sea during the rainy season and remain as arid salty desert during the rest of the year. Pakistan staked its claim on half of this area on the ground that it was an arm of Arabian Sea and the international border should run along the middle of it. After some minor skirmishes in the summer of 1965 the issue was referred to a Tribunal which awarded to Pakistan three years later an area covering about 780 sq. km. much less than what Islamabad had claimed. Both parties accepted the verdict and accordingly India transferred that territory to Pakistan.
17. The violence that accompanied the partition of the Indian Subcontinent was unprecedented in human history. Hundreds of thousands of people were massacred and more than ten million people crossed borders in what has been described as the largest migration in the history of Mankind. There is hardly any family on both sides of the Radcliffe Line in Punjab, which was not a victim of violence. Thus the birth of the independent states of India and Pakistan

was accompanied by religion-triggered bloodshed that left deep scars on the minds of their people.

18. India got full utilization rights on the three "eastern rivers" –Ravi, Beas and Sutlej.
19. Some of them are: Hoffmann, Steven (1990), *India and the China Crisis*, Oxford University Press, Delhi; Lamb, Alastair (1964), *The China–India Border: The Origin of the Disputed Boundaries*, Oxford University Press, London; (1966), *The McMahon Line*, 2 Vols., Routledge and Kegan Paul, London; (1975), *The Sino Indian Border in Ladakh*, University of South Carolina Press, Columbia; Maxwell, Neville (1970), *India' China War*, London; Swamy, Subramanian (2001), *India's China Perspective*, Konark Publishers Pvt. Ltd., New Delhi; Woodman, Dorothy (1969), *Himalayan Frontier*, Barrie and Rockliff; London.
20. A Boundary is a geographic line agreed to in diplomatic negotiations (delineation), jointly marked out on the ground (demarcation), thereafter visualized on a map (cartography), and accurately formalized between two sovereign governments (treaty), in which each thus recognised the limits of its own and that of its neighbour's territory. See: Swamy, Subramanian, (2001), *India's China Perspective*, Konark Publishers Pvt. Ltd., New Delhi, p. 39.
21. Perhaps the first ever linear boundaries in continental Asia were established by the Russians to separate their newly conquered Central and Northeast Asian territories from Sinkiang and Manchuria of imperial China in the second half of the 19th century. British and French colonizers followed suit in Southeast Asia at the end of that century.
22. The areas lying south of the Himalayas and north of the Assam plains were not parts of Tibet in strict sense. Arunachal Pradesh, as that region is known today was fragmented and was under the control of several tribal chieftains. These chieftains in turn owed their allegiance to the Tibetan rulers in Lhasa.
23. In other words the boundary line that now separates India's two north-eastern states of Assam and Arunachal Pradesh was roughly the boundary between British India and Tibetan territories.
24. The threat the British rulers were apprehensive of at that time was in fact not coming from either the Chinese or the Tibetans. The Imperial Russian advance into Central Asia had begun in the middle of the 19th Century. The Russian campaign was swift and decisive and by late 1880s the Russians annexed what are now called Central Asian Republics and their armies were knocking at the doors of Kashmir and Chinese Turkestan. A Russian army led by Captain Grombechevsky actually landed in Hunza in Northern Kashmir in 1888. At the same time Peking's authority over the remote western province of Sinkiang was gradually weakening because of various politico-social, ethnic and religious reasons. There was a danger of Russians extending their sway over that region and then entering into the adjoining Tibet. Had they succeeded in that adventure then they would have posed serious threat to both Northern and North-eastern regions of India.
25. NEFA was a part of the stare of Assam for some times. In 1972 it was accorded the status of a Union Territory with a new name of Arunachal Pradesh. Full statehood followed suit fifteen years later in 1987.
26. The Chinese army came right up to Bomdila, just 80 kilometre north of Tezpur and 40 kilometres away from oil fields at Dig Boi and thus threatening to enter the Assam plains.
27. Though the Chinese have not given up their official claim over Arunachal Pradesh yet, the fact remains that they have not done anything significant to disturb the McMahon Line since 1962 despite their overwhelming superiority against the Indians as far as military strength is

concerned. Though the Somdorong Chu incident of 1986 created some resentment in New Delhi it was amicably settled by the end of the year and was soon forgotten.

28. Kolkata, or Calcutta as it was know till recently, was the capital of the British Indian empire during the 19th Century and it enjoyed that position until the capital was shifted to the newly built city of New Delhi in 1911.
29. Aksai Chin is a triangular elevated tableland lying between the Karakoram Mountains in the west, Tibetan Plateau in the east, and Kuen Lun mountain range and low lying Uyghur Xinjiang (Sinkiang) beyond in the north. Geographically it is an extension of the great Tibetan plateau. It is easily accessible from the Chinese side whereas the high-rise Karakoram Mountains deny India similar easy access.
30. These names were coined by Alastair Lamb in his book: *The China–India Border: The Origin of the Disputed Boundaries*, Oxford University Press, London, 1964.
31. This line is called "Ardagh-Johnson Line" as it was prepared way back in 1863 by Survey of India explorer W. H. Johnson and later proposed to the government of India in 1897 by the chief of British military intelligence in London, Major General Sir John Ardagh. See: Woodman, Dorothy (1969), *Himalayan Frontier*, Barrie and Rockliff; London, pp. 360-65.
32. This line was suggested to the Viceroy Lord Elgin by George Macartney, the British representative in Kashgar and proposed to the Chinese, on behalf of the viceroy, by Claude MacDonald, the British minister in Peking.
33. This line was drawn by the India Office cartographer Trelawney Saunders for the Foreign Office in 1973.
34. The full text of Viceroy Elgin's official communication to London can be found in Dorothy Woodman, (1969), *Himalayan Frontier*, Barrie and Rockliff; London, pp.364-65.
35. One of the two patrols that went towards the southern section of Aksai Chin reported in October that the Chinese had indeed built a road there. The other patrol that went to the north disappeared. It was later learnt that they had been detained and later `deported back' to Indian territory by the Chinese. The unfortunate patrol team was lucky to be discovered and rescued after being dumped by the Chinese at the Karakoram Pass far away from any nearby Indian post.
36. Karakoram Mountains are the second highest mountain ranges in the world next only to the Himalayas.
37. For the full text of this Agreement, see: Sali, M. L., (1998). *India-China Border Dispute- A Case Study of the Eastern Sector*, (A.P.H. Publishing Corporation, New Delhi, pp. 288-92.
38. It's interesting to note that Indians learned of Chinese presence in Aksai Chin only when Beijing officially announced in mid-50s that it had completed the construction of a road in that region.

**References**

Ahsan, Aitzaz, "The Indus Person" in *On the Abyss: Pakistan After the Coup*, (2000) Harper Collins Publishers India, New Delhi.

Ali, Rahmat (1933): *Now or Never*, Monograph, Cambridge.

Aziz, K. K. (1967): *The Making of Pakistan: A Study in Nationalism*, Chatto and Windus, London

Barnds, William J (1972): *India, Pakistan and the Great Powers*, New York.

Davies, C. Colin (2nd Edn. 1959): *An Historical Atlas of the Indian Peninsula*, Oxford University Press, Oxford.

Chadha, Vivek (1989): *Low Intensity Conflicts in India,* Sage Publications, New Delhi.

Chapmann, G. P. (1990): "Religious v. Regional Determinism: India, Pakistan and Bangladesh as Inheritors of Empire", Ch. 6, pp.108-134 in Chishom, M. and Smith, D. *Shared Space: Divided Space*, Unwin Hyman, London.

——(2000): *The Geopolitics of South Asia: From Early Empires to India, Pakistan and Bangladesh*, Ashgates Publishing Company, Burlington.

Coupland, R. (1943): *Reports on the Constitutional Problems in India, Pt I The Indian Problem 1833-1935, Pt. II Indian Politics 1935-1942, Pt III The Future of India*, Oxford University Press, London.

Ganguly, Swagato, "Grouchy Tiger, Misread Dragon" in *Times of India*, (Chennai), 8 October 2009.

Godbole, Madhav (2006): *The Holocaust of Indian Partition: An Inquest*, Rupa & Co., New Delhi.

Habibullah, A. B. M. (1961): *The Foundation of Muslim Rule in India: A History of the Establishment and Progress of the Turkish Sultanate of Delhi, 1206 - 1290*, New Delhi.

Hardy, P. (1972): *The Muslims of British India*, Cambridge University Press, Cambridge.

Hodson, H. V. (1969): *The Great Divide: Britain – India – Pakistan*, London.

Hoffmann, Steven (1990): *India and the China Crisis*, Oxford University Press, Delhi.

Jha, Prem Shankar (2004): *The Origin of a Dispute: Kashmir 1947*, Oxford University Press, New Delhi.

Lamb, Alastair (1964), *The China – India Border: The Origin of the Disputed Boundaries*, Oxford University Press, London.

—— (1966), *The McMahon Line*, 2 Vols., Routledge and Kegan Paul, London.

——(1975), *The Sino Indian Border in Ladakh*, University of South Carolina Press, Columbia.

Luce, Edward (2006): In Spite of the Gods: *The Strange Rise of Modern India*, Little, Brown, London.

Maxwell, Neville (1970): *India's China War*, London.

Michel, A. A. (1967): *The Indus Rivers: A Study in the Effects of Partition*, Yale University Press, New Haven and London.

Pirzada, S. S. (1963): *Evolution of Pakistan*, The All Pakistan Legal Decisions, Lahore.

Razvi, Martaza (1971): *Frontiers of Pakistan*, National Publishing House, Karachi.

Sali, M. L., (1998). *India-China Border Dispute- A Case Study of the Eastern Sector*, (A.P.H. Publishing Corporation, New Delhi.

Swamy, Subramanian (2001), *India's China Perspective*, Konark Publishers Pvt. Ltd., New Delhi.

Taylor, David and Yapp, Malcolm (Eds.), *Political Identity in South Asia*, Curzon Books, London.

Tayyeb, A. (1966): Pakistan: A Political Geography, Oxford University Press, London.

Wirsing, Robert G. (1994): *India, Pakistan and the Kashmir Dispute*, Macmillan, New Delhi.

Wolpert, Stanley (2006): *Shameful Flight: The Last Years of the British Rule in India*, Oxford University Press, London.

Woodman, Dorothy (1969): *The Himalayan Frontier: A Political Review of British, Chinese, Indian and Russian Rivalries*, Barrie and Rockliff, London.

# PART IV

# INDIA AND SOUTH ASIA

# 14

# India's Threat Matrix and South Asia

M.D. Nalapat

Towards the end of the 1980s and into the 1990s, when the rest of the world and much of this country was pessimistic about India, this essayist wrote that the country was on track to be a superpower. The country confronts a worsening internal and external situation which the country's institutions are either incapable of, or unwilling to, rectify, while the overwhelming majority of the population live in either ignorance or denial about the threats to the future that confront them and the country. The global financial crisis which erupted into open virulence in 2008 was caused by a sacrifice of the medium and long term for enhancing to the maximum possible level, benefits received in the short run. It was analogous to an individual using up his life savings in order to have a lavish holiday that his circumstances cannot afford. Indeed, this is exactly what several individuals in the US who had been given liberal loans seem to have done. Such a concentration of attention on the short term usually becomes the precursor to a period of depletion of resources and the process of slowly and painfully building up a reservoir of savings once again. While the short term is important - after all, each of us lives in the present - yet this needs to get balanced by an appraisal of the longer and medium term, so that actions that compromise the future are avoided. On a broader scale, the difficulties being experienced by present-day human settlements as a consequence of climate change has been caused by a similar short-term focus on immediate needs, to the neglect of the future.

One of the most important threats to the future of India is the concentration of attention of the top political layer of decision-makers on the short term; their refusal to consider either the effect of short-term palliatives in the long term, or the need to ensure that the basic conditions to a problem get eliminated, rather than a few symptoms for what is usually a short period of time. Even on questions of national security, the reluctance in taking a longer view than (at most) the next election cycle has meant the turning away from solutions towards worsening problems such as illegal migration into India and deepening of fissures existing between different social groups. The concentration on the immediate often means a neglect of problems that require longer-term solutions. To this can be added the cost of regarding delay as a virtue, when in a large number of cases, it may exacerbate a problem, thus making the implementation of a solution in future more difficult. 'Well begun' may be half done, but in the case of India, an announced-and 'firm' policy usually takes less than six months before a dilution or a complete reversal takes place. An example of this being the post-Mumbai-November 26-28 2008 attacks which has led to a freezing of talks with Pakistan 'till the perpetrators are brought to justice'. Having nothing significant to show on this front other than the reinstating with courtesy by the venerable Chief Justice of Pakistan, of the Army Chief, along with the release of the Lashkar-e-Toiba Chief Hafeez Sayid from custody, India reversed its policy stance on July 15 at Sharm-el-Sheikh.

Such a high incidence of flip-flops has damaged India's credibility as a country perseverant in the defence of its interests, and has led to Delhi's initial bouts of bravado being ignored. Even in the field of national security, effective (though most often less than adequate) action is avoided until a crisis takes place, after which the search is more for palliatives than for effective long-term remedies. This emphasis on the short term is creating problems not only in reacting to external challenges to national security, but to internal threats as well, of which regional passions are an example. The rapid rise of the Maharashtra Navnirman Samiti (MNS) in Maharashtra has resulted from a demagogic tapping into resentment among Marathi-speaking residents against migrants from Hindi-speaking states. The MNS is the creation of Raj Thackeray, who has built a voter platform for himself that is going largely unobstructed by the more conventional political class. Judging by the lenient way with which he has thus far been treated by the state administration, when added to the various restrictive measures against migrants from other states into Maharashtra, in what should remain a genuine Union of India, it would appear that even some 'mainstream' politicians are happy to form a part of the Thackeray bandwagon. The consequence of this has been to give oxygen to regional impulses in Maharashtra, which may fan such sentiments in other parts of the country.

While the concept of a united India does bubble on the surface of the consciousness of citizens, regional impulses nevertheless form the substratum. Such impulses are thinly countered by the federal idea for many throughout the country. Should the MNS succeed in Maharashtra on the lines of the Shiv Sena, other states may experience backlashes directed against those settled there from other parts of the country. States in the northeast as well as Kashmir, where many have yet to reconcile themselves to the Union would find the federalist space diminishing.

Apart from regional exclusivism, another factor that has received less attention than it merits with regards to national security is that of caste. This development has been an anachronism. That which is said to have been primordially flexible turned rigid with time and calcified as it were. This is another cleavage that is exploited. There now needs to be a policy matrix that is neutral not only to the caste factor, but also to those of region and faith. Tolerance has been the foundation of Indian culture, and today, almost every citizen has within him or her cultural DNA, the three strands of the Vedic, Mughal and Western civilizations, the main premise of what I term 'Indutva'. Sadly, rather than an emphasis on this confluence there has been increasing polarization between faiths. Geopolitically, to demonize the Christian community in the way some 'Hindutva' elements are doing is to run the risk not only of alienating Christians in India (which is itself indefensible) but also the wider Christian-majority world, on whom India depends for much of its markets and technology. Similarly, verbal and physical attacks on Muslims have their repercussions on India's relations with other countries, specifically the Muslim-majority world. This is undoubtedly harmful to India's national interests. In the words of John Donne, 'No Faith is an Island', and an attack on one should be treated as an attack against all. Unfortunately, in India, several seem to take a 'segmented' view of this, responding only when their own faith is seen to be under threat.

The link between a stable, tolerant and a syncretic society and national security is a factor that needs to be stressed. The mindset that would promote this thought needs to get inculcated at a young age. Sadly, the country's educational institutions have such curricula that in effect divide Indian history into what may be termed as Hindu, Muslim and Christian periods. This encourages adherents of these three faiths to subliminally regard 'their' particular segment as the Golden age, and to stigmatize the rest. The history of India needs to be treated as an unbroken continuum, rather than as segregated into three phases, a classification that exacerbates faith-based perceptions of difference that ought instead to be reduced. Just as the epics from India's past belong to all Indians, and not just to those belonging to a single faith, so too must each citizen understand as an entirety the entire current of Indian history, rather than relate to merely one faith-based segment of it.

Ideally, citizens of India would follow the syncretic model (still extant but now under threat from Wahabbis). However, instead of such a coming together, what appears to be taking place in present-day India is a growing societal difference between people of different faiths. This is taking place even in places where 'secular' parties have always formed the government, such as West Bengal and Kerala. Actions and words that fuel feelings of exclusivism and victimhood in any community need to be eschewed, along with the short-term gains they may bring. Although security analysts routinely - and often with justification - point to Pakistan, Bangladesh and other neighbours as examples of societal instability, they need to recognize that India's dysfunctional institutional structures have converted what was a difference in kind within India into a difference in degree.

Another factor that needs attention is the doing away with feudal exploitation in the farm sector. It is such cruel practices that have created a pool of recruits for 'Maoist' parties. In addition to this, the increasing linkage between 'Maoists' and Wahabbi fanatics, it is essential to address the social roots of the Maoist problem. The opportunity to participate in economic growth is usually an antidote to extremism among disadvantaged populations, and this could be served by a vigorous program of road-building and other infrastructural activities, especially in the north-east. Such efforts at creating road links and other infrastructure need to go international and promote connectivity between India and the ASEAN, India and Myanmar and so on.

If much of this analysis seems a digression into sociology. The reason for this being that internal security is best preserved within a societal matrix that does not discriminate between individuals on the basis of region, caste or faith and is best helped through a system of administration capable of identifying problems and opportunities, and dealing effectively with both. Although, as the other sections of this essay indicate, India faces a threat from external players as well, yet the virulence of such challenges can be mitigated by changes in internal conditions. To look beyond the country's shores for solutions to threats to security ought not to divert attention away from the need for domestic action.

A final word is needed on a potent security threat, which is the influence of terrorist organizations and their controllers in the informal money laundering networks that exist throughout India. Unfortunately, policymakers within the country have tended to focus on 'soft' targets (such as the business and professional class) rather than pay attention to terror linkages. As a consequence, the record of India in stanching such fund flows and prosecuting those responsible has been dismal, in contrast to the success achieved by countries such as the US.

**China**

China has seldom been included in traditional discussions on threats to India, and where it has, the discussion has usually been on its military capabilities. The reality is that it is the internal situation in the country that can drive its external actions, exactly as they did in 1962, when adverse views about the efficacy of the policies adopted by the then Chairman Mao Zedong, helped to tip the balance towards a war that served as the lightning rod for neutralizing dissent. Should political and social stability in China falter on account of lower economic growth or for other reasons, an intensification of the Sino-Indian problem may be the preferred way of winning back public and party cadre support, through the unity against an external foe. That the PRC has thus far refused to settle the border issue with India the way it has with the Russian Federation and Myanmar is an indication that the tinder is being kept dry for possible use later.

What are the fault lines in the Peoples Republic of China (PRC) that could lead to an intensification of public unrest and dissent within the party? The most obvious would be a slowdown in economic growth. Although it had its origins as a traditional 'peasants and workers' party, today's Chinese Communist Party (CCP) has as its base the urban middle and upper classes, who have benefited from the Deng Xiaoping reforms of the 1980s. These individuals, most of whom are convinced of the presumed link between democracy and instability, as well as the link between authoritarianism and growth, are accommodative of the monopoly that the CCP has over the political and policy space. Should there be a reversal of the post-1980s trend of constantly rising standards of living, this group would begin to lose confidence in the CCP and many may turn to an acceptance of other forms of governance as a solution to the economic travail. The only emotion that could dampen these feelings (for a length of time sufficient for the party to work out a policy response to the unrest within this erstwhile core of support) would be a conflict or a near-conflict that could erupt into hostilities at any time.

The reason for this may be traced to the effective core ideologies of the CCP, the development of Han nationalism and triumphalism. This in many respects has a substantial basis. In his writings, Samuel Huntington talked of two potential sources of conflict for the western world, the Islamic and the Sinic. This was prescient. For, rather than the Islamists who are seen as the major threat, it is the Sinic peoples who are demonstrating the potential to challenge and perhaps replace the western world as the Lead Civilization (in terms of material advancement and the generation of new knowledge). The PRC is home to more than 85 percent Sinic peoples of the world, and should such a challenge to the primacy of the West emerge, the PRC will be at the forefront. Over the past decade, the process of inculcation of Han exceptionalism within the population was initiated, and has been accelerated under Hu Jintao. The CCP has in effect identified itself with the aspirations of the Han people, and has as a subtext conveyed the message that only the party can assure the steady rise of the Han.

The ideology of Han exceptionalism has entered universities and the academia as well, with researchers in economics at Tsinghua for example (in the February 2007 India-China-US conference organized at Kochi, India), attributing the 'better' highway system in the PRC to its 'social cohesion', as compared to the medley of cultures and peoples in India, a country with a much less impressive record in highway and other development. Although such race-centric world views may have been warranted in countries such as Germany, Italy and Japan during the 1920s until the mid-1940s, it must be remembered that these fascist ideologies were in essence the extreme development of the theories of Western exceptionalism that have continued to linger Similar world-views are held by some extremist religious groups even in the Middle East and in India. Paradoxically, it is not the rise of China that can push it over the edge of safety for the international community, but a fall, that disrupts social cohesion. Economic conditions are the prime consideration that could create such a dangerous situation. In a situation of global downturn, the risk of such a contingency becomes higher.

This is especially the case because, the downturn in the United States had its toxic effect on the PRC's principal market-the lower and lower-middle classes, who form the major chunk of consumers of China's low-cost manufactures. Several enterprises in the PRC have been forced to further cut prices (and costs) or close down. Workers are usually the first victims of either course, seeing either their wages reduced or, in the latter case, eliminated. However, it needs to be remembered once again that workers (or peasants) are no longer the primary focus of the CCP, but the owners and managers of the numerous enterprises that have powered the rise of China into the second-most important country in the world. A prolonged international slowdown would lead to several enterprises closing down, or else the state would have to print enough money to sustain them in a situation where international demand for their products has become drastically low. Such conditions may fuel inflation and higher unemployment, replaying the situation in Germany during the years between World War I and II.

Graft is prevalent in the CCP, as it is in many other ruling parties in other countries. Ironically, the success of the drive against corruption led by current President Hu Jintao has led to a reduction in the morale and willingness of the lower and lower-middle cadre of the CCP to go the extra mile in protecting the party and in carrying out its directives. The reason is that, since the 1990s, the access to sources of graft of such cadres has come down substantially, because of the centralization of decision-making. The result is a sense of being wronged felt (by not being given access to graft the way higher levels still have) by the lower cadres whose impact is being gradually felt on the effectiveness of the party machine in confronting a situation. The result is that problems that were once cut off at the source now fester for long periods, and subsequently explode, such as what took place in Tibet in 2008 or in Xinjiang in 2009, where timely inputs from the base may have led to correctives being applied before the situation having gone out of control. Honesty, it would seem, and the meagre lifestyle that this mandates, has become a factor in reducing the morale and the motivation of those at the lower levels of the CCP. A consequence of this has been a greater propensity towards instability in a situation where the system has not been reconfigured so as to eliminate or at least substantially reduce the potential for graft at the higher levels.

The PRC has, since the Hong Kong handover of 1997, showed an increased assertiveness in publicly defending its interests and in carving out an international space for itself. This is not a surprise. The generation of school kids during the Cultural Revolution of the 1960s, developed through experience contempt for authority that manifests as yet. This can be said by the confidence with which international 'authority' represented by the West led by the US is frequently rebuffed. Their leadership has now assumed confidence in their ability to checkmate countries and groups seen as standing in the way of China's rise towards the leadership position now assumed by the US. The impact of such inner assurance on policies towards India could be significant, for within Asia, in the context of a stagnant Japanese economy, India is the only country that can count as a potential equal of the PRC. Clearly, this would represent a setback for the PRC. And hence the efforts at ensuring that Pakistan and now Bangladesh, have the strike capability to paralyze India so as to prevent it from taking action against them for having harboured terrorists. Also, despite the linkages between both militaries and organizations facilitating terror attacks against India, the PRC continues to supply sensitive communication and other equipments that could have the dual use of being utilized both by the regular military as well as by terrorist organizations. In addition to this are the persistent efforts aimed at displacing India as the primary external player in Nepal, Sri Lanka and the Maldives.

The 'Manifest Destiny of the Han' that lies at the core of the CCP ideology represents a challenge to Indian security and this country's long-term future, especially in a context where several policymakers believe that it is the US and not the PRC that is evolving as the partner of choice for Delhi. Is this welcome? There is no doubt that the United States will be India's most significant partner in the coming decades, given the myriad links that exist between the two countries. However, such a partnership does not mean automatic acquiescence in all the policies of the US towards other countries. There will be instances where an approach different from that of the US is mandated by national security needs, such as for example Iran. While giving up 'Non-alignment', India needs to adopt a foreign policy that is 'aligned', but to its self-interests and to these alone.

**Pakistan**

Since its creation in 1947, Pakistan has sought to define itself through its opposition to India. Islamabad's ambition is parity between the two states, an objective that became even more definite after the 1971 Bangladesh war. The military in Pakistan is a player independent of the elected government, and controls foreign, defence and security policy. In furtherance of its goals, there is no hesitation within the military in using Terror and other non-conventional methods to ensure that India becomes sufficiently off-balance to make the country's longer-term prospects for global power status, unfeasible. In 2003, constrained by the US from continuing its then level of assistance to the insurgency in Kashmir, the ISI appears to have broadened its focus from that state to the whole of India, specifically the larger urban agglomerations that house the bulk of India's top manufacturing and service providers. The spate of attacks across the country since then, which has made India the biggest victim of mass terror attacks after Iraq, Afghanistan and Pakistan itself, have been a demonstration of the ISI's capability in securing local assistance from individuals of multiple faiths in order to ensure a sufficient flow of terror significant into major Indian cities. Mumbai (November 26-28, 2008) has been the most spectacular of these, creating a much larger international footprint than previous attacks, because of the deliberate targeting of Westerners by the commandos who carried out the attack.

However, since the 1950s, it has been US backing for Pakistan, especially to the military of Pakistan that has allowed it to emerge as a significant threat to India. In other words, the propensity of US policymakers to avoid a clear examination of the basic intentions of their Pakistani interlocutors has developed into a threat to India's security. An example is Kashmir, where the new Obama administration has intensified the prodding on Delhi to come up with a 'solution' to the 'Kashmir dispute' that would satisfy the Pakistani army. And what is the Pakistani Army's rationale for an 'appropriate' resolution of the dispute? It is that terror groups within Pakistan are mostly motivated by the Kashmir cause, and cannot be placated except by getting satisfaction on Kashmir, in other words, by the conversion of that state to an approximation of Taliban-controlled Afghanistan. Would such a result be in consonance with the national security interests of the US? The answer seems obvious, and yet the US continues its backchannel efforts to find a solution that would in reality placate not simply the Pakistani army, but also the clients of the military in Kashmir-the terror groups operating within the state. Lack of any coherent effort by India within the ranks of the US policy community and opinion channels has helped such misperceptions to continue within key segments of the US policy community.

Diplomacy has to be judged not by the quality of those involved in the process, but by their success or lack of it in meeting objectives. Judged by such a yardstick, Indian diplomacy towards the US has been a failure. There is a blind spot in the research carried out in the US with regards to Pakistan. There is still a gap in the 'ozone layer' of analysis because of which the Pakistani military continues to support individuals frenzied by terrorist activities. China is a partner of the Pakistan military in such asymmetrical activities, in the sense that equipments (including sophisticated communications kits) get transferred to Pakistan that very soon reach terror groups operating in India. Because the Pakistan army is seen by several US commanders through lenses provided by that very institution, there is no protest from the US at such transfers, even though some of those equipments could get diverted to terror groups in theatres other than India. The China-Pakistan link in conventional and non-conventional capabilities, when combined with the inertia displayed by the US, represents a potent threat to India.

As is the case with China, any increase in domestic instability would raise the possibility of increased recruitment into terrorist pools in Pakistan. In the case of the PRC, there seems to exist an influential lobby that focuses on the perceived need to ensure that India does not progress to a level where it can challenge the primacy of China in Asia. In the case of Pakistan, the threat to India is Pakistani military's constant search for ways in which to cut India down to a strategic size that matches Islamabad's desire for parity with India. Should there be a 'resolution' of the Kashmir 'dispute' (by India agreeing to the Roben Raphel formula of converting it into a Talibanised state under the control of Jihadi groups, Pakistan army's obsession with parity would still drive Pakistani policies on paths hostile to Indian interests, as demonstrated by the activities of the Inter-Services Intelligence (ISI) in Kashmir and elsewhere in India. Until the hated 'Other' (India) becomes an enfeebled and divided state or the Pakistan Armed Forces change into accepting the need for good relations with India, such operations will not cease.

The Pakistani military-specifically the army-has a command structure that in effect is designed to ensure continued overlordship of the Punjab over other provinces as well as to prevent substantive action by the civilian administration against terror groups that are the army's auxiliaries in the covert war against India.

The military and security services are also linked to terror groups by a money trail that is an amalgam of moneys received for the jihad against India from the Middle East, SE Asia and elsewhere, as well as the financial rewards for facilitating the region's trade in narcotics. Now that restrictions have been placed on the military's control over enterprises in Pakistan, the pair of 'jihad donation-narcotics' sources of money provide the bulk of the unrecorded income of several within Pakistani military and this is also one reason why they are unlikely to terminate support to terror groups even should India give them satisfaction on the Kashmir issue in the way some Obama policymakers (following on from the Clinton years) want.

Unlike India, where a significant part of the country has made substantial progress in agrarian reform and industrial relations, in Pakistan control of the levers of civilian power remains in the hands of the feudal elite. Interestingly, it was from such an elite group of Muslims in India that M.A. Jinnah secured support for his plan of bisecting India into a Muslim and a Hindu state. At the base of the occupational pyramid in Pakistan, there remains a vacuum in opportunity, especially in access to modern education that is getting filled up by religious teaching, often of an extreme exclusivist kind, in the urban areas. In rural areas, the control of the feudal elite over the rest of the population has made membership in extremist religious organizations the best available escape route to the stagnation in opportunity that feudal constraints bring along. In today's Pakistan, it is only such organizations that claim to pose a challenge to the feudal elite, even though such opposition is more symbolic than substantive. This stance wins them immense popularity.

Unless measures are taken to bring modern education within the reach of common citizens in Pakistan, and correctives are applied to the stifling control of the feudal elite over the rest of the rural population, extremist organizations will continue to get a substantial flow of recruits. The other escape route for those outside the circle of the feudal elite who are seeking some degree of social standing and empowerment is the military, and it is not a surprise that the world view of a major portion of recruits to the lower ranks is similar to that held by those in extremist religious groups. The pool of manpower is the same, as is the social and school education imparted to them. Sadly, far from seeking to create in recruits a world view consonant with the needs of development and social progress, most commanders in Pakistan have instead encouraged the instilling of an extremist religious mindset within the pool of recruits to the military.

With more than sixteen million young people in Pakistan believing in the extremist vision of a world that can be made 'healthy' (in their view) only by the creation of a Talibanised state, and with more from the rest of the population joining them in such a belief, demography in Pakistan represents a significant threat to India, a threat that can manifest itself in the form of illegal migration that forms networks of extremist ideology and facilitates terror. Unless (1) the feudal elite in Pakistan follows the example of the Afrikaners in South Africa and voluntarily surrender policy space to the rest of the population (2) the educational system becomes geared to modern needs and is made accessible to the general population and (3) the military regards the defence of Pakistan its main priority rather than obsessive pursuit of a policy that seeks only to checkmate the rise of India; the threat from Pakistani military and its jihadist auxiliaries will continue-talks or no talks, Kashmir 'solution' or no solution.

**Bangladesh**

The primary 'threat' to Indian security is the tepid response of the Indian policy establishment towards the need for secure and sanitized borders with Nepal and Bangladesh. In particular, the open India-Nepal border is a major gap in this country's defences against an external security threat, as is the undefended, unpatrolled, unfenced nature of much of the Indo-Bangladesh border. Securing of borders has to be a priority, especially in the context of expected population shifts as a result of weather factors.

However, this does not mean a downgrading of links. On the contrary, better road and other links need to be created between India and these two neighbouring states, perhaps through the private sector for several segments. Because the Indian establishment has shown an almost pathological aversion to the display of the 'stick' (even in cases where such action is clearly warranted), Bangladesh continues to put aside its own national interest (that mandates closer links with India) and has instead protected the objectives of the Pakistan military by refusing cooperation with India in creating better roads and other links. Carrots are of much less value in the absence of sticks, and unless there be costs to the Bangladesh military for its connivance with groups hostile to India, such misdirected behaviour is likely to continue. Misdirected because each other country in South Asia requires cooperation with India if it is to develop in a rapid manner. Both Bangladesh and Pakistan have lost out substantially by rejecting an expansion of economic and other linkages with India. Sourcing production from India rather than from more distant markets would result in lower costs as well as greater competitiveness within Pakistani industry. Similarly, in the case of Bangladesh, a meshing of that country's resources with India's needs and vice-versa would accelerate growth for both. Should Bangladesh continue to avoid an optimal economic linkage with India, a strategy may need to be put in place that bypasses that country while creating roads and other links to ASEAN. Should Bangladesh be a part of such a plan, that country would gain significantly.

No major country in the world so exemplifies the doctrine of 'turning the other cheek' as vividly as India. Despite repeated rebuffs and active participation of Pakistani military's non-conventional plans against India, thus far Pakistan or

Bangladesh have not suffered any ill consequence as a result of Indian action. Unless there be an Indian response to negative acts by Dacca or Islamabad, these are likely to continue, in view of the servility with which sections of the ruling establishment treat the Punjabi elite in Pakistan. These sections have a strong 'Stockholm Syndrome' towards the Punjabi elite, despite (or perhaps because of) the genocidal fury of the (then West) Pakistan response to the victory of Sheikh Mujibur Rahman in the 1970 election. The ethnic hatred of sections within the (then West) Pakistan elite towards the Bengalis resulted in the illegal countermanding of the elections and the subsequent military action against the population of Bangladesh. Despite this history, a leading political party in Bangladesh, as well as the country's army, exhibit an extra-territorial loyalty towards the Punjabi elite in Pakistan, a mindset that has made them collaborators in the non-conventional war against India.

Unless there are proportional Indian responses to hostile actions from within Bangladesh, these will continue. One suggested course would be a vigorous action to identify, quarantine and deport citizens of Bangladesh who are illegally residing in India. These constitute a security danger in view of the commitment of the Bangladesh military and a section of the political establishment towards hostile activities against India. Both-the Pakistani as well as the Chinese militaries and the pro-Punjabi sections in Bangladesh have all been participants and joyful onlookers respectively of the continued sabotage of India.

Simultaneously with an effective response to hostile action, the advantages of a better relationship with India need to be shown to the people of that country. The rapid development of links with ASEAN as well as with friendly South Asian countries would highlight the sacrifice being made by Bangladesh as a consequence of that country's 'Stockholm Syndrome' and nudge that country into a closer relationship with India.

# 15

# Struggle for Democracy in Myanmar: India's Response

V. Suryanarayan

When Aung San Suu Kyi, the Nobel Laureate and the tallest leader fighting for the restoration of democracy in Myanmar was sentenced to eighteen months imprisonment (house arrest) in early August, I was reminded of the two quotations given in the beginning of this essay. The frail, but indomitable, Burmese leader, has spent thirteen of the last fifteen years in prison, mostly under house arrest. The court found Aung San Suu Kyi guilty of violating the conditions of her house arrest, after an uninvited American journalist spent two nights in her house in May 2009. She was sentenced to three years imprisonment, but the sentence was reduced to eighteen months' house arrest. The ruling military junta wanted to show to the international community that they have taken a lenient view of violation of the State Protection Act of 1975. As Ms. Irene Khan, the Secretary General of the Amnesty International, has rightly pointed out, it is not leniency. To quote Irene Khan, "it is not and must not be seen as leniency, especially by ASEAN and UN. Daw Aung San Suu Kyi should never have been arrested in the first place. The only issue here is her immediate and unconditional release".

For nearly three decades, the Army Generals, whose hands are tainted with the blood of thousands of innocent civilians, have doggedly held on to power in Rangoon. (Yangon). Neither the sanctions imposed by the United States and the European Union nor the incentives held forth by the member states of ASEAN have resulted in any meaningful restoration of democracy. Myanmar's isolationist Generals continue to be indifferent to both carrot and the stick. As a result, *Suvarnabhumi* (land of gold), as Burma was known in ancient times, has become one of the most economically destitute nations. The degeneration of Burma and the stranglehold that the organized criminal groups have over the country was succinctly summed by the Congressional Research Service in August 2008.

To quote, "Transnational organized criminal groups in Burma (Myanmar) operate a multi-billion dollar criminal industry that stretches across Southeast

Asia. Trafficked drugs, humans, wild life, gems, timber and other contraband flow through Burma, supporting the illicit demands of the region and beyond. Widespread collusion between traffickers and Burma's military junta, the State Peace and Development Council (SPDC), allows organized crime groups to function with impunity. Transnational crimes in Burma bear upon US interests as it threatens regional security in Southeast Asia and bolsters a regime that fosters a culture of corruption and disrespect for the rule of law and human rights".

**Political Developments in Burma since Independence**

In terms of natural resources, Myanmar is richly endowed and if it were administered well, the country could easily have become one of the most developed countries in Asia. Known as the Union of Burma for many years, the name of the country was changed by the military junta to Pyidaungzu Myanma Naingngandaw (Union of Myanmar). The name has been promoted by the ruling clique since 1989. The decision to change the name was arbitrary, for it was not ratified by Parliament. Many countries, including the United States, have not approved the new name. The rich natural resources include petroleum, timber, tin, antimony, zinc, copper, tungsten, lead, coal, marble, limestone, precious stones, natural gas and hydro power.

Myanmar is a multi-ethnic, multi-religious and multi-lingual country. It has a population of 48 million. The population consists of Burmans-68 percent, Shan-9 percent, Karen-7 percent, Rokhine-4 percent, Chinese-3 percent, Indians-2 percent, Mons-2 percent and others comprise 5 percent of the population. In terms of religion, Buddhists constitute 89 percent, Christians constitute 4 percent (Baptist 3 percent, Catholic 1 percent), Muslims constitute 4 percent, Animists constitute 1 percent and others constitute 2 percent of the population. After independence, attempts made by the government to build the nation on the basis of the language and culture of the majority community were resisted by the minority groups. They resorted to armed struggle to protect and foster their separate identity. Equally important, the Chinese community dominates the economy and has amassed considerable wealth disproportionate to the number of their population. The Indians played a significant role in the political and economic life of the country before the Second World War, but their number has rapidly declined; many of them were edged out of the country as a result of nationalization of retail trade pursued by the Socialist Government. The position of the Indians is deplorable in Myanmar. Nearly 400,000 of them, belonging to the fourth and fifth generations, still remain stateless. There is hardly any Indian representation in the administrative services, armed forces and the university system. Unfortunately the Government of India is more interested in befriending the military government than in protecting the interests of the Indian minority groups.

Burma came under British occupation by stages over a period of 62 years-1824 to 1886-and was incorporated into British India as a province. It remained a province of India until 1937. Due to the demand put forward by Burmese nationalists, backed by sections of British administrators that Burma was receiving step motherly treatment from the British Government in India, Burma was separated from India under the provisions of the Government of India Act of 1935 which came into force in 1937. The prolonged anti-colonial struggle, combined with the exigencies of the post-war situation compelled the British to grant independence to Burma in 1948.

The early years of independence were a period of political turbulence. Aung San, the great nationalist leader, was assassinated and he was succeeded by U Nu. The Burmese Communist Party started an armed struggle for capturing power; it was followed by revolts led by the Kachins, Karens and the Shans for independence from the Union of Burma. Compounding the complex situation was the presence of Chinese Kuomintang troops in the northern parts of Burma, which contributed to strains in relations between Burma and the PRC. The political instability and the consequent economic ruin paved the way for the Burmese military to capture power in 1962.

The ideology of the new military regime was published in a document called the Burmese Way to Socialism. It was a curious mixture of Buddhism, Marxism and humanism. However, in reality, Burma withdrew into diplomatic isolation and the economy declined to the point of bankruptcy. All banks and private enterprises were nationalized and Burma's vibrant free press was strangled. The long spell of military rule only enabled a small coterie to enrich itself. Finally General Ne Win's regime collapsed under the weight of popular discontent and it was replaced by a regime which was ostensibly a liberal regime. Even under the new dispensation, General Ne Win effectively controlled the administration from behind the scenes. As David Steinberg has written, "It was a last ditch attempt by an economically and politically bankrupt government to save itself from extinction at the hands of a disillusioned urban populace".

September 2007 witnessed prolonged protests in Myanmar in nearly twenty years of repressive regime. Small scale demonstrations triggered by a hefty fuel price increase in mid-August 2007 gathered momentum and on September 6 the army fired over the heads of protesting monks. At their peak, there were thousands of demonstrators marching daily. The military regime started a crack down on September 25. Soldiers flooded the streets of Rangoon, blocking off the access to Shwe Dagon Pagoda and other religious places which acted as the safe sanctuaries for the demonstrators. Many were killed and many more were detained. Following international protests, the United States, European Union, Australia and Japan imposed sanctions on the military regime. In the 13th ASEAN Summit held in Singapore on November 17, 2007, the ASEAN urged the military regime to enter into a constructive dialogue with Aung San Suu Kyi and work towards 'a peaceful transition to democracy'.

**Aung San Suu Kyi and the Second Struggle for Independence**

Aung San Suu Kyi returned to Myanmar from her home in Oxford in April 1988 in the midst of political upheaval in her motherland. The military authorities had carried on a sustained vicious campaign against her alleging that she was a stranger to Burma, had married a foreigner and had spent most part of her life abroad. Deriving inspiration from her father Aung San's contribution to Burmese struggle for independence, she declared, 'People have been saying that I know nothing of Burmese politics. The trouble is that I know too much. My family knows better than any, how devious Burmese politics can be and how much my father had to suffer on that account'. The demonstrators gathered near the Shwe Dagon Pagoda cheered her wildly and the cheer reached a crescendo when she concluded, "The present crisis is the concern of the whole nation. I could not, as my father's daughter, remain indifferent to all that was going on. This national crisis could, in fact, be called a second struggle for independence". No wonder she was able to immediately establish rapport with the people, emerge as the leading voice of the opposition and demanded the restoration of democracy in the country. What is more relevant, the pro-democracy movement, which hitherto was functioning in fits and starts because of the lack of proper leadership, became more organized and principled. Aung San Suu Kyi insisted on the Gandhian form of struggle, more remarkable because in India, Mahatma's own country, people have started to abandon the Gandhian form of struggle and are resorting to increasing violence to express their protest.

On September 24, 1988 the National League for Democracy was officially formed and the party soon spread its roots throughout the country. The army viewed Aung San Suu Kyi's increasing challenge with suspicion and put her under house arrest on July 20, 1989. The international media began to give more publicity to the developments in Myanmar and compared Aung San Suu Kyi with various other great nationalist leaders, to George Washington and James Fonda in the United States, to La Passionaria in France, to Benazir Bhutto in Pakistan and Corazon Aquino in the Philippines.

Aung San Suu Kyi was only three years old when her father Aung San was assassinated. When he was killed Aung San was only 34 and left behind his wife,

Khin Kyi and three small children, two sons and a daughter. Khin Kyi was one of the outstanding leaders of Burma; she soon entered public life, worked for the government in several capacities before being appointed as Burma's Ambassador to New Delhi, the first Burmese woman to be appointed as an Ambassador. Aung San Suu Kyi completed her school education in New Delhi and joined the Lady Shri Ram College for higher education. In the college she was adjudged as a bright student. It was during her stay in India that she got fascinated with the Indian struggle for independence. She developed lasting admiration for the principles of non-violence as embodied in the life and political philosophy of Mahatma Gandhi.

Aung San Suu Kyi soon left for higher education in England. In 1964 she graduated in philosophy, politics and economics from St Hugh's College in Oxford. She worked as a research assistant for a brief interval in the University of London. During 1967-71, she held various positions in the UN Secretariat in New York before marrying Michael Aris, a British theologist, in 1972. Her marriage with a foreigner created a lot of controversy in Burma. The military regime, as mentioned earlier, has accused her on several occasions of being 'un-Burmese'. It must, however, be highlighted that Aung San Suu Kyi visited Burma regularly, retained her Burmese citizenship and sent her sons to become novices in Buddhist monasteries in Rangoon. As Bertil Lintner has pointed out she never lost her Buddhist identity. Her intellectual inspiration, during her long stay abroad, came from the Civil Rights Movement of Martin Luther King and the ideas, ideals and practices of Mahatma Gandhi. She also spent some time as an academic in Australia and Japan and was also a fellow in the Indian Institute of Advanced Study in Shimla. Among her published works during this period was a comparative study of Indian and Burmese nationalist movements.

In April 1988, Aung San Suu Kyi returned to Burma to visit her ailing mother, who suffered a stroke. Gradually she was drawn into the vortex of the democratic movement. Her agony and anguish at the deteriorating situation in Burma came out vividly in one of her essays, "The economy has not been well managed and Burma is not a prosperous nation. However, with its wealth of natural resources, there is always hope for the future. And that future lies in the hands of its peoples".

Under the dynamic leadership of Aung San Suu Kyi, the National League for Democracy (NLD) began to occupy the centre stage in Burmese politics. She became increasingly outspoken in her criticism of the Burmese government and began to accuse Ne Win of being responsible for the economic and political miseries of her people. Though Ne Win was pretending that he had retired from politics, he was virtually the power behind the government. The elections held in

1989 witnessed a massive turn out and the NLD won 392 of the 483 seats in the 492 member state assembly. The National Unity Party (NUP, the new incarnation of the BSPP) won only 10 seats. The ruling military junta did not want to transfer power to the elected representatives and turned its back on the popular mandate. The era of tyranny and oppression continued and Aung San Suu Kyi continued to languish under house arrest. In May 2008, Myanmar was struck by cyclone Nargis which left over 90,000 dead and 50,000 injured. Despite this tragedy, the junta continued with its constitutional referendum and is currently setting the stage for parliamentary election in 2010. Sixty nine years after independence, Myanmar has not sorted out any of the major problems—popular representation, ethnic discontent, military-civilian relations and removal of poverty.

In an article in *Asian Survey* in July 1990, Prof. Josef Silverstein had raised the basic question, "Is Aung San Suu Kyi Burma's woman of destiny? It would appear so at this time. There is no other person who has achieved her status, love and respect from the people of Burma and support from foreign governments, who have appealed on her behalf. She is her father's daughter-intelligent, honest, tough and fearless. Most of all, she has no past connection with the failures of the democratic government of U Nu or the corrupt, incompetent and brutal dictatorship of Ne Win. For many Burmese she appears the reincarnation of her father and is destined to carry out his unfinished work of leading Burma into the modern world".

**International Response**

When General Ne Win captured power in 1962, there were other military regimes elsewhere in Asia. While these military regimes trusted the advice of the technocrats, presided over long periods of economic growth and allowed the development of civil society, the military regime in Burma became more and more oppressive. The developments in Indonesia and Pakistan deserve special mention. Under General Suharto, Indonesia was a show case for the Western world led by the United States; there was apparent political stability and substantial economic growth. However, it soon became clear to discerning observers that behind the façade of apparent stability and prosperity, the Suharto regime concealed serious political, economic and social distortions. And when the Asian Economic Crisis engulfed the country and spontaneous political protests became the order of the day, the Suharto regime collapsed like a pack of cards. The developments in Pakistan during the last five years are also illustrations that Western support and backing to military dictators is no alternative to democratic governments backed with popular mandate.

In addition to the brutal suppression of democratic aspirations, the flow of refugees, including political dissidents, helped to internationalize the issue. The United States, European Union and Japan reacted strongly against the autocratic tendencies of the military regime. The Treasury and the State Department prepared a list of Generals and government servants who were denied visa to the United States. The Burmese financial assets in the United States were frozen and these governments approached the United Nations Security Council and made an appeal that sanctions should be imposed against Myanmar. Though these countries imposed sanctions on their own volition, their efforts to invoke UN sanctions did not succeed because of the stiff opposition by China, backed by Soviet Union. The sanctions did not mean complete ban of the Burmese imports nor did it affect private investments in Burma.

The ASEAN differed from the United States on the question of imposing sanctions. Some of the member states of ASEAN are headed by authoritarian governments of varying degrees, naturally there was not much concern on issues like dismantling of democratic structure and violation of human rights. The ASEAN leaders believed that the policy of isolating an already isolated country would be counterproductive and dangerous. They further were of the view that the opening of the space for civil society and gradual democratization of the political system could take place by constructive engagement with the Burmese government. If the military government is given multiple options, its dependence on China could also be reduced. It was in furtherance of these goals that Myanmar was admitted into ASEAN, despite strong reservations expressed by the United States and the European Union. The military junta welcomed these initiatives because this enabled it to come out of international isolation, provided more avenues for export and import and the government could attract foreign direct investments from relatively more advanced countries like Malaysia, Singapore, Indonesia and Thailand. But the policy of constructive engagement pursued by ASEAN could not make much headway and Myanmar doubled its efforts to put down democratic aspirations. This policy provided legitimacy to the Burmese government and there was no dialogue or engagement with the regime on the question of political reforms. The business community in ASEAN reaped a lot of economic benefits. They could get lucrative contracts for the building of hotels and factories in Myanmar.

The military regime is able to sustain itself politically and economically because of the solid support by the Government of the Peoples Republic of China. In the United Nations and other international organizations, China maintained that the developments in Burma and the Governmental response are strictly 'internal affairs' and that China would not interfere in the 'internal affairs' of another country. China appealed for restraint and called for reconciliation of various political forces within Myanmar. On the nature of Government, China made it clear that Burma should strive for a democratic process 'appropriate for the country'. The solid support extended by China to the Burmese government must be seen in the context of China's brutal suppression of pro-democracy elements within China Itself. As Bertil Linter has pointed out, "The present Burmese junta which seized power on September 18, 1988, after crushing a nationalist uprising for change, clearly saw in China a political ally, especially when the leaders in Beijing staged a very similar massacre of pro-democracy activists in June the following year".

The Burmese army, which has expanded considerably during recent years, is provided with fighter planes, patrol boats, tanks and ammunition in addition to sophisticated military equipments. China has emerged as Myanmar's major economic partner; it imports considerable raw materials and supplies most of the consumer goods. China is also evincing a lot of interest in Burma's infrastructure including the construction of roads from the Yunnan province to Rangoon. It is also involved in the upgradation of Burmese ports. Burmese government has also permitted China to exploit its natural resources in the ethnic minority areas along the Sino-Burmese border. The Burmese leaders have frequently declared that China is the 'most trusted friend' of Myanmar.

**What Should the Indian Response be?**

A matter of great concern for New Delhi in the coming years will be the developments in Myanmar, a country with which India shares land and maritime boundaries. As early as 1944, Sardar KM Panikkar had focused attention on the strategic significance of Burma to India. To quote Panikkar, "The defence of Burma in fact is the defence of India and it is India's primary concern no less than Burma's to see that its borders remain inviolate. In fact, no responsibility is considered too heavy for India when it comes to the question of defending Burma".

Why is Myanmar so strategically important to India? Ranjit Gupta, an astute observer of Asian political development, sums them up as follows. Myanmar is important in the context of India's territorial integrity; in the context of the security, stability and economic development of India's north-eastern states; in the context of India's security interests in the Bay of Bengal and the eastern Indian Ocean, including the security of the strategically vital Andaman and Nicobar Islands; in the context of India's energy requirements; in the context of India's Look East Policy as Myanmar is the geographical bridge between India and ASEAN and in the context of checkmating China's increasing influence in Southeast and South Asia.

An equally important point in this connection is the stake that India has in promoting and fostering democratic regimes in India's neighbourhood. In this connection, it is necessary to recall the fact that India played a pivotal role in bolstering Burma politically and militarily in the early years of independence. As pointed out earlier, independent Burma was beset with manifold problems. The assassination of Aung San was followed by revolts by Karens and the communists. The security of even Rangoon was threatened by rebel forces. Indian concern was naturally sharpened with the emergence of PRC which shared borders with both India and Burma. Thanks to Nehru's initiative, the Commonwealth countries were persuaded to provide military and economic aid to Burma. Indian assistance to Burma encompassed military and economic assistance and also bolstering of the U Nu regime. This policy was naturally aimed to have a friendly regime between India and China, but also prevent destabilization of the northeast India, where the Nagas and the Mizos were straddling the India-Burma border. It may also be mentioned that the Government and people of India also assisted the people of Nepal in getting rid of Rana's despotism.

A survey of recent political developments in South and Southeast Asia clearly brings out the fact that sooner or later the authoritarian regimes will be swept away by democratic forces. Marcos in the Philippines, Suharto in Indonesia and General Musharaff in Pakistan; though it seemed that they had become permanent fixtures; they were swept aside when the people revolted against them. It will be a tragic day, if India, like China and ASEAN, also adopts a foreign policy of opportunism and cynicism. It is undoubtedly true that the pro-democracy movement in Myanmar has seen ups and downs. But temporary setbacks had been a regular feature in pro-democracy movements in several parts of the world. The logic of history and the justness of the cause will surely bring about a turn in the tide in Burma. As Aung San Suu Kyi pointed out in the Joyce Memorial Lecture, "The dream of a society ruled by loving kindness, reason and justice is a dream as old as civilized man. Does it have to be an impossible dream? Karl Popper, explaining his abiding optimism in so troubled a world as ours, said the darkness had always been there, but the light was new. Because it is new, it has to be tended with care and diligence".

The need of the hour is for various political parties, media, trade unions, NGOs and student's Unions to rally round Aung Saan Suu Kyi and her comrades. This will also be in conformity with our nationalist heritage and the Gandhi-Nehru legacy.

Aung San Suu Kyi, to quote Vaclav Havel, "is an outstanding example of the power of the powerless". She is Burma's woman of destiny and is the hope and inspiration of her people. Given our nationalist heritage, more so, Gandhi-Nehru legacy, New Delhi owes to itself and the struggling people of Myanmar that it should immediately initiate steps to mobilize international opinion so that pressure is brought upon the military junta to restore democracy and human rights. It is amazing that New Delhi has become insensitive to the flagrant violations of human rights in Myanmar. The Doctor in Albert Camus's book, *The Plague,* has the following advice, 'All I maintain is that on this earth there are pestilences and there are victims, and it is up to us, so far as possible, not to join forces with the pestilences'.

# 16

# Nation-building and Foreign Policy Behaviour of India in the Regional Setting of South Asia

P.M Joshy and Mohanan B. Pillai

---

## Introduction

The states of the South Asia stumble on a complex social frame in which ethnicity, religion, caste, language etc., play a decisive role. The configuration of these complexities and diversities most often precipitates political polarizations and mobilizations which quite often lead to violent conflicts among different communities of the region that cut across state borders. Generally speaking, these conflicts are a modern phenomenon and are intertwined with the logic of nation-building and interest articulation within a competitive capitalist system. As far as South Asia is concerned the cartographical setting of the present state system is a product of late colonialism and in the post-colonial period the old political practices got transformed into more sophisticated mobilizations and manoeuvrings. However, the linkage between internal complexities and foreign policy is a matter of dispute because, conventionally, foreign policy is an art by the elite for the elite section in the society. In South Asia, to a greater extent, foreign policy is interconnected with the process of nation-building. The foreign policy of a nation could contribute to internal coherence and regime legitimacy of the ruling class. The very logic of foreign policy and nation building shares a common platform that both-make and sustain the 'us' and 'them' in its area of action. So, the overall process brings forth several 'others' both within and outside the nation. This seems to be the core determinant of politics and foreign policy behaviours in South Asia.

During 1990s, the states of South Asia started integrating their economies with the world capitalist system. It is a well known fact that both state and market function on diametrically opposite directions; state fragments territory and market integrates. Coincidently, the process of globalization considerably decreased statist sovereignty and that very much reflected in their foreign policy behaviours. The aggressive foreign policy posture of the former National Democratic Alliance (NDA) Government in India is an example. Here, we can see a shift in the fundamental nature of the state, i.e. a shift from a developmental state towards a facilitator for global finance capital. As a result the responsibility of the state has been redefined as the sole manager of market functions. In other words, the state in its managerial role devote time for the better execution of neo-liberal policies in the society and accordingly the state has become more militaristic in orientation and thus embroiled in the implementation of the laws and treaties of the market.

In this scenario, we are going to look at the foreign policy behaviours of the South Asian states in general and the responses of the Indian state in particular.

**State and Society in South Asia**

As is well known, South Asia is a region of rich diversity which encompasses eight states-India, Pakistan, Bangladesh, Nepal, Sri Lanka, Bhutan, Maldives and Afghanistan. The multi-ethnic/religious/linguistic/racial composition of the region brings forth strengths as well as weaknesses. The region consists of a number of religions that originated in the Indian subcontinent like Hinduism, Buddhism, Jainism and Sikhism as well as those religions that arrived here like Islam, Christianity and Judaism. This religious diversity has had clear cut influence on the social fabric of South Asia. India has a multi-religious composition in which 80.46 percent of the total population is Hindu, 13.46 percent are Muslims, 2.34 percent are Christians, 1.875 percent are Sikhs, 0.41 percent are Jains and the remaining 0.65 percent belong to other faiths. Pakistani society too confronts linguistic, ethnic, cultural diversities even within the dominant Islamic religion. The Punjabis (60 percent), Sindhis (12 percent), Pukhtuns (14 percent), Baluchis (4 percent) are the four ethnic groups in Pakistan. Mohajirs, the Indian migrants in Pakistan, comprise 8 percent of the total population. Hindus and Christians are tiny minorities in Pakistan. Needless to say, all the South Asian states are plural in social composition. For instance, it has been noted that 61 ethnic groups exist in the small state of Nepal. However, religion plays a major role in South Asia not only as belief systems of the people but also as agents of convergence within the state. Islam is the official religion of Pakistan and the Maldives, Hinduism is the official religion of Nepal. Mahayana Buddhism is the official religion in Bhutan. During the regime of General Ziaur Rahman in Bangladesh, Islamic identity got prominence. Both India and Sri Lanka follow secularism as their state policies [Momin, 2009:21-38]. In this scenario, the majority-minority relations are controversial topics for research. Scarce resources and competing claims in the society always perpetuate conflicts and tensions. The internal dynamics of the South Asian states, especially its ethnically blurred boundaries, always propels inter-state conflicts and tensions and it seems to be one of the core determinants of foreign policy behaviour of these South Asian states.

**Pakistan**

The relations between India and Pakistan are a matter of great concern in the region. The overall image created during the past sixty two years fixed them as 'enemy states.' This enemy image has historical roots which go back to the period of then Indian nationalist struggle. The nationalist struggle had progressed along the dominant secular line. It bifurcated, creating another stream of thought-Muslim religious nationalism, under the leadership of Jinnah which culminated into the Muslim League's demand for a separate nation-state, where it believed that Muslim religious identity could be safeguarded. The creation of Pakistan was legitimized on the pre-supposition that the linguistic and ethnic divisions could be surpassed by the dominant Islamic identity. This nationalistic perspective took an intolerant attitude towards hybridism and diversity. But the assertion of the Bengali linguistic identity over the dominant religious identity paved the way for the creation of Bangladesh in 1971 [Sheth, 1989: 383; Mishra, 2000]. However, even though Pakistan remains Islamic, Punjabi ethnic identity is the core determining factor in the affairs of the state. 80 percent of the army and 55 percent of the federal bureaucracy is from Punjab. Punjabi domination in state affairs is being legitimized by equating Punjab's interest with that of Pakistan's. Here ethnicity and nationalism come into coexistence with the Punjabi ethnic group proclaiming itself as the vanguard of Pakistani nationalism. The assertion of other ethnic groups is considered as 'anti-national', implying that they are pro-Indians [Samad, 2009:208-214]. Indeed, the Pakistani national self is moulded by positing India as it's 'Other.' Pakistani ruling elite has been using the anti-India card for regime legitimacy for quite long. In fact, there is tension hanging over the constraints of nation-building, regime legitimacy and the growing urge for democracy.

**Afghanistan**

Afghanistan is a land locked and mountain-studded country which borders with Iran (west), Uzbekistan, Tajikistan and Kirghizstan (north), Pakistan (south) and China to the east of the Wakhan Corridor. It had historical land contacts with India and China, which lost importance with the discovery of sea roots to India. Afghanistan is one of the richest countries in Asia, because of its treasure of natural resources, but remains underdeveloped (Chopra 1998:23-24). The geopolitical position of the state had caused many twists and turns in its long history. During the nineteenth century both Britain and Russia played a decisive role in determining the destiny of the country and Cold War real politics dragged it into the containment strategy of the US. In 1979 the rebel combat units operating in Afghanistan were well trained by the US and its allies (ibid: 29). However, these forces themselves became a challenge to US supremacy in the post-Cold War era.

Before 1919, the state was a tribal confederacy. It was so weak that it could not extend its control over the other parts of the country. Each part of the country was controlled by their respective land lords until King Abdur Rahman forcibly cowed tribal chieftains and the feudal lords during his twenty-one years rule (1880-1901). The basic foundation for a modern nation-state was laid when the state achieved its independence from the British colonialists in 1919 under the leadership of King Amanullah (Pavithran 2008:257). During the Cold-War years Afghanistan was a major site of super power engagement. With the end of the Cold War, Afghanistan witnessed the Talibanisation of the state and the society. The role of Pakistan was very important because it hosted the Mujahedeen factions during the Soviet intervention. Following Soviet withdrawal, the Taliban defeated the warlords and captured Kabul in 1996. But Taliban did not succeed in its efforts to integrate the whole nation under the Islamic ideology professed and practiced by it. In its dealings with the smaller ethnic identities, Taliban pursued a policy which had a strong Pushtoon bias (Bahadur 1998:63-9). However, the Taliban debacle in mid September of 2001 gave way to the emergence of a new dispensation in which the American interests became predominant.

The celebrated 'War on Terrorism' by the US and its allies brought forth new dimensions to international politics. Afghanistan was the first target and the Taliban regime was replaced by a puppet government under the control of the US. However, the humanitarian situation in Afghanistan has worsened and as a result life has become miserable. In this situation, the Taliban has been growing rapidly and it has strong holds in some of the tribal areas and it is also penetrating to other areas. Recently, a reporter shared his experiences in a Taliban camp, "The tribal areas were more developed and the Taliban more sophisticated than I expected. They browsed the internet and listened to hourly news updates on Azadi Radio" (David Rhode 2009). As far as India is concerned the developments in Afghanistan always put its interests in a tight spot because of the very presence of Pakistan and its involvement in the issue. Generally speaking, India also has partaken in the US led war on terrorism.

### Sri Lanka

India and Sri Lanka have had centuries of people-to-people relations with Tamil ethnicity becoming the core determinant in the post-colonial period. Sri Lanka consists of 74 percent Sinhalese, mainly concentrated in the south, west, and central parts of the country; and Hindus and Muslims besides Christians comprise almost 26 percent of the total population. The Tamils comprise 12.6 percent and it is these linguistic and religious cleavages that prompted them to settle in the northern and the eastern parts of the island nation. [Kukreja, 2008:237]. The British colonialists politically integrated the island nation in 1831.The impact of this political unification was far reaching. The Jaffna Tamils spread all over the island nation and became an elite section during the colonial era. They (specifically Vellalas, the dominant caste within the Tamils) got English education from American missionaries and became a strong presence in the colonial administrative service. During this colonial administration, a new Sinhala entrepreneurial class had been ascending. In the first half of the 20th century colonial power was transferred to this class combine. The social condition of the Tamils of the east coast was different from Jaffna Tamils. They were migrant labourers from South India who came there as workers in British tea plantations. On the eve of independence in 1948 the total number of Indian Tamils was slightly higher than Sri Lankan Tamils. However, during the colonial period, Sinhala-Tamil distinction did not play an important role [Kloos, 2009: 186-87]. In the post-colonial era due to large scale marginalization, Tamils asserted for equal rights. They were discriminated against through governmental policies especially in the five major areas of land, language, education, employment, and power sharing. This eventually turned into violent conflicts [Kukreja: 237]. The ethnically blurred boundaries as well as its strategic position in the Indian Ocean prompted India always to keep an eye on the island nation. However, India's stand on ethnic conflicts in Sri Lanka was more pragmatic. It stood for the territorial integration of Sri Lanka and also considerable devolution of powers to the Tamil minorities. The end of the military conflict has opened up new horizons for India-Sri Lanka relations and new possibilities of handling the ethnic issue within the constitutional framework.

**Bangladesh**

The state of Bangladesh is a counter symbol of pure religious nationalism. In 1971, the territorial-ethno-linguistic and cultural nationalism gave birth to Bangladesh. Bengali nationalism dominated in the nationalist struggle against Pakistan. However, Islamic and Bengali identities joined together in the articulation of a national identity. Muslims comprise 86 percent of the total population, Hindus 13 percent, and tribals 1 percent. The tribal population also enjoys linguistic-cultural-religious variations [Momin: 34]. There are four major Tribal communities in Bangladesh-the Chackmas, Marmas (Maghs), Tipparas (Tipras) and the Mros (Moorangs). Chackmas and Marmas are dominantly

Buddhists, Tipparas are basically Hindus. Mros are considered as the original inhabitants of the Chittagong tracts. The rest are presumed to have migrated from India and Burma [Phadnis, 2001:70-71].

Two thirds of the tribal populations are located in the Chittagong Hill tracts. This border area is conflict prone because these tribal sections have been revolting against the state's attempts of 'Bangladeshisation'. They are afraid of the loss of their identities because of statist interference. Statist modernization discourses have distorted the traditional mode of agriculture and employment possibilities through constitutional and extra-constitutional measures [Phadnis, 1986:18-20] adopted by the state. The total marginalization of these minority sections thus, cause violent revolts and consequently, refugee flows, especially into the states of West Bengal and Assam.

**Nepal**

Nepal is a country of hybrid ethnic and linguistic groups. Urmila Phadnis broadly classifies the population of Nepal into three categories- Tibeto-Burman, Indo-Aryan and Austro-Asiatic [2001:72-73]. The power structure in Nepal is oligarchic which comprises three dominant caste groups, Brahmins, Kshatriyas and Newars and the monarch is the apex of the system. The economic resources are concentrated in the hands of a tiny section in the Terai area. The slow pace of societal change and non-competitive nature of Nepali economy have been the principal causes of inter-ethnic conflicts in Nepal. The monarchy has been playing as an overarching role in the society and has given a poignant edge to the political integration of the country (Phadnis 1986:14-16). The 'Jan Andolan' or a people's movement launched by the political parties including the Maoists in March-April 2006 brought forth a qualitative change in the existing power structures. The monarchy is no longer portrayed as a symbol of national unity and territorial integrity. The role of the civil society and the media, in general, has become vital to this movement. Though, the movement alone could not change the society, gains from the movement deserve wholehearted legitimacy, consolidation and institutionalisation (Baral 2009:74-87).

**Bhutan**

It is a North-eastern Himalayan state, sharing borders with India, Nepal and China. The Bhutanese society emerged as a result of co-mingling of various ethnic groups which are identifiable across the region [Phadins, 2001:71]. Bhutan's population comprises of three major ethnic groups-Bhutiya (50 percent), Nepalese Grung (35 percent), Sharchops (15 percent) [Momin: 34]. The Bhutanese polity is a coalition of different elite sections of various communities legitimized by those communities [Phadnis, 1986: 16]. The development of Bhutanese infrastructure facilities and communication networks has very much altered the traditional system [ibid]. The state of Bhutan has had an image of sacrosanctity till the 1980s. Because of its ethnic complexities and feudal structure it has generated its own form of ethnic conflicts [Sinha, 2008:282-308]. Bhutan witnessed ethnic tensions during the 1990s, in the aftermath of the new citizenship act, which marginalized many members of the minority Nepali community located in the southern part of country by making them stateless. Because of the ethnic conflict, thousands of Nepali refugees fled from Bhutan to Nepal from the period stretching from 1993 to 1998 [Momin: 36].

**Maldives**

The people of Maldives are mainly migrants from Sri Lanka, Arabia and Africa-which renders a multi-ethnic texture to that state. Around the 12th century, people of this nation were massively converted into Islam even though ethnic diversity has prevailed in the state. The Divehi language essentially derived from Elu (an old form of Sinhala) has provided a greater degree of cultural homogeneity to the state despite its regional and dialectical differences in the north and in the south. Phadnis views that both the Islamic religion and the Divehi language provide a strong national identity and cultural distinctiveness to the state [1986:17; 2001: 75]. During the 16th and 17th centuries Maldives was under Portuguese and Dutch colonialism. It was a British protectorate from 1887 to 1965 and in 1968, following a referendum it became a republic [Momin: 26].

**India and Its Neighbours**

As far as South Asia is concerned democracy is not strong and healthy enough except in India and Sri Lanka. The rest of the South Asian states have experienced undemocratic regimes and of course, there have been struggles for democracy within the civil society. However, as a strategy to legitimize their regime, the ruling classes of these states have been using the 'anti-India' card. Because of the blurred ethnic boundaries between India and her neighbours, the internal developments in these countries have ramifications in India. In these pluralistic societies the process of nation-building is running on the majoritarian line and most often the minorities are excluded from this process. The insider/outsider image plays a vital role in the process of nation-building in South Asia. Sajal Nag notes,

"The project of all nation states is nation-building by which it is constantly shedding portions of its own people from its purview and thereby creating its own outsiders. The nation-states spearheaded this process because it emanated from logical requirements of an industrial system. This state formation requires homogeneity; it also requires loyalty. Therefore dissent was a disqualification for its citizenship" [2001: 4758].

The homogenizing imperative of the modern nation-state is employing the process of coercion as well as consensus. Often minorities are labelled as 'anti-national'. The Mohajirs in Pakistan, the Tamil minority in Sri Lanka, the Nepalese in Bhutan and the Chackmas in Bangladesh are best examples. According to Hindutva nationalists in India, Muslims and Christians and other minority communities are outsiders to the Hindu body politic. Of course, internal politics of these societies have clear cut influence on their foreign policies. Sankaran Krishna notes,

"...to speak of foreign policy presupposes the availability of a given specialization of the world in terms of 'us' and 'them.' In the modern, post-Westphalian world of nation-states, foreign policy constitutes the actions of state elites who try to maintain, at minimum, something called 'our national security' and to further, at every opportunity, something called 'our national interest' [2000: 3].

Foreign policy is thus, a tool at the hands of national elites to sustain regime legitimacy and internal coherence. The state of Pakistan emerged by legitimating religious nationalism. During its nation-building stage, it lost its supreme leader, Jinnah. Pakistani politics had been facing deeper systemic crisis displaying a bewildering array of shifting allegiance and alliances. In its half a century of existence, Pakistan has been administered by martial law regimes for nearly 30 years. At other times, the army has more directly pulled the strings of puppet democratic dispensations. The great influence of the military always keeps the Pakistani state as praetorian. The state upholds a 'political economy of defence' over a 'political economy of development' [Talbot, 2003: 1-3]. The dominant influence of the Punjabi ethnic community over military and the bureaucracy is a major determinant of the political horoscope of Pakistan. So people's aspiration for democracy and the ruling class interests that strongly support an Islamic authoritarian state, have always been in conflict. Veena Kukreja notes,

"Pakistan's traumatic and uncertain political history exemplifies a struggle between the forces of authoritarianism and constitutionalism, or a conflict between state and civil society" [2003:×II].

In this scenario, the Pakistani elites have been positing India as its 'other' and have been pursuing aggressive foreign policy postures. In fact, the forces which are acting against the possibility of a sound democratic system in this country are the forces which are always thwarting a peaceful dialogue between India and Pakistan. Both India and Pakistan have waged five major and minor wars and a proxy war is still going on, on the issue of Kashmir. The nuclear explosions in 1998 contributed new dimensions to their foreign policy behaviour.

India supported the liberation struggle in Bangladesh which culminated in a war between India and Pakistan from the December 4 to the December 16, 1971. The secession of East Pakistan from West, strengthened hostility between India and Pakistan and generally it was viewed as a setback in the promulgated dominant Islamist nationalism; the very raison d'être of the Pakistani state was questioned. Even though, India tried to follow good relations with Bangladesh, the latter was suspicious about the hegemony of India in South Asia. The political elite of that country have also been using the 'anti-India' card as the key to mobilize people. The Farraka dam agreement between India and Bangladesh is seen as India's hegemonic bilateralism [Mishra: 2000]. The internal ethno-political turmoil very much reflected in Bangladesh's foreign policy. For most of its history Bangladesh has 'oscillated between unstable democracy (1972-75 and 1991 onwards) and benign authoritarianism (1975-1990 except for four months of Abdus Sattar's civilian rule)' [Kukreja, 2008:105]. The Mujibur era was a definite period for India's friendly relations with Bangladesh. His successors tried to convert the country into an Islamic one and the anti-India propaganda heightened. The political elite of the country highlighted bilateral issues to generate anti-India sentiments. Issues like the Farakka Barrage, Chakma refugees, New Moore Island Controversy and the Tin Bigha Corridor issue are the major determinants of India's relations with Bangladesh. India has also been facing problems such as illegal drug trafficking, the problem of refugees, trafficking of women and children and most importantly terrorist activities emanating from Bangladeshi soil, in its relations with the said.

The geo-political, geo-strategic position of Sri Lanka in the Indian Ocean and also the ethnic linkage between Indian Tamils and Sri Lankan Tamils has prompted India to keep an eye on this country. However, both these countries have deep rooted historical relations. The ethnically blurred boundaries between India and Sri Lanka have very much influenced the foreign policy behaviour of both countries. The Indian state of Tamil Nadu and Sri Lanka have had historical relations. Sufferings of Tamil people in Sri Lanka, also has a long history. In the post-colonial period the new constitution of Sri Lanka has totally colonized Tamil Minorities and this has resulted into large scale protests by various Tamil groups and later on it was taken over by the LTTE under the leadership of Prabhakaran.

The Indian involvement [1987] in Sri Lanka's ethnic conflict is a part of its wider and long term perspective on the foreign policy front. It strongly stood for the unity, sovereignty and territorial integrity of the island nation. India's stand for democracy and pluralism always contradict with that of the LTTE's, which stood for a one-party dictatorship. However, initially as a strategy to protect the interests of the Tamil minorities in the state India extended its hand of help to that militant organization. But in the post-Rajeev period India changed its attitude towards this militant organization and it was banned in India soil.

The military conflict in Sri Lanka has come to an end with the killing of LTTE's top leaders including Prabhakaran. Consequently, the defeat of the LTTE has come as a setback to its attempts at carving out an autonomous Tamil state in the island. The post-LTTE debacle scenario brings forth several questions concerning the Tamil minority in Sri Lanka. What will be the approach of the majoritarian Sinhalese government towards this Tamil minority? An inclusive policy adopted by the Government might bring back the Tamils to the mainstream. For reconstructing the economy and rehabilitating the internally displaced groups, Sri Lanka needs strong international support, without which it cannot accomplish the set goals. In this scenario, the nations of the world and donor agencies can pressurize the Sri Lankan government for the devolution of power and this way the Tamils can foster their identity within the framework of the broader Sri Lankan nation. India can play a crucial role in the reconstruction of post-conflict Sri Lanka. The India-Sri Lanka accord of 1987 contains important provisions for the devolution of power to the local bodies. The implementation of the 13$^{th}$ Amendment to the constitution is viewed as an important step towards decentralization. The sharing of power between the majority and the minority, centre and the provincial councils is an apt solution to the ethnic problem.

As far as Nepal is concerned the conflict between people's aspiration for federalizing state power and the very foundation of the state- religion, caste, ethnicity and other forms of divisions yields a contradiction between the very existing state and the spirit of the modern democratic state [Baral, 2009:69-90]. The peoples struggle for democracy in Nepal has its reverberations in India.

In 1960s Bhutan broke its isolationist policy and it became an active participant in international forums like the SAARC, UN and the NAM. A rising China and its invasion of Tibet increased its anxieties. This prompted Bhutan to come closer to India. However, Bhutan was so sceptical about India that it had been facing a foreign policy dilemma as how to sustain a balanced relationship with China as well as India. Unlike Bhutan, the Maldives is not affected by Indophobia. Instead, it also seeks India's support for its security and development.

**Nation-building and Foreign Policy of India**

The states of South Asia have been facing two overlapping problems, namely

(1) the internal constraints over developing and sustaining a nationalist image and (2) legitimately positing the nation-state in the web of a modern world system. The very notion of the nation-state is a modern western phenomenon and the states of South Asia owe their energies as 'nations' to western modernity. The colonialists ruled these societies with their rationalist discourses and to a great extent questioned the legitimacy of these societies to become nation-states because of their multi-ethnic composition. Here the notion of the nation-state was posited against a pluralist reality. Against this backdrop the states of South Asia emerged with an emphasis on the possibility of a rational socio-political order above multiple ethnic structures. The contradiction between the attempts to homogenize and the resistance directed against it, in favour of heterogeneity determined the future course of South Asian politics.

In India, the contradictory policies of colonialists in their dealings with natives had given considerable inputs to the emergence of the nationalist movement. The colonialists legitimized their regime in the colony with the support of the western rationalist paradigm. Modernity envisaged the rational equality of all individuals. But colonialists subjugated the natives and this was questioned by the newly emerging middle class. This sentiment spread as a mass movement especially under the leadership of Gandhi and Nehru.

There were three 'master narratives' in Indian nationalism. One was a secular nationalism propagated by the Indian National Congress; the other was religious nationalism-mainly in two streams: Hindu nationalism and Muslim nationalism. The third one was caste based assertions of the deprived sections [Varshney, 2002:55-59]. All these streams evolved in their opposition to colonialism. The secular-nationalist version of the movement was also ambiguous regarding its approach to western modernity. Both Gandhi and Nehru had different approaches regarding the role of western modernity in Indian society. However in post-colonial India, Nehruvian notions regarding state, economy and foreign policy dominated. According to this strand of thinking, western modernity would transcend parochial societal divisions and it would develop the Indian society into a modern nation-state.

Religious nationalism evolved along with the dominant secular-nationalism. The roots of Hindu nationalist sentiments go back to the writings of Dayananda Saraswathi, Swami Viveknanda, and Sri Aurobindo and also to the writings of Bankim Chandra Chatterjee [Sharma, 2003]. The 19th century Indian thought was a response to the logo centric view of the Indologists, whom viewed India as a static and superstitious social formation and thought that it could not be developed into a modern nation state. Thinkers like Vivekananda and Dayananda Saraswati defended themselves by reinvoking the Indian tradition, by which they constructed an Indian past which was characterized by its rational order and vehemently criticized the present Indian Society for obscuring this glorious past with the present superstitious belief system. However this line of thought culminated into extreme Hindutva posturing at the beginning of the $20^{th}$ century. Golwalkar, Savarkar and Hedgewar were the prime ideologues of Hindutva. The Hindutva version of nationalism stands for a strong centralized state, primarily on the logic of the insider-outsider. In this view Muslims, Christians and Communists are the outsiders of the wholly Hindu nation and India is only for the Hindus who are the original inhabitants of this country [Savarkar, 1942, 1984, 1989; Golwalkar, 1939, 2000]. However, as a movement Hindutva lost its glamour with the assassination of Gandhi. It was also overshadowed by the power of the dominant nationalist ideology and the Nehruvian consensus within that frame. Hindutva reasserted itself during the 1980s when Congress' ideological hegemony was questioned from different quarters. The assertion of the Hindutva during the 80s and 90s contributed towards a different texture of India's foreign policy.

The other stream of pre-independence nationalism based on Muslim identity culminated into the partition of India and the birth of a new nation-state, Pakistan. The partition caused massive bloodshed on both sides. The large scale displacements, refugee flows, pain, miseries, all generated deep rooted psychic assault against the people of both countries. The problem of Kashmir has sustained itself as a 'burning site' of that great tragedy, partition. The question of Kashmir is the core determinant of relations between India and Pakistan and the elites of both these countries have been manipulating this issue for regime legitimacy. Indeed, nation-building is vexed with regime legitimacy of the ruling class.

The dawn of India, a new nation-state in the web of world nations was a period of drastic changes. The atomic horror, end of the World War, a shift in the world capitalist system towards American centrism, communist revolutions in Russia and China, the beginning of the Cold War, the de-colonization of many states of Asia and Africa and the beginning of a new age of international relations all highlighted the inevitability of newly emerging nations to engage with other nations. India's foreign policy was a mixture of idealism and real politic during the Cold-War, which owed itself to the ideas of the great independence struggle and the necessities of an infant nation-state.

Nehru, the architect of India's foreign policy, had absorbed lessons from the independence struggle and gently understood the complexities of international relations of his time. He moulded the foreign policy of India from his own experiences as a western educated intellectual and as one of the leaders of the freedom struggle. A recent book on India's foreign policy says, "The strategic culture influencing India's foreign policy under Nehru was-for all intents and purposes the strategic culture of Nehru" [Engelmeier 2009: 198]. We cannot discover Nehru as different from the constraints of a new nation. Nehru as a statesman was moulded by various factors which included power relations in the international system, the necessities of a new independent capitalist class in India, the legacies of the independence struggle, the ascendancy of socialist ideas at the international realm and most importantly his fascination with the modern western socio-economic development paradigm. However, the post-colonial elites of India confronted mainly two issues, (1) how to construct and sustain a nation in the pluralist Indian society, (2) how to put up legitimate foreign policy patterns which protect the interests of the nation.

The nationalist struggle created an ideological hegemony in the society. New terms like 'national development' and 'national security' had totalized the security thinking in India, especially in the post-colonial period. In contrast with Gandhi's visions on development, Nehru promulgated a new, modern, developmental nationalism which had a 'silencing effect' on the society. He envisaged a modern developed India with heavy industrialization and big dams which were labelled as 'temples of development'. Rightly speaking, he had simplified persisting social realities in India with an argument that the heavy industrialization would replace the caste and religious identities with class based identities. However, this developmental nationalism was preoccupied with the process of nation-building and owed itself to western modernity. Indeed, this process could not be detached from regime legitimacy of the ruling class.

Since independence, the foreign policy behaviour of India is intertwined with nationalist imaginations. The dominant nationalist ideology which evolved from the anti-colonial movement had a universal approach, which emphasized upon peace and prosperity of all nations. The foreign policy is a sphere by which the ruling class makes sure of legitimacy from the people and also seeks recognition from other nations of the world. During the Cold War, India had championed Non-Alignment as the basis of its foreign policy. It seems to be a strategically useful position not to join either of the camps of power politics and that added an aroma to India as a nation with a difference. There is a correlation between Nehruvian domestic politics and foreign politics-and that is consensual. On the domestic front, India adopted a mixed economy, ideologically, a liberal capitalist development with a socialist flavour and in foreign relations, it followed a consensual pattern which was ideologically and strategically suited to the new nation. However, the Nehruvian approach to foreign policy was more global than regional.

During the 1980s Nehruvian consensual politics lost its glamour, and the 'Congress System' failed to sustain its hegemony upon Indian society and politics. In this scenario, many groups in politics became prominent, which included movements of the deprived sections like lower caste groups, tribals, women etc. They questioned the very orthodoxy of conventional politics and some movements emerged as mass political movements threatening traditional hierarchies. However, the opening up to the global economic system and the overall developments in the international realm like the collapse of Soviet Communism generated a legitimacy crisis in the Indian socio-political system. In this situation India faced a foreign policy crisis also because India's promulgated Non- Aligned foreign policy behaviour was questioned and the socialist/planned economic system lost its relevance. The newly emergent forces within the society became a threat to the existing system as well as stumbling blocks on the path to better implementation of the neo-liberal policies. In this scenario, a new wave of Hindutva politics has emerged in the name of a 'true nationalist' party and has claimed to return the lost honour of India in the international realm. This seems to be a shift in India's foreign policy behaviour from the Nehruvian consensual pattern of politics towards an aggressive posture in foreign policy.

This 'aggressive foreign policy posture' of the BJP government is required to be seen from three important points; (1) regime legitimacy, (2) projected difference with the previous regimes (3) a display of its capacity of 'governance' to the world. The BJP government pursued a full-scale liberalization policy. As a result some kind of insecurity prevailed among the common psyche. At the same time, there was criticism from the Sangh family on the question of liberalization and in order to escape from this 'legitimacy crisis', the Sangh came out with its 'Security' project. Pratap Bhanu Mehta notes:

"The installation of a BJP led government at the centre was supposed to have a profound impact on at least one area of governance, defence. Here was a government committed to more self-confident and aggressive foreign policy posture, unencumbered by idealistic pieties in international relations, openly confrontational in its approach to Pakistan, and given to a shrill rhetoric of militarism. When India conducted its nuclear tests, many feared that it would be engulfed by a rising tide of militarism, a security obsession that would adversely affect its development priorities. The rhetorical postures of the government, its open commitment to 'coercive' diplomacy, and loose and wild talk threatening war, all seemed to signal the onset of a new militaristic state." (2003)

In a congratulatory letter addressing the Prime Minister of India AB Vajpayee, HV Sheshadri (Sarkayavah of the RSS) said, "...all the world has got a loud and clear message that India can no more be treated as a second or third rate nation now" (1998:3).

The celebration of a strong militaristic state and aggressive foreign policy posturing are reflections of the legitimacy crises of the ruling class. At the same time, the Vajpayee Government had pursued a full scale liberalization policy. The ruling class hoped that aggressive postures in foreign policy would bring some coherence to the society, which would smoothen the process of liberalization and privatization. However the threat perception of the Vajpayee government, positing 'China and Pakistan as major threat to India', created an insecurity complex in the region. L.K. Advani linked the nuclear explosions to the Kashmir issue and Fernandez, the Defence minister of the Vajpayee government, specifically commented that 'China is No.1 threat to India' (Bidwai & Vanaik 2001:55-6). This appears to be a major change in India's foreign policy from its old Non-Aligned posturing to an interest shown towards being a partner in the global US strategy.

The UPA government has moderated the confrontationalist foreign policy stance of the previous BJP led government and has fine tuned it to an acceptable level of cooperation. The managerial functions of the state with regards to the society/market have increased in the context of the integration process vis-à-vis the capitalist world system. In this process, state sovereignty has been eroded considerably and that has led to a rethinking on regional cooperation efforts. The newly emergent political climate in South Asia featuring a new wave towards democratization, has been contributing positively to renewed efforts at regional cooperation. The restoration of democracy in Pakistan, the end of the ethnic conflict in Sri Lanka and the developments in Nepal, are all contributing towards newer frontiers of friendship and cooperation. The UPA Government in India has retracted from its hard power approach that was followed by the previous NDA Government and has adopted a soft power approach towards its South Asian neighbours. This could definitely contribute towards regional cooperation. However, the disparities in power relations between India and her neighbours, bilateral issues and ethnically weakened boundaries are all standing in the way of closer South Asian integration. The growing urge for integrating the South Asian economy and knowledge of the contradictions within the system, brings forth new questions and dilemmas in foreign policy making.

**References**

Baral, Lok Raj (2009): Nepal: Political Dynamics and challenges, in Tan Tai Yong (ed), Socio-Political And Economic Challenges In South Asia, New Delhi : Sage.

Bidwai, Praful & Achin Vanaik (2001): "South Asia on a Short Fuse: nuclear Politics and the Future of Global Disarmament", New Delhi: Oxford University Press.

Dhakal, Ameet (2006): Nepal Maoists sign historical deal, The Hindu, Nov. 9.

Engelmeier, Tobias F., (2009): Nation-Building and Foreign Policy in India: An Identity-Strategy Conflict, Delhi: Foundation Books.

Golwalkar, MS (1939): We or Our Nationhood Defined, Nagpur: Bharat Publications.

Golwalkar, MS, (2000): Bunch of Thoughts, Bangalore: Sahitya Sindhu Prakasana.

Jha, Nalini Kant (2008): Domestic Turbulence in Nepal: Origin, Dimensions, and India's Policy options, in Veena Kukreja (2008).

Kloos, Peter: Sinhala and Tamil Youth Violence in Sri Lanka, in Momin [2009].

Krishna, Sankaran (2000): Post Colonial Insecurities: India, Sri Lanka, and the Question of Nationhood, New Delhi: Oxford University Press.

Kukreja, Veena & Mahendra Prasad Singh [2008]: 'Sri Lanka: To Federalize or Not to Federalize? in Veena Kukreja& Mahendra Prasad Singh, *Democracy, Development And Discontent In South Asia,* New Delhi: sage Publications.

Kukreja, Veena (2003): Contemporary Pakistan, Political Process, Conflicts and Crisis, New Delhi: Sage.

Kukreja, Veena (2008): Democracy and Authoritarianism in Bangladesh, in Kukreja (2008).

Mehta, Pratab Bhanu (2003: "Where is the strong defence? " The Hindu, June 26.

Mishra, R.C. [2000]: Security in South Asia: Cross Border Analysis, Delhi: Authors Press.

Momin, A.R. [2009]: *Diversity, Ethnicity and Identity in South Asia*, New Delhi: Rawat Publications.

Nag, Sajal (2001): Nationhood and Displacement in Indian Sub-continent, Economic and Political Weekly, December 22.

Phadins, Urmila [1986]: Ethnic Tensions in South Asia-Implications for Regional Cooperation in Bhabani Sen Gupta: *Regional cooperation and Development in South Asia: Political, Social, Technological and Resource Aspects*, Vol. 2, New Delhi: South Asian Publishers.

Phadins, Urmila& Rajat Ganguly [2001]: Ethnicity and Nation-Building in South Asia, New Delhi: Sage Publications.

Samad, Yunas: Pakistan or Punjabistan: Crisis of National Identity, in Momin [2009].

Savarkar, V.D (1984): Hindu Rashtra Darshan, Bombay: Veer Savarkar Prakashan.

Savarkar, VD (1942): Hindu Padashahi or a Review of the Hindu Empire of Maharashtra, Poona: Published by Manohar Mahadeo Kelkar.

Savarkar, VD (1989): Hindutva: Who is a Hindu, New Delhi: Bharati Sahitya Sadan.

Sehth, D.L [1989]: Building in Multi-Ethnic Societies: The Experience of South Asia, *Alternatives,* Vol. 3, No.4, October.

Sharma, Jyotirmaya (2003): Hindutva: Exploring the Idea of Hindu Nationalism, New Delhi: Penguin.

Sheshadri, HV (1998): "India can no more be treated as a Second rate nation", Organizer, Vol. XLIX, No. 43, May 24.

Sinha, Awadesh Coomar: Ethnic Engagement in Bhutan and Its Regional Consequences, in Veena Kukereja [2008].

Sukumaran Nair, P (1997): India and Bangladesh in 1990s, in Raman Pillai (ed), Indian Foreign Policy in the 1990s, New Delhi: Radiant Publishers.

Talbot, Ian (2003): Pakistan, A Modern History, New Delhi: Oxford India Paperbacks.

Varshney, Ashutosh [2002]: Ethnic Conflict and Civic Life, New Delhi: Oxford University Press.

# 17

# Conflicts and Co-operation on Trans-boundary Waters in South Asia

Deepa Karthykeyan

## Section I: Introduction

Water holds a vital place in the survival of a nation on account of being the only scarce resource with no substitutes. Rivers have cradled the birth of numerous civilizations and continue to be dynamic elements that permeate into every aspect of an individual's social, political, cultural and economic life. Traditional wisdom acknowledges this special and all-encompassing role played by water and encourages all stake holders to share and use the same on a sustainable basis.

However world water usage is 35 times higher today than just a few centuries ago and has grown twice as fast as world population in the twentieth century. [1] The rapid rise in industrialization and technological development on account of the increasing functional integration of the global economy has made nations lustful and short sighted making irresponsible exploitation of scarce resources the sovereign right of a state. This has led to the dilution of our traditional understanding of water and has instead replaced it with a neo-liberal statist one. The evolution of such a limited 'nation-centric' understanding of water is often seen as a direct product of the gradual world-wide depletion of natural resources like water. The rising demand for water complemented by the relatively unchanging supply of the same compels nations to pre-dominantly focus on the role of water as a mere input in the growth process of an economy. This contributes to the polarization of popular opinion that continues to place the use of natural resources and economic development as incompatible opposites. Wendell Berry in his piece 'Getting along with nature' points out to the irony of this polarization. Here he states, "*the defenders of nature and wilderness- like their enemies the defenders of the industrial economy – sometimes sound as if the natural and the human were two separate estates, radically different and radically divided. The defenders of nature and wilderness sometimes seem to feel that they must oppose any human encroachment whatsoever, just as the industrialists often apparently feel that they must make the human encroachment absolute or, as they say 'complete the conquest of nature'. But there is danger in this opposition, and it can be best dealt with by realizing that these pure and separate categories are pure ideas and do not otherwise exist".* [2]

The evolution of such a narrow approach to the development and use of water sacrifices the cultural, social and environmental dimensions of the same at the altar of economic progress. This may disrupt and destabilize the delicate social fabric that continues to evolve around the usage of water. The connection between water and society is a complex historical, sociological and regional one, providing the centre piece for social theories of civilization and state, community and collective action, culture and prosperity. [3] Every river along with its silt carries with it the histories of millions of men, women and children whose lives continue to be intertwined with it. They implicitly encourage people to forget their differences and co-operate to fulfil their needs. The number of co-operative incidents on water sharing that outnumbers the conflicts stands as a testimony to this strange yet beautiful tendency of water to unite even while it divides. Sadly a state led definition of development, does not reflect this harmony, making the discourse on water sharing a minimalist one that ignores the cultural and social aspects. Explaining the phenomenon Ramaswamy. R. Iyer states, "W*hat lies at the heart of water conflict is greed....Agreements, accords and treaties may temporarily bring peace, but conflict will erupt unless we learn to redefine development".* [4]

Thus a development led 'state-centric' understanding of an extremely dynamic concept like water which has no regard for boundaries makes the sharing of international rivers in a manner that is both equitable and sustainable, a difficult proposition. Most actors involved in the process of evolving a framework for the sharing of international waters often find themselves in a political quagmire on account of a narrow 'nationalistic' view that predominates the discourse on sharing common rivers.

This is all the more manifest in the context of South Asia as issues of trans-boundary water sharing continue to be seen with the narrow lens of 'sovereignty'. The tense political atmosphere in South Asia that dominates individual and collective interests of the region tends to further perpetuate these state-led misconceptions associated with water use and development. The political space amongst the nations in South Asia is one defined by hostility and a long history of political rivalry.

The shift in political boundaries that followed partition had a disrupting influence on the historical continuity and the geographical contiguity of the territories within the region, making political relations that persist between India and her neighbours, one of mutual suspicion and hatred (with the exception of

Bhutan). This has reinforced the state-led militaristic discourse on water in the region.

An attempt is made in this paper to trace the political and economic bottlenecks that prevent a peaceful sharing of trans-boundary water resources within South Asia. It takes a brief look into the history of water disputes in South Asia, the treaties that were signed, the difficulties encountered and a critical understanding of the solutions put forth with a special emphasis on the Ganges Water Treaty. Section II of the paper begins by providing a brief background to trans-boundary water sharing in South Asia with some emphasis on the Indus and Mahakali rivers.

This might provide us with a good template to enable a comparative understanding of the various issues of conflict and cooperation on trans-boundary water sharing in the region. A detailed description of the events that culminated in the signing of the Ganges Water Treaty along with its major features is discussed in Section III. Section IV critically analyzes the role of good water economics and politics in establishing cordial relations between India and her neighbours in South Asia. Section V briefly summarizes the conclusions.

**Section II: Background on Trans-Boundary Water Sharing in South Asia**

The Northern part of the Indian sub-continent in South Asia consists of two major water systems that commonly originate in the Himalayas and are trans-boundary in nature. For almost half the world's population, water-related dreams and fears intersect in the Himalayas and the Tibetan plateau. [5] On the Western side of this region, is the Indus river system with its extensive network of tributaries namely the Ravi, Beas, Sutlej, Chenab and Jhelum that begin in Tibet and flows out into the Arabian Sea near the Karachi port. On the Eastern side one finds the Ganga-Brahmaputra-Meghna river system that is commonly shared among Nepal, Bangladesh and India and supports the largest number of the world's poor in one region. The Indus river system in the West finds its origin in the Tibetan plateau in the vicinity of China, runs a course through the Ladakh district of Jammu and Kashmir, and finally merges into the Arabian Sea near Pakistan's port city of Karachi.

The water dispute over the sharing of the Indus traces its origin to the extensive development of irrigated agriculture in the undivided Punjab basin. While partition disrupted the consolidated development of irrigation, the dispute over water sharing in the North Western region contrary to popular perception was not a direct result of partition but preceded it. A notable example of this phenomenon was the dispute between the provinces of Sind and Punjab as early as 1935. [6] The Indian Independence Act of 1947 created the State of Pakistan and merely internationalized the dispute adding a 'statist' element to the already complex problems of water sharing.

The major bone of contention over the use of the Indus waters in the West revolved around the strong dependence of both the newly formed nations on man-made irrigation projects as the major source of water supply, given the semi-arid climate of these regions. Initially in the absence of any agreements, any effort at diverting water to maintain the irrigation works in the Indian region automatically reduced water flow to Pakistan. This fuelled the already growing discontent amongst Pakistanis against India, the upper-riparian state and a regional rival.

**Indus Water Treaty**

In 1948 a 'Stand Still Agreement' was signed between the two riparian countries. In accordance with this Agreement, while India conceded to release waters to Pakistan it maintained that Pakistan could not claim any share of the waters as a matter of right. Pakistan highly displeased with such a legal status quo pushed for a more equitable distribution of all the common rivers. This culminated in the signing of the Indus Water Treaty on September 19, 1960 with the active intervention of the World Bank. The water sharing formula prescribed by this Treaty was quite simple, three Western rivers namely, Chenab, Jhelum and the Indus were allocated to Pakistan and the three Eastern rivers, the Ravi, Beas and Sutlej were given to India. The treaty also provided for an Indus River Commission with representatives from both Pakistan and India. It was responsible for periodical exchange of data and resolution of disputes if any.

The powers of upper-riparian India were restricted through the insertion of conditions in the Treaty. The World Bank also provided the two parties with enormous financial assistance to develop their rivers for non-consumptive purposes as long as they fell in line with the conditions laid out by the Treaty. This helped to ease Pakistan's insecurity vis-à-vis India and provided a strong base for cooperation.

**Lessons**

The Indus Water treaty of 1960 is often cited as an example of bilateral cooperation even when conflicting situations exist. This Treaty despite all its shortcomings set a precedent for the amicable sharing of water resources in South Asia. While power inequities and political antagonism do continue to slow down the process of negotiation, a full-fledged confrontation between the two nations on the water front has not been witnessed. This again does not imply that the Indus Water Treaty has been successful in preventing the two nations from engaging in water disputes. There are certain contentious issues that keep coming up on the political scene like the Salal hydro-electric project in Jammu and Kashmir, the Tulbul project (known as the Wular Barrage in Pakistan) and more recently the Kalabagh controversy. These remain unresolved on account of the lack of a comprehensive dialogue between the nations on the issue of trans-boundary water sharing and a concerted national policy on assessing the human and environmental impacts of large supply side-interventions through the construction of dams. The Indus Water Treaty is also often criticized for being a sub-optimal solution that disregards principles of integrated water management. However despite these short comings one cannot marginalize the important role played by the Indus Water Treaty as it continues to be an interesting template to compare and contrast other water treaties in the South Asian region.

**Sharing the Mahakali**

Now turning to the East, we have the Ganga-Bramhaputra-Meghna basin. This system of rivers cuts across China, Nepal India, and Bangladesh. Nepal shares with India a total of 264 rivers all of which form a major part of the Ganges system. It occupies around 13 percent of the Ganges basin and supplies almost 47 percent of its water. [7]

While statements such as 'water is to Nepal as oil is to the Arabs' tends to distort the Nepali water reality, the rivers that emanate from the Himalayan region and flow down the mountains of Nepal do have a tremendous potential for generating 'hydro-electric' power and is the chief earner of foreign exchange for the country.

The case of trans-boundary water sharing between India and Nepal serves as a good template to understand the dynamics of formulating a comprehensive water treaty in the presence of geographical and power asymmetries between countries. The development and use of the Mahakali river (known as Sarada in India), a boundary river is an interesting one on account of a set of unique features that characterize it.

Firstly in the context of the Mahakali water dispute, Nepal is the upper riparian and holds a geographical advantage vis-à-vis India, while India is far more superior to Nepal in terms of economic and military strength. The water dispute over the Mahakali river provides an interesting case as the lower riparian, here India, being militarily more powerful did not resort to military coercion against Nepal as Israel did against the Arab countries.

Secondly the issue of sharing a trans-boundary river basin between India and Nepal is not one based on the actual volumetric division of the river but on the question of cooperation on deriving the benefits from the water resources by way of hydro-electricity, flood control, irrigation etc. [8] This makes the allocation of the economic benefits of sharing between the two countries relatively more simple than the actual volumetric division of the river by itself.

Finally, these countries unlike India and Pakistan share a relatively less difficult political situation as the two nations have been integrated economically for most of the last 60 years. This integration has made cooperation relatively less cumbersome in the context of Indo-Nepal bilateral relations. However despite these favourable political and economic conditions, inter-state interaction between the two countries has not been without hiccups and low periods. Nepal being a nation sandwiched between two giants (namely India and China) is always a little wary of getting too close to one or the other.

**Treaties**

The Sarada barrage project along with the two Kosi and Gandak treaties that were signed in 1920, 1964 and 1966 respectively were controversial. The Government of Nepal alleged that the Indian Government conferred substantially more benefits on India than on Nepal. [9] Moreover the Tanakpur barrage controversy that used a small (577m) portion of Nepalese territory to construct an eastern afflux bund raised questions of internal sovereignty and adequate compensation amongst the Nepali opposition. Between 1976 and 1996, efforts were made to meet Nepal's needs in terms of 'equity' over the Tanakpur Barrage and the potential Pancheshwar Dam. The Mahakali treaty was finally signed in 1996 between his Majesty's Government of Nepal and the Government of India to bring about the integrated development of the Mahakali. This treaty was concerned with the operation and augmentation of two existing facilities namely the Sarada Barrage and the Tanakpur barrage and the future construction of a large multi-purpose dam, the Pancheshwar project.

A closer look at the various aspects of the treaty brings out the subtle additions that have been made to the treaty to accommodate the special needs of both countries. The Mahakali treaty is equitable in terms of power generation at Pancheshwar and contains modest consideration for in-stream flows. It takes into account seasonal variability and provides for a joint river commission with strong recommendation powers 'guided by the principles of equity, mutual benefit and no harm to either party'. It also has a meaningful dispute resolution mechanism and is accommodating with respect to local users and their water needs. It is also somewhat flexible in that either party is able to demand a review of allocations at 10-year intervals, and is supposed to be in effect for 75 years upon ratification. [10] Amongst other things, the Mahakali Treaty called for the creation of the Mahakali River Commission (MCR). [11]

The Mahakali Treaty continues to be a well drafted piece of literature on trans-boundary water sharing however with little or no impact on the integrated development and usage of the Mahakali River. The construction of Pancheshwar, the highest dam in South Asia continues to be embedded in controversy on account of the environmental and human impacts of the same. The absence of bilateral dialogue on the issue of Kalapani, a disputed territory between India and Nepal and internal political instability within Nepal caused by the Maoist insurgents has further deepened the rift between the two nations making the dialogue of cooperation on the water front a painfully slow one.

While the sharing of the Indus and the Mahakali waters both provide scope for improvement and better engagement, they are relatively less complex when compared to the difficulties involved in the sharing of the Ganges-Meghna system between India and Bangladesh.

**Section III: Ganges Water Treaty: The Farakka Controversy**

With about a hundred urban settlements on its banks and a population of more than 120 million people, the Ganga is the longest river in India and one of the most important rivers in South Asia. The river by virtue of its strong mythical connections to various Indian God heads has evolved to acquire a deep cultural and social content that goes beyond its utilitarian one. Taking the example of the Ganga, Ajaya Dixit points out that, "*For the present day Bangladeshi, Nepali, Sri Lankan, Pakistani, or Indian, the Ganga is a denominative absolute, be it the Burhi Ganga of Bangladesh, the Trisuli Ganga of Nepal, the Mahaweli Ganga of Sri Lanka, the Sindhu Ganga of Pakistan, or the Cauvery Ganga of peninsular India. The Trisuli Ganga hurtling past the gorge evokes in the Nepali villager the same sentiment as the Ganga entering from upstream to join the Bay of Bengal does in the Bangladeshi farmer*". [12]

Such is the power of the Ganges to unite a people divided by culture, religion, race, territory and various other man-made boundaries. Despite the cultural and social connotations associated with this river, the sharing of its waters continues to be a bone of contention between India and Bangladesh. There are fifty-four rivers and streams that cross the Indo-Bangladesh border. The partitioning of Bengal (into West Bengal and East Pakistan, later to declare independence as Bangladesh) by the Radcliffe line in effect divided the delta region of the Ganga basin, severing river networks of the Ganga, Brahmaputra and Meghna, and leaving Bangladesh with little control over fifty-four of its rivers. The careless partition of the Bengal region into the Indian state of West Bengal and East Pakistan(now Bangladesh) complicated by the anti-Indian overtones of Bengali nationalism added to the already complex problems of trans-boundary water sharing.

Thus along with the traditional problems associated with upper and lower riparian claims, the two nations also faced regional pressures driven by domestic politics against cooperation with one another. To understand the political and technological nuances of the dispute one must begin with a reiteration of the various historical events that culminated in the formulation of the treaty.

**History**

The dispute over the sharing of the Ganges waters like most other problems that plague the Indian sub-continent, traces its roots way back to the colonial period in late nineteenth century, when Calcutta (now Kolkata) port was first established in 1890. The tendencies of the river to migrate eastwards near the Hooghly-Bhagirathi basin added to the large deposits of silt that continued to get accumulated on the river bed. The decision to build a barrage at Farakka near the Indo-Bangladesh Border was first made in 1951. The barrage was to have a length of 7363 ft, and was designed for a maximum design discharge of 27, 00,000 cusec and had a head regulator with a diversion capacity of 40,000 cusec flow to enhance the navigability of the Hooghly. [13] Protests against the construction of such a barrage by Bangladesh (erstwhile East Pakistan) were initially drowned by the Indian claim that such concerns were only hypothetical given the preliminary stage of the Farakka project proposal.

Official meetings on the issue only began between the two countries in 1960. Till then India saw the usage and development of the Ganges as a pre-dominantly Indian affair. Meetings continued until 1970 without much progress. Failure by the two nations to resolve the issue peacefully led Bangladesh to raise the issue of Ganges water sharing in the UN General Assembly session in 1976. Confronting adverse international opinion, India finally signed an *ad hoc* agreement for 5 years on Ganges water sharing in 1977 .The basic principles of 1977 agreement included dividing the lean period water flow from January 1 to May 31 into 15 slots having ten days each. The sharing was supposed to be on the basis of 75 percent of the dependable flow at Farakka from 1948 to 1973 and the sharing proportion of Bangladesh and India was 60:40 respectively with a minimum flow of 34,500 for Bangladesh and 20,500 cusec for India. In the case of a decrease in flow at Farakka under extreme situations, Bangladesh was guaranteed with 80 percent of its share during each of the slots.

The 1977 Agreement expired in 1982 and India refused to extend it. The then military ruler General Ershad succumbed to mounting Indian pressure and signed a MOU scrapping the 1977 agreement where the interest of Bangladesh was compromised and the guarantee clause was excluded. The MOU signed in 1982 expired in 1985 and was extended to 1988 through two other similar extensions. However 1989 onwards India refused to come to any deal with Bangladesh on the sharing of the Ganges waters.

It was only in 1996 with the installation of a new government in Bangladesh under the stewardship of Sheikh Hasina Wajid did the negotiations on the water sharing front begin. Finally an agreement was reached and the Ganges Water Treaty was signed by the two countries on December 12, 1996. The basic principles of the Treaty included calculating the flow at Farakka on the basis of the average flow for the period from1948 to 1988. The proportion of sharing between the two countries was now fixed at a ratio of 45:55 generally and 30:70 in some cases. During the period from March 1 to May 31 the sharing was on the basis of a hydraulic cycle. Here when one side had a guaranteed flow of 35000 cusec, the other side received the rest of the flow. In such a cycle when the flow is 50,000 cusec, India will receive 35,000 cusec and Bangladesh will receive only 15000 cusec. However, when the flow falls below 50,000 cusec no sharing principle will exist, and Bangladesh and India might have to meet and negotiate a settlement on the equitable sharing of the river.

The Ganges Water Treaty has been functioning fairly smoothly for several lean season periods (except the 1997 period when the downstream water flow reached its all time low) and focuses on the volumetric division of the water resources to share the burden of lean season flow in the Ganges. While the Ganges Water Treaty attempts to address some of the major problems associated with the lean season availability and sharing of water between the two nations, to regard the whole dispute as having wholly disappeared would be a mistake.

While division of resources in the short-run has been settled, the two nations are beginning to embark on an ambitious strategy to augment the dwindling water levels in the Ganges basin in the long run. This has led to yet another impasse on the sharing and management of the Ganges waters. The two countries have not been able to amicably arrive at mutual consensus on the means through which such an augmentation program must take place. The Indian proposal to augment the water-short Ganga is mainly through the construction of a link-canal between the Ganga and Brahmaputra Rivers from Jogighopa to Farakka, running right through Bangladesh, while Bangladesh instead proposes to use the storage capacities of the numerous dams in Nepal.

Beyond the issues of augmenting the rivers, there are also issues of sharing and management on other rivers namely the Teesta River on which a sharing agreement has become a matter of urgency as both India and Bangladesh have barrages on the river and are beginning to develop irrigation in their respective commands. [14] Similarly the construction of the Tipaimukh dam on the Barak

River which forms a part of the Meghna system has also attracted a lot of controversy over failing diplomatic relations between the two states and the environmental and human impact that might follow such a large supply-side intervention.

These new and more complex issues on the sharing of the Ganges can be summarized in the words of Binayak Ray. Ray traces the problem of water-sharing between the two neighbours to three factors: one real, second perceived and third practical. First, the Indo-Bangladesh river basin has the largest concentration of world's poorest people with a high rural population density, making water an extremely sensitive political issue. Second, Bangladesh being the smaller neighbour often treats India with suspicion, making it difficult to conduct discussion on common interest issues in good faith. Third, the large number of riparian countries involved in the processes of multilateral diplomacy and negotiation further entrenches the difficulties involved in arriving at an agreement and complicates processes. [15]

Given the mutual interplay of these various complex factors, one needs to identify specific bottlenecks that stall the negotiation process and identify the role played by good water economics and politics in easing even if not resolving the current stale mate.

**Section IV: Good Water Economics**

Water possesses certain unique features that tend to make its management a special affair in economics. While applying theories of economics, water is often seen as neither a public nor a private good on account of two fundamental attributes that are often associated with water. The first one is in allusion to its property of 'non-excludability' as water (unlike certain other resources such as oil) flows across boundaries, making it difficult if not impossible to assign property rights on the same. Moreover water while non-excludable is subject to competition and rivalry, disqualifying it from assuming the status of a public good which are in general assumed to be non rival. This ambiguity often associated with the nature of water has led to the understanding of it as a common pool resource [16] whose economic implications entail a situation of finite and often stochastic supply of water combined by a rising and often exaggerated demand.

The unfinished debate on water as a private and public good thus precludes pure market-based solutions and creates problems of allocation as the indiscriminate use of such a finite common resource by one riparian will necessarily diminish the benefits accrued to the others. Taking the example of the Indo-Bangladesh dispute on the sharing of the Ganges waters and the provisions of the Ganges water treaty one can notice that these unique attributes of water have been sidelined. By setting a fixed volumetric bench mark on the division and sharing of the river, the treaty ignores the highly stochastic and unpredictable shifts in the supply component. This is seen in the formulas provided in Annexure I and II where conclusions based on the fairness of the treaty are based on comparisons made between the actual water flow into Bangladesh and average flow set in the treaty over a certain period of time. [17] The crucial assumption here lies in the equalization of 'average flows' to 'expected flows' which might lead to erroneous conclusions on the fairness of the treaty often projecting India as a 'bully state' for no fault of hers.

Another problem with the formulation of large supply led interventions to store, augment or divert waters from a river is the lack of sufficient scientific studies to understand the linkages between the various uses of water that might be derived by the construction of a dam or a barrage. Water unlike most commodities is used by a large number of users, and a variety of uses over various geographical areas. The *raison d'etre* behind the Farakka barrage was to enhance the navigability of the Kolkata port and reduce the salinity levels in the water used for drinking and industrial purposes. The irrigational advantages that went with the diversion of the river were only an added incentive. Today the increased sedimentation of the Hooghly-Bhagirathi basin despite the diversion of waters from the Ganges through a feeder canal has made the Kolkata port inefficient for the handling of large cargo. Most of the heavy cargo is now carried through the Haldia dock complex which is around 104 kilometres downstream from Kolkata. The irrigational incentives that accrue from this diversion however cannot stand out as the *raison d'etre* for the barrage as there are much less controversial and cheaper alternatives to irrigate the districts of West Bengal that fall along the area that is currently being irrigated with the water diverted from Farakka. This shows the lack of a scientific and comprehensive analysis of supply led interventions in the form of dams and barrages and the weak linkage between the various uses accrued from the same. This might often result in the escalation of the operation and maintenance costs of the project while the overall benefits accrued to the system of users from the same may be minimal, thereby defeating the very purpose of its existence. However, now given that the construction of the barrage cannot be reversed, one needs to look beyond its presence and focus on effective demand-led management of domestic and trans-boundary water resource. A demand driven water management policy will reduce the reliance of these countries on mammoth supply led interventions that are often expensive and possess massive human and environmental repercussions.

However demand-led water policies are harder to sell politically both within the nation and among states. Water is often considered an inalienable right which should be made freely available to all citizens by governments. Given this general mindset amongst the people in South Asia, the evolution of a strong formal/informal market for water while not absent is very slow and highly unorganized in India.

The absence of comprehensive water laws and high transaction costs also prevents the evolution of an efficient price mechanism to allocate scarce resources. Alternative demand-driven policies however include taking a closer look at the actual demand for water as against the demand projected by nations. Structural shifts in the demand for water through the usage of more efficient and less water consuming varieties of paddy in the West Bengal and Bangladesh basin and the adoption of better patterns of irrigation might help reduce the often exaggerated projection of the water demanded. International financial institutions like the World Bank and the Asia Development Bank must facilitate the development of such irrigation and agricultural projects.

Sadly, despite the availability of sound demand led alternatives the lack of political will to implement demand-led water management policies on account of domestic political compulsions to sustain party regimes and the multiplicity of laws that guide water management within states have contributed to the current crisis in the sharing of both trans-boundary and intra-state water resources. The national water policy of 2002, while a huge improvement over the previous draft of 1987, still does not address the problems associated with the highly segmented, overlapping and cumbersome atmosphere of regulations that guide the management of water resources in India.

Moreover these domestic policies however are only necessary but not sufficient conditions in defeating the 'Water Wars' prophesy of Boutros Boutros Ghali. To extend the benefits of an efficient domestic water management system to a more peaceful sharing of trans-boundary waters India needs to take a more pro-active stance in terms of formulating its foreign policy vis-à-vis its regional neighbours. Diplomatic engagement on the water resource front can yield enormous economic gains to all parties involved and bring about the sustainable development of the entire water basin as an integrated whole.

India must convince her neighbours about the vast economic benefits that may be reaped through regional or sub-regional cooperation on trans-boundary water sharing. For example Nepal has tremendous potential to generate hydroelectric power and the sale of power to energy starved India would help Nepal generate wealth beyond its dreams. Similarly sub-regional cooperation with Bangladesh on the Ganga-Brahmaputra-Meghna basin would help tap the benefits of inland water transport for purposes of industry, commerce and help uplift the lives of millions of people who live by the banks. Moreover through cooperation, Assam's famed tea could be shipped downstream to Bangladesh and sent to other parts of the world. Oil from the Numaligarh refinery, also in Assam, can be exported in river barges to meet Bangladesh's energy needs. These simple but effective measures might help provide access to important Bangladeshi transit routes and might help strengthen connections between India's seven isolated North Eastern states with the ports of Kolkata in India and Chittagong in Bangladesh. This would generate employment and revive the economies of marginalized communities. [18] These economic incentives could further promote cooperation on the sharing and usage of the trans-boundary water resources setting. However despite the significant role played by economics in Hydro-diplomacy, the absence of a congenial political environment acts as an obstacle to regional cooperation.

**Good Water Politics**

There is growing international consensus on the idea that 'good water economics' would automatically lead to 'good water politics'. However in South Asia any attempt to apply principles of economics to trans-boundary water sharing pre-supposes political stability. The domestic politics within nations in the region play a significant role in determining inter-state relations. Again taking the example of India-Bangladesh relations on the question of trans-boundary sharing of water, one observes the massive politicization of water within both nations and all the more so in the case of Bangladesh. In fact the decisions made by the two nations in the negotiation process shows that Bangladesh and India might have even gone to the extent of keeping the water disputes alive for internal political reasons. Moreover the waning of Sino-Soviet rivalry, the strengthening of Bangladeshi ties with China and Pakistan's acquisition of nuclear weapons-making capabilities, have added to Bangladesh's problems of finding a rational solution to security issues.

The unfortunate story of antagonism between the two riparian countries and the passive/reactive stance adopted by India in the formulation of its foreign policy have added to the difficulties involved in water sharing amongst the two nations. This can be traced by taking a look at the various exchanges that took place between the two governments around the Farakka issue. The Farakka barrage first conceived by the then Prime Minister Nehru, was never seen as an issue that involved Bangladesh as the Ganges was never construed as a trans-boundary river but an Indian one, giving the Indian state complete jurisdiction over its use and development. Protests from Bangladesh (then East Pakistan) resulted in the breaking of that illusion and talks between the two states officially began in 1960 and continued till 1970 without any real progress. In 1971, talks were suspended when the East Bengali political forces under the Awami League initiated a separatist movement that culminated in the separation and independence of East Pakistan later renamed as Bangladesh. Initially Bangladesh's independence from Pakistan signalled an era of good relations between the two nations, but the issue of sharing the Ganges continued to be excluded and was only taken up at the Prime Ministerial level in 1974. By 1975 the construction of the barrage was completed and became operational. This coincided with the victory of the Awami League and the election of Mujibur Rahman, a pro-Indian leader. He initially agreed to the operation of the barrage in May 1975 on trial basis for a period of 41 days to assess the impact of such a diversion on both nations. However Mujib's assassination on August 15, 1975 put the clock back. His death was followed by a turbulent phase of coups and counter coups and worsening relations between Dhaka and New Delhi.

It was only in 1977 that a new phase in this inter-state dispute was initiated with a shift in the foreign policy strategy of India on account of the formation of a new government at the centre led by Morarji Desai. [19] This led to the signing of the Ganges Water Agreement along with its 80 percent guarantee clause for a period of five years. The next change in relations between the two countries arose in 1985 when Rajiv Gandhi initiated steps that led to a MOU for sharing water in the lean season, with Bangladesh receiving a falling share of dry season flows. The agreement was valid till 1988, and after the stipulated period, no efforts were made to renew the agreement or extend it. In the absence of any progress the BNP-led coalition government attempted to internationalize the issue, raising it in the UN General Assembly and the Commonwealth Summit in 1993. Mounting international pressure, change of central government in India, the concerted efforts of I.K Gujral along with the then West Bengal chief minister Jyoti Basu and the victory of a relatively more pro-Indian government in Bangladesh led by Sheikh Hasina, all culminated in the signing of the Ganges Water Treaty in 1996.

A quick glimpse at the sequence of events that led to the signing of the Ganges Water Treaty points to the emergence of certain new trends in the understanding of security within South Asia.

Firstly while an oversimplified 'nationalistic' view on issues of trans-boundary water continues to guide the bureaucratic and political processes in both countries, there has been a slow yet nuanced shift in the understanding of what beholds security amongst the fellow riparian countries. This has led nations to place greater weight on the non-traditional threats to security like terrorism, environmental degradation and illegal migration in the formulation of their foreign policy.

Secondly while countries like India still tend to over-emphasize the need for a bilateral process of negotiation, the role played by Track II diplomacy in overcoming mutual hatred through facilitatory efforts at both official and non-official levels is gaining popularity to arrive at political rather than technocratic settlements between nations. The recent support extended by the Indian Government to Bangladesh in the Wake of Cyclone Sidr, and its decision to lift the ban on the export of five lakh tons of rice to Bangladesh and adopt ten severely affected villages for rehabilitation entails a strong step in this direction. Apart from this, efforts are also being made by several Non-Governmental Organizations and Agencies of Governments to tap on the multi-faceted historical relationship and the common values shared between the two nations to strengthen cooperation on a range of areas.

Thirdly the fact that a sustainable arrangement was arrived at with the signing of the Ganges Water Treaty (despite its shortcomings) by the two nations on account of changing domestic politics recognizes the fundamental underlying truth that 'it is not always a case of conflicts over water that worsen political relationships but on the contrary it is more a case of a difficult political relationship that renders water disputes more intractable'. [20] This therefore places a tremendous amount of pressure on nations to establish 'good water politics' as the foundation for constructing the edifice of 'good water economics' which might often in turn reinforce better political relations between nations leading to the conscious internalization of domestic politics into the dialogue on trans-boundary water sharing through diplomatic engagement.

Finally, a closer look at the various events that culminated in the signing of the various water treaties in South Asia show the need for a broader and a more flexible understanding of what constitutes sovereignty. The revision of a state-led militaristic discourse on water to accommodate the complex and dynamic nature of trans-boundary rivers will encourage nations within the region to manage and develop the entire water body as a single integrated whole. Closer linkages between nations through the exchange of economic, political and cultural ideas would help to make these boundaries less sacrosanct. The establishment of a window to facilitate trans-boundary water sharing within the SAARC might even actually help facilitate this exchange and strengthen linkages.

A sub-regional or regional approach to the management of water basins thus holds tremendous potential for the resolution of non-conventional threats to security. A sustainable solution to the ongoing water disputes might even provide countries with a strong premise to solve the problems of illegal migration across the porous borders between India and Bangladesh. This will in turn act as a confidence building measure that might even assuage Bangladesh into allying with India to combat cross-border terrorism and other issues that continue to destabilize India from within.

**Section V: Conclusion**

The complex orientation of the rivers in South Asia that cuts across a number of countries in the region complemented by a tense and uncompromising political situation amongst the fellow riparian countries brings out the strategic role played by 'water' in the region. The growing body of literature on conflicts over scarce water resources and their 'security implications' point out to the growing significance of such a 'water-led' discourse in the foreign policy formulation of countries. While India has conventionally preferred a bilateral approach in dealing with its neighbours on issues of sharing trans-boundary waters, such a stance will make it increasingly difficult for India to negotiate sustainable solutions with her neighbours on areas of common interest. This does not imply that a multi-lateral or regional approach, on account of being the next best alternative, is the only way to attain sustainable solutions in all circumstances. A diligent understanding of the necessary diplomatic tools, whether bilateral or multilateral in nature, should be employed by India by de-linking herself from a 'one size fits all' attitude in the formulation of her policies with respect to neighbouring countries.

To arrive at a pragmatic solution to inter-state water disputes India must thus overcome her 'statist' hangover in the formulation of her foreign policy stance and accommodate various conventional and unconventional alternatives to deal with her fellow riparian countries so as to enable the efficient and sustainable sharing of trans-boundary waters in South Asia as Water by its very nature should help dissolve boundaries not create them.

**Notes**

1. Joshua. S. Goldstein, *International Relations,* 5th edition , (New York, 2004), p. 436.
2. Wendell Berry, "Getting Along With Nature", in *Home Economics*, 1st Ed. (San Francisco, 1987), p. 6.
3. Kuntala Lahiri-Dutt, "Introduction: Placing Water First", in *Water First: Issues and Challenges for Nations and Communities in South Asia*, Kuntala Lahiri-Dutt and Robert J. Wasson, Ed. (New Delhi, 2008), p. xx.
4. Ramaswamy Iyer, "Trans-boundary Water Conflicts: A Review", in *Water Conflicts in India: a Million Revolts in the Making,* Joy, Gujja, Paranjape, Gould and Vispute, ed. (New Delhi, 2008), p. 375.
5. Kenneth Pomeranz, "The Great Himalayan Water shed: Agrarian Crisis, Mega Dams and the Environment", *New Left Review*, vol. 58, July-August 2009.
6. Aaron.T. Wolf and Joshua.T. Newton, " Case Study of Trans-boundary Dispute Resolution: The Ganges River Controversy".

7. Glen Hearns, "The Mahakali River Treaty: Applying a New Lens to Past Efforts for Future Success", in *Natural resources security in South Asia: Nepal's Water,* Fiona Rotberg and Ashok Swain, Ed. (Stockholm, 2007), p. 143.
8. Ramaswamy. R. Iyer, "Conflict Resolution: Three River Treaties", *Economic and Political Weekly*, vol. 34, Jun. 12-18, 1999, p. 1510.
9. According to India observers however the Nepali allegation was not a reasonable claim given the vast difference in irrigation and power demand between the two countries.
10. Glen Hearns, "The Mahakali River Treaty: Applying a New Lens to Past Efforts for Future Success", in *Natural Resources Security in South Asia: Nepal's Water,* Fiona Rotberg and Ashok Swain, Ed. (Stockholm, 2007), p. 144.
11. Despite Indian initiatives in 1997, the Mahakali River Commission is yet to be created.
12. Ajaya Dixit, "Rivers of Collective Belonging," Essay, *Himal South Asia*, Kathmandu, August 2003.
13. Ganges Water Sharing Treaty - A Critical Evaluation, Compiled and Edited by the Engineers Association of Bangladesh, (Dhaka, 1997).
14. Ramaswamy. R. Iyer , Conflict Resolution: Three River Treaties, *Economic and Political Weekly*, vol. 34, Jun. 12-18, 1999, p. 1514.
15. Binayak Ray, "Global Conventions and Regulations on International Rivers: Implications for South Asia", in *Water first: Issues and Challenges for Nations and Communities in South Asia*, Kuntala Lahiri-Dutt and Robert. J. Wasson, Ed. (New Delhi, 2008), p. 84.
16. Jasper. M. Dalhuisen, Henri. L.F. De Groot and Peter Nijkamp, "Economics of Water : A Survey of Issues", *International Journal of Development Planning Literature*, (Netherlands, 1999), Available: https://www.researchgate.net/publication/4794732_The_economics_of_water__a_survey_of_issues
17. Ramaswamy. R. Iyer, "Conflict Resolution: Three River Treaties" ,*Economic and Political weekly*, vol. 34, Jun. 12-18, 1999, p. 1515.
18. Sanjoy Hazarika, "South Asia: Sharing the Giants, Water Sharing of Indus, Ganges and Brahmaputra Rivers." *UNESCO Courier*, (October, 2001).
19. Douglas Hill, "The Regional Politics of Water Sharing: Contemporary Issues in South Asia", in *Water first issues and challenges for nations and communities in South Asia*, Kuntala Lahiri-Dutt and Robert J. Wasson, ed. (New Delhi, 2008), p. 71.
20. Ramaswamy. R. Iyer, Conflict Resolution: Three River Treaties, *Economic and Political Weekly*, vol. 34, Jun. 12-18, 1999, p. 1516.

# 18

# Regional Integration in South Asia: Reflections on EC/EU Paradigm

Jayaraj Amin

South Asia, comprising about 20 percent of global population and 2.7 percent of world area but only about 2 percent of world GNP was conspicuous due to the absence of a regional organisation until mid- 1980's. After its inception in 1985 the South Asian Association for Regional Cooperation (SAARC), the only regional organisation of South Asia, has made progress in some areas; yet the overall situation of South Asia has constrained its pace. It has not assumed a central role in South Asia either as a conflict resolution body harmonising differing perspectives of member states or as a springboard for the economic progress of the region. In other words, SAARC is yet to emerge as a visible entity in the developmental agendas of member states.

The tardy progress of SAARC has not proved beneficial to the region or to member states. Elsewhere, most countries and regions of the world have sought to protect their interests through a regional cooperative endeavour when confronted by common challenges. But in South Asia internal bickering is so intense despite apparent conciliatory moves that they find it hard to accept common moves at the regional level as a useful leverage to face common problems. The national interest defined in realist terms and the accompanying tensions and military expenditure coupled with the connivance to words military threats emanating from economic insecurity, social unrest and ethno-cultural factors is proving detrimental to the interests of member states as well as the region notwithstanding some progress in selected areas in SAARC. The recent developments in South Asia involving acts of terrorism coupled with the impact of the global recession have brought about a real danger of South Asia being marginalised in the community of nations.

Hence, improving the overall situation in South Asia for peace and progress is absolutely essential. Making countries convinced of the regional approach for mutual benefit though appears an arduous task given the delicate bilateral relations has nevertheless become inevitable. This primarily involves strengthening of the SAARC and increasing the scope and pace of SAARC activities. Though regionalism could be argued as not an effective substitute for bilateralism, in South Asia, SAARC activities can help member states to realise their common purpose better by providing larger economic space and a leverage to deal effectively with emerging global market upheavals as well as issues of peace, development and human security. It is through regional cooperation that the member states would be better equipped to deal with domestic inadequacies and international pressures. Hence strengthening of the SAARC could benefit member states the most.

Conditions in South Asia are far from being satisfactory for regional cooperation. The detached, at times hostile response of political elites to regional issues frustrates the drive towards further improving the effectiveness of the SAARC. Although the rhetoric of strengthening is constantly maintained by political elites in South Asia the action plan in concrete terms is found wanting. Lack of common perception with regards to the role and efficacy of SAARC in South Asia with countries like India stressing on economic, cultural and technological aspects, and Pakistan, desiring the expansion of the scope of SAARC to include political and even bilateral aspects have only complicated problems.

Hence, the search for additional or alternative strategies to strengthen the SAARC has become inevitable without which the interests of the region as well as of the member states are likely to be jeopardised. Apart from others, looking-up at other regional organisations and learning from the developmental experiences of other organisations and applying such knowledge relevantly to the progress of the SAARC could be one useful and effective way of promoting the SAARC. Although there exist many regional organisations to look towards, it is the European Community/European Union (EC/EU), a pioneer in regional integration, that is worth a close observation because of its remarkable and successful growth in a continent otherwise known for conflicts and competition and its role in the promotion of economic progress, political stability and development of the region ensuring peace, prosperity and progress. Certainly, SAARC could reflect on the developmental pattern and experience of the EC/EU and derive certain ideas for its progress. This calls for an understanding of the distinct aspects of the developmental strategy of the EC.

**EC/EU: Developmental strategy**

It is axiomatic that the EC/EU was instrumental is restructuring intra-European relations. EC/EU has given a distinct identity to Europe and has become a major force in international relations. Since its inception EU has sufficiently 'widened' to include most parts of Europe by successive enlargements and 'deepened' the relations among member states coupling their interests within the larger framework of a regional organisation.

However, the evolution of EC/EU was not a smooth, unilinear progress. It reflects the amalgamation of ideas, situations, diverse responses and even experimentation that has made the EU to be what it is today. The making of EU is riddled with idealism, pragmatism, contestation, compromises, compulsions etc. Nevertheless, the EC/EU has made distinct contribution to the regional integration process, some of which are also its unique features. Discerning such unique contributions/bequests is important to understand its relevance to the promotion of SAARC.

**Rapprochement:** EC and its forerunner, the European Coal and Steel Community (ECSC), are known for bringing about conciliation between age-old enemies, France and (West) Germany. The interests of these former enemies were innovatively entwined by placing coal and steel industry in a supranational (regional) framework under a common authority of the ECSC, which foresaw the complementarities between French iron ore and German steel thus ensuring economic progress in Europe, and making war not only 'unthinkable but materially impossible'. In other words, regional framework was seen as an effective conflict preventive and beneficial mechanism. The EC, emerging from Franco-German rapprochement in the context of East-West conflict, has subsequently progressed horizontally (by successive enlargements) and vertically (by deepening relations) facing new challenges with time. But the Franco-German solidarity still remains central to the European integration process though other countries including smaller ones have their share of influence in European dynamics. Integration in EU has, hence, become an ongoing process to safeguard their interests against re-nationalisation or emergent nationalism – the biggest fear in Europe. [1]

The EC/EU thus demonstrates a case where initial rapprochement could develop into a closer net of cooperation and transformation of the political map of the region into a zone of peace and stability. The EC/EU though has not replaced nation states as the centre of citizen's loyalties, it is at least, seen as a catalyst of European peace and progress and as a medium of lessening the rigidity of national boundaries and narrow national assertions.

**Primacy of Ideas:** The success of the ECSC, and subsequently the EC project, is a testimony to the visions of European statesmen like Monnet, Schuman, Adenauer, de Gasperi etc. Their ideas may not have been elaborate or even original but the contextual advocacy and the appropriateness of the ideas to the situation are note worthy. It is true that there were many congenial factors for the success of the EC like the cold war situation, American support etc., but without clear ideas supplemented by concrete work the EC would not have taken off or progressed.

In this endeavour, significantly, the historical European identity with roots in the Greco-Roman and Judeo-Christian civilization, its humanists tradition, its faith in progress and its technical and industrial development, was sought to be developed into 'European consciousness' without affecting the national sentiment. The 'European', for whom the idea of Europe was hitherto predominantly cultural with no motivation to turn it into political since Europe which took itself for the world, was shocked by the two World Wars, decolonisation and the Cold War, which eroded his 'superiority complex' and hegemony. Now there was a realization that further decline could be prevented and European interests could be safeguarded only by agreeing to unite amongst themselves. [2] It was here that the supranational regional framework was thought to be effective and a suitable framework was adopted. [3]

The EC was a demonstration of the inevitability of ideas i.e. articulation of interests relevant in the changed context for initiative as well as for success of regional organisation. This is not to imply that the movement of any regional organisation would be unilinear or teleological. As EC/EU process highlights, different situations and contexts would have the share in shaping the regional integration/cooperation process; yet, without a vision construction of regional framework for cooperation would be defective or the motivation for further cooperation would be minimal with no commonly felt tangible or intangible benefits and articulation of group identity or purpose.

**Functional Strategy:** A significant aspect of the EC is the strategy that was adopted to realize the objectives of peace and prosperity. Convinced by the failure of the European Defence Community (EDC) in 1955 that the states would not forsake areas central to sovereignty, the makers of Rome Treaty found that the ECSC strategy was the most suitable and adopted a less controversial economic route to peace and progress although it had implicit political consequences. The strategy of incrementalizm, which was in tune with neo-functionalist assumptions largely proved to be a success although at times the nature and reach of the EC into national sovereign arena was contested. Even sceptics like Britain became part of the EC and in the process a complete interdependency in the EC/EU has emerged along with the number of areas dealt by the EC/EU and its influence in the national sphere has gradually increased.

The success of the EC/EU thus reflects the rationale that once the integration process in initiated, even though it may be for the self interest of the participants, it would develop its own processes, logic and incentives for further integration. The final form may not be clear, but integration is bound to proceed by leaps and bounds depending upon the political climate and the regional organisation would be recognised as inevitable in the national developmental process.

**Institutional Structures and Processes:** The EC, despite supranational objectives, could foresee the adverse effect of thrusting supranational institutions on member states; hence, it settled for a balance between supranational institutions (Commission, European Parliament, European Court of Justice etc.) and intergovernmental Council of Ministers. Though the creation of Council of Ministers was a result of the demand of smaller Benelux (Belgium, Luxembourg, and Netherlands) countries, it did prevent a sense of 'domination' and 'dominated' from arising without missing the supranational thrust.

Hence institutional design of the EC/EU could be argued as a major factor in promoting and sustaining integration, for, trade offs between them could result in a higher phase of integration. Intergovernmental cooperation provided a healthy environment for a commonly accepted move towards the next stage of supra nationalism and processes have resulted in increasing communitarization of policies on agreed areas without creating ill will.

While the increasing legitimacy of the community institutions and communitarization of policies are evident in the Single European Act (SEA), Maastricht Treaty on European Union (TEU), Treaty of Amsterdam (TA) and the Lisbon Treaty, significantly the Community also accepted the principle that member states would not block others from going ahead on an issue to which they would not consent ('constructive abstention'). The subsidiarity principle in the EU again confirms the idea that a regional organisation can better deal with those issues which individual nations states are unable to deal with effectively.

In other words, EC/EU institutions are shaped not only to have flexibility - a great strength of institutions - but also autonomy of their own. Such flexibility and autonomy of EU institutions removed ill will and facilitated unwilling ones to join the stream for common benefit. These internal adjustments and compromises reduced frictions and due to increased interdependency, communitarization of policies and impact of one states' policy on other's common perspectives on issues began to develop. Such an approach had a great impact on the consolidation of the organisation as well as its capacity to adjust to changing situations.

Such an orientation was supplemented by the lack of intrusiveness on the part of the EC and sufficient space for member states to pursue their domestic agenda, which allowed for contestation, as well as compromise and new experiments in forms of cooperation. At the same time new tasks were aimed to be completed in a time framework compelling countries to be materially and psychologically ready to accept changes according to the timetable. That is, while gradual convergence of ideas for common good was allowed, the objective was not compromised and it was sought to be achieved in a time frame once the goal was set. Consequently the competence of the EC/EU has grown significantly but without affecting national peculiarities. National and coordinated policy instruments continue despite the thrust towards communitarian dimensions.

Thus it is clear that the EC/EU in its developmental process has been able to converge not merely economic policies but also political perspectives to a large extent, though not without stress and debate. Partly, this has been so because the EC has been instrumental in evolving a complex interdependency both among its member states and also between itself and member states. Its activities today cover practically every area of governance. 'Regional' co-exists, competes and at times shares responsibility with the 'national'.

It is through the EC/EU, that the European member states have irrevocably coupled their interests and prosperity strengthening not only their position but also the image of Europe. By gradually increasing its economic and political weight the EC/EU has largely emancipated Europe from internal feuds, economic weaknesses, and pressures from the Soviet Union during the Cold War and the domineering role of the US and has increased its bargaining power against major powers and trading blocs.

**Making of the EC/EU: Compelling factors**

It is important to note that, in spite of its appealing and interesting aspects, the growth of the EC/EU has not been unilinear or smooth. Its progress was often conditioned by the domestic, European and international situations. But the EC/EU is often presented as a success story of an organisation, as a lesson and a model for emulation by others for peace and progress. The universal applicability of its model as implied in EC's own advocacy of a regional organisation (as evident in its most region and country specific strategy papers and other development perspective documents) is mostly shaped by its preference and advocacy of compatibility between regionalism and multilateralism, a scenario which appears to suit the EC's interest the most. [4] The ground realities in different regions are different and the context, pressures and the support, which the EC had during its development, do not exist in other regions. Hence, the success of the EC need not get reproduced in other organisations that emulate the EC.

Therefore, before applying the EC/EU developmental experience to the SAARC it is pertinent to know the concrete situation that shaped the EC integrate so as to better understand the suitability of the EC model to the SAARC condition. In its eagerness and tremendous capacity to advocate the viability of regional organisations the EU itself does not sufficiently highlight the systemic factors that proved conducive to the success of the integration and these are also not adequately focussed upon by other narratives on the EC/EU. [5]

The context of the Cold War, fear of Soviet expansion, the American support to the EC project and the French concern regarding the US suggestion for rearming (West) Germany as a check against potential Soviet westward expansion, for instance, do not get sufficient attention. More than Soviet aggression it was the fear of resurgent Germany that made French leaders to align with Germany as an insurance against the latter's revival. Therefore, it is necessary to note that French national interests were paramount in the French suggestion for a supranational sectoral integration rather than an idealism of supranational Europe and European identity which were only the means for serving national interests a fact which is often underplayed. The EDC failed not because it was not supranational but because it failed to address French national apprehensions.

Further, the proposed customs union was to accrue benefit to the French steel industry by expanding production and shedding protectionist tendency as well as helping in containing the re-emergence of German industry. Aware of British non-participation in the customs union project, for the French aligning with a still weak Germany was a means of asserting the dominant role of France in Europe whereas for Germany it was a desperate attempt to establish equality with others and remove wartime restrictions. So supra-nationalism served immediate national interests of key countries rather than European interests. Even Benelux countries were guided primarily by nationalist considerations. Hence regional/European interests were seen as a means of protecting national interests or reviving the faith in the nation state that had been badly damaged by the Second World War especially by its advocates. [6]

Subsequent to its formation, the EC's progress varied in different contexts and political configurations. While personalities like de Gaulle and Margaret Thatcher were not happy with the increasing independence and power of the 'Brussels' institutions and sought to assert national control, it was the economic and political conditions of the 1980's and 1990's that helped the EC in strengthening its institutional mechanism. But subsequently when integration was seen as touching won the core areas of nation-states, national assertions were again made and the pace of integration receded. This was evident in the French and Dutch rejection of the EU constitution as well as the Irish response to the Lisbon Treaty. Therefore, the idea that the creation of institutions in itself can promote and sustain the progress of regional organisations does not hold good.

Hence, the EC/EU trajectory itself suggests on a closer examination that the integration and progress of regional organisations depends on situations and political perspectives and there can be no unilinear movement. Since the present situation in South Asia is very different from that of the EC in its formative stage or later, duplication of the EU model in South Asia is difficult and any attempt towards emulation is unlikely to yield expected dividends.

**EC's Relevance to SAARC: Some Reflections**

Though the EC/EU model does not appear to suit South Asia because of different contexts and conditions, the EC integration process could certainly be a source of inspiration and a reference point for SAARC. Moreover, the EU trajectory does provide certain insights that are useful in the South Asian Context. The SAARC process perhaps needs to consider these in its developmental pattern with relevant adjustments. Hence, identifying relevant aspects and learning from the EC's developmental experience could be beneficial to SAARC's progress. Some of these are:

**Motivation:** Generally strong and self-confident states as well as weak or small countries would be reluctant to irreversibly transfer sovereignty to such an organisation which would be self-regulating. In the EC's case, Britain, that was less affected by the war, for instance, was not willing to join an emerging supranational organisation like the ECSC or the EC in the beginning. The Benelux countries' insistence on the creation of the Intergovernmental Council of Ministers in the EC spoke of the apprehension of the smaller countries regarding domination of the organisation by bigger countries. So in the normal situation there may not be motivation for states to opt for regional integration or enhance cooperation within a regional framework unless certain advantages are foreseen. Bilateralism may still be preferred to regionalism.

In South Asia too a similar situation can be found. India and Pakistan, relatively stronger countries in South Asia, appear to have no motivation for strengthening the regional organisation and do not take SAARC as inevitable for their progress. In the initial stage, India did not like to be tied up with an organisation in which it would not have complete freedom of action and thought its interests would be adversely affected in case neighbours use the regional platform to 'gang up' against India. Hence was India's insistence upon the non-inclusion of bilateral and contentious issues within the SAARC framework. Pakistan too, apprehensive of India's domination in the organisation, was unenthusiastic about the proposal for a regional organisation although other countries thought it to be an effective instrument against big power domination and a mechanism to ensure equality in the region.

But as the experiences of the EC or the SAARC suggest countries of the region would not like to bear the cost of non-inclusion and they would become the part of the stream however grudgingly it is. This is because of the realisation that (a) other's move could affect their interests significantly or (b) later they can not join the organisation on their terms or (c) inability to face emerging domestic or external challenges/crises individually.

Therefore, countries would not pursue regional cooperative endeavour intensely unless there is an expectation of benefits or compulsions of the situation. In the case of the EC the crisis situation of the post Second World War period created a conducive environment. Cold War pressures, American support, fear of resurgent Germany, advantages of economic cooperation all proved to be compelling factors for the creation of an integrated regional framework-the ECSC and the EC.

Subsequent to the formation of the EC the realisation of the inability of the states to meet certain contingencies gave a forward push to the 'deepening' as well as 'widening' of the EC. For example, the stagnation of the European economies resulted in the adoption of the SEA in the 1980's. Similarly Post-Cold War developments accompanied by ethnic conflicts in Eastern Europe and refugees as well as rising number of applicants prompted adoption of the Maastricht TEU and the TA in the 1990's. The failure in the attempts to have a European constitution to streamline the working of the EU and to have a definite direction and identity led to the Reform (Lisbon) Treaty in 2007. Therefore the crisis situation and realisation of internal inadequacy to meet emerging challenges can enable common action and strengthening of regional frameworks.

This common action to meet common challenges needs to be considered in South Asia as well. In South Asia too crises situations, although of a different nature, exist. The socio-economic backwardness of the region in the context of the globalisation process which is capable of homogenising cultural patterns along with its emphasis on western capitalist orientations is affecting the collective interests of the SAARC member states in the absence of an effective regional strategy towards the issue. The militaristic approach to security with nuclear explosions in the region in 1998 by India and Pakistan and the stalemate over the issue of terrorism have only pushed up the tension in the region as well as defence and unproductive expenditures for stopping infiltration, counter propaganda etc.

The threats emanating from non-militarist sources like poverty, unemployment, ethnic problems etc., have increased manifold and states are unable to curb them individually as these often have trans-national dimensions. The domestic and bilateral disputes have not only affected peace and stability in the region but also global investments. When other regions are protecting/advancing their interests through regional organisations, failure to do so by further strengthening of the SAARC by its member states, despite the realisation of the futility of the individualist approach, has put them in real danger of being sidelined by the global community.

Therefore, conducive (crises) atmosphere as well as the chances of benefit by cooperation do exist in South Asia for 'deepening' of relations; but, SAARC member states are yet to make up their mind for realizing the benefits of collective action. The disparate developmental strategies in South Asia have already resulted in duplication of efforts and higher costs of providing public goods and services, increasing dependence on extra-regional markets, higher costs and lower efficiencies of national infra-structural and developmental projects; inward political orientations resulting in domestic unrest, political chaos, strained bilateral relations, slow down in regional economic development and development in social and related sectors. [7] Therefore it is necessary to move towards finding regional solutions to common problems.

However, as the EU experience suggest it is not mere by a conducive atmosphere that is required for 'deepening' relations but also the willingness on the part of political elites to go beyond the present stalemate. The mutual conflictual situation need not necessarily be a hindrance to regional cooperation as it is sometimes believed. [8] Bilateral relations could strengthen along with or as a consequence of strengthening regional organisations if there is a political will.

**Core Group Initiatives:** In regional organisations though all member states are equal participants, a thrust into internal dynamics is often provided by few major states which might have grater stakes in integration. In the EC's case, Franco-German rapprochement not only created the EC but also provided an impetus to its integration. But in inter-governmental SAARC, unlike the EU, despite instances of joint communiqués of ministerial meetings on the environment, WTO related issues etc., member states pursue opposite or contradictory policies that prevent SAARC from realising its best.

This is because the two major countries of the region-India and Pakistan-who ideally should have taken the lead in promoting the SAARC are, in fact, not very enthusiastically involved in the progress of the SAARC. Their bilateral adversarial relations often take precedence over regional cooperative endeavour. Unless these two countries agree to cooperate and promote the SAARC, the SAARC and the region's progress is bound to be tardy because as former Secretary-General of the SAARC, K.K. Bhargava argues, "even though the (SAARC) charter specifically states that bilateral and contentious issues are to be excluded from the deliberations, we have to reckon with the fact that a symbiotic relationship exist between tension-free ties among member states and healthy regional cooperation". [9]

It is here again the actions and attitudes of France and Germany becomes important as a guiding force. France and Germany in spite of their centuries of conflict decided to bury hatchet in the post Second World War period and link their interests to a regional framework for peace and progress. The same drive on the part of India and Pakistan could help South Asia to overcome much of its problems. As Rummel puts it, "it can be an asset rather than a hindrance if a regional organisation has one or two leading countries to drive the cooperative process. It requires, however, that they refrain from power demonstrations and accept compromises. It also requires that they have more advanced mechanisms and a higher degree of cooperation than the rest of the group, see Franco-German Elysee Treaty. If not, they risk to block the cooperative process and the whole enterprise is doomed to fail". [10]

But how to bring these two adversaries together for regional well-being with India not in favour of a third-party mediation? Some apparently taking a clue from Franco-German rapprochement propose linking of Indo-Pak national interests under a common framework. [11] However, these measures appear difficult to be realized if analysed in the context of present developments in South Asia. Obstacles to regional cooperation in South Asia are basically political and psychological and the state driven SAARC process is unlikely to perform a managerial role. The regional bilateral differences, especially between India and Pakistan at times touch the core areas of nation state. Pakistan's insistence on the centrality of the Kashmir issue in Indo-Pakistan relations and India's stress on the end of 'cross-border terrorism' and non-acceptance/denial of each others demands have made relations intractable. Ignoring such issues central to the perception/ideological basis of each state has not been easy for them both.

Nevertheless, the appeal of 'burying the hatchet' as in the case of Franco-German conciliation can not be ignored and India and Pakistan need to consider this strongly for regional as well as their own progress. If immediate goodwill is not possible at least they need to cooperate in strengthening the SAARC process and their bilateral disputes need to be put in the backburner as in the case of the EC's founder members. Given the political will narrow national considerations could be prevented from affecting broader regional interests and, similar to France and Germany in the EC, India and Pakistan could effectively propel the SAARC towards progress.

**Strategy for Cooperation:** Since its inception the EC aimed to achieve a customs union first and an abstract 'ever closer union of the people' with political connotations which necessitated the states to come together for realising common objectives. But with stress on economic integration and the pushing of bilateral conflicts to the backburner, political issues were tactically avoided. In this strategy of achieving higher forms of integration, starting from the least controversial sectoral ('low political') integration, a step-by-step approach was adopted in which the present stage of integration was hoped to create conditions for the next stage of integration ('spill-over effect'). In this strategy, which is in tune with neo-functionalist assumptions, sovereignty instead of being surrendered is only asked to be pooled up to the extent required for joint performance of functions.

In the South Asian context, the neo-functional strategy is difficult to be replicated since every area including water, health, population, technology etc. are related to national development and are nationally sensitive. Therefore 'high' and 'low' sectors are difficult to distinguish. But, at the same time, it is necessary to look beyond the mere intergovernmental, state-driven process of regional cooperation and the essence of neo-functionalism here could be relevantly applied.

In South Asia, it is essential to move the cooperation beyond the official national confines especially in those areas which are beneficial to all or many, if regional cooperation has to be meaningful. The present cooperation in SAARC under the Integrated Programme of Action (IPA) is mostly confined to official interactions and other programmes are affected by a lack of political support. Therefore it is necessary to go beyond official confines under the IPA as well as promote cooperation in other areas having regional implications. [12] This could be in the area of river water harnessing, industrial and technological up-gradation in a regional framework strengthening cooperation in national planning processes and poverty alleviation and so on.

Once cooperation is effected keeping in mind the regional rather than narrow national interests, such cooperation over a period of time tends to develop its own logic, pressure and incentives for further progress notwithstanding possible official sanctions. Here bilateral conflicts need not preclude the negotiation on such areas if regional cooperation is perceived as a positive development. [13] Therefore, the present SAFTA endeavours can go a long way in sustaining and promoting regional cooperation. The 'deepening' of regional cooperation process can help member states to understand each other better and prepare ground for reconciliation gradually but willingness to cooperate in the mutually beneficial areas is a pre-requisite.

In this context recommendations of the SAARC Group of Eminent Persons (GEP) are important. In the economic area, for instance, the GEP suggests that SAARC needs to realise not only South Asian Free Trade Area (SAFTA) but also move beyond it towards Customs Union and South Asian Economic Union. [14] Such concrete moves not only would benefit people but also would create interest in regional integration due to their tangible and intangible benefits resulting in reduction of bilateral conflicts and transformation of attitudes.

Further, the SAARC has to move not only towards higher forms of cooperation/integration but also, like the EC, move within time framework. This would enable states to be ready for the changes and to effect suitable policy measures at the domestic level. The deadlines have to be realistic but once decided should not be extended. Therefore, it is imperative that the SAARC takes up only those areas which are feasible and workable, as its success could result in a conducive atmosphere for increased cooperation in other areas.

**'Deepening' Relations:** In the EC while official interactions continued, the integration process has slowly percolated into the civil society. Over the years, a number of interest groups have emerged showing interest in and seeking to influence the integration process. [15] The networks that begun to develop across member states were enduring and it could sustain itself even when official interactions were at an ebb, often influencing policy processes in favour of closer cooperation. Though the EC/EU is not seen as a panacea for all problems, its role has come to be increasingly recognised and the EU is seen mostly as inevitable.

On the other hand, the EU is also eager to move closer to the people and increase the legitimacy of its actions by encouraging them to internalise the EC through sustained campaigns, media programmes and other socialisation techniques impressing people of its desirability. Though it is not totally successful, the EU is consistently striving to overcome its perceived 'legitimacy crisis' and 'democratic deficit'. The EC institutions are also increasing transparency in their proceedings and the EC holds open and structured dialogues with interest groups. The EC Commission has also made available a list of non-profit interest groups to both - officials and the general public and the access to internal documents of the European Commission are regulated by a set procedures.

On the contrary, South Asian cooperation has not gone beyond state-managed processes and interactions and at non-official levels remain minimum. The Civil society is yet to internalise the SAARC or develop an idea that the SAARC is instrumental to progress or at least see its presence as inevitable to progress. The SAARC Documentation Centre is setup in Delhi to make science and technology information available to interested parties. But, unlike the EC, there is no code of conduct with regard to the access to SAARC documents for scholars and Non-Governmental Organisations (NGOs). The impact of SAARC Audio-Video Exchange (SAVE) programme is insignificant and the SAARC's drive to reach people has been poor. Consequently, the SAARC process has failed to get the recognition and the importance it deserves.

Hence, SAARC like the EC needs to adopt measures to make the cooperation process in South Asia not only durable but also effective. Such measures could supplement official processes of cooperation and primarily aim at reaching and involving people in the cooperation process. This includes, among others, active involvement of NGOs and interest groups, easing of travel restrictions and, as in the EC, orienting educational systems and media programmes to foster regional cooperation. Reaching the civil society, hence, is inevitable for SAARC success. Significant undercurrents of mutual understanding facilitated by unnatural boundaries, shared social and cultural characteristics, broadly similar levels of economic deprivations, concern for stability and prosperity and deeply entrenched historical linkages etc. which Prof. Muni terms as 'Pull factors' could supplement the process. [16]

**Institutions and Institutionalisation:** The framers of the EC deemed it necessary to create separate institutions for the management of EC affairs that would be independent of member states. What finally emerged was a balance between supranational (Commission, European Court of Justice, European Parliament etc.) and intergovernmental (Council of Ministers) institutions. However, hopes were pinned on the Commission, which was regarded as the motor of European integration. But as events in the EC revealed, the Council did not lag behind in involving and directing the integration process through its own bureaucracy-COREPER (Council of Permanent Representatives) and suitably modifying its decision making structure, from unanimity to Qualified Majority Voting (QMV) as the situation demanded.

What ensued was a competition between the Commission and the Council to direct and shape the integration process which increased not only the authority of both but also held them together in a closer net of competing as well as converging interests. Wherever convergence was established higher phases of integration followed. Here the Intergovernmental Council did not prove to see an antithesis to the supranational Commission; rather complementary, since many of the programmatic actions were debated and approved in the Council, sorting out the differences among member states and proving to be conducive to the advance towards the next stage of integration.

Along with these the assertive Court of Justice and the influential European Parliament sustained those vested interests which advanced economic and political integration and generated community bureaucratic ambitions. In other words, EC institutions and the institutionalisation process established bureaucratic specialists who had interests and knowledge to further shape the integration and legislation. The elite socialisation of the EC and the internal dynamics of the EC often influenced the political perception of member states and manipulated their choices. The credit of promoting, sustaining and advancing the integration process can not be given solely to EU institutions, for, contexts and circumstances were equally important. Nevertheless, there is no gainsaying that proactive EC institutions and institutionalisation of the integration process did make the integration process not only irreversible but also forward-looking.

While the EC institutions have given rise to mutually reinforcing process of institutionalisation and bureaucratisation of the integration, at the non-official and civil society level there have emerged many interest groups with a stake in the integration process. The interaction and networking among them has proved conducive to the integration and the institutionalisation of interaction and cooperation has made the integration process stable, dynamic and irreversible.

Therefore, it is clear that the EC institutions and institutionalisation process although devoid of power have begun to control their own resources, accumulate knowledge and exert authority. The whole process, although at times assumes diverse forms and appears to take the EC/EU process in different directions, it nonetheless impresses upon the public mind that the EU and the integration as inevitable, if not legitimate. This has further helped in advancing the integration process. But what is important is that the whole process has acquired a distinct identity and autonomy of its own, independent of national official processes.

The institutionalisation and bureaucratisation of the integration process has led to accusations of rigidity in the integration process and 'integration from above'. Nevertheless, momentum of integration is sustained and people's perceptions in favour of the integration have largely emerged as a consequence of such institutionalisation. People and interest groups have foreseen advantages in such a process. Institutionalisation, hence, has helped the integration process and the SAARC needs to intensify such a process.

However, in SAARC, the member states are still the driving force behind the cooperation process and their mood and political climate to a large extent shape the nature and pace of cooperation in South Asia. Moreover, the SAARC - unlike the EC - emphasises on intergovernmental 'cooperation' rather than supranational 'integration'. Hence, it is not a surprise that SAARC institutions, unlike most EC institutions, are not endowed with any authority of their own or the power to initiate, direct or enforce the integration process.

Even in formal cooperation processes not much consistency could be found. Complete and sustained support to SAARC activities especially by the bigger countries hardly exist. The Summit meetings - important platforms for formal and informal interaction among leaders and a 'forward push' to the cooperation -

themselves are becoming irregular and when held are devoid of the cooperative spirit. At Summits, sometimes substantive issues are discussed but initiative and implementation largely rest on national bureaucracies rather than the SAARC secretariat. Consequently regional institutions including the Secretary-General are constrained by the considerations of 'national interests' and are unable to shape or influence the member states' policy perspectives towards regional concerns.

In SAARC the secretariat is the only regional institution of SAARC and other SAARC institutions such as the Council of Ministers, Standing Committee etc., work more as coordinating agencies of national perspectives. There have been no moves made to introduce other regional institutions like a SAARC Parliament despite the suggestions by the academia which actually could have increased the legitimacy and initiatives of the SAARC. Agencies outside the SAARC have their own limitations—financial, legitimacy and reach—in furthering the SAARC process and thus, are not very effective.

Hence it is necessary to strengthen existing SAARC institutions as well as support regional endeavours which could develop interest in sustained regional cooperation. Learning from the experience of the EC/EU, it is necessary to endow regional institutions with certain autonomy to perform regionally oriented activities, encourage non-governmental initiative on regional activities and attempt to bring the SAARC process closer to the people so as to make it effective and durable. These might require, among other things:

- Endowing the SAARC, particularly the Secretary-General and his team, with certain freedom and powers at least to suggest measures for enhanced regional cooperation and implementation similar to, if not exactly like, the European Commission. Role of the Secretary-General and staffing of the SAARC Secretariat need to be reviewed as an essential element of capacity building; [17]
- Strengthening the SAARC regional institutions to truly make them nodal points of SAARC activities in concerned areas rather than duplicate national institutions and evolving an acceptable procedure for official and public access to information;
- Actively involving and giving more role to NGOs and professional bodies like the SAARC Chamber of Commerce and Industry (SCCI), Association of SAARC Speakers and Parliamentarians, SAARCLAW (Association of persons of legal communities) etc., in SAARC activities. Networking should be encouraged in these bodies so that an institutionalized process could become supplementary to SAARC activities and at times could exert pressure

for increased cooperation. Besides, the institutionalized interactions among media professionals, business class as well as police, customs officials etc., could be encouraged to facilitate the SAARC;

- As the EU experience suggests convergence/harmonizing policy perspectives not only provide greater leverage to deal with issues but also increase the bargaining power of the region. Therefore, in SAARC the existing procedure of consultation and discussion among the Commerce ministers to evolve a regional viewpoint before WTO meetings, SAARC's informal discussions with the EC, ASEAN etc. and the coordination among SAARC planning ministers, finance ministers etc. should be regularised and allowed to take an institutionalized form. This not only presents SAARC as a visible entity inside and outside South Asia but also helps SAARC member states to evolve common viewpoints and approaches towards the issues which will help in sustaining and enhancing the momentum of SAARC cooperation;
- Set up a representative (parliamentary) body for SAARC with the possible extension of the present Association of SAARC Speakers and Parliamentarians.

Once these programmes, some of which are already through, are initiated, intensified and encouraged, as the EU experience suggest, regional institutions and institutionalisation would over a period of time de-link themselves from national official points-of-view and begin to develop their own rationale and processes for integration/cooperation often influencing political perceptions of member states and manipulating their choices. Regular, institutionalised interaction, therefore, not only facilitates exchange of ideas but also exercises conflict prevention. Moreover, the elite socialisation thus promoted could, as in the EU, become a major force in sustaining and promoting further advances in regional cooperation/integration.

At the same time SAARC should be able to construct an increasingly dense network of interdependent bargains making it difficult for member states to pursue exclusionary politics. Eventually all these might lead to 'domestication of the SAARC' as in the EU the 'domestication of Europe' and, if not subsidiarity, at least perception of inevitability of increased presence of the SAARC in certain areas. The increased institutionalisation process, therefore, not only makes integration/cooperation process irreversible but also furthers it.

Hence, EU's developmental experience could be relevantly applied to the South Asian context. In addition to the above mentioned areas, taking a clue from EU's approach towards (intra-European) regions, the SAARC also need to have a policy towards the region and strengthen its present position i.e. though two does not exactly mean a 'sub-regional approach', there could be an emphasis on growth triangles or quadrangles or alternatively sectoral integration among three or four countries which could focus on locally available resources like water, hydropower, iron and steel etc. These measures could effectively harness local resources and benefit the South Asian region, for example, water in the Himalayan region. Such increased collaboration could take place even among the areas of cooperation covered under the IPA and efforts could be boosted by mutually eliminating/reducing tariff and NTBs and agreed upon investment incentive measures.

These measures, as in Franco-German relations or Benelux within the EU, could help in experimenting with certain aspects of integration on a smaller scale, and subsequently it could exert pressure for extending such cooperation on a larger scale in the organisation. Moreover, as the EU experience shows disparity within the region need not be a hindrance to closer cooperation and member states within the SAARC like the EU could go at varying speeds with integration within the broader framework and help others to raise the level of participation. Therefore, bilateral/trilateral cooperation within the region like Indo-Sri Lankan Free Trade Arrangements or Bangladesh-Bhutan-India-Nepal Growth Quadrangle (BBIN-GQ) need not be seen as antithesis to regional cooperation and the SAARC emphasis on consensus should not be an impediment to such moves. [18]

Nevertheless, to avoid existing discrepancies from widening and disturbing the regional cooperation process and to help relatively backward countries to effectively participate in the SAARC process, a SAARC Fund (which is already contemplated) on the lines of the EU structural and cohesion fund need to be setup. This fund could be used for different purposes such as developing certain regions and sectors. The existing South Asian Development Fund (SADF) for instance, could be broad based on the lines of European structural fund to assist vocational training, to undertake new forms of agriculture, fishing etc., besides regional and joint venture projects. In the given structure although states might be the ultimate beneficiaries of the assistance, the fund could increase SAARC's legitimacy by acting as a developmental and re-distributive agency that promotes its visibility in the process of states donating, appealing and bargaining for funds, drawing attention of even the public towards the SAARC. The resources of the fund could be raised by the contributions of member states, but external funding need not be rejected if given for developmental purposes, a proposal that has also been made by the GEP with regards to the SADF. [19] This SAARC Fund could help in building the organisation as well as in nation-building by overcoming uneven and imbalanced development.

**India's Role**

In the regional endeavour India which has stronger presence in South Asia by virtue of its size, economic and military power, with a stable democracy and political system and experiences in pluralism could help in fostering relations by opening up sufficiently to South Asia. Depending upon the context such moves could be even unilateral or without much stress on reciprocity as had been done during I.K. Gujral's tenure first as Foreign Minister and then as the Prime Minister, which helped in improving India's image in South Asia. [20] India's initiatives would be crucial for instance, in economic integration of South Asia. Therefore, India needs to take interest and initiative in furthering economic integration of South Asia and such a measure would certainly be supported by others, especially by small countries of South Asia. India that has already granted tariff concession to a large number of items for trade in South Asia could extend it to many more items or abolish tariffs. India's large market and its trade with the region makes a difference to the overall intra-regional trade in South Asia since in its absence, the South Asian market becomes limited coupled with foreign account restraints or low market demands of other importing countries of South Asia. Already Bilateral trade agreements of Nepal and Bhutan with India have been arrived at. Bangladesh and Sri Lanka too are willing to increase their trade with India.

Hence, it would not be fair on the part of India to insist on reciprocity and trade advantages and to look from a purely commercial point of view because many of its neighbours being LDCs have supply side constraints and India also is self sufficient in most items. India is in a position to supply industrial inputs and capital goods at competitive prices which has close correlation with fixed capital formation in these countries and India needs to increase its trade with South Asia from its present level of exports worth mere $US 4262 million (in 2004) to SAARC countries out of its global exports worth $US 75384 million exports (i.e. 5.6 percent) and $US 848 million worth imports from SAARC countries out of its global in parts worth $US 99833 million (i.e. 0.8 percent). [21] More than trade benefits, such measures have intangible benefits of stability and goodwill in the region.

Therefore, such postures supplemented by exploratory/interactive dialogues could help in overcoming most of the existing problems and every initiative/proposal from her neighbours for regional cooperation need not be suspiciously seen. India perhaps has nothing to fear or loose by such gestures and reluctance would only help anti-Indian hawks, particularly Pakistan. Increased relations based on goodwill would not only help in strengthening regional cooperation and the SAARC but also tend to benefit by such global politics and the world market that put a premium on inter-regional and intra-regional cooperation.

India's initiatives might be viewed as hegemonic; but, lack of initiative would also be blamed as lack of sincerity. Therefore, it can be hoped that such gestures gradually would tend to make neighbours reciprocate and realise the futility of harping on asymmetry and perceptions of dominance and instead, may prompt them to realise the value of collective solidarity in the face of global changes and challenges as well as national inadequacies. Here the experiences of the EU may be considered. As Rummel observes that, "A single country i.e. India in the SAARC or Germany in the EU, is a major challenge to the other members of the regional group. Germany which in several respects a dominant country hardly launches unilateral initiative but looks for a partner, big or small, to join. Bonn is also prepared to go along with other member state's initiatives. Certainly, the asymmetry and the dominance of India in the SAARC are much more visible and can not be altered, but the success of the SAARC will be decisively dependent on the way New Delhi handles this fact. It is also a question of other members and their perception or instrumentalization of India's dominance." [22]

Therefore, India needs to initiate measures that promote South Asia's progress and improve its overall relations with South Asian neighbours. Since economic progress is likely to benefit all, India's initiatives in the economic sphere are likely to be supported by others. Pakistan by harping on the Kashmir issue may refuse initially to join the stream but conciliatory stance of India could make Pakistan to put bilateral conflicts onto the backburner to reap the benefits of cooperation. Although issues related to terrorism and 'K' (Kashmir) often upset the cooperative spirit of India and Pakistan, both need to assess and react to the issues realistically and rationally. In this regard conciliatory moves of Pakistan's new democratic regime towards India in improving relations need to be reciprocated by India. This would help Pakistan's new democratic regime eventually to strengthen its position vis-à-vis hawkish elements in its army and the ISI (intelligence agency) as well as fundamentalist forces. Hence, it is in the interest of all that countries of the region set aside their conflictual issues and concentrate on issues of common concern and benefit.

All these efforts could make SAARC a composite bloc and a visible entity enhancing its legitimacy in international relations. As could be seen in the EC/EU, the strengthening of regional organisation need not be a zero sum transfer of power leading to a weakening or a restricting of the autonomy of states or denial of their sovereignty. When a region progresses, it is the people and the member states that progress. Therefore, the region and member states can witness economic progress, region-wide space, peace and stability and collective strength to bargain and to interact with the rest of the world, which in turn can strengthen the capacity of the states to act in diverse areas with greater vigour. This, in fact, adds to the essence of the concept of sovereignty. Thus regional cooperation can lead to mutual and balanced gains, if not equitable benefits; and the returns from investment in regional cooperation could be diverse-peace, stability, market space and other varying economic dividends because of trade-offs. So strengthening of regional organisations and regions would in a way mean strengthening of constituent member states and what is transferred is returned by way of increased capacity of the states to act, which is back by the strength of regional space, resources and good will.

Therefore, a closer look at the EU suggests to us the benefits of the SAARC and the cost of 'non-SAARC.' This should enable member states to strengthen the SAARC as an investment in mutually profitable processes. In this process there could be debates and contestations but there can be no denying of the fact that facilitating the SAARC is the facilitation of the members' own good. Hence, SAARC member states, particularly India and Pakistan—two important countries in the region whose support is absolutely essential to the success of SAARC—need to shed the perception, as evident in their action, that the SAARC is a peripheral institution not important in any national developmental process and that the strengthening of the SAARC accrues no obvious advantage. If not they would not be any better than what they would be, by strengthening the SAARC in an irrevocable manner.

Success of the SAARC, therefore, mainly depends on member states' willingness to promote increased interaction in South Asia at different levels—governmental, private sector, civil society—for mutual benefit and for strengthening the SAARC so as to realise the objectives for which it was created. In pursuing objectives, each region has to have its own path of development as conditions across regions vary. Nonetheless, insights from the EC/EU's developmental process could be relevantly applied by South Asian countries to their own if the regions' progress is considered as important by them.

**Notes**

1. See, Reinhardt Rummel, "Transformation of EC in to EU: Its Salience and relevance to regional peace and development in South Asia", In L. L. Mehrotra, H.S. Chopra and Gert W. Kueck, eds., *SAARC 2000 and beyond* (New Delhi: Omega Scientific, 1995) pp. 286-89.
2. The development of European consciousness now came to be based on what Robert Frank identities as four rejections—the rejection of war in 1920, reactivated in 1945; fascism; Russian imperialism during the cold war; and non-acceptance of the relative decline of the European nation-states. See, Robert Frank, "European Identities, Consciousness and Construction: Harmony and Disharmony between Politics, Economics and Imagination", in

H. S. Chopra, Robert Frank and Jurgen Schroder, eds., *National Identity and Regional Cooperation: Experiences of European Integration and South Asian Perceptions* (New Delhi: Manohar, 1999) pp. 44-48. In fact, Delanty argue that idea of Europe (cultural) existed long before people identified themselves as Europeans. But the idea of Europe failed to become a cohesive collective identity, for, instead of European unity configurations of national identities were formed. Strategically this was developed in to European identity ('Self conscious political identity') as a form of consciousness. See, Gerard Delanty, *Inventing Europe: India, Identity and Reality* (New York: St. Martins Press, 1995).

3. Jean Monnet, *Memoirs,* Richard Mayne, trans., (New York: Doubleday, 1978), p. 298; Richard Mayne, "The Role of Jean Monnet", *Government and Opposition* (London), vol. 2, no. 3, 1966-67, pp. 349-71. For Schuman plan see, *Documents on American Foreign Relations,* 1950, vol. 12 (Massachusetts, 1951), pp. 85-87.
4. See, Jayaraj Amin, "Inter-regional cooperation: A study of EU-SAARC Relations" in Rejendra K. Jain, Harmut Elsenhans and Jayaraj Amin, eds, *The European Union in Transition: Economy, Politics and Society*(New Delhi; Radiant, 2007) pp. 33-38; Jayaraj Amin, "The European Union and SAARC: Estranged Inter-Regional Partners?" in Rajendra K. Jain, ed., *India and the European Union Building a Strategic Partnership* ( New Delhi; Radiant, 2007) pp. 13-32.
5. See, Klaus-Dieter Borchardt, *European Integration: The origins and growth of European Union*, 4th edn., (Luxembourg: Office for Official Publications of the European Communities, 1995); Hans Von der Groeben, *The European Community, The Struggle to establish the Common Market & the political union (1958-1966)* (Luxembourg: Office of the official publication of the European Community, 1986); Neill Nugent, *The Government and Politics of the European Union* (London: The Macmillan, 1995): Martin Holland, *European Community Integration* (London: Pinter, 1993).
6. See, Alan S. Milward, *The European Rescue of the Nation state* (London: Routledge, 1992) especially pp. 318-44.
7. See, Arif A. Waqif, "Costs and Benefits of Regional cooperation in South Asia", In L.L. Mehrotra, et al, eds., *SAARC 2000 and beyond* n. 1, pp. 131-40.
8. Moonis Ahmar, for instance, points out the problems in South Asia such as suspicion and mistrust while contrasting the EC without considering the fact that EC emerged among the former adversarial states. Moonis Ahmar, "European Union as a model for SAARC", In K. B. Lall, H. S. Chopra, Thomas Meyer, eds., *The European Community and SAARC* (New Delhi: Radiant, 1993) pp. 44-45, 53-54.
9. K. K. Bhargava, "The SAARC: Challenges and opportunities", in K.B. Lall, et al eds., *The European Community and SAARC*, ibid., p. 25.
10. Rummel, n. 1, p. 294.
11. See, H. S. Chopra, "The Franco-German Reconciliation: Its relevance to the Indo-Pak Perspectives on South Asian Peace Order", in Mehrotra, et al., eds., *SAARC 2000 and Beyond,* n.1, pp. 350-55.
12. Lama and Lavakare opine that South Asia could benefit from programmes similar to EUREKA which are based on the collaborative spirit and willingness of member states to look at long term gains rather than short term inconveniences. See, Mahenda P. Lama and Prabhakara J. Lavakare, "Technology Missions for South Asia: Cooperation in the high tech domain", In Mehrotra, et al, eds., *SAARC 2000 and beyond*, n. 1, pp. 167-99.
13. Pakistani Scholar Iqbal Cheema, for instance, argues that bilateral disputes need to be

subjected to collective discussion and the exclusion of bilateral and contentions issues by SAARC charter is a 'problem'. Pervaiz Iqbal Cheema, "SAARC needs Revamping", in Eric Gonsalves and Nancy Jetly, eds., *The Dynamics of South Asian Regional Cooperation and SAARC* (New Delhi: Sage, 1999), pp. 97-93, 103. But resolution of bilateral conflicts though could be conducive need not be a precondition for increased regional cooperation.

14. *SAARC vision beyond the year 2000: Report of the SAARC Group of Eminent Persons Established by the Ninth SAARC Summit* (Delhi: Shipra, 1999) p. 53-57.
15. See, Percy Allum, *State and civil society in Western Europe* (Cambridge: Polity Press, 1995) pp. 281-83; Laura Cram, *Policy making in the European Union, Conceptual lenses and the integration process* (London: Routledge, 1997) pp. 123-53; Sonia Mazey and Jeremy Richardson, "Pressure groups and lobbying in the EC," In Juliet Lodge, ed., *The European Community and the Challenge of the future*, 2nd edn., (London: Pinter, 1993) pp. 37-47.
16. S. D. Muni, "Regional Conflicts in South Asia and Role of SAARC in their Management," in Lall, et al., eds. *The European Community*, n. 8, p. 61; SAARC Vision, n. 14, pp. 48-51.
17. See, Kant Kishore Bhargava, Heinz Bongartz and Farooq Sobhan, *Shaping South Asia's Future: Role of Regional Cooperation* (New Delhi: Vikas, 1995) pp. 34-37.
18. The idea of BBIN-GQ was resented by Pakistan, Maldives, Sri Lanka and also within Bangladesh as such going against the SAARC spirit. In 1997 in Bangladesh when Prime Minister Sheikh Hasina was supportive of the idea, leader of the Opposition Begum Khalida Zia was bent on its opposition. See. Abdul Kalam, "Sub-regional Cooperation in South Asia in comparative perspective: Ideals and Realities", in B.C. Upreti, ed., *SAARC Dynamics of Regional Cooperation in South Asia,* Vol. I, Nature, Scope and Perceptions (New Delhi: Kalinga, 2000) pp. 109-143. Three of the SAARC members are also part of another sub-regional grouping (outside SAARC forum) called BIMST-EC (Bangladesh, India, Myanmar, Sri Lanka, Thailand Economic Cooperation) whose inaugural ministerial meeting took place in Bangkok in June 1977.
19. SAARC Vision, n. 14, pp. 70-71.
20. *Economic Times* (New Delhi) 12 May 1997; Rajan Harshe, "South Asian Regional Cooperation: Problems and Prospects", *Economic and Political Weekly* vol. 34, no. 19, 8 May 1999, pp. 1100-05: Padmaja Murthy, "The Gujral doctrine and beyond," *http://www.idsa-org/an-jul* 9-8.html.
21. This appears slightly an improvement compared to 1999 figures of US $ 2331 million as against its global trade of US $ 84079 million that represent just 2.7 percent. Yet it is far from satisfactory. Compilation based on *IMF, Direction of Trade Statistics Quarterly* (Washington), June 2000 and March 2001 and IMF, *Direction of Trade Statistics Year Book, 2005* especially pp. 251-53.
22. Rummel., n.1, p. 294.

# PART V

# INDIA AND SRI LANKA

# 19

# Emerging Trends in Sri Lanka: An Indian Perspective

R. Swaminathan

A quarter century of LTTE-led militancy and terrorism in Sri Lanka came to an end in May 2009. Some of the trends that have been and are emerging in 'Post-War' Sri Lanka need to be noted and considered by policy-makers in Sri Lanka, India and elsewhere.

## Sri Lankan Government

The armed forces of Sri Lanka are entitled to their happiness and pride in having 'eliminated' the capabilities of LTTE to mount conventional military operations. Some competent analysts have gone to the extent of praising President Rajapakse as the first leader to have successfully terminated terrorism by military means alone. The Sri Lankan Government (SLG) has claimed that the armed forces of some countries have approached Sri Lanka for training in counter-terrorism techniques. With the 'intoxication' induced by all these goodies, the doubt arises as to whether the overall vision of SLG is becoming blurred by 'triumphalism' and/or by the 'chauvinistic' demands of its supporters, leading to the ignoring of ground realities. The president and his advisers seem to have concluded that the military defeat of LTTE has at the same time ended the struggle of the Tamils for 'equal' citizenship. I would like to sound a note of caution that, while the militant leaders of a major terrorist group have been eliminated or neutralized, the seeds of militancy and terrorism will remain as long as the basic grievances and deprivations are not addressed and effectively resolved. The seemingly low priority accorded to any meaningful progress in evolving a consensual political solution to the Tamil ethnic issue poses the threat that, with the basic causes existing and a solution by peaceful dialogue being indefinitely delayed, other groups or leaders may emerge who once again feel pushed into militancy. US Assistant Secretary of State for South Asia and former Ambassador to Sri Lanka (Robert O Blake) has also warned that Sri Lanka's failure to share power with minority Tamils after the end of the war could lead to renewed violence.

History has shown that a political solution, delivered or credibly promised, is an essential component of reconciliation, in situations as in Sri Lanka. Positive and negative examples can be found in India (the partition of India instigated by the British policy of 'divide and rule' when discussions-as advised by Rajaji-might have resulted in an indigenous solution, secessionist and anti-north noises in Tamil Nadu, militancy in Punjab and Mizoram, etc.), erstwhile Soviet Union, China and in many other areas of the world. History has also shown that a mono (ethnic/linguistic/theistic/ideological) State cannot survive for long in a nation whose people are multi (ethnic/linguistic/theistic/ideological). Such states have either to perish (as in the Soviet Union) or change (as in USA in mid-1880s, China during its economic turn-around); but nations survive, with their multi ethnic/linguistic/theistic/ideological nature intact. The lessons of history can be ignored only at one's own risk.

War consists of a series of actions by the parties involved in the confrontation, but peace is a combination of a state of mind and harmony between all the different ethnic groups that populate Sri Lanka. The president had earlier hinted that a political solution would be offered once the military operations ended. There was also the hint that when the report of the All Party Representative Committee (APRC-under Tissa Vitharana) was finalized, it would be implemented. Later, the non-participation of the TNA in the formulation of a policy for reconciliation was stated to be delaying progress. The president subsequently convened the All Party Meeting for Development and Reconciliation-without any linkage between political solution (power devolution) and reconciliation. Meanwhile, local body elections were held in Jaffna and Vavuniya without a clear definition of the issues, with very low turnout and with mixed results. President Rajapakse has also reportedly stated that he needs a fresh mandate for working towards a political solution. It is difficult to comprehend as to why separate mandates are required to wage war and to make peace, as making peace is the natural culmination of a successful war effort. These apparently dilatory tactics generate scepticism about a real intention to evolve an equitable political solution. Robert Blake has also warned that if SLG keeps on delaying announcing a political solution, "there is a possibility that they will alienate the Tamil community further and again exacerbate the divisions, and perhaps even give new opportunities to the LTTE".

It should be obvious that rehabilitation, reconciliation, development and restoration (of democracy) are the most essential measures to be taken without delay. There should be no rigidity in attempting these measures sequentially, as apparently opined by SLG, and efforts need to be made to tackle them almost simultaneously. With the elimination of the military capabilities of the LTTE, SLG can negotiate from a position of strength. It should recognize that the LTTE had indeed brutalized Tamils everywhere and that the LTTE, despite its own grandiose claims, was never synonymous with all Tamils of Sri Lanka. The Sinhalese can and should deal with their Tamil fellow-countrymen in a non-patronising but magnanimous manner and seek national reconciliation. Although the president has repeatedly promised to be generous to the Tamil minority, the fine points of the government's position are yet to emerge. The deep disappointment of USA with President Rajapakse for relegating the devolution of power in the Tamil majority areas to the backburner until after the presidential election has been publicly expressed by Robert Blake. He has urged that SLG should figure out ways to have an early dialogue with the Tamil community.

The decision to prohibit the use of ethnic or linguistic identities in the names of political parties is fraught with dangerous possibilities in a multi-ethnic and multi-lingual country. One can only hope that better counsels would ultimately prevail.

**Armed Forces**

It is not unknown for grateful governments to grant higher ranks to military leaders who have successfully led the armed forces to a significant victory. However, the quick restructuring of the command setup, with the appointment of General Fonseca as Chief of Defence Staff and the vesting of extraordinary powers in the CDS and the Defence Secretary, are intriguing. The accountability of the armed forces to the civilian authority of a cabinet may be diluted.

Normally, the end of war operations results in the reduction in the strength of the armed forces, through demobilization and diversion of excess manpower. However, SLG proposes to expand the armed forces and regularly deploy military units in the north and the east. These new (permanent) deployments are likely to be in the nature of cantonments, i.e. family stations. Depending on the ethnic profile of the deployed forces, this may become another cause for resentment. Also, apart from any effect on the demographic profile of these areas, these trends raise the distinct possibility of the armed forces becoming an additional and credible power centre in Sri Lankan politics.

**Internally Displaced Persons (IDP)**

More than 250,000 refugees (somewhat euphemistically referred to as Internally Displaced Persons-IDP) are in 'relief' camps and additional thousands had been semi-permanently 'displaced' in earlier years. There are credible reports that the conditions in these camps are as good as could be expected in the current circumstances, but there are contradictory reports (including one by a BBC correspondent who had recently visited one of the camps) that these are in fact internment camps. The president has said that these IDP cannot yet go back to their homes, which (in his words) are 'jungles'. A delay in total de-mining of their home areas is one of the reasons cited for their continuing in the camps. The 'screening' of the refugees is another cause for delaying their rehabilitation. The claim that more than 40,000 Tamil families have already been rehabilitated in their homes severely strains the credibility of an analyst.

Makeshift hovels in unsatisfactory conditions would be fertile breeding grounds for resentment and the seeds of further future unrest would be nurtured there. The frustration, anger and neglect of legitimate grievances of an already marginalized Tamil population are bound to make ethnic reconciliation and lasting peace distant dreams. There is need for a sense of urgency in resettling the refugees in their old homes. International support and help would certainly be available if the SLG comes out with viable and verifiable procedures. In the meantime, SLG could usefully bring in more transparency in the administration of these camps, by forming monitoring groups with members from different shades of the political spectrum, including Tamils.

The US has also demanded that steps should be taken to ensure that the international community, the United Nations and the International Committee of the Red Cross and others have access to the camps, so that it could be verified that everything that goes on in these camps is up to international standards. The Tamil leadership should, at the minimum, pursue this idea vigorously. They should also demand that their representatives should have access to the camps and to the refugees.

## Human Rights

A certain amount of restrictions on human rights would have to be expected when a government is prosecuting a war. The situation should, however, be reversed as soon as possible, after the war ends. On the contrary, the current indications are that the president and SLG are becoming increasingly intolerant of criticism or dissent, particularly from the media. The 'white car' activity and 'missing persons' phenomenon are said to be continuing. Except during Eelam War IV, Sri Lanka has had a fairly good record in the area of human rights – if one considers ethnic violence from both sides as an unfortunate national aberration. President Rajapakse would be well advised to take personal initiative to improve respect for the human rights of all citizens and residents of Sri Lanka.

## Economy

Every war imposes severe economic hardships on all citizens. Conversion from a war-driven economy to a peace-dictated economy is normally slow and painful. The general downturn in global economic activity would make it even more difficult for SLG. There is a school of thought which believes that, if the policies of SLG do not bring about a quick turn-around in the peace-time economy, the sufferings of the people would increase. The possibility that economic discontent may bring the Sinhalas and the Tamils together in their common disaffection against the SLG's handling of the economic difficulties is also being spoken about. In my personal view, the ethnic division has been made so deep-rooted in the last few decades that the economy has probably reach a near-collapse situation, for the ethnic animosities to be forgotten in attempts to forge a common anti-SLG front. The highly developed survival instinct of the president and his supporters may not let such a situation come about.

**Tamil Leadership**

The civil leadership of Sri Lankan Tamils had surrendered, not necessarily voluntarily, their leadership role to the LTTE for more than twenty years. They now seem unable to recognize their opportunities and discharge their new (but natural) responsibilities. Their public inactivity and seeming non-involvement in the speedy evolution of a political solution, coupled with the president's ability to take unquestioned unilateral actions, give the impression that they also subscribe to the SLG's view that the entire Tamil movement had been defeated when the LTTE was administered its military defeat. It is time that the Tamil leadership get out of their LTTE-imposed stupor and start functioning again as responsible leaders of a marginalized and 'deprived' community.

It would perhaps be out of place for me to suggest courses of action to the Tamil leadership, but they could usefully consider some of the following measures:

- Openly and clearly disown the militancy of LTTE and seek a peaceful resolution within the framework of a unified Sri Lankan nation.
- Use the delays imposed by the president, to organize themselves into cadre-based parties working amongst the people, with whom they have had little interaction or meaningful contact for two decades.
- Be politically active and mobilize public opinion throughout Sri Lanka, in favour of ethnic reconciliation at the national level.
- Consider a coordinated effort by all the Tamil parties, through a 'Joint Action Committee', to demand and urge forward a movement on the package for political devolution- instead of merely waiting for crumbs to fall from the presidential table.
- Behave as 'Sri Lankan' political parties and not look for inspiration and support from outside the country.

## Sri Lanka-India

The emerging trend seems to be to sideline India as much as possible. In the field of economic relations, India is increasingly being relegated from its traditional 'first choice' role for collaboration in major projects, particularly in the field of infrastructural development. Reports speak of Sri Lanka and China having signed agreements worth USD 350 million relating to the bunkering facility at Hambanthotta and the expressway from Colombo to the Kattanayake Airport. While the Hambanthotta deal can be understood as being part of a composite project, it would be difficult to justify the exclusion of Indian companies from bidding for the expressway project. The Government of India and Indian companies have to take note of this disturbing trend and devise measures to restore India's leading role in Sri Lanka's economic development. Special emphasis would be necessary on projects related to the Tamil-populated areas. Preparedness on the part of Indian companies to make significant investments in Sri Lanka and tax incentives for such investment may be useful steps. Essentially, India could try to be more cooperative and helpful on the economic front.

Politically, India has little option but to continue her unobtrusive, non-interventionist, persuasive role in working towards the Tamils being treated as equal citizens the same as the Sinhalas, Muslims etc. The recent statement of the Indian High Commissioner (Alok Prasad), linking a broad-based political settlement to the resettlement of war displaced, should be welcomed. India would not be alone in such an approach. Robert Blake has bluntly stated that continued US aid to Sri Lanka would depend on how expeditiously the Rajapakse government alleviates the lot of the hundreds of thousands of internally displaced Tamil refugees and 'on the progress that it makes towards political reconciliation and devolution of power.'

In matters relating to relief and rehabilitation, India could and should be much more pro-active, supportive and involved. It should never be forgotten that Sri Lankan Tamils are natural allies of the Indian people and the government, and that India cannot but help them to attain their legitimate aspirations.

## Conclusion

In this critical crossroad of Sri Lankan history, it is for President Rajapakse to decide on his place in that history. Does he want to be known as the Sri Lankan version of Abraham Lincoln, who rendered justice to all citizens irrespective of their ethnicity and helped build a unified multi-ethnic Sri Lanka? Or would he be satisfied with being the president who perpetuated the ethnic division and fractured the country for a long time to come?

# 20

## Is Tamil Nadu the Villain in India-Sri Lanka Relations?

V. Suryanarayan

---

In a country of continental proportions like India, which shares land and maritime boundaries with Pakistan, China, Nepal, Bhutan, Bangladesh, Myanmar, Thailand, Indonesia, Sri Lanka and Maldives, bilateral relations will have their inevitable fallout on contiguous Indian states. Thus relations with Pakistan will have its fallout on Punjab, Rajasthan. Gujarat and Jammu and Kashmir; relations with Nepal will have its fallout on Sikkim, Uttar Pradesh and Bihar, relations with Bangladesh will have its fallout on Assam, West Bengal, Manipur, Meghalaya, Tripura and Mizoram; relations with Bhutan will affect West Bengal and Sikkim; relations with Myanmar will affect Manipur, Mizoram, Nagaland and Arunachal Pradesh, relations with Sri Lanka will affect Tamil Nadu and Kerala will be affected by development in the Gulf countries. In the years of one-party dominance in New Delhi bilateral relations were determined solely by what the Central government perceived as India's national interest. On many occasions the interests of the contiguous Indian states were sacrificed and consequently there were strains in centre-state relations. The mass upsurge in Assam over the illegal infiltration by millions of Bangladeshis is a telling illustration of New Delhi's neglect of Assam.

With the formation of coalition governments and regional parties becoming partners in the central government, the equation has undergone a fundamental transformation. Regional inputs are being made into the making of India's neighbourhood policy; what is more, the central government has also, on several occasions, contributed to the softening of the chauvinist foreign policy perceptions of regional actors. For the successful conduct of foreign relations, it is essential that there should be benign interaction between central and state governments. If such an interaction has to take place, there must be vibrant think-tanks in regional capitals. The Universities, which have departments specializing in international relations, strategic studies and area studies, should play a greater role in sensitizing public opinion on major foreign policy issues. However, if one surveys the achievements of these departments in various South Indian Universities, the balance sheet is not very commendable. For want of qualified faculty, dynamic and imaginative leadership and dearth of library resources, many departments are languishing. The tragic fact remains that even after sixty two years of independence, we do not have in South India an institution similar to the Institute of Southeast Asian Studies in Singapore or Australian National University in Canberra.

This essay is an attempt to study the interaction among the Central Government, the State Government of Tamil Nadu and the political forces in the State in the making and unmaking of India's Sri Lanka policy.

**Recent Trends**

Speaking in the Tamil Nadu Legislative Assembly recently, Chief Minister M. Karunanidhi, who is also the President of the Dravida Munnetra Kazhagam (DMK), pointed out that in the post-LTTE era, attaining the goal of Tamil Eelam was not a realistic goal. He advocated the pursuance of a 'flexible policy', where the Tamils should avoid critical comments about the Sinhalese 'out of anger and hatred', because it may have 'adverse effect' on their well being. The need of the hour, Karunanidhi underlined, is for the Tamils to carry on their struggle 'for equal rights, equal status for their language and devolution of power at the regional level'.

Discerning students of Tamil Nadu politics, especially those analyzing the role of Tamil Nadu in the Sri Lankan ethnic conflict, are intrigued by the transformation that has taken place in the DMK perception on Sri Lanka. It may be recalled that following the communal holocaust in July 1983, Karunanidhi and Anbazhagan resigned their seats in the Legislative Assembly to protest against New Delhi's lukewarm response to the sufferings of the Sri Lankan Tamils. On August 27, 1983, the DMK passed a resolution, which stated that a 'separate Tamil Eelam shall be the only remedy and paramount solution'. Speaking in the Marina beach on the next day, K. Anbazhagan demanded Indian 'military intervention' to put a halt to the 'genocide' taking place on the island.

The DMK, in the long years when it was in opposition, used to be severely critical of the policies and programs of the central government; more relevant from the regional perspective, the Party used to accuse the AIADMK government of sacrificing the interests of their Tamil brethren across the Palk Strait. After coming to power, in 1989, Karunanidhi wanted to prove his pro-Tamil credentials. When the Indian Peace Keeping Force (IPKF) returned from Sri Lanka, Karnunanidhi did not have even the courtesy to receive them, for he accused the Indian Army of committing 'atrocities' against the Tamils.

Far worse things are happening in Sri Lanka today. As the Sri Lankan military offensive gathered momentum, the war against the Tigers degenerated into a war against Tamil civilians. The hapless Tamils were caught virtually between the Sinhalese Lions and the Tamil Tigers. Hundreds of them lost their lives as a result of savage bombing and many were fatally injured. As A Sivanandan, Director of the Institute of Race Relations, London, states, "It is difficult to talk dispassionately about what is going on in my country, when the horror of what the government is doing to a civilian Tamil population – already shelled and burned out of their existence and now herded into concentration camps and starved of food and medicine...".

The Government of India should have tried to evolve an international mechanism, acceptable to the Sri Lankan Government and the Tamil Tigers, to rescue the trapped Tamil civilians from the war zone and escort them to refugee camps manned by the UN organizations. It may be recalled that when large scale riots took place in Colombo in 1958 and Tamil residents were scared of their lives and security, the Indian High Commissioner, YD Gundevia, along with other friendly countries, persuaded the Governor General Olivier Goonetileke, to accept the offer of ships to transfer the Tamils to the safety of the Tamil areas in Jaffna peninsula. India, along with other countries, arranged ships and those Tamils who wanted to leave Colombo were taken to Kankesenturai. When normalcy was restored, the Tamils returned back to the city. No such initiative was taken by New Delhi this time. The response of the Government of India, backed solidly by the Tamil Nadu government, was only to express 'concern' at the plight of the Tamil civilians. The maximum that Karunanidhi could accomplish, after his famous hunger strike, was the assurance from President Mahinda Rajapakse that there will no military offensive for three days.

How does one explain the paradigm shift in New Delhi-Chennai equation? Was it due to the 'coalition dharma' practiced by the central government, in which the DMK is an important partner? Was it due to Karunanidhi's keen desire to strengthen his political links with Congress President Sonia Gandhi at a time when sections within the Congress were toying with the idea of a coalition with the AIADMK in the post election scenario? Was the policy dictated by the Chief Minister's desire to ensure important cabinet berths to his near and dear ones in the Central Government?

**Basic Realities**

In order to provide a rational explanation, it is necessary to highlight certain stark realities in India-Sri Lanka relations. The role played by Tamil Nadu in fashioning India's Sri Lanka policy is a subject matter of great controversy. The Sinhalese have always maintained that Tamil Nadu was invariably the villain in the deterioration of Sri Lanka - India relations in the post independence period. Prof. K.M De Silva, the well known Sri Lankan historian, in his book, Managing

Ethnic Tensions in Multi-Ethnic Societies, Sri Lanka, 1880-1985, has written, "The increasingly turbulent politics in Jaffna peninsula began to be treated as an integral part of the internal politics of Tamil Nadu. The DMK, effectively checked from pursuing its separatist goal in India, took vicarious pleasure in giving encouragement and support to separatist tendencies among the Tamils of Sri Lanka". Prof. De Silva added, "Once a separatist movement emerged among the Tamils in Sri Lanka, it was fostered, nurtured and protected by Tamil Nadu".

For entirely different reasons, JN Dixit, former Indian High Commissioner in Sri Lanka, also endorses this view. Speaking in the United Services Institute, New Delhi on March 10, 1989, J.N. Dixit highlighted the problems associated with Sri Lankan Tamil ethnicity and its repercussions on Tamil Nadu as important determinants in India's Sri Lanka policy. To quote Dixit, "The first voice of secessionism in the Indian Republic was raised in Tamil Nadu in the mid-sixties. This was exactly the same principle of Tamil ethnicity, Tamil language. So in a manner, our interest in Sri Lanka, Tamil aspirations in Sri Lanka were based on maintaining our own unity, our own integrity, our own identity, in the manner in which we have been trying to build our society". Based on this premise, Dixit stated that if New Delhi did not support the cause of the Sri Lankan Tamils, the Tamils in India would feel that 'we are not standing by our own Tamils', and if that is so, then in the Tamil psyche, Tamil subconscious, the question arose, "Is there any relevance or validity of our being a part of a larger political identity, if our deeply felt sentiments are not respected? So it was a compulsion, which could not be avoided by any elected government in the country".

The explanations provided by Prof. KM De Silva and Ambassador JN Dixit are over simplifications of a complex issue. When I analyze the triangular relations among New Delhi, Chennai and Colombo in a chronological perspective, I come to the following conclusions: On the broad canvas of India-Sri Lanka relations, the role of Tamil Nadu was peripheral in the fashioning of India's Sri Lanka policy. In fact, on crucial issues, the interests of Tamil Nadu were sacrificed by New Delhi in the name of good neighbourly relations. Take the case of the Sirimavo-Shastri Pact, 1964 and the subsequent Sirimavo-Indira Gandhi Pact 1974. These two Agreements converted the people of Indian origin in Sri Lanka into merchandise and they were divided, without ascertaining their wishes, between the two countries. All political leaders in Tamil Nadu, irrespective of their political affiliations—C. Rajagopalachari, Kamaraj Nadar, C.N. Annadurai, V.K. Krishna Menon and P Ramamurthy—opposed the inhuman agreement. But Prime Minister Lal Bahadur Shastri, guided by the advice of the then Commonwealth Secretary C.S. Jha, signed the agreement in

October 1964. It should also be pointed out that the agreement was a betrayal of the Gandhi-Nehru legacy. Jawaharlal Nehru consistently maintained that the people of Indian origin in Ceylon, most of them belonging to the third or fourth generations, because of the long years of residence and their contributions to the development of the economy, had every right to become citizens of that country. The second major issue where the interests of Tamil Nadu were not kept in mind by New Delhi was in the delimitation of the maritime boundary between India and Sri Lanka. The 1974 and the 1976 Agreements not only ceded the island of Kachchativu, which was a part of the Zamindari of Raja of Ramnad to Sri Lanka, they also failed to uphold the traditional fishing rights of Indian fishermen in those waters. Tamil Nadu fishermen still continue to suffer because of the failure of New Delhi to uphold their interests.

Despite geographical proximity and close cultural linkages, the Sri Lankan Tamil nationalism had an autonomous momentum of its own. The two political movements took diametrically opposite courses. In India, the demand for a separate state died a natural death; today the Dravidian parties not only rule in Tamil Nadu, they also share power in New Delhi. In Sri Lanka, on the other hand, the consensual politics has given way to conflictual politics. The dynamic changes in the Indian political system illustrate the success of the nation building experiment. On the other hand, a close study of the developments in Sri Lanka illustrates the perils of majoritarian democracy. A political system which does not take into consideration the aspirations and sensitivities of minority groups is bound to face serious challenges.

The decision to pursue the mediatory-militant supportive policy towards Sri Lanka at the end of July 1983 was taken by New Delhi with absolutely no inputs from Tamil Nadu. The decision was taken in a meeting attended by Prime Minister Indira Gandhi, G Parthasarathy and A. Amirtalingam. The views of the Government of Tamil Nadu on the subject were never sought. According to informed sources when Tamil Nadu Chief Minister MG Ramachandran came to know of the decision he was extremely unhappy about the attitude of New Delhi.

The volatile politics in Tamil Nadu can be understood only if we keep in mind the competitive politics among the two Dravidian parties, namely the AIADMK and the DMK. Equally relevant were the Congress party's attempts to rebuild itself in Tamil Nadu by lending support to the Sri Lankan Tamil cause. In the game of one upmanship and competitive mudslinging, rhetoric was more important than reality.

A close analysis of the policies and programs of the LTTE clearly bring to light that Prabhakaran steadfastly retained his independence of action. He was willing to take help from all quarters, including from President Premadasa (to get the IPKF out of Sri Lanka). When he realized in the beginning of 1987 that Chief Minister M.G. Ramachandran, in the final analysis, has to follow the dictates of New Delhi, he not only returned to Sri Lanka, but also built up the international network which financed the LTTE and fuelled its war machine. He still hoped to use Tamil Nadu as the sanctuary and as the supply base and maintained his close contacts with supporters like Nedumaran and Vaiko. When international supply lines got dried up during the Fourth Eelam War, Prabhakaran was hoping that the pro-LTTE forces will sweep the polls in Tamil Nadu; he was also hoping that the Congress party will lose and a government more sensitive to Tamil aspirations will come to power in India. His fond hopes were shattered when the Congress returned to power.

Unlike the era of one party dominance, wherein the interests of Tamil Nadu were ignored by New Delhi, the era of coalition governments, which began in 1979, brought about salutary changes. The regional partners began to make inputs into the making of foreign policy. What is more, the Central Government also began to influence the regional partners and brought about changes in their way of thinking. Few illustrations are given below. The inclusion of the Sethusamudram project in the common minimum program, the non-conclusion of the defence agreement between India and Sri Lanka, the dropping of the idea of a land bridge between India and Sri Lanka and the decision not to resume shipping between Tuticorin and Colombo and Rameshwaram and Talaimannar—are illustrations where one can clearly discern the influence of Tamil Nadu. Equally relevant, the Man Mohan Singh government has been able to persuade the DMK, especially the Chief Minister, to conform to and support the policies of the central government towards Sri Lanka, which upholds the unity and territorial integrity of the State, zero tolerance for the acts of terrorism committed by the Tigers and fashioning of a new political order, based on the implementation of the 13th Amendment.

**New Delhi's Ignorance of Basic Realities**

New Delhi found itself in a quagmire in Sri Lanka following Mrs. Indira Gandhi's assassination, because some of the important decision makers in the Indian Foreign Office were not conversant with the complexities and realities of Sri Lanka. Two incidents, mentioned by J.N. Dixit in his book Assignment Colombo, are worth repeating. The first relates to Romesh Bhandari, Foreign Secretary, one of the main architects of India's Sri Lanka policy during the stewardship of Rajiv Gandhi. Bhandari, who brought about radical shifts in foreign policy, claimed, "India intends to have an Indian rather than a Tamil Nadu policy towards Sri Lanka". To quote Dixit, "...he asked me whether I had informed the moderate Tamil leaders about the contents of the Non-Paper which were conveyed to the Sri Lankan Government. I told him I had not because I had no such instructions. This was where his vague knowledge about Tamil leadership found expression. He said, "Mani, as soon as you reach Colombo hand over the documents to Chelvanayakam". I pointed out that Chelvanayakam had died nearly two decades ago. So handing over the papers to him was not possible. I said perhaps he meant that I should hand over the paper to Dr. N. Thiruchelvam. Bhandari was impatient. He said, "Give the paper to Chelvanayakam, Thiruchelvam whosoever it is. All these South Indian names are very confusing". I assured him that I would carry out the instructions".

The second incident pertains to General K. Sundarji, Chief of the Armed Forces. What was General Sundarji's assessment of the fighting capabilities of the Tigers? According to Dixit, General Sundarji told Prime Minister Rajiv Gandhi, "If the LTTE decided to take on India and Sri Lanka militarily, Indian armed forces would be able to neutralize them militarily within two weeks. So there need not be any serious worry on this score". Unlike General Sundarji, who had a poor opinion about the fighting capabilities of the Tigers, perceptive Sri Lanka watchers in India were aware of the single-minded determination of Prabhakaran to carry on the struggle for the attainment of the Tamil Eelam; they were also conscious of the fighting capabilities of the LTTE guerrillas. The task before the Indian Peace Keeping Forces was not easy, many lost their lives and finally they had to return from Sri Lanka without attaining the objectives which the Government of India had set for them.

**Cultural and Political Interaction**

The cultural and political consciousness of the Sri Lankan Tamils had always been influenced by developments across the Palk Strait. This applied to politics as well as to culture. The main events in India, both in the north and the south, had their impact on the Tamil community. The founding of the Arya Samaj, the changes within the Hindu community brought about by the Ramakrishna Mission; the emergence of the Indian National Congress; the teachings of Gopal Krishna Gokhale, Mahadev Govind Ranade, and Aurobindo; the leadership of Mahatma Gandhi; the non-cooperation and Satyagraha movements all of them had their impact on the Tamil community. Equally relevant were the social and political movements in Madras Presidency—the emergence of Periyar Ramaswamy Naicker and his teachings, the self respect movement, the formation of the Dravida Kazhagam and later the Dravida Munnetra Kazhagam also contributed to the rise of the political consciousness of the Tamil community in Sri Lanka. However, we have to keep in mind differing political developments in

Sri Lanka and South India. In Sri Lanka the Tamil political leaders moved away from collaboration with the Sinhalese political elite and started demanding a separate state when the nation building experiment started on the basis of Sinhalese language and Buddhist religion. Whereas, contrastingly in India, political developments resulted in Tamil leaders moving away from the demand of a separate state. What is more, they became the upholders of the status quo by joining the national mainstream.

While explaining the interaction between the political developments in Tamil Nadu and the Tamil areas of Sri Lanka, we have to distinguish between rhetoric and reality. From the 1960's, the protagonists of a separate state of Tamil Eelam used to assert, based more on imagination than on facts, "In India the south fights for independence from the north; in Sri Lanka, the north fights for independence from the South". The Dravidian leaders used to highlight the 'sacred duty' of Tai Nadu (motherland) to protect the rights and interests of the Tamils scattered in different parts of the world. In the popular Tamil film, Parasakti, the script of the film was written by Karunanidhi, hero Gunasekaran (played by Sivaji Ganesan) poses the question, "why is the water of the Bay of Bengal saline? Is it because of the tears of overseas Tamils?"

**Tamil Nadu and Ethnic Conflict in Sri Lanka**

The communal holocaust which took place in Sri Lanka in July 1983 and the mounting tragedy in the island had its inevitable fallout in Tamil Nadu. As mentioned earlier, Tamil Nadu politics during this period can be understood only in terms of competitive politics in the state. The response of the DMK/AIADMK was motivated mainly by their desire to score debating points and stage one-upmanship upon the opponent. During 1983-1987, the debate cantered round as to who was the greater champion of the Sri Lankan Tamil interests. As M.R. Narayan Swamy writes in Tigers of Lanka: From Boys to Guerrillas, 'There was no love lost between MGR and Karunanidhi, and both tried to score points over each other using the Tamil issue as a chequer board. Whatever MGR did for the Tamils was not enough for Karunanidhi; and anything that the DMK leader said or did was seen by the Chief Minister as play acting. In the long run both began to view the Eelam campaign with an eye on the elections. Unfortunately Tamil groups also courted them'. The Tamil United Liberation Front (TULF) was close to the central government; Amirtalingam tried to maintain good equations with both DMK and the AIADMK; the LTTE and its leader Prabhakaran became very close to MGR; the Tamil Eelam Liberation Organization (TELO) had the patronage of Karunanidhi; the Peoples Liberation Organization of Tamil Eelam (PLOTE) under Uma Maheshwaran had the blessings of Somasundram of the

AIADMK; the Eelam Peoples Revolutionary Liberation Front (EPRLF) under Padmanabha, because of its leftist ideology, came close to the CPI and later the UCPI; only the miniscule Eelam Revolutionary Organizers (EROS) under Balakumar, kept a safe distance away from all political forces. With the blessings of the Chief Minister M.G. Ramachandran, the LTTE began to register an astounding growth. Prabhakaran adopted ruthless methods to annihilate political opponents and eventually emerged as the single most important factor in the Tamil areas.

It should be kept in mind that in terms of electoral support, the most ardent supporters of the LTTE in Tamil Nadu have never been able to get elected to the Legislative Assembly on their own. P. Nedumaran and S.D. Somasundaram contested the 1989 elections to the Legislative Assembly on the Tamil Eelam platform, but the electorate decisively rejected them. The charisma of MGR overshadowed the political scene. The author recalls one occasion, when MGR undertook a hunger strike before the Anna Samadhi in Chepauk in support of the Sri Lankan Tamils cause; thousands thronged the scene, the mere sight of MGR sent them into frenzy; all shouted slogans in support of MGR; they forgot the cause for which the hunger strike was undertaken.

The LTTE built its vast network in different parts of Tamil Nadu. Tamil Nadu was not only a sanctuary, but also became a safe haven from which the Eelam struggle derived its vocal and material support. Prabhakaran exploited to the full the contradictions in the Indian political scene–between the AIADMK and the DMK, between the central and state governments and between RAW and the IPKF. What is more, the efficient network which the LTTE painstakingly built in Tamil Nadu–comprising smugglers, fishermen, political activists, transport operators, business men and corrupt officials–provided support and backing to their war machine. Through the 'Prabhakaran trail', stretching from the arid areas of Coimbatore, Salem, Erode through Karur and Trichy on the Cauvery banks to the coastal village in Vedaranyam, explosives, hand grenades, food, medicines, fuel and diesel oil were moved and from Vedaranyam to the Jaffna peninsula. The long coastline in Tamil Nadu, with innumerable fishing harbours, provided a safe haven to the LTTE's fast moving boats. An efficient communication system linking Jaffna to the outside world through Tamil Nadu was built up. The four principles of ancient Indian statecraft–Sama, Dana, Bheda and Danda-were employed by the LTTE to retain Tamil Nadu as a sanctuary and a supply base.

The IPKF's plea to successive governments in Tamil Nadu–AIADMK, DMK and even President's administration–to curb the activities of the LTTE fell on deaf ears. It is a strange paradox, but true, that Indian soldiers in Sri Lanka were getting maimed and killed by the explosives and grenades manufactured in Tamil

Nadu. What is more, the wounded Tamil guerrillas were getting treated in Tamil Nadu hospitals.

## DMK Adopts Pro-Tiger Stance

When the DMK came into power in Tamil Nadu in 1989, the party began to adopt a pro-Tiger stance. The decision taken by the Government of Tamil Nadu to boycott the functions in connection with the return of the IPKF has to be seen as an attempt made by the DMK to get closer to the Tigers. However, the LTTE continued to remain intransigent. The LTTE's policy of flouting all canons of civilized behaviour became evident when in June 1990, the LTTE guerrillas murdered the EPRLF leader Padmanabha and his comrades in cold blood at Kodambakkam in Chennai. The well-knit LTTE network enabled the assassins to escape from the scene of murder without any difficulty. The contempt that the LTTE had for the DMK can be understood from the fact that on the day of Padmanabha's assassination, Karunanidhi was pleading with his allies in the National Front in New Delhi to accord permission to the LTTE to bring the sick and the wounded to Tamil Nadu for medical treatment. Even after Padmanabha's assassination, security in the State was not tightened and streamlined. And the killing of Rajiv Gandhi at the prime of his life was the culmination of the overt and covert Indian involvement of Sri Lanka and the equally despicable activities of the LTTE in Tamil Nadu. From the security angle, it should be mentioned that if on that fateful night in Sriperumbudur, female security personnel would have physically frisked all women who wanted to greet Rajiv Gandhi, we may not have lost a political leader of great promise, at the prime of his life. Another failure of Tamil Nadu Security needs a mention; among the accused in the Rajiv Gandhi assassination case, six of them were registered as refugees in the state.

## Rajiv Gandhi's Assassination and After

The assassination of Rajiv Gandhi in May 1991 turned the tide against the LTTE. The sympathy and support that Sri Lankan-militants, refugees and ordinary civilians, enjoyed, evaporated immediately. The Sri Lankans found it difficult to get houses on rent. What is more, the two Dravidian parties began to delink themselves from the LTTE. Chief Minister Jayalalitha stepped up pressure on the central government and the LTTE was banned as a political organization. She also demanded that the Sri Lankan Tamil refugees be sent back to the island and the process of repatriation of refugees commenced in January 1992. The media reported high handed methods adopted by the Government of Tamil Nadu to send back refugees. The Tiger network in Tamil Nadu was destroyed and many who extended their support to the LTTE were detained. Following the publication of the Jain Commission Report, a dislike for the Tamil cause increased further. The DMK and the AIADMK claimed innocence and began to accuse each other for extending support to the LTTE. The cumulative result was that, except for the fringe elements of ardent LTTE supporters, the politicians in Tamil Nadu did not get actively involved in the political developments in Sri Lanka. Resultantly, impact of Tamil Nadu in India's Sri Lanka policy declined.

**Resurgence of Interest in Tamil Nadu**

When the Eelam War IV began and the Sri Lankan Government began to resort to savage bombing of the Tamil areas in the northern part of Sri Lanka, the political parties in Tamil Nadu began to express deep concern. In August 2006 when news about the air attack on Sencholai orphanage and also a school meant for the internally displaced children reached Tamil Nadu, there was righteous indignation. Almost all political parties came together and the Tamil Nadu Legislative Assembly passed a unanimous resolution. The resolution characterized the air attack as 'barbaric, uncivilized and inhuman.' The resolution also requested New Delhi to step up pressure on Colombo to cease fire immediately and try to arrive at a negotiated settlement.

As the conflict intensified and the war against the Tigers degenerated into war against Tamil civilians, the political parties in Tamil Nadu began to step up their agitation. The Sri Lankan issue became enmeshed in electoral politics. Even Jayalalaitha, the leader of the AIADMK, who used to scrupulously avoid any mention of Sri Lanka in her statements, began to speak about the atrocities against the Sri Lankan Tamils. Obviously she did not want her party to get alienated from public opinion. Competitive politics sharpened further as with the approach of the polling day, the general feeling in Tamil Nadu as reflected in the media was, that the AIADMK led alliance will sweep the polls in the State. Even sections in the Congress believed that the DMK-Congress led alliance may not fare well in the polls. In order to strengthen the claims to form a government at the Centre the Congress leaders began to send feelers to the AIADMK for a possible post poll alliance. A shrewd politician that Karunanidhi is, he resolved to express concern for the sufferings of the Sri Lankan Tamils, while at the same time extending solid support to the central government's policies on Sri Lanka. The end result was the DMK completely toeing the central line on Sri Lanka issue. Observers of Tamil Nadu politics could not escape the inference that from Karunanidhi's point of view, power is the greatest aphrodisiac and, as stated at the beginning of the essay, he was willing to radically revise the party's policy towards Sri Lanka. The ultimate losers were the Sri Lankan Tamils, who virtually became pawns at the hands of opportunistic politics of Tamil Nadu.

**Post-LTTE Phase**

The Fourth Eelam War came to an end with the entire leadership of the Tigers, including Prabhakaran, getting killed. The victory represented an end to the military dimension of the fratricidal ethnic conflict, which brought about death, destruction and untold suffering to thousands of people-Tamils, Muslims and Sinhalese alike. The war has ended, but the immediate task, equally important, is to win peace.

Winning peace is difficult, and at the same time, a multi-pronged task. It involves the de-mining of the war zones; rehabilitation of the 2,80,000 civilians who today live in unhygienic surroundings in relief centres manned by the Sri Lankan army; restoration of agriculture and fishing; reconstruction of houses, hospitals and places of worship; creation of new employment opportunities and putting the economy of the north and the east back on track. Sri Lanka cannot accomplish this task alone and it requires massive investment of capital and foreign technical expertise.

Given the geographical contiguity and ethnic affinities, the government and people of Tamil Nadu can and should help their brethren in their hour of need. Tamil villages can be adopted by various organizations and the reconstruction of the economy and ushering in of a new order can be facilitated by Tamil Nadu. In order to prioritize the short term, medium term and long term needs, it is essential to send a team of Tamil speaking specialists from India and the team, with the assistance of Sri Lankan specialists can chalk out the short term and long-term plans of action. What is required in Sri Lanka is a massive Marshall Plan.

But the task of economic reconstruction can only take place if the Government of Sri Lanka ushers in a new chapter in its political history and wins the hearts and minds of the Tamil people. This task can be accomplished only by the introduction of far reaching political reforms and substantial devolution of powers to the Tamil regions. Unfortunately, according to Indian observers of the Sri Lankan scene, President Mahinda Rajapakse is keener to consolidate his political power on a chauvinist triumphalist platform. Soon after the victory in the Fourth Eelam War, Prof. M.S. Swaminathan, father of India's Green Revolution, visited Sri Lanka and submitted a detailed report to the Government of India on the development models required for rejuvenating agriculture and fishing. He also added that the development can take place only after a union of hearts between the Government and the Tamils has taken place. Disappointed by some of the recent steps taken by the Sri Lankan Government, Prof. Swaminathan has disassociated himself from the Sri Lankan Government. So also Narayanamurthy, Chairman of the INFOSYS, who was invited by Colombo to render advice on how information technology could be channelized for developmental purposes.

According to a report published by the IANS, Narayanamurthy has stated that development should not lead to exploitation of the oppressed people.

India, especially Tamil Nadu, should clearly adopt a policy which should make a viable political solution that is acceptable to the Tamils, a pre-condition for developmental assistance. In the moment of victory, if the President does not display magnanimity towards the Tamils, the reservoir from which the Tamil militancy can draw its strength will remain. The distinguished Indian jurist, Soli Sorabjee, in one of his recent essays, has given expression to the dangers inherent in the situation. To quote Sorabjee, 'LTTE has been vanquished by the Sri Lankan army and its chief Prabhakaran is dead. The Tamil cause, however, remains alive. If the legitimate aspirations of the Tamils in Sri Lanka are not fulfilled, the deadly seeds of conflict that Prabhakaran implanted will continue to simmer. The Sri Lankan Tamil minority will draw inspiration from Prabhakaran as a hero and a martyr and there will be more Prabhakarans in the future'.

# 21

# Maritime Dimensions of Indo-Sri Lanka Relations

R.S. Vasan

*"Geographically the security of Tamil Eelam is interlinked with that of its seas. It is only when we are strong on the seas and break the dominance the enemy now has that we will be able to retain the land areas we liberated and drive our enemies from our homeland."* Late Prabhakaran, LTTE Leader

The relations since time immemorial between India and its southern neighbour Sri Lanka have largely been dictated by geography and the proximity of the Island nation to its big neighbour. If Buddhism travelled to the Island and became a major religion, Tamils who crossed over from Tamil Nadu either on their own or because of the colonial masters who needed indentured labour, became an important community. All the communities lived in relative harmony at different phases of the history of the Island till Sinhala majoritarianism raised its ugly head and by its partisan policies started alienating the Tamils who till then were contributing in a major way to the economy, education and the well being of the country.

The persecution of the Tamils led to blood-letting and hatred. With the policy of targeting the minority Tamils, they were driven to a state of despair and were forced to take up arms. The creation of the LTTE was both a result of the failed policies of Sri Lanka as well as India's interest in the welfare of Tamils in its immediate neighbourhood.

The long and protracted war for a separate Tamil Eelam claimed nearly 80,000 lives and has displaced more than 3 lakh Tamils from their own homes. The entire effort was mostly supported by the seas. It is evident that the Sea that sustained the momentum also swallowed the efforts in the final phase of the war. Fisheries and livelihood issues have haunted the fishermen on both sides and has also at times influenced the stance taken by the State with the Centre in Indo-Sri Lankan relations The strategic location of Sri Lanka has also invited extra regional players and the present century would witness power play in our neighbourhood. The paper examines this maritime context of Indo-Sri Lankan relations and the international dimensions in the run up to the LTTE defeat and thereafter.

## Geography

The tear shaped Island which is just half the size of Tamil Nadu has immense geo strategic importance for both India and Sri Lanka. The Palk Strait separates the two countries, though many feel that instead of dividing it, it actually unites the people of the two countries. The countries have by and large enjoyed healthy relations for centuries. The spread of Buddhism has been a major factor for Sri Lanka to relate historically to its religious roots in India.

Figure 1: Sri Lanka

The landscape is characterized by:

- Shallow straits.
- The presence of uninhabited small Islets.
- Kachchativu, a barren Island but a rich fishing ground which has remained a source of contention.
- A mere 16 kilometres distance separating Dhanushkodi from Talaimannar.
- Trincomalee-a Major Natural Harbour.
- Kankesanthurai-another important port with strategic importance.
- Fishing villages on both the Indian and Sri Lankan coast facing each other

across the strait.

The Palk Strait has remained the source of livelihood for communities on both sides of the International Maritime Boundary line which was demarcated only in 1974 after the ceding of the Kachchativu Island. While fishing remains a major vocational activity, the narrow straits have also served the cause of smugglers who routinely indulge in transferring goods to either coast driven by profit as the motive. During the LTTE struggle and the Eelam wars, the seas have continued to play a vital role in enabling the LTTE to obtain military hardware and essential supplies in a clandestine manner by its operatives operating around the world.

**Geo Strategy**

Both India and Sri Lanka have the geographic advantage of being in a position to keep the Sea Lines of Communication (SLOCs) and all that is carried through them under observation through means of surveillance. In addition, the following factors have a bearing on the actions of the two nations both in the Palk Bay and in the Gulf of Mannar:

- **Presence of Hydrocarbons/gas in Palk Bay Area:** There are high expectations that the Palk Bay area may be holding large volumes of energy (gas/oil) resources. With the conclusion of the Eelam war, there would be renewed efforts to tap the energy resources in the region by joint/mutually agreed areas under the NELP.
- **Sethusamudram Project:** While the SSCP took off in a big way, this has now got muddled in various issues including religious and environmental objections. It is not clear as to what shape it would take in future. It has also become important to undertake a fresh survey of the concerned areas of SSCP post Tsunami as the Environmental Impact Analysis was carried out before the Tsunami struck. There are expectations that the underwater profile in the areas would have undergone changes and there are also fears of what impact would any future Tsunami strike have, if the SSCP is implemented. There was a proposal by Ranil when he was the President for consideration of a land bridge between the two nations. If the SSCP is likely to be abandoned altogether, there lies a need to have another close look at the land bridge proposal. Technology today enables such connectivity while retaining options for vessels of a particular size to travel beneath such a bridge.
- **Declaration of the Marine Bio-sphere, Development of Tuticorin and Deep Water Ports:** The declaration of a portion of the Gulf of Mannar as a marine Bio-Sphere would ensure that there are no developmental activities.

There, however, the two nations may be in a position to invest in environment-friendly ventures of tourism in the area.

- **IOC Tank Farm in Trinco:** The tank farms in Trincomalee invested in by the Indian Oil Corporation have a strategic angle and would provide the required leverages in bilateral relations. The stocking of the IOC farms would need to be done by the sea routes for the moment.
- **Extra Regional players (China, US, Pak, UK etc):** With excellent geographical vocational advantage enjoyed by Sri Lanka, this continues to interest Extra Regional Powers who would like to engage Sri Lanka to ensure that their options are open depending on future global strategy driven largely by energy and economic interests. These interests mainly relate to the safe use of the seas along the established SLOCs. Over 80 percent of the worlds merchandise still moves through the medium of the seas from the African/Arabian coast to the Pacific nations.
- **Hambanthotta Port:** It is no gainsaying now that China has come in to our neighbourhood. As per records, it is clear that India let go of an opportunity to invest in Hambanthotta. It is only because of the bureaucratic bungling from the Indian side that China was able to get a strategic foothold in Sri Lanka. However, it is now necessary to ensure that India's interests are protected by pro-active strategies with respect to the Island nation which has enjoyed historical and cultural relations with India since times immemorial.
- **Sri Lanka's training of the Pakistani Army:** The success of the Sri Lankan forces has evoked interest in the globe as it is a rare case of success against a well trained determined Guerrilla force by a conventional army. The request therefore by Pakistan Army to be trained in such operations would take the defence cooperation between the two nations to a higher level. India would need to be watchful of the developments in her neighbourhood.

On the Indian side, since the IPKF operation in 1987, seven naval detachments were set up on the Tamil Nadu coast. The Coast Guard also set up two stations namely CGS Mandapam in the Palk Bay and CGS Tuticorin in the Gulf of Mannar. The Naval Air Station at Uchipalli in Ramnad district served the purposes of both the Navy and the Coast Guard for 'basing' their air elements as well as staging through operations for those aircrafts operating from Chennai/Kochi and Arakkonam. It is only recently that the Naval Air Station was commissioned as INS Parindu.

### Improvisation and Innovation by the LTTE

Post-war scenario, it has come to light that the LTTE adopted novel ways to equip itself in all the three media and used the strength of its Diaspora for gaining access to technology and funds.

Figure 2: Improvised Submarine

Figure 3: Stealth Boat

Many of the boats were designed based on the books and manuals published in the west indicating the technological prowess and grasp of its committed cadres who left no stone unturned in obtaining the necessary inputs from required sources/Diaspora.

For example the titles shown below illustrate how the LTTE went about building boats in the areas held under its control by using illustrative books.

- Boat Designs
- Build New Instant Boats
- Boat Data Book
- How to design a Boat
- Start with a Hull
- Fiberglass Handbook
- Glen-L Marine Design

In addition, the LTTE was also able to import small aircrafts and modify them ingeniously by which they could use them to drop bombs even at night. There were limited successes in some of the attacks undertaken by the Air Tigers.

The LTTE held territories in the North and the East were progressively taken over till the LTTE was driven towards Mullaittivu and then defeated by the Sri Lankan Army. The Eelam war IV, as it was called, came to a conclusion with the death of Prabhakaran on 19th May 2009.

**The LTTE Defeat**

Many reasons have been put forward as reasons for the defeat of the LTTE. Some of the important ones in the assessment of the author are to follow in the succeeding paragraphs.

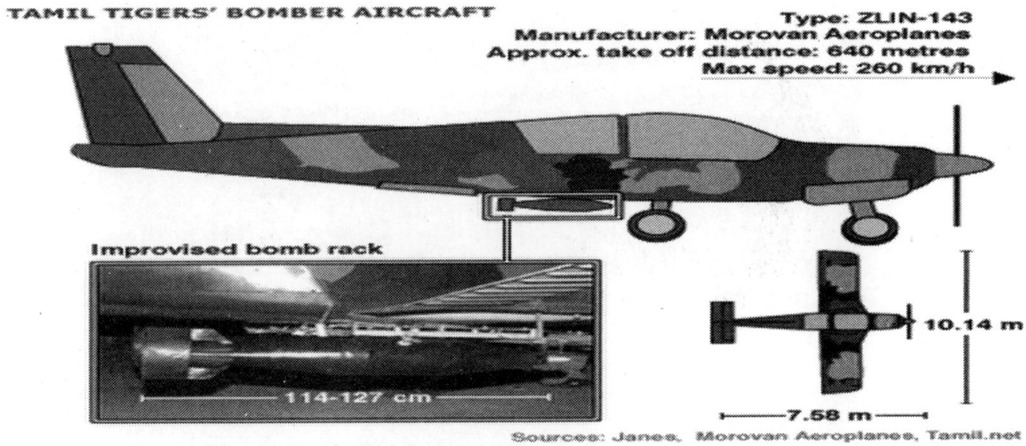


Figure 4: Zlin 143 aircraft modified to carry bombs

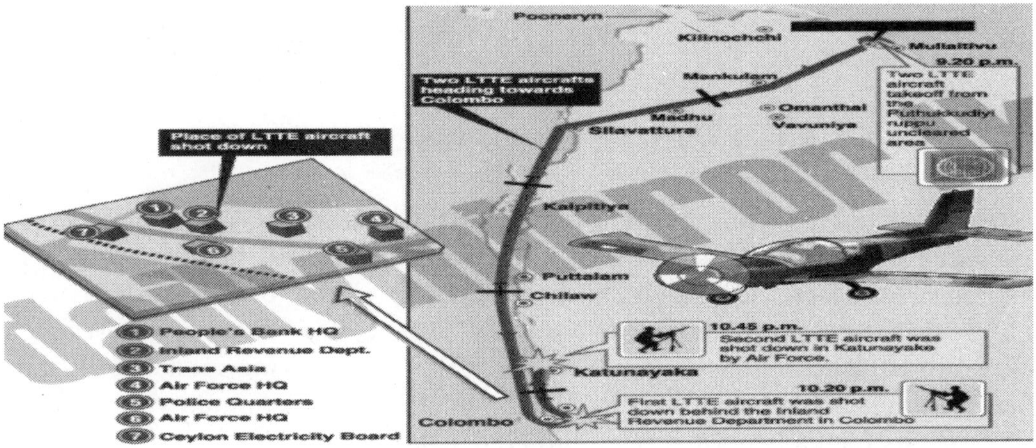


Figure 5: Attack on Katunayake and Colombo

Figure 6: Black Air tigers who died in the attack on 20 Feb 2009

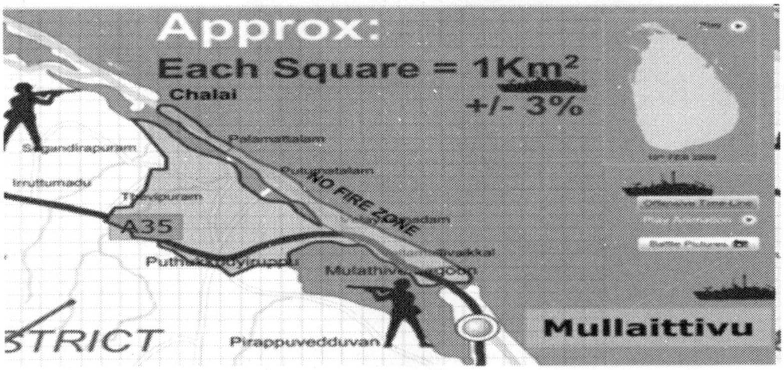


Figure 7: Final phase of War: Shrinking LTTE territory

- Responses post 9/11-Global War on Terrorism measures (GWOT): The world at large had become intolerant of terrorism and initiated many measures to combat terrorism. USA which was attacked on its own soil led many initiatives to combat terrorism in what was called the Global War on Terrorism. The actions at home by the LTTE in attacking innocent citizens and politicians hardened the stand of the international community against the LTTE. Sri Lanka benefited from the hard stand of the global community and was able to get the LTTE proscribed in over 32 countries around the world. Such branding as a terrorist organization enabled host nations and Interpol to keep closer watch on the activities of the LTTE particularly on efforts to acquire weapons and systems from the west. Also, financial transactions came under scrutiny, making it difficult to carry on in a manner it did prior to 9/11.

- Break away of Karuna: It was initially assessed that the breaking away of Karuna would not affect the manner in which the LTTE carried out its war efforts. However, it is clear that Karuna did provide the military edge to the SL Army as he was fully aware of the tactics and the level of preparedness of the LTTE. The inside knowledge of means and methods helped the SL Army to go after the LTTE with thorough preparation.
- Election of Mahinda thanks to the LTTE: It is ironical that the election of Mahinda was facilitated by the LTTE leader who called upon Tamils not to vote and participate in the electoral process, which ensured a clear victory for Mahinda who proved that he was more than a match for Prabhakaran.
- Cooperation by military of China, Israel, Pakistan, India. Despite the political and military differences that China, Pakistan and India have on many issues, Sri Lanka was helped by all these countries in terms of building up a credible force with required weapons to take on the guerrilla force. Sri Lanka also played its cards well and was able to get the best from all the regional and extra regional players. There was criticism from Tamil Nadu about the nature of weapons supplied. But in the long run, this had little impact on the decisions taken by the Centre.
- Neutralization of FOC ships and war making machinery.

Figure 8: Sinking of FOC ships

During the heydays prior to 9/11, the LTTE ruled the seas and was able to transact with any country/group of its choice to obtain military hardware by employing its own ships. It has been estimated that over a dozen ships were routinely employed in obtaining military weapons from South-eastern countries and other groups involved in such activities. The provision of intelligence regarding the movement of such ships carrying weapons was crucial in neutralizing the ships at a safe distance, including the high seas. The Sri Lankan Navy and the Air force operated in tandem to sink ships at distances not attempted hitherto.

Actions were also initiated by the Government of India to reinforce security measures particularly post the assassination of Rajiv Gandhi. The list includes the following measures:

- Setting up of seven naval detachments along the Tamil Nadu coast. These were set up along the coast and manned by the Navy. The state government also funded the revenue expenditure of these assets and provided necessary help in running them. The navy on its part positioned personnel on a rotational basis and also used commercially hired trawlers/boats to augment the surveillance capability along the coast.
- Optimal use of CGS Mandapam in Palk Bay and CGS Tuticorin in the Gulf of Mannar for better surveillance and for support of surface operations.
- Activation of NAS Ramnad (INS Parindu): Both, the Navy and Coast Guard air assets were deployed as required for carrying out aerial surveillance in the Palk bay and other areas of interest.
- Greater interaction with civil authorities (Customs, Police, State Administration and NGOs): The enhanced levels of communication and interaction amongst the agencies involved, allowed for speedy decision making and implementation of such decisions.
- Intelligence sharing: This played a crucial role in preventing the LTTE from having unfettered freedom in smuggling of essentials from Tamil Nadu and from other countries.
- Sensitizing fishermen along the coast: Many fishermen, who indulged in smuggling items to the LTTE, did so either due to sympathy or due to commercial reasons. However, the LTTE did not enjoy support across the board, particularly when it was established that the LTTE did not hesitate to kill Tamil fishermen for furthering its own agenda.
- Induction of the Hovercraft to overcome shallow water limitations: The LTTE as well as the smugglers were safe in the relative comfort of shallow waters and were able to use the shallow waters to evade arrest and detection. The induction of the Hovercraft changed this situation and the coast guard was able to chase suspects even in shallow waters.
- Regular IBL meetings with their naval counterparts on a regular basis for a review of the arrangements. This arrangement stood the test of time and quarterly meetings were held on the IBL-alternatively on either a naval ship or a coast guard vessel. The close coordination and frank discussions enabled

many measures to be implemented without bureaucratic impediments.

## Fishing in Troubled Waters

For centuries, fishermen on both sides have been routinely fishing in areas in the Palk Bay. The insensitivity of the Central Government and the inaction by the State Government led to a situation of gifting away Kachchativu to the Sri Lankans in the interest of having a settled maritime border. However, this has caused undue hardships to fishermen from Tamil Nadu, who now accused of straying into Sri Lankan waters intentionally. During the different phases of the Eelam war, this remained a contentious issue. Fishing in the Palk Straits is characterized on both sides by:

- Fishing communities comprising of around 35,000 people.
- 8,000 sea-going fishermen.
- Distance of only about 16 km to Talaimannar in Sri Lanka.
- The lack of fish on the Indian side of the IBL.
- Centuries-old practice of fishing around Kachchativu.
- Use of fishing boats for smuggling, refugee landing and clandestine activities.

A ban was imposed by Sri Lanka on its own fishermen. Indian fishermen carried on fishing in these disputed waters with near impunity though there were incidences of firing by either the Sri Lankan Navy or the LTTE. Many of the firing cases reported remained unsolved as it was difficult to establish who actually carried out the firing. The proof provided by fishermen in the case of MV Krishna clearly established that the LTTE had killed the fishermen and had taken over their vessel during May this year.

## Recent Developments

It would be interesting to examine some of the recent developments of significance to both the nations in the post-War phase. These include:

- **Creation of a Coast Guard by Sri Lanka:** Sri Lanka has announced setting up of a Coast Guard. This would enable Sri Lanka to entrust peace time tasks to another designated maritime security agency with a human face. The tasks of Search and Rescue, Marine Pollution etc., are best handled by the Coast Guard with low value investments.
- **Greater Role for the Military:** 50 percent increase in Military Strength was envisaged. The announcement that the strength of the armed forces would go up to 3 lakh is something that has a potential to upset the democratic process and governance in the Island. The strengthening of the military which played a decisive role in the Eelam war IV comes with the possibility of greater role

for the Armed forces which does not augur well in a democracy. After having defeated the LTTE the need for increasing the strength by 50 percent defies logic in a democratic set up. If this force was in the form of home guards or the police, it would have been quite understandable.

- **Upgradation of Military Posts:** The upgradation of the posts for the Armed Forces, the creation of the Chief of Defence Staff etc., is not on unexpected lines as the Government wanted to recognize the exemplary services rendered by the top military leaders. Yet, this has the prospect of allowing the military to have a greater influence in day-to-day governance.
- **Formation of the LTTE Government in Exile:** Observers around the world also took note of the announcement of the creation of a LTTE Government in exile. It only shows that the movement can still bounce back depending on the actions or lack of them in the Island. Also, according to credible inputs, there is still a lot of money available under different heads and there is some kind of power play to take control of the funds raised during the struggle stretching across almost three decades.
- **Arrest of KP:** The arrest of KP, the master planner and the key figure for arms procurement has dented the efforts of the organization to restructure itself. The Diaspora and the LTTE remnants would be examining all options to see that the movement is sustained. This can only be prevented if the Sri Lankan Government is serious about its role and commitment to the Internally Displaced Persons of the Island who are waiting to return to normalcy.
- **Trapped Civilians (IDPs) and Misery:** The harsh environment in the camps and the international criticism about the treatment has not helped the Government in its effort to relocate its citizens. However, there is an immediate need to see that the rehabilitation efforts are intensified with outside assistance. Any delay or negligence on this account would help those sympathetic to the LTTE cause to regroup together and think again about self-determination.
- **Action by Tamil Diaspora:** The diaspora was angry that there were no returns on their investment as it were and tried to bring about greater pressure on the Sri Lankan Government through the Red Cross and global organizations. The Diaspora is also divided on the way ahead. While some are supportive of the Sri Lankan Government's efforts many still feel that the Tamils will not live in harmony and dignity as a vanquished race.
- **Regional Politics:** While there were lots of expectations that Tamil Nadu would burn if anything happened to Prabhakaran, nothing of that nature took

place. This was indicative of the lack of support to the violent ways of the LTTE. The regional parties continue to whip up emotions to derive political mileage. However, Sri Lanka is being engaged by the Centre to ensure that the relations remain on an even keel and are taken to the next level of performance.

**Conclusion**

Having examined the overall picture related to the defeat of the LTTE, there are certain issues that merit immediate attention.

First and foremost, the rehabilitation of war ravaged civilians' needs to be accorded the highest priority. This has become even more important in the face of monsoon showers. The international community has to play an important role in helping Sri Lanka in demining the areas to help speedy return of the IDPs.

Devolution of power to restore equality, dignity and pride to the Tamils as citizens of a Unitary State: This has become a little more complicated as there is fresh thinking on the very need for such devolution. The President has gone on record to say that there is a need to get a fresh mandate post elections for actions that are required to be taken to help the Tamils.

Action and help by the International community is required for expediting the process of rescue and rehabilitation.

There is need to develop strategic counters in the IOR. From the Indian point of view, it has to be alert about the developments in the Island that may be inimical to the security of the country.

Engaging our southern neighbour to improve maritime safety and security in the region. With the excellent level of cooperation that existed while defeating the LTTE, there is a need for India not to lose the momentum and have a strategic long-term partnership with Sri Lanka that would enable a concerted effort to keep the Extra Regional Powers at bay.

# 22

# Post-war Challenges in Sri Lanka: Policy Options for India

S.Y. Surendra Kumar

The advent of Mahinda Rajapakse as President (November 2005) marked a fundamental departure from previous governments in its approach towards the ethnic conflict. His strategy was based on a realist paradigm i.e., military victory and deterrence form the back bone of peace and security. Thus, in July 2006, Rajapakse declared the 'War for Peace' [Eelam War IV] against the LTTE and ultimately declared the end of war in May 2009 with the capture of LTTE-controlled areas and elimination of the top leadership of the LTTE, including its chief, Prabakaran. The military success in a short period was possible due to President Rajapakse's determination and commitment to end the conflict by eliminating the LTTE. Subsequently, his core group constituted younger brother Gotabaya Rajapakse, as Defence Secretary and Sanath Fonseka as Army Chief who took most of the decisions without any opposition within the government. Moreover, President Rajapakse was in charge of the defence portfolio and his brother as defence secretary ensured that budget was no constraint. Hence, free flow of economic resources for the Sri Lankan armed forces ensured successful attacks on the LTTE, resulting in the end of the LTTE. In addition, the Rajapakse government established the Media Centre for National Security (MCNS) in June 2006, to counter the LTTE's propaganda. At the same time, despite the pressure from international community, civil society, Tamil diaspora over the civilian casualties and human rights violations during the course of the war, Rajapakse did not bow down to these pressure tactics and took bold steps to finish the war.

Although, the Rajapakse government has successfully defeated the LTTE, it does not mean the end of the conflict, rather it is the beginning of another phase of conflict in which the government is confronted with many challenges outlined below.

## Humanitarian Crisis

The 'war for peace' has caused large scale civilian casualties and displacement. For instance, most of them from Killinochchi and Mullaitivu have been displaced and as of now there are more than 2.8 Lakh Internally Displaced

Persons (IDPs) in Sri Lanka, currently housed in 29 temporary camps in the districts of Vavuniya, Mannar, Trincomalee and Jaffna. [1] However, the majority of IDPs, estimated at 230,000 individuals, reside in Manik Farms IDP camp in Vavuniya District. Unfortunately, most of them are put up in temporary welfare centres or camps, erected hurriedly to house the fleeing civilians from the rebel controlled areas at the borders of the conflict zone. Moreover, those 100,000 people, who were displaced during 2008 are still lodged in welfare camps in Vavuniya and other places and are leading a miserable life without proper resettlement and reunion of their family members.

In response to the humanitarian crisis, the Rajapakse government has initiated measures like mobilizing international aid for providing basic amenities to displaced persons residing in various camps. IDP return packages that have been initiated comprise of shelter material, cash grants equivalent to US$220 with additional subsidies for farmers, and a six-month food supply, including USAID/FFP commodities, distributed by the U.N. World Food Program (WFP). [2] Apart from this, the government has even gone to the extent of assuring the international community of resetting all the displaced within 180 days. As a result, in July 2009, the Government of Sri Lanka had announced preparations to return approximately 75,000 IDPs to areas of origin in Eastern and Northern provinces. Subsequently, it is confirmed by the Government of Sri Lanka that more than 4,076 IDPs have returned from Vavuniya camps to areas of origin in Ampara, Batticaloa, Jaffna, Trincomalee districts and to other areas in Eastern Province. [3]

Despite these measures, the Rajapakse government is confronted with many stumbling blocks in resettling the IDPs before December 2009, such as the removal of landmines in the northern region, which still remains a major problem, as the LTTE before fleeing the areas had heavily mined them. De-mining is done manually by the Army and eight other organisations. Since it is manually done, 10 square metres can only be demined in one day, resulting in the prolonging of the de-mining process in the northern region. Moreover, de-mining is very expensive. Clearing of just one square kilometre costs US$10,000, and around 3,000 square miles including Mannar, Killinochchi, Mullaithivu and parts of Jaffna districts are yet to be demined before the Tamils return. [4] Nevertheless, to overcome this problem, in September 2009, the Government of Sri Lanka initiated the process of importing five de-mining automatic machines from Slovakia, which would clear 5,000 square metres a day. Thus, it would expedite the de-mining process and ensure that civilians are safe and secure after resettlement. [5]

Although GoSL launched the 'Return in 180 days' plan with much fanfare, it is yet to provide a comprehensive framework for the implementation of the proposed returns plan and enhance coordination with humanitarian agencies. As a result of this difficulty, the Government of Sri Lanka is emphasising that at least 60-80 percent of the displaced would be resettled before December 2009. At the same time, the government needs more international aid for building infrastructure, facilities and a source of livelihood for the returnees. In this regard, most of the donors, including India and US have informed GoSL, that aid would be subjected to early political solution to the ethnic crisis, failing which aid would be stopped. Hence, ensuring safety and providing basic amenities to the displaced persons, remains the biggest challenge.

India has always responded positively to humanitarian crisis in Sri Lanka and continues to do so. Even in the present crisis, India has sanctioned Rs. 500 crore relief, reconstruction and rehabilitation package for displaced persons. It has also sent a 60-80 member military medical team and increased the number of de-mining teams that are presently operating in the island to ensure that civilians have access to more safe areas. In addition, the Tamil Nadu government has separately announced a package of Rs. 250 million as humanitarian relief. Apart from these gestures, India has very rightly conveyed to Sri Lanka that 'broad-based political settlement' of the ethnic conflict would enable it to utilise the Rs. 500 crore package for the displaced. [6] Thus, Sri Lanka has a huge task of not only resettling the IDPs but also of finding a lasting solution to the ethnic problem.

**Political Solution**

With the military victory President Rajapakse is now confronted with the challenge of evolving an amicable solution to the ethnic strife. Even India and the international community have been insisting Rajapakse to work towards a politically negotiated settlement acceptable to all sections of the Sri Lankan society, but within the framework of an undivided Sri Lanka. In this regard, President Rajapakse during the course of Eelam War IV had assured India and the international community that he would work towards the implementation of the 13th Amendment, one of the recommendations made by the APRC. However, implementation of the 13$^{th}$ Amendment would be a difficult task, since the main political parties such as UNP, JVP, SLMC and TNA were not part of the APRC deliberations. Further, managing the hard core ethnic and religious minded JVP and JHU and its break away groups are destined to be problematic. The JVP and JHU fear that giving provincial autonomy and power to the Tamils may open the path to separatism and Indian influence, is unfounded. However, this argument is weak, as the election in the Eastern province shows that there is no separatism developing and the provincial administration is fully accepted by the local population. [7] Another aspect of the 13th amendment is that it is a result of the Indo-Sri Lanka Peace accord of 1987, which paved the legitimising of Indian military intervention to prevent a Tamil state at Sri Lanka's door steps. This was also a rejected policy measure by every stakeholder to the conflict including Rajapakse himself. Hence, implementation of the APRC recommendations is unlikely.

Moreover, with the electoral victory in the Eastern Province, President Rajapakse had promised to implement the $13^{th}$ Amendment in both letter and spirit. Ironically even after one year, the police and land power has not been devolved in the eastern province. [8] At present several powers of the provincial councils, such as health and education, have been re-centralised by the central government. The flow of economic resources from the central government to the provincial councils has been abysmally poor. The funds allocated are grossly inadequate for effective developmental work to take place out of any of the existing provincial councils. [9] Unfortunately, till now only 6 percent of the EPC's operating budget has been passed by the Central government, due to excessive delays on the part of the latter. As a result, this has led to the EPC being unable to implement even small developmental projects and has led it to depend on the central government or multi-lateral donors. [10]

Apart from this, from time to time Rajapakse's speeches with regard to finding an amicable political solution have not been encouraging. For instance, soon after the defeat of the LTTE in May 2009, President Rajapakse announced the 'de-existence' of minorities in Sri Lanka. In his formal address to the Parliament to announce the end of the war, the president said, "We have removed the word 'minorities' from our vocabulary three years ago. No longer are there Tamils, Muslims, Burghers, Malays or any other minorities. There are only two peoples in this country. One is the people that love this country. The other comprises the small groups that have no love for the land of their birth." [11] Furthermore, President Rajapakse in an interview with *The Hindu* newspaper stated, "I have a solution, but want it from the people", this indicates that a political solution would be put forward only after the next Presidential elections", which might take place early next year. Moreover, he also emphasised on a home-grown solution to the ethnic problem, in a way indicating less or no role for external actors like India or Norway.

In addition, in August 2009 the local government elections were held in Jaffna and Vavuniya, where the government led alliance, United People's Freedom Alliance (UPFA) and EPDP led by the Social Welfare Minister Douglas Devananda emerged victorious in Jaffna and the TNA in Vavuniya. [12] Thus, with the government's military victory over the LTTE; the electoral victory in the eastern and northern provinces coupled with Rajapkse's own Sinhalese-supremacist notions, it is very unlikely that the Rajapakse government will evolve a political solution to the ethnic problem based on devolution, including the full implementation of the 13th Amendment. Hence no amount of Indian and Western pressure will make Rajapakse concede to this vital issue; it will merely make him seek refuge in evasive tactics. Despite these developments, India and the international community should continue to pressurise the Government of Sri Lanka to work towards a political settlement that meets the aspirations of all sections of the Sri Lankan society.

**Economy**

The Sri Lankan economy is in a bad shape, mainly due to two decades of ethnic conflict, which eventually hindered its economic growth by seriously affecting vital economic sectors like fishing, agriculture, textile and tourism. Subsequently, high defence spending by successive governments to fight the LTTE had a negative impact on the economy. For instance, in the 2009 Budget, the defence allocation was Sri Lankan Rs. 1.771 billion, despite the economy being weak; inflation being all time high and there having been acute shortage of essential commodities. [13] In addition, the global recession has also affected the economy badly. For instance, the EU and the US accounted for 62 percent of its total exports comprising mainly of garments, gems and tea. With rising unemployment and low consumption in the US and the EU markets, the demand for Sri Lankan products has gone down and adversely affected the economy. [14]

Fortunately, to a certain extent with the defeat of the LTTE and the tight monetary policy adopted by the Central Bank, the economy has been somewhat strengthened. The Economist Intelligence Unit forecasts the GDP growth rate at 2.5 percent in 2009, which might accelerate to 5.7 percent, in 2010. [15] The rate of unemployment has continued with its declining trend and reached the lowest rate in 2009. Even inflation, which was 28 percent in 2008 has come down to less than 7 percent and the current-account deficit will narrow down to 2 percent of GDP this year. [16] Moreover, the end of the conflict has increased confidence of the international community to grant more aid and invest in the island. For example, the IMF on July 24, 2009 approved a US$ 2.6bn loan to the Sri Lankan government. The 20-month standby facility is intended to bolster dwindling foreign-exchange reserves, and may indirectly relieve the country's burgeoning fiscal crisis. [17] Even the Asian Development Bank (ADB) plans to increase its lending to Sri Lanka by 50 percent to help rebuild it after ending its 26 year conflict. It also plans to raise Sri Lanka's annual allocation to US$ 300 million in

2010 from US$ 200 million, to fund roads, power, water and sanitation projects in the island's north and the east. [18] Thus, Sri Lanka should initiate more policy measures to boost the economy.

Although, India's trade with Sri Lanka constitutes only 2 percent of the total trade, [19] India has signed many agreements to advance economic cooperation with Sri Lanka, like the free trade agreement (FTA); a double taxation avoidance agreement; and a series of bilateral agreements in the areas of small-scale industries, agriculture, tourism, space and information technology and air travel facilities. [20] Despite this, India should further strengthen its economic relations through trade and investment in Sri Lanka. Subsequently, India should certainly help Sri Lanka increase its involvement in the SAARC and BIMSTEC, which will also strengthen bilateral relations.

Apart from these challenges, since the beginning of Eelam War IV the international community and civil society groups both within Sri Lanka and aboard have been very critical of perpetual human rights violations and lukewarm steps of the Government of Sri Lanka in preventing it. As result, most of the donors have warned the Government of Sri Lanka to prevent human rights violations and find an amicable political solution at the earliest, or else aid would be stopped. Thus, the Government of Sri Lanka has a difficult task of convincing the international community and donors so as to make them support its actions against human rights violations.

### China's Growing Influence in Sri Lanka

In the recent years, the Chinese influence in Sri Lanka has been increasing. This is not a challenge for Sri Lanka, but is a major concern for Indian strategic interest in Sri Lanka and the Indian Ocean. The year 2007, marked the 50th anniversary of the establishment of diplomatic ties between Sri Lanka and China. As a result, the year was also declared as the Year of China-Sri Lanka Friendship. Although, both the countries share strong diplomatic ties, it was President Rajapakse, who successfully established stronger economic, military and political ties with China.

### Economic Ties

On the economic front, China is heavily investing in the field of infrastructure, for instance, the Norochcholai power plant which is to be completed by 2010 to meet Sri Lanka's power requirements. The expressway from Colombo to the Katunayake airport is being built with Chinese assistance. China is also extensively involved in building the Hambantota Port worth US$ 1 billion. This will be significant in connecting the southernmost part of the island with the existing shipping lanes and also provide China a firm ground in the Indian Ocean and in turn reduce its dependence on the existing routes. When this port is completed, it is expected to have a container port, a bunkering system, an oil refinery, an airport in addition to other facilities that are expected to transform it into a major trans-shipment location. [21] The bunkering terminal, which is expected to be completed in 39 months, provides for the terminal to handle up to 500,000 metric tons (mt) of oil products a year. [22] Recently, Sri Lanka allocated an exploration block, in the Mannar Basin, to China for exploring oil resources. [23] Furthermore, to encourage growing Chinese investment, the Sri Lankan Board of Investment (BoI) has also taken important steps to facilitate the needs of investors from China like the demarcating a separate zone for Chinese investors at Mirigama, establishing an investment promotion office in Shanghai and earmarking a special five-year visa for investors. [24] Thus, Sri Lanka-China economic ties now have grown stronger than before.

Although, growing economic ties between Beijing and Colombo is not a concern for India, the construction of Hambantota port by China has serious security implications on India's interest in the region. During the construction of the port a large number of Chinese experts are expected to be present in the region, which is a security concern for India. [25] Subsequently, these ports are to be linked through a land link/oil pipeline from China to gain direct access to the Indian Ocean. And during war, these infrastructural assets will become military/naval assets. [26] However, both China and Sri Lanka have consistently maintained that the port is a commercial enterprise and not necessarily a military port. For example, Sri Lanka's Ports Minister, Chamal Rajapaksa, a brother of President Mahinda in response to India's concern about the presence of Chinese technicians in Sri Lanka, stated, "They [Chinese] are here to build the Hambantota Port and it is a development project and has nothing to do with military purposes". [27]

Although, it will be difficult for India to contain the Chinese influence in Sri Lanka, but India can develop Trincomalee on the eastern coast of Sri Lanka as a major commercial hub for Indian Ocean traffic. This would balance Chinese influence. Furthermore, it is not just increasing Chinese influence, the Rajapakse government is strengthening its relations with Iran, Pakistan, Saudi Arabia and Malaysia. For example, Iran is slowly beginning to play an important role in the oil refining sector and it is only a matter of time before it starts demanding a role in the retail sale of oil, a sector in which the Indian Oil Corporation presently has a pre-eminent role. Thus, increasing Sri Lankan economic relations vis-à-vis other countries have vast implications for Indian interests. As a result, India needs to be proactive in containing growing influences of China and other external actors in Sri Lanka.

**Military Ties**

The Eelam War IV, which began in July 2006, also provided an opportunity for expanding Sri Lanka-China military relations. For example, in 2008 Sri Lanka signed an arms deal worth US$ 37.6 million with Beijing-based Poly Technologies. The arms sale included Chinese Jian-7 fighters, JY 11-3D air surveillance radars, armoured personnel carriers, T-56 assault rifles, machine guns and anti-aircraft guns, rocket-propelled grenade launchers and missiles, which were beneficial for Colombo in defeating the LTTE. Moreover, it is alleged that Beijing went to the extent of providing six fighter aircrafts (F-7 jets) free of cost. [28]

There are vital reasons for the rapid expansion of Sri Lanka-China military ties: it was convenient for Sri Lanka to approach China, as Chinese arms are readily available at cheaper rates in the global arms market. Consequently, Sri Lankan troops were familiar with the usage of Chinese weaponry. Unlike India, China does not have any internal compulsion like the Tamil Nadu factor in preventing arms sale to Colombo. Moreover, Sri Lanka being an independent and sovereign nation, it has every right to buy weapons from any country it wants to. As a result of these compulsions, India was not able to prevent Sri Lanka-China military relations from growing.

Although India unlike China did not supply arms and ammunitions to Sri Lanka during its fights against the LTTE, India did provide radars and other non-weapon military aid for the SLAF. Subsequently, it was widely acknowledged that the intelligence agencies of India and Sri Lanka worked closely in the SLN's elimination of the LTTE naval and maritime strength. [29] Thus, India's military support to Sri Lanka was limited due to the internal political compulsion [Tamil Nadu factor].

India in response to growing Chinese military activities, including developmental activities in Sri Lanka, is planning to establish a naval base and listening post in the Maldives. Indian officials are now in talks with their counterparts in the Maldives to boost security for the tiny island, which has been targeted by drug smugglers, terrorists and pirates, and also to develop a new vantage point to protect its own coastal waters. [30] Under the plan, India wants to develop a former Royal Air Force base on the islands, and integrate the Maldives into its own coastguard system. The Indian defence minister, A.K. Anthony, visited the islands in August 2009 to discuss the deployment of surveillance aircraft and ships, as the Maldivian government is unable to police its own waters. Although this step is a small one, it would go a long way in strengthening India's security interests in the Indian Ocean region.

**Political Relations**

On the political front too, both the countries are making a headway, as a number of high level meetings have been taking place between Sri Lanka and China. For example, recently the Defence Secretary, Gotabhaya Rajapakse visited China and thanked Beijing for its 'steadfast support' in strengthening the 'war on terrorism'. At the same time, China has also used it veto power in the United Nations Security Council (UNSC) to block the discussion on steps undertaken by the Sri Lankan government in its fight against the LTTE. This action by China has strengthened bilateral relations. In addition, as a result of successful Chinese initiative, Sri Lanka has been granted the dialogue partner status in the Shanghai Cooperation Organization (SCO). In return, Sri Lanka along with Pakistan is keen on China's entry into SAARC, because of which India is unhappy. Thus, Chinese influence in Sri Lanka would continue and India needs to evolve new strategies to balance China's presence in the region.

In a nutshell, the defeat of the LTTE has not just resolved the conflict, but has also created a golden opportunity for the Rajapakse government and the people of the island to genuinely address the legitimate grievances and aspirations of the Tamils. Even the TNA has extended support to the Government of Sri Lanka in finding a political settlement at the earliest. If Rajapakse fails to capitalize upon this opportunity, then there are chances of LTTE's re-emergence not in the present form but in any other form, which would intensify the conflict in the long run and Sri Lanka would be back to square one, where innocent civilians would be at the receiving end.

At the same time, India should be proactive in persuading the Government of Sri Lanka to work towards a broad based political settlement at the earliest. India should continue to provide humanitarian aid and assistance to displaced persons. Subsequently, to contain increasing Chinese influence on the island, India should strengthen its bilateral relations with Sri Lanka, particularly political and economic relations and also explore new areas of cooperation with Sri Lanka both on strategic and security aspects which would meet India's security concerns.

**Notes**

1. *M. Mayilvaganan,* "Masses in Flight: The Crisis of Internal Displacement in Sri Lanka" May 5, 2009. Available at www.idsa.in/publications/stratcomments/mmayilvaganan050509.html. and B. Muralidhar Reddy, "Devastated Lives", *Frontline*, 22 May 2009, p. 7.
2. USAID Report, *Sri Lanka: Complex Emergency*, 10 August 2009. Available at www.usaid.gov

3. Minister Mahinda Samarasinghe "Govt's goal resettlement of IDPs in original areas of residents" August 21, 2009. Available at www.priu.gov.lk/news_update/Current_Affairs.html
4. B. Muralidhar Reddy, "Unsettled Questions", *Frontline*, 25 September 2009, p. 28.
5. B. Muralidhar Reddy, "Campaign to Tarnish Image: Sri Lanka", *The Hindu*, 6 September 2009, p. 12.
6. B. Muralidhar Reddy, "Deal Key to Relief Package: India", *The Hindu*, 16 August 2009, p.12. N. Manoharan, "Post-LTTE: India's Policy Options on Sri Lanka's Ethnic Issue, May 20, 2009.
   www.ipcs.org/article_details.php?articleno=2874&cid=8
7. Tisaranee Gunasekara, "Soft Anarchy ", *Himal South Asian*, September 2009.
8. V. Suryanaraya, Is it the End of the Struggle", *The New Indian Express*, 19 May 2009, p.8.
9. Jehan Perera, "Implementing 13 Amendments through Northern Elections", *Himal South Asian,* 15 June 2008.
10. Malathi de Alwis "The Eastern Equation", 20 July 2009. Available at www.lines-magazine.org/?p=1197
11. Tisaranee Gunasekara, op.cit.7.
12. B. Muralidhar Reddy, "Surprise results", *Frontline*, September 11, 2009, p.52.
13. Ajay Lele, "Time to Win the Peace", *The Pioneer,* May 2, 2009.
14. Bharti Chhibber, "Indo-Sri Lankan Economic Cooperation: Contemporary Scenario", *Mainstream*, Vol XLVII, No 32, July 25, 2009.
15. Economist Intelligence Unit, *Sri Lanka: Economic Forecast Outlook for 2009-10*, May 26, 2009. Available at www.economist.com/countries/Srilanka/profile.cfm?folder=Profile-Forecast
16. Address of Hon. Prime Minister of Sri Lanka at the *Sri Lanka Economic Summit - 30th June 2009.*
17. MCM Iqbal, "Devolution of Powers under the 13th Amendment – Fact or Fiction ?", 14 August 2009. Available at lines-magazine.org/?p=1234
18. Dr. S. Narapalasingam, "Prospect for Peace and Progress in Post-War Sri Lanka", Available at www.transcurrents.com/tc/2009/08/prospect_for_peace_and_progres.html
19. India exports to Sri Lanka varieties of goods and services including transport equipment, cotton yarn, fabrics, readymade garments, iron and steel, machinery and instruments, sugar and wheat, drugs and pharmaceuticals, chemicals, glass and glassware, ceramics, cement and paper and wood products; and imports non-ferrous metals such as copper, spices, electronic goods, electrical machinery, scrap metal paper pulp and chemicals.
20. Bharti Chhibber,op.cit.14.
21. Gunjan Singh, "Growing Chinese Influence in Sri Lanka", June 08, 2009. Available at www.idsa.in/publications/stratcomments/gunjansingh080609.htm
22. B. Raman, "China Doing a Myanmar in Sri Lanka?" Paper no. 2748, 27-June-2008, www.southasiaanalysis.org/ percent5Cpapers28 percent5Cpaper2748.html
23. Amit Kumar, "China's Growing Influence in Sri Lanka: Implications for India", July 26, 2006. Available at www.ipcs.org
24. Bharti Chhibber, op.cit.14.
25. Gunjan Singh, op.cit. 21.
26. Col. R. Hariharan, "Media Bytes on Chinese Influence in Sri Lanka", Available at www.southasiaanalysis.org/ percent5Cnotes6 percent5Cnote522.html
27. Sathy Moorthy, "101 members of Western Provincial Council are going to China", *Daily*

*Mirror* August 22, 2009. Available at www.dailymirror.lk

28. B. Raman, "China Doing a Myanmar in Sri Lanka?" Paper no. 2748, 27-June-2008, www.southasiaanalysis.org/ percent5Cpapers28 percent5Cpaper2748.html
29. Sathy Moorthy, op.cit. 27.
30. "India Plans Naval Base On Maldives To Contain Chinese Influence", *Daily Mirror,* August 22, 2009. Available at www.dailymirror.lk.

# 23

# Human Rights Situation in Sri Lanka and Indian Response: Narratives of Refugees/Survivors

Ramu Manivannan

There is a big change in the flow and pattern of arrival of Tamil refugees from Sri Lanka in the last few months. This is due to the fact that the entire area has been cordoned off by the military as high security zone with little or no opportunities for the civilians to flee. Civilians involved in the present conflict situation, were for long confined to areas controlled by the Liberation Tigers for Tamil Elam (LTTE) and they moved along as the LTTE retreated from the Jaffna area to Killinochi and finally to Pudukudirrupu. These people distrust moving into government camps even under the present circumstances of extreme gloom and destitution. But the Sri Lankan Government insists on keeping them inside the camps or leaving them dead in open fields. There is still a trickle of ten to fifteen people arriving at Tamil Nadu everyday. The movement of refugees has also shifted from the conventional boat trail from Thalaimannar-Rameswaram to Mullaitevu-Nagapattinam due to geographical proximity in a renewed context. There are at least two hundred and fifty thousand people who are now either confined to government camps or being pushed around.

There is no single truth as there are many. Truth above all is the first martyr in a war. The lives of these civilians for long have revolved around the influence and control by the LTTE. There are other fifty thousand people whose lives were intertwined with the rise and fall of the LTTE as a fighting unit during the last phase of Eelam IV war as they had their kith and kin fighting the liberation struggle.

Refugees attribute this factor as one of the reasons that the Sri Lankan Government distrusts the stranded civilians in the Pudukudirrupu areas. The Sri Lankan government has always treated the Tamils in the north and the east with suspicion and contempt underlined by its fear of infiltration by the LTTE among the civilian population. The opposite factor influences the psychological conditions of the civilians including those in the Pudukudirrupu area-the fear of revenge and retaliation by the Sri Lankan military. The civilians are also familiar with the conditions of torture and concentration camp like situations inside government camps. The civilian casualty in the last stretch of twenty-five miles of Eelam-IV has been exceptionally high because of mutual perceptions of both-the Sri Lankan government and the civilian population. There were at least two hundred civilian deaths every day spanning over for several months in the Vanni region. The US based Human Rights Watch has responded to the satellite pictures contained in the report of April 26 of the United Nations Institute for Training and Research (UNITAR) as being an 'incontrovertible evidence' of government bombing of civilians. The UNOSAT images showed deep craters, two to nine meters wide, caused by aerial bombardment.

A comparison of two images of March 29 and April 19 revealed the destruction of temporary refugee shelters in Valaignarmadam. This is another clear evidence of the Sri Lankan Air Force having bombed the highly populated No Fire Zone (NFZ) while continuously maintaining before the global audience that the LTTE is keeping the civilians as human shields inside the NFZs. Human rights advocates believe that the satellite images could constitute a crucial evidence of violation of international humanitarian law in bombing areas identified as heavily populated by unarmed civilians.

In Mullaitevu, the Sri Lankan government had announced 20 sq. km area as the NFZ but conducted aerial attacks through cluster bombs and tank fire without any restraint within the declared NFZ. The government then maintained that this NFZ has been reduced to less than 5 sq. km (2 km length X 1.5 km width). It was believed at this stage that the Tigers were confined to less than a few miles of territory. It was within this newly demarcated 'safe zone' that the bloodbath took place from the evening of 9th May to the morning of 10th May 2009. The victims were all civilians including women, children and elderly people. International agencies estimated the death toll at around 2000, including the deaths of more than 200 children. Gordon Weiss, UN spokesperson observed on 11th May 2009, after this horrendous mass destruction of civilians by the Sri Lankan Armed Forces, that 'the bloodbath has become a reality' with the steady increase in civilian deaths over the last few months.

United Nations has clearly gone on record to condemn this monstrous act by the Sri Lankan Armed Forces. The Sri Lankan government, on the one hand, was playing media diplomacy by inviting the UN Secretary General to engage with the rehabilitation process and on the other hand, continuing its shelling of safe zone. It was feared that there was a likelihood of 1,30,000 people being trapped within this stretch of few miles. The experience of cluster bombs and artillery fire along with the tactical unleashing of chemical warfare made the situation in the north alarming for remaining civilians and survivors. Refugees account that regular human rights violations by the Sri Lankan Armed Forces made them numb and also drove them to believe that the Sri Lankan Government was utterly inhuman.

A recent arrival from Mullaitevu, Vanni responded by saying, 'if you want to know about what is war, you must go and see Vanni'. The continuous search for food, medicine, the fear of cluster bombs and sexual abuses by the soldiers have all made people behave like the mentally retarded moving around an open mental asylum. There are no boundaries to this war except the ethnic reference of Tamil speaking territories, breaching all universal norms of war. The mean and dehumanized existence of life is a new reality in their home land. They were caught between the slow and painful death of hunger and the sudden death by aerial attacks including cluster bombs. There were innumerable instances of older people dying in fear at the sound of aircrafts flying low over their heads as they kept moving from one place to another in search of safety and food. We heard a young woman living in a refugee camp narrate the death of her mother by a heart attack on hearing the sound of KFIR jets. People were also been denied access to food and basic medicines. Starvation deaths were quite high since the last months of the war. There were incidents of people dying after consuming poisonous plants. They could barely distinguish between food and poison driven by hunger and the fear of death as they marched from one place to another. They were not spared even bunker deaths, snake bites and deaths by water borne diseases. Neither school buildings nor hospitals were spared during aerial rides conducted by the Sri Lankan Air Force.

This was a war that was meticulously planned and executed through both-military and non-military means, including tactical employment of lies, deceit and misinformation. In many ways a war of this nature has never been waged by any government against its own people, the Tamil ethnic minority in this case. All acts indicate a systemic genocide of the minority ethnic community in Sri Lanka, executed in the name of counter terrorism. There was little truth in the announcement by the Sri Lankan Government that it would restrain from the use of heavy weapons including cluster bombs. Soon after the announcement by the Sri Lankan Government an aid of one hundred crore Indian Rupees towards rehabilitation work in the north was declared by the Indian Government. Sri Lankan military forces began to use heavy weapons including KFIR jets and cluster bombs from the same evening of April 27, 2009 resulting in the death of more than one hundred civilians.

There is a need to educate our governments and the world community that cluster bombs were banned during the Second World War. It is difficult to believe how international organizations and major states were unable to prevail upon the Sri Lankan Government so as to prevent it from using cluster bombs.

There were reports of chemical warfare being waged by military forces through smouldering gas which is known to cause the Hiroshima effect. Usage of venomous gas and chemical bombs by the Sri Lankan Armed Forces was common knowledge among the Tamils caught in the war zone. ICRC (Red Cross) Committee Chairperson Peter Harpy had also observed that white phosphorus bombs were being used by the Sri Lankan government in areas inhabited by civilian population. The usage of white phosphorus bombs is restricted to direct combat against enemy's installations when facing each other on the battlefield. There are certain international regulations to be observed by parties to the conflict in the usage of white phosphorus bombs in the battlefield. This basic warfare norm was violated by the Sri Lankan Armed Forces as growing number of victims of this chemical warfare began to be treated by doctors.

A team doctors from the French supported hospital in Settikulam area have confirmed the usage of white phosphorus bombs as they conducted tests among victims. The same information has been shared by the refugees and survivors who have escaped from the Mullaitevu area recently. But their statement would not have had legitimacy but for the statement of the ICRC Chairperson and the verifications from the field like the one made by the French supported hospital in Settikulam. The usage of *Sarin* chemical bombs during the last phase of Eelam-IV by the Sri Lankan Artillery was also recorded. *Sarin* is a nerve wrecking chemical weapon banned through an international agreement. *Sarin* bombs have the potential to affect people staying within the radius of five kilometres. The oppressive military administration and absence of media freedom made it possible for the Sri Lankan Government to deny access and knowledge about the nature of the warfare and the ethnic genocide taking place in Sri Lanka.

The Sri Lankan Government has long been pursuing the strategy of 'smoking the opponents out' inspired by the American pursuit in the hilly, mountainous and uninhabited terrain of Afghanistan, in search of Osama Bin Laden and top Taliban leaders in hiding. This strategy of 'smoking the opponent out' in an area where there is a huge civilian population including women, children and older people has created havoc and deep scare in the minds of survivors. .The Sri Lankan Government used smouldering gas and chemical bombs during the last stretch of this battle maintaining that they wanted to capture, the remaining LTTE cadres and the leaders, dead or alive. The government wanted no compromise in this pursuit though the means and methods applied were highly questionable. There was no military rational for having used cluster bombs and poison gas. Civilians have also been the target of the Sri Lankan Government for more than one reason-especially their knowledge and familiarity of the LTTE and their identification with its political goal of a separate state, Eelam.

Survivors narrate that there is a sense of undisguised hatred and cruelty in the treatment of the Tamil civilians by the government forces. Refugees defend that people at large are hesitant to go to government camps and even preferred to die trapped inside open battle zones than walk into well known conditions of torture, sexual abuses and humiliation in the camps. People are kept like cattle in the camps without any basic hygiene and living amenities. IDPs also suffer from the phobia of animals tied together for slaughter. The government, on other hand, wants them either inside the military camps or dead because it has not been able to distinguish between the LTTE cadres who may have dropped their weapons and the general population. Therefore the military forces are angry and frustrated against everyone. It costs almost one hundred thousand to three hundred thousand Sri Lankan Rupees to travel from Mullaitevu to Nagapattinam in Tamil Nadu. The charge for this uncertain journey from Mannar to Rameswaram would usually cost Rs.10,000-Rs.15,000 in Sri Lankan Rupees. New arrivals bring with themselves more telling images and sorrowful memories revealing the bitter conditions of human life in the north.

Their narrations of the war and the camps remind us of Germany in 1942, when the successful Nazi war campaigns and the extermination of Jews went hand in hand. The early appeasement of Germany and its subsequent refusal to withdraw its policies of discrimination against the Jews was similar to the situation in Sri Lanka when the government refused to bring the war to an end unmindful of the appeal from several nations including the United Nations. Refugees fear that the Sri Lankan government wants to keep surviving Tamil civilians perpetually in camps. These twin goals are to be achieved in the name of anti-terrorism and the rehabilitation of the civilian population with an aim of obtaining assistance for both functions from all quarters and without exception from those countries which advocate peace and democracy in the island nation. The post-war reconstruction in Sri Lanka needs to be addressed from these two opposite but related realities.

First the LTTE as a representative of the Tamil people will now be re-examined and readdressed. The search will bring close allies of the Rajapakse administration to the forefront in the north and the east who will have to reconcile with the division of Karuna and Pillaiyan factions under Colombo's seeming strategy of divide and rule. Secondly, the rehabilitation question has several implications including development and resettlement issues. There were five hundred thousand Tamils in the north living as Internally Displaced People (IDPs) and now we need to add another two hundred and fifty thousand to three hundred thousand people to this number. This means eight hundred thousand people will be destined to stay in the camps for a very long time. This is one of the reasons that east will be the focus of post-war reconstruction than the north because majority in the north have either left or have been killed or stay in camps. The Jaffna Peninsula for all practical purposes remains the Sinhala colony manned by the Sri Lankan Armed Forces. The Sri Lankan government is deliberately defying the truth about the role of people in future political processes and reconstruction work in the north. Every third house in Jaffna remains occupied by the armed forces and every civilian is confined to army camps in Killinochi and beyond. This is another side of the political process that the Sri Lankan government is talking about. The United Nations and other humanitarian agencies should demand a fresh population census and status of Tamils living in the north and the east before determining the nature of development and reconstruction work to be undertaken. It was sad to hear a refugee speak about the future of Tamils in Sri Lanka which would be decided without taking them into account-a common question being where are the people whose future that the Sri Lankan government is talking about?

The Sri Lankan Government and international agencies are now talking about rehabilitation of civilians and post-war reconstruction. The voices of Internally Displaced People in Sri Lanka and the refugees living elsewhere need to be heard. Though the Internally Displaced People have little freedom and literally no will to speak, there is an appeal for global intervention in the administration of IDP camps in future. The United Nations should step in to monitor and protect the Internally Displaced People in Sri Lanka. Every refugee who has left the shores of Sri Lanka taking a secret boat either from Thalaimannar or Mullaithevu fears that Tamils cannot live in the camps without any fear of torture, sexual abuse and frog marches. Anything can happen anytime, they feel. All young men and women are routinely dragged out in the name of investigations. Small girls, young women including pregnant women have continuously been assaulted sexually by decadent soldiers. There are many of us who remain indifferent to this sexual assault committed by the soldiers as though it is a universal phenomenon common to all wars in the world. There are incidences of forced sterilization of men and birth control operations (tubectomy) performed on young Tamil women to prevent the future generation of ethnic Tamils. These are the factors that determine the nature of this conflict in Sri Lanka. Posters depicting the victory of the Sri Lankan Armed Forces as the success of the Sinhala race against the Tamils are also signs of this mindset. These are not simple political rumours but non-military methods of bringing the ethnic question in Sri Lanka to its dead end. There are clear reports of tubectomy being performed on innocent women in Vavuniya and Mannar government hospitals by the Sri Lankan medical staff.

The Sri Lankan Government and other countries, such as India and China, supporting the military efforts of Sri Lanka and must genuinely address the conditions of IDPs and the trauma of the Tamils. People need to go to their homes and cannot be confined to camps forever. They cannot to be forced out of the political process in future. If the conditions are not right, the United Nations or internationally coordinated monitoring agencies have to be employed to administer these camps with eight hundred thousand civilians stranded in them. Governments including those of the U.S and France have repeatedly been asking the Sri Lankan Government to allow their representatives to visit the north and especially the Internally Displaced People living in government camps. The Sri Lankan Government has however, simply been dodging international public opinion and the appeal for more civilized treatment of these Tamils. The Indian Government recently asked for permission to visit the civilians stranded in the north. The eternally disguised diplomatic gesture by the Sri Lankan Government towards the Indian government came out with the government asking for better understanding of the circumstances than making demands at this crucial stage. The Indian Government must ponder over the meaning of political, economic, military support and other logistics extended by it in the last few years leading to the complete victory of the Sri Lankan government forces over the LTTE. Indian Government may also realize now that it has very little or no role in determining the political process in the Island nation. A large number of people are confined to military camps and will remain out of the political process for a long time to come.

The people living in the camps are subjected to several types of hardships including political suspicion, economic deprivation and often denied access to meet other family members. They fear that if there is no international intervention, they will end up living as slaves of the medieval period comparable to the conditions of people conquered by the enemy. They do not see any political future or any signs of democratic politics in Sri Lanka. The Indo-Sri Lanka accord of 1987 has long been diluted beyond recognition through a systematic undermining of the provisions of the treaty. The integration of north and east and the politico-administrative reforms as advocated by the 13$^{th}$ amendment have also been foreclosed with the intervention of the judiciary and the continued opposition from the radical Sinhala elements. The dilemma of the Indian Government arises from the absence of political conditions and the continued failure of the Sri Lankan Government to address the genuine aspirations of the Tamils in Sri Lanka. The post-war reconstruction in the Sri Lankan context implies at large the isolation of the Tamil population from any immediate involvement in the political process. The entire North for all practical purposes has been an open prison for the Tamils and the high security zone for the Sri Lankan government resulting in deprivation of normal life and livelihood opportunities for the people.

Let me sum up this narrative of the survivors by citing the parts of a last editorial written by Lasantha Wikramatunga for the Sunday Leader Newspaper before being killed by suspected Sinhala fascists' coterie in Sri Lanka. Lasantha who was posthumously awarded the UNESCO Award for Freedom of the Press for this year wrote in his last editorial, "*the LTTE are among the most ruthless and bloodthirsty organizations ever to have infested the planet. There is no gainsaying that it must be eradicated. But to do so by violating the rights of Tamil citizens, bombing and shooting them mercilessly, is not only wrong but shames the Sinhalese, whose claim to be custodians of the Dhamma is forever called into question by this savagery, much of which is unknown to the public because of censorship. What is more, a military occupation of the country's north and east will require the Tamil people of those regions to live eternally as second-class citizens, deprived of all self respect. Do not imagine that you can placate them by showering 'development' and 'reconstruction' on them in the post-war era. The wounds of war will scar them forever, and you will also have an even more bitter and hateful Diaspora to contend with.*"

There is a growing evidence of genocide in Sri Lanka. Most Human Rights advocates agree that the means and methods employed by the Sri Lankan government in the name of counter terrorism amounts more to war crimes and crimes against humanity. The process of ethnic cleansing has been pursued by the Sri Lankan State with the connivance of military and political institutions as done by the Nazis in Germany during the Second World War. Refugees ponder hesitantly and ask, 'we do have a question to the Indian government; why and how did it choose to disrespect the sentiments, family ties, cultural and historical bond of the Tamils in Sri Lanka with Tamil Nadu and the country at large by extending its military support to the Sri Lankan government?' The Indian government remained a silent witness to the sufferings of the Tamils while countries like France, Britain, Germany, Switzerland and the United States pulled up the Sri Lankan government for its excesses. Is this a final solution to the LTTE or the Tamil question in the island nation or to both? How should we respond to the acts of State terrorism and the on going genocide of Tamils in Sri Lanka? How many more innocent lives should be sacrificed before the global community recognizes the genocide in Sri Lanka? How do we ensure the accountability of the Sri Lankan State for its acts of oppression, State terrorism and genocide of the ethnic Tamils. The Indian government will need to reflect on these questions as it will have much less time to grabble with the consequences of its action in the next few years.

A final but a haunting question that the enlightened refugees/survivors ask is about the rehabilitation of the poor Sinhalese, given the state of war economy, media, political freedom, racist religious order and the war obsessed elites of the country? It is time that global civil society and governments around the world begin to recognize that Sri Lanka is not only a partisan but also a savage state whose existence defies the principles of political democracy in a plural society and the survival of the civilized notion of the state itself.

# 24

# India-Sri Lanka Relations: Impact of Ethnic Conflict in Sri Lanka

Jacob Ashik Bonofer

## Introduction

For the Tamils in Sri Lanka and also the Tamil Diaspora, India has always come under their larger homeland umbrella mainly due to the umbilical cord that joins them both. India is their closest neighbour to whom they can always lookup for help. Despite these close relations, India's policy towards Sri Lanka has always had a negative impact on the latter. The love-hate relationship compounded with the fear of a big brotherly attitude has always made Sri Lanka look at India with suspicion. India although being in an advantageous state did little to facilitate the creation of hope but her short-sighted policies have always antagonized her southern neighbour.

The ambiguous role played by the Central Government in New Delhi and the Tamil Nadu Government towards the protracted ethnic conflict between the Tamils and the While the ethnic crisis is an emotional issue between both India and Sri Lanka, Indian policy towards Sri Lanka has also been based more its strategic interests in the Indian Ocean.

The Sri Lankan Government should also be given equal credit for contributing towards this love-hate relationship. Despite her awareness on India's security concerns, Sri Lanka has always tried playing a divisive role in allowing external actors to interfere in the affairs of the Indian Ocean and act against India's interest. A telling example of this attitude was evident with Sri Lanka allowing Pakistani Air Force to refuel during the Bangladesh war of 1971. Thus, Sri Lanka's self interest is also one of the reasons of India's over-arching security concerns regarding external interference.

The Indian intervention in Sri Lanka, which is claimed as inevitable, could have been avoided for good. The Indian forces sent to Sri Lanka became a victim to hasty and restricted policies of India. Having fought against the LTTE on behalf of the Sri Lanka Government, the IPKF was sent out unceremoniously by the Sri Lankan Government. The Tamils who had welcomed the IPKF, with open arms also played their part in getting the IPKF out of Sri Lanka, bringing an end to India's involvement in Sri Lanka.

The end of the Eelam War has opened a new chapter in India Sri Lanka relations. Now, India need not be worried about the presence of a third Navy (Sea Tigers), Air Force (Air Tigers) and suicide cadres in the Indian Ocean. But the absence of LTTE does not mean that there is no threat arising from the Indian Ocean, rather, growing relations of Sri Lanka with China and Pakistan have increased strategic concerns for India. This paper studies the challenges facing India-Sri Lanka relations, based on the Historical context and its impact on the current situation. The paper would also deal with various facets that influence India's current policy changes towards Sri Lanka.

**Various Phases in India's Policy towards Sri Lanka**

*"Sri Lanka is as important strategically to India as Eire is to the United Kingdom or Taiwan to China.... As long as Sri Lanka is friendly or neutral, India has nothing to worry about but if there be any danger of the island falling under the domination of a power hostile to India; India cannot tolerate such a situation endangering her territorial integrity."*- A Former Commander of the Indian Navy

Since the Independence of India in 1947 and Sri Lanka in 1948, both nations have been enjoying ebb and flow of closer relations with each other. Security interests and the shared ethnicity of Tamils living in southern India and in northern and eastern Sri Lanka are the two major factors in Indo-Sri Lankan relations. After the British vacated the Indian Ocean Region (IOR), India and Sri Lanka increasingly came to share regional security interests. [1] Though India looked into this issue keeping in mind her strategic concerns, Sri Lanka feared that India would exercise a hegemonic attitude towards her. Majority of the Sri Lankans, be it Sinhalese, Tamil or Muslim, belong to the same ethnic stock as India's population, and cultural affinities extend not only to religion, but also to language-Tamil being common to Tamil Nadu as well as the north and the east of Sri Lanka, and Sinhala being related to the North Indian vernaculars such as Hindustani, Marathi, Gujarati, Bengali and so on. [2] Despite these close relations, Indo-Sri Lankan relations have always been overshadowed by distrust and mutual suspicion.

Indo-Sri Lankan relations can be divided into four phases; first, Nehruvian, starting since the Independence of both the nations until 1970's; second, the phase where India was following the policy of involvement; third, post-IPKF till the 2002 peace process and fourth, the Eelam War IV, when India was not directly involved but was actively present. The end of Eelam War IV may be said to have ignited the next phase in India-Sri Lanka relations.

The first phase of the relationship comprised of clearing the colonial baggage and formulating the policy of Non-Alignment. The first issue to arise between India and Sri Lanka was that of the 'People of Indian Origin'. The first bilateral agreement between India and Sri Lanka, the 'Nehru-Kotlewala Agreement on Persons of Indian Origin in Ceylon' was signed in 1954. This agreement dealt with the problems of illicit immigration and proposals for granting them citizenship. According to the agreement, persons of Indian Origin who desired to get Indian citizenship were to be registered under the Indian and Pakistani (Citizenship) Act, and it was expected to be completed within two years. But not all the persons of Indian Origin came forward to register. Prime Minister Mrs. Srimavo Bandaranaike in a statement in the Senate said,

*"The registration of Citizens under the Indian and Pakistan Residents (Citizenship) Act is now complete. Over 134,000 Indians have been registered as Ceylon Citizens. The Indian High Commissioner has in the meantime only registered 50,969 persons as Indian Citizens."* [3]

As 9,75,000 persons did not register under this agreement, they were declared stateless. The process of registration and repatriation to India had to be restarted again under the Indo-Ceylon (Sirimao–Shastri) Agreement of October 30, 1964. Under this agreement out of a total of 9.75 lakh stateless persons in 1964, 5.25 lakh were to be repatriated to India over a period of 15 years. At the same time and in agreed proportion 3 lakh stateless people would be given Sri Lankan citizenship. The status of further 1.50 lakh was to be determined later by negotiations between the two countries. From the date of the pact up to the 1$^{st}$ of January 1973, 70,621 persons were repatriated to India and Sri Lanka had conferred nationality on 40,268 persons.

The problem became a little more complicated by the April 30, 1970, which was the deadline for applying for Indian citizenship, when only 4 lakh people had sent their application for an Indian Passport though India had agreed to take in 5.25 lakh people and 6.25 lakh applied for Sri Lankan citizenship as against the quota of 3 lakh agreed upon the pact. Because of this India had to reopen the Indian register for fresh applications. As difficulty arose over the question of reopening of the registration no definite decisions could be taken and the solution was left to the Prime Ministers of the two countries who were scheduled to meet later that year.

Mrs. Gandhi visited Sri Lanka on the April 27, 1972 on a goodwill visit for 3 days. During this visit issues pertaining to repatriation of people of Indian origin, Kachchativu and untapped avenues for economic cooperation were discussed. This visit of Mrs. Gandhi was more to assure Sri Lanka that India was open to more repatriation of people of Indian Origin and that India would not involve itself in Sri Lanka's internal problem, as it did in Bangladesh. Despite India's categorical opposition to Tamil moves, the Sinhalese were always suspicious of India encouraging the Tamils. For this reason Mrs. Gandhi refused to meet the Tamil leader S.T.V Chelvanayakam during this visit. [4]

The second phase of relations started with the ethnic crisis in Sri Lanka intensifying in mid and late 1970s and by early 1980s.This period also witnessed the ethnic situation reaching a point of major explosion when a number of Tamil militant leaders and their associates left for Madras so as to acquire training in carrying out their struggle against the Sri Lankan state. This season witnessed an involvement-of not only the Indian Government but also the Tamil Nadu government and the people.

**India's Reaction to the Sri Lankan Ethnic Crisis**

In the last week of July 1983, massive ethnic violence broke out in Sri Lanka, with its epicentre in Colombo. This violence was directed towards Tamil life and property. India was directly affected as a result of this violence. The victims of the ethnic holocaust included not only the Sri Lankan Tamils but also estate workers of Indian origin; Indian nationals, both Tamil estate workers and casual visitors, members of the Indian High Commission including the Indian establishment in Sri Lanka which was also badly gutted in the violence.

The ethnic issue stretched beyond Sri Lankan boundaries and threatened India's regional security as well as ideological sensitivity. The Sri Lankan government initially went out of its way to seek political and military aid from external actors especially the USA, the UK, China, Pakistan, Bangladesh and Malaysia. It deliberately kept India out of this due to the latter's inclination towards the Tamils of Sri Lankan. Mrs. Gandhi in her conversation with President Jeyewardene on the 5th of August strongly disapproved of Sri Lanka seeking external military support. [5] Despite India's protests, President Jayewardene also launched a diplomatic offensive. He went to Beijing in May and extracted promises of military and moral support. Encouraged by his trip to China he undertook a three-nation tour to the US, UK and India in June. In this trip he got little help from both-the UK and the USA, and with India he was more concerned with requesting '*India not to involve in the Sri Lankan issue*'. [6]

Pakistan also came to help Sri Lanka during the ethnic crisis. Though initial reports claim that Sri Lanka sought Pakistan's help, the former denied the same. Pakistan granted Rs.10 million towards relief assistance and military equipment. In addition to this, the Sri Lankan Army Chief visited Pakistan and a Pakistani Naval ship made a goodwill visit to Sri Lanka. This increased international involvement in Sri Lanka's ethnic crisis slowly became a threat to India's security and one of the reasons for India to enter into the Sri Lankan issue.

The official Indian rationale for India's involvement in the Sri Lankan crises was the influx of Sri Lankan Tamils to India as refugees. As the civil order in the north and in the east was completely disrupted due to the armed conflict, some Tamil people escaped from the crisis-ridden land and sought refuge in South Indian soil. [7] Mrs. Gandhi in her statements and action made it clear that she regarded India as a principle mediator rather than a neutral one. Throughout the period stretching from 1983 to 1990, India never abandoned her role of being the principle mediator of the interests of the Tamil Minorities in the island. [8]

President Jayewardene, during his visit to Delhi in November 1983, on the sidelines of the Commonwealth Heads of Governments meeting, met Mrs. Gandhi for the first time after the 1983 riots. The meeting with Mrs. Gandhi served to underline the weakness of his position in negotiating with the Indian government on the resolution of the political crisis in Sri Lanka stemming from the ethnic conflict. He tentatively accepted the set of proposals embodied in a document, which came to be known as 'Annexure C,' wherein the framework of a settlement with the Tamil groups was outlined. The merger of the northern and eastern provinces into a single Tamil whole was also included in this agreement. This single Tamil ethno-region [9] that was implied in this document was one of its controversial features. As a result, Sinhalese opinion steadfastly refused to accept a politically viable proposition, elevated to the position of a cardinal principle of a political settlement with the Tamils.

After the assassination of Mrs. Gandhi, Mr. Rajiv Gandhi as the Prime Minister of India, made a positively encouraging impression on Sri Lankan politicians and diplomats who met him during his early months in office. Among his first decisions on the Sri Lankan affairs, was the appointment of Romesh Bhandari, India's Foreign Secretary, as principle mediator in place of G. Parathasarathy, a move that was clearly intended to signal the arrival of new policies in a more cordial atmosphere.

The meeting between Prime Minister Rajiv Gandhi and President Jayewardene in New Delhi in June 1985, for the first time took place in a greatly improved atmosphere. This was followed by Mr. Bhandari's visit to Colombo for talks with the Sri Lankan President. The talks resulted in a major breakthrough with the latter being persuaded to let his government begin talks with those Tamil groups engaged in violent confrontations with the Sri Lankan security forces. The increase in the number of spokesmen for the Tamil minority had some predictable consequences, beginning naturally with a struggle for dominance and a quest for the position of the sole spokesman. The LTTE eventually pushed ahead to a position of dominance largely because of its strong and expanding bases in Jaffna.

Two sets of talks between representatives of the Sri Lankan government and the various Tamil groups claiming to speak on behalf of the ethnic group, took place in July and August 1985 at Thimpu, the capital of Bhutan. These talks did not yield any positive result, but Mr. Bhandari used the opportunity this provided to continue negotiations with the Sri Lankan delegation at New Delhi. These talks were more fruitful. The new agenda for reconciliation yielded a framework for a realistic devolution of power in Sri Lanka. The draft Accord came to be known in official circles as the Delhi Accord of August 1985. One of the most significant features of this meticulously drafted agreement was that the unit of devolution was to be a province and no longer the district. Initiated on the 30th of August, this draft Accord became the basis of all future negotiations between the two governments on Sri Lanka's ethnic problems concerning the Tamil minority. The actual signing of the Accord, which Bhandari hoped would crown his efforts, confronted a major obstacle, if not refusal, in the form of not being accepted by the Tamil groups who were represented at Thimpu to give their consent to it. [10]

Meanwhile the outbursts of ethnic violence, especially in the north and east of the Island led to clashes between the security forces and Tamil groups. The Tamil groups in Sri Lanka had their supporters among the political parties of Tamil Nadu. Tamil Nadu continued to serve on three grounds; firstly in providing sanctuary; secondly, in providing the base for training and thirdly, supplying arms and funds.

The Sri Lankan army having become aggressive over the Tamils in Jaffna, the Indian leaders started thinking of direct intervention. Plans for such intervention were finalized by March 1987 and Colombo was warned rapidly to desist from attempting a military victory over Jaffna. However, when Sri Lanka did not heed to the warning, India intervened directly in June 1987, in the name of dropping relief supplies to the beleaguered Jaffna-first through naval boats and when these boats were stopped by the Sri Lankan Navy, then by air under the cover of Indian Air Force planes. This intervention brought the Sri Lankan military operation in Jaffna to an end and led to the conclusion of the Indo-Sri Lanka agreement in July 1987. [11]

**Tamil Nadu Factor**

Tamil Nadu's role in India-Sri Lanka relations can never be ignored. Due to the close ethnic and geographical proximity of the state, Tamil Nadu has always tried to have a say in India's Policy towards Sri Lanka, however in many occasions New Delhi has tried to bypass Tamil Nadu in its crucial decisions.

In the initial stages of the ethnic conflict while Tamil Nadu and the central government in New Delhi were keeping a close watch on developments in Sri

Lanka, they scrupulously refrained from doing anything that could be considered as interference in Sri Lankan affairs, despite there being a tremendous support from the opposition party and other key parties of Tamil Nadu. [12] However, Tamil Nadu's role became inevitable only after the infiltration of Tamil militants into Tamil Nadu. Their presence in Tamil Nadu activated the Tamil social constituency in India and many Tamil public figures, media organizations and even local politicians started sympathizing with them.

The Tamil Nadu factor although inevitable should be analyzed on the premise of two important factors; first, the role of Tamil Polity in both Tamil Nadu and Sri Lanka during the initial period of the ethnic crisis and second: their role during the start of military conflict in Sri Lanka. Until the movement of Tamil militants into Tamil Nadu, the Government of Tamil Nadu was only offering lip service and not really involving itself, especially in terms of the creation of a Tamil Eelam. This was clearly mentioned in Prof. A.J Wilson's book: SJV Chelvanayagam-The crisis of Sri Lankan Tamil Nationalism 1947-1977,

*"Given the nearness of the South Indian mainland, it has to be expected that when Chelvanayagam conceived the idea of a federation, he would think of a relationship with Tamil Nadu in India and the Tamil areas of Ceylon forming a unit of the Indian federation. However, he withdrew from this position as soon as the politicians from Tamil Nadu, who questioned on the subject by pro-government press, 'expressed disapproval"'. He adds, "He made no reference in public speeches and statements to Tamil Nadu as representing a fallback position. He did not wish to use it as a lever. It was his view that the Tamils people in Ceylon must struggle for their freedom by themselves." [13]*

However, this position of non-involvement changed with the presence of Tamil Militants on the Indian soil. Since their presence, a major section of the Tamil Polity has been advocating for Eelam or autonomy for the Tamil region or federalism in Sri Lanka. This situation has of course changed over the years. The economic growth of India has made Indian more inward. Hence Vaiko claiming a 'blood bath' in Tamil Nadu if the war in Sri Lanka were to intensify had no real base.

### IPKF's Role in the Ethnic Conflict

Within 24 hours of signing the Accord, [14] the Indian Peace Keeping Force landed on the northern and eastern provinces to establish peace and normalcy in Sri Lanka, which was ravaged by an extended conflict between the Tamil minority and the Sinhalese majority. Following the Indo-Sri Lankan Accord, cessation of hostilities proved a unilateral affair-the IPKF alone endeavoured to enforce peace in Tamil provinces.

The IPKF's mission was inherently complex and unusual. Added to this complexity was India's complete inexperience as a peacekeeper during civil strife in a neighbouring country. Though Indian forces were in other countries as part of peacekeeping missions, in all those cases, it was a part of multinational forces under the UN Resolution or Multinational Agreements. In the case of Sri Lanka, the IPKF had to work under a bilateral agreement, and there it not only had mutually incompatible relations and linkages with the contending parties but also had its own objectives. [15]

The IPKF was to act on behalf of India in executing and assuring the performance of everything included in the Indo-Sri Lankan agreement. Thus the mission and the objectives, scope and functions of the IKPF became broad and general, not precise and restrictive. Several in the island however understood the IKPF's exercise in a different light. A general obligation was undertaken by India to guarantee an observance of the resolutions and in the annexure to the agreement was a pledge of assistance through Indian forces to secure a halt to fighting within Sri Lanka. [16]

While the situation in the north and the east was returning to normal, the suicide of 17 LTTE cadres who were arrested by the Sri Lankan navy while the cadres were returning in an armed boat, made way for the LTTE to revert to taking up arms. [17] Evidently the IPKF also grew impatient waiting for the LTTE to conform to the agreement, surrender arms and follow its provisions. But soon it became clear that the LTTE was going back on the agreement. They either had to be forced by the IPKF to do so or eliminated so that the agreement could be executed through other small Tamil militant factions. For this reason, the IPKF's operational aspects soon turned out to be offensive in combating an intractable enemy, the LTTE in the northeast. To the LTTE, the settlement to the ethnic conflict contained in the Indo-Sri Lankan agreement was unacceptable. It was unsatisfactory.

In addition to this, President Jayewardene, on the contrary asserted that, he on sensing the threat to the people wanted to counter the same, and thus, had invoked military assistance immediately, and subsequently affirmed that, "The entry of the IPKF was a military act and it was the decision of the President". When the LTTE dishonoured the agreement, 'in November, Rajiv Gandhi had to disarm them according to the terms of the Agreement.' He also disclosed the reason for providing Indian Military assistance, as, 'Consequently from a Sri Lankan view, the IPKF's mission and objectives were to render the LTTE military inactive, and also save Sri Lankan citizens from Janatha Vimukthi Peramuna's rebellion'.

The sudden change in the political situation had its impact on the affairs of the IPKF. With the departure of President Jayewardene from office, the commitment to the Indo-Sri Lanka Accord at the highest level of the Sri Lanka government was bound to ebb, especially because his successor had never shown much enthusiasm for it. Moreover with President Premadasa's election into office in December 1988, the IPKF's continued presence on the island had become a point of contention between the Indian and the Sri Lankan governments. Eventually the vicissitudes of electoral politics in India, which saw the defeat of Rajiv Gandhi's government and the formation of a new coalition under V.P. Singh, also changed the situation. Soon the IPKF was withdrawn on the basis of a timetable drawn by V.P. Singh's government under the key negotiator for India I.K. Gujral, the then Minister for External Affairs. The process of withdrawal of the IPKF was completed in March 1990.

The IPKF's presence in the north and the east of the island was not without its advantages to the Sri Lanka government. Sri Lanka's defence expenditure dropped noticeably after mid-1987. The Indian government bore the heavy expenditure involved in this. At the time of the IPKF's arrival on the island, only the Sinhalese were hostile and opposed to its presence. But soon, even the Tamils who originally welcomed them as liberators alienated themselves from them. [18]

The withdrawal of the IPKF and the assassination of Rajiv Gandhi by the LTTE in May 1991 in Tamil Nadu, marked the end of an era of India's active involvement in the Sri Lankan ethnic problem, a process that stated after the July 1983 ethnic riots. Before its total withdrawal, India tried to prop up a pro-Indian provincial administration in the north and the east headed by the EPRFL and also an army called the TNA. But both the organizations collapsed even before the departure of the IKPF. India's failure to bring about satisfactory solutions to the ethnic problem in the island led to a qualitative change in world opinion regarding India's future role in Sri Lanka. [19] Subsequently the LTTE was banned also in India.

**Post-IPKF Tenure**

The exit of the IPKF and the assassination of Rajiv Gandhi started the third phase of Indian Interests in Sri Lanka. After India withdrew from Sri Lankan peace talks, third party involvement in Sri Lanka was put on hold until the involvement of Norway. The Norwegian government acted as a facilitator in reviving the interrupted communication between parties to the conflict. The MoU of 2002 marked the first success of Norway's facilitating efforts.

Since the accession of Chandrika Kumaratunga as the President of Sri Lanka, Indo-Sri Lankan relations experienced an upswing. President Kumaratunga made numerous trips to India to chart out closer ties with India. With the LTTE gaining more power than the Sri Lankan defence forces and their capturing of several places in the northern coast, made the Sri Lankan government seek Indian help in 2000. Even though India did not help Sri Lanka, it was felt that Indian help was needed to counter the LTTE.

Although India had clearly expressed its position on non-involvement in Sri Lankan affairs, due to strategic reasons it remained a spectator to Sri Lankan affairs. The Norwegian mediators, Sri Lankan authorities and other international organizations, throughout the peace process visited India, so as to inform it about the status of the peace process. President Chandrika Kumaratunga in an interview to Frontline said, *"India does not participate in our conflict-resolution (process) except that it wants to be kept briefed and it wants to know what is going on since it is very closely related to us and also because of its geographic concerns."*

The November 17, 2005 Presidential election saw a change in the political set-up of Sri Lanka. The new President Mahinda Rajapakse, who was regarded as a realist by the LTTE came to power with the promise of ending the ethnic war. The initial step taken by the new government was to start the peace process; however the LTTE in all its undependability began to attack people and Government establishments in the months following the presidential elections.

Since the unofficial declaration of the Eelam War IV India had been extremely unhappy about developments in Sri Lanka. Security concerns went up with the change of events. This was mainly due to the fear of infiltration of the LTTE into India as refugees. In addition to this, the sophistication of the LTTE, especially in its air wing, prompted India to tighten its screws on coastal security.

Although India did not openly support Sri Lanka in the Eelam War IV, its subtle involvement was clearly evident. Initially there were repeated denials from the Government of India on the supply of arms to Sri Lanka, however newspaper reports show that India in addition to sharing of intelligence also gives tactical weapons to the Sri Lankan Armed Forces.

**Instruments of Policy**

Three major factors still remain the determinants of Indo-Sri Lankan relations. These factors not only have an impact on the lives of Sri Lankans but also of Indians. With the end of the military phase, these issues would play a major role in determining India-Sri Lanka relations. Although these issues do not form the trump cards of the subject of this essay, these issues have impacted upon Indo-Sri Lankan relations, something that is likely to continue in the coming years.

**Fishermen Issues:** Fishermen issues have deeply affected the history, economy and culture of the coastal regions of both-Tamil Nadu and northeast Sri

Lanka. Due to ceding of the Kachchtativu Island in the 70s to Sri Lanka, the livelihood of Tamil Nadu fishermen has been badly affected. The fishermen of both these countries have not respected the maritime boundary at all. Despite the historical linkages between the fishermen of both Tamil Nadu and North-eastern Sri Lanka, they still see their comrades as martyrs and those on the other side of the international boundary line as aggressors. Sri Lankan fishermen poaching in other countries' waters have been more widespread than that of Indian Fishermen. Tamil Nadu Fishermen on the other hand, even today invoke historical rights and routinely stray into Sri Lankan waters for fishing. This has led to apprehension by the Sri Lankan Navy and in some cases even shooting. Another factor that makes Indian fishermen cross into Sri Lankan waters is the possibility of a better catch both-in quantity and quality. On the other hand, Sri Lankan fishermen have also often crossed over into Indian waters near the Lakshadweep Islands for Tuna fish.

These issues are reflected in the media but not in a major way. There is a need for Southern states like Tamil Nadu and Kerala and the Centre to come to grips with the problem and resolve this issue on a lasting basis. Various proposals have been made from time to time to obtain fishing licenses for the fishermen of the area. A proposal for lease in perpetuity or reciprocal licensing has also been mooted. All this requires concerted action by Governments.

The main problem with fishing rights in the Palk Bay is that of the laws binding the law of the sea and traditional fishing rights. Historically Indian fishermen and Sri Lankan fishermen have been fishing in the Palk Bay with occasional fights between both these groups, [20] however with the ceding of the Kachachativu to Sri Lanka in 1974, fishing has become an issue of contention between both India and Sri Lanka. The LTTE in the capacity of a third navy in India's backyard increased the complexities of this. The protracted ethnic war having come to an end, fishing rights is likely to be a major issue that both nations would need to sort out at the earliest. A solution to this issue is only possible if there is a proper agreement on the possibility of fishing around Kachchativu Island. The following section would give a brief background to the issue of Kachchativu.

**Issue of Kachchativu:** Kachchativu is a small island in the Palk Strait situated to the north-east of Rameswaram, about 11 nautical miles from the Indian coast and about 10 nautical miles from the south-western part of the Sri Lankan Island of Delft. There is no source of drinking water and the only building is the poorly maintained St. Anthony's Church. By tradition, the island had been used by fishermen from Tamil Nadu as a staging post to dry nets and to celebrate the St. Antony's festival. He was considered as a patron to seafarers.

The issue of sovereignty over the island of Kachchativu has been emotionalised to a considerable extent in Tamil Nadu and in Sri Lanka. The maritime boundary in these 'historical waters' was fixed in accordance to the relevant provisions of the UN Convention on Territorial Sea and the Contiguous Zone, 1958.

It is claimed that Kachchativu was originally part of the Zamindari of the Raja of Ramnad and that the people of Rameswaram and other coastal areas regarded the area as part of their traditional fishing grounds. Kachchativu was essentially an integral part of the Zamindari of Raja of Ramnad which was ceded to Sri Lanka, initially in the years 1880 and 1885, for the collection of roots for dyeing purposes and in 1913 for the full exploitation of *sankha* shells. Five decades lapsed between this and Sri Lanka's laying claim to the island in 1921 and the discussions leading to the 1974 Agreement. During this period, neither the Zamindari of Ramnad nor the Government of Madras/Tamil Nadu, as the successors to the Zamindari, moved any court in India or in Sri Lanka to establish ownership rights over the island. The Government of Tamil Nadu also did not mount any judicial challenge to the Central Government's decision to accept (in the 1974 agreement) Sri Lanka's claims of sovereignty over Kachchativu. [21]

The issue of Kachchativu was discussed at the highest political level for the first time in November-December 1968, during the visit of Prime Minister Dudley Senanayake to India. The formal official talks ended in a deadlock. Indian Foreign Secretary T.N. Kaul informally elaborated on certain proposals made by him earlier. One suggestion was the lease of the island in perpetuity, either by Sri Lanka to India or by India to Sri Lanka. As this involved modification or denial in some degree of Sri Lanka's claim of sovereignty over the island, it was not acceptable to Sri Lanka.

Meanwhile Indian Foreign Secretary Kewal Singh had discussions with Jayasinghe in Colombo on December 24, 1973, after delivering Indira Gandhi's letter dated December 18, 1973 to Mrs. Bandaranaike. He repeated the proposals made by his predecessor in 1968. One of them was that India had sovereignty over Kachchativu, but will give it to Sri Lanka on perpetual lease on nominal rent or without rent. He, however, apprehended that Tamil Nadu may object even to this and that the Madras High Court may intervene and the Supreme Court may allow a writ, but Sri Lanka did not agree to this proposal. From then on Kachchativu has become an area of dispute between Indian fishermen and Sri Lankan fishermen.

**Refugee Issues:** The official Indian rationale for India's involvement in the Sri Lankan crises, at least in the beginning, was the case of Sri Lankan Tamil refugees. [22] The Sri Lankan refugees as Prof. V. Suryanarayan opines, "come from a poor country to a poorer country". Their journey is not all the way roses; [23] however security for their lives makes them undertake this daring and violent passage through the Palk Strait to land on the shores of their fatherland-Tamil Nadu as Anoton Balashimgham puts it. A typical life of the Sri Lankan refugee is best described by VIS. Jayabalan as:

"My son is in Jaffna wife in Colombo father in the Wanni mother, old and sick in Tamil Nadu relatives in Frankfurt a sister in France and I Like a camel that has strayed in Alaska am stuck in Oslo. Are our families cotton pillows to be torn scattered by the monkey fate"? [24]

Sri Lankan Refugees arrived in India in phases. The first phase was from 1983 to 89, where 1,34,053 persons arrived from Sri Lanka. The second phase was from 1989 to 91, where 1,22,078 persons came to India. From 1991 there was a significant drop in the refugee influx till 1996. The third phase was from 1996 until 2001, where 21,940 refugees arrived in India. [25] At present there are 73,241 refugees in 115 camps in 26 districts and 31,802 [26] of them are living outside camps in Tamil Nadu.

Sri Lankan Refugees can be broadly divided into camp refugees and non-camp refugees. The camp refugees live mostly on dole and non-camp refugees live mostly in rented houses or with friends and relatives. The treatment that is given to Sri Lankan refugees living in camps in India has had its ebb and flow. This is mainly because of the lack of a Refugee Law in India. Following Rajiv Gandhi's assassination there were reports of camp refugees in Tamil Nadu being forcefully repatriated. Many of the repatriated refuges reverted to India because of uncertainty in Sri Lanka. During these forced repatriations many refugee's families broke down, and many of them came back to in India in a pitiable condition.

Life as a Refugee in India is also not easy. Most of these camp refugees, although are allowed to work, in some occasions are forced to stay back in their camps. During Jayalalitha's tenure as the Chief Minister, even education was not affordable due to restrictions imposed on the opportunities for higher education. However, these stringent rules have now been removed and education has been made available to all Sri Lankan refugees, including higher education.

Ill treatment of Tamils in Sri Lanka has made these innocent victims of war seek refuge in Tamil Nadu. The Government of Tamil Nadu as well as the Central Government have the vital task of equipping these people intellectually and as skilled labourers so as to rebuild their homeland on their return in the near future. However it is also important to know that with Sri Lanka planning to resettle Sinhalese soldiers along with their families in the north would discourage the rehabilitation of Tamil refugees languishing in camps in Tamil Nadu.

**Conclusion**

*History will have to record that the greatest tragedy of this period of social transition was not the strident clamor of the bad people, but the appalling silence of the good people.*- Martin Luther King, Jr.

From the days of non-involvement in Sri Lanka's policy Indo-Lanka relations have come a long way. Politics and ethnic conflict have become one of the facets of bilateral relations. Since the end of the Eelam war IV a new chapter has begun in India-Sri Lanka relations. It is likely that this period would not see the policy of involvement but rather of mutual growth and harmony.

It is important that India looks at the issue of Internally Displaced Persons numbering almost 300,000 in Sri Lanka. Their needs are enormous and immediate and any delay in offering help to these people would put them into enormous trouble. The Sri Lankan Government with all its insincerity in giving a proper political package in the past has promised a political package to the Tamils. But the fear in most of these Tamils is that the Sri Lankan Government would again deprive them of a package unless there is no Indian involvement.

Having said so, it is imperative that India has a pro-active policy towards Sri Lanka, in order to not only save the people but also for its own security reasons. Economy could be a big trump card in India's policy. Indian corporate houses have shown interest in investing in Sri Lanka. There is also a favourable mood in Colombo in allowing Indian houses to invest. India can use this leverage to not only develop the north and the east that has been affected by the protracted war but also protect it from external influence.

With the end of the War, Sri Lanka has come closer to China, Pakistan and Israel because of their support during the Eelam War IV. China building the Hambothota port cannot be ignored by India. Hence it is important that India looks at these developments with great caution and ensures a proper policy towards her closest southern neighbour. As said above, India needs to invest in Sri Lanka so as to keep the latter in the zone of its influence. Timely Indian help during the Tsunami proved to the world that India is capable of handling challenges facing this region. Having proved ourselves, it is important that India consolidate this good it enjoys vis-à-vis its neighbours.

**Notes**

1. www://countrystudies.us/India/125.htm
2. Shelton U. Kodikara, *Foreign Policy of Sri Lanka, A Third World Perspective,* Chanakya Publications, (New Delhi, 1982).
3. ed., Amal Jayawardane, Documents on Sri Lanka's Foreign Policy 1947–1965, Regional Centre for Strategic Studies, (Colombo, 2004).
4. Ram Sharma, *Indian Foreign Policy, Annual Survey: 1973*, Sterling Publisher, New Delhi,

1977.

5. Ibid.
6. Rajesh Kadian, *India's Sri Lanka Fiasco, Peacekeepers at war*, Vision Books, (New Delhi, 1990).
7. Gamini Keerawella, "India's Involvement in the Sri Lankan Ethnic Crisis", in eds, Mahinda Werake et al, *Security Dilemma of a Small State*, South Asian Publishers (New Delhi, 1995).
8. K.M. De Silva, *Reaping The Whirlwind,* Penguin Books (New Delhi, 1998).
9. Hugh Tinker, *The Baniyan Tree,* in K.M. De Silva, *Reaping The Whirlwind,* Penguin Books (New Delhi, 1998).
10. K.M. De Silva, *Reaping The Whirlwind,* Penguin Books (New Delhi, 1998).
11. S.D. Muni, *Pangs of Proximity, India and Sri Lanka's Ethnic Crisis*, Sage Publications, (New Delhi, 1993).
12. S.D. Muni, *Pangs of Proximity, India and Sri Lanka's Ethnic Crisis*, Sage Publications, (New Delhi, 1993).
13. V. Suryanarayan, Dilemmas of India's Sri Lanka Policy.
14. Gamini Keerawella, "India's Involvement in the Sri Lankan Ethnic Crisis", in eds, Mahinda Werake et al, *Security Dilemma of a Small State*, South Asian Publishers (New Delhi, 1995).
15. S.D. Muni, *Pangs of Proximity, India and Sri Lanka's Ethnic Crisis*, Sage Publications, (New Delhi, 1993).
16. Bertram E.S.J. Bastiampillai, "Indian Peace Keeping Force in Sri Lanka", in eds, Mahinda Werake et al, *Security Dilemma of a Small State*, South Asian Publishers (New Delhi, 1995).
17. S.D. Muni, *Pangs of Proximity, India and Sri Lanka's Ethnic Crisis*, Sage Publications, (New Delhi, 1993).
18. K.M. De Silva, *Reaping The Whirlwind,* Penguin Books (New Delhi, 1998).
19. Gamini Keerawella, "India's Involvement in the Sri Lankan Ethnic Crisis", in eds, Mahinda Werake et al, *Security Dilemma of a Small State*, South Asian Publishers (New Delhi, 1995).
20. V. Suryanarayan and R. Swaminathan, *Contested Territory or Common Heritage? Thinking out of the Box*, Ganesh and Co, Chennai, 2009, p.14.
21. Lok Sabha Debates, 17 May 1966, Cols. 1683-84.
22. Gamini Keerawella, "India's Involvement in the Sri Lankan Ethnic Crisis".
23. V. Suryanarayan, Dilemmas of India's Sri Lanka Policy, *Agni.*
24. V. Suryanarayan and V. Sudersen, Between Fear and Hope: Sri Lanka Refugees in Tamil Nadu, T.R. Publication, (Chennai, 2000), p. 55.
25. Repatriation of Sri Lankan Refugees, Economic and Political Weekly, Vol: XXXVIII, No: 24, June 14-20 2003.
26. http://timesofindia.indiatimes.com/india/Grant-permanent-residential-status-to-Lankan-Tamil-refugees-Karuna/articleshow/5193167.cms

# PART VI

# INDIA, US and EUROPE

# 25

# Contemporary Developments in US-Pakistan Relations: Impact on Indian Foreign Policy

M.J. Vinod

---

United States-Pakistan relations have been distinguished by a long history of 'trust' and 'mistrust', ups and downs. It has been difficult to say anything with 'finality' as an 'element of elusiveness' has always existed in the relationship. Pakistan has remained in the storm due to what the former Pakistan Ambassador to the US calls the 'tyranny of geography'. Besides, Pakistan is situated in a very volatile part of the world which leads Pakistan to be a critical player in both regional and global security (Lodhi Maleeha: 2009). The US approach to Pakistan has also been heavily influenced by 'personal relationships' at the top. The relationship has also been highly 'militarized' and 'centralized', with very little trickling down to the average Pakistani.

Since 9/11 US-Pakistan ties have entered a new phase, primarily driven by the US response as the 'war on terror'. Since then Islamabad has assumed a strategically vital role in Washington's foreign policy calculations to combat terrorism. The US government since the 9/11 incident has declared that its larger strategic policy objectives toward Pakistan are grounded on the following five goals:

1. Global War on Terrorism.
2. Non-proliferation of WMDs.
3. Managing Pakistan-Afghanistan ties.
4. Maintaining peaceful relations between India and Pakistan.
5. Strengthening the democratic fabric in Pakistan.

However, given Pakistan's track record so far, it is bound to pose one of the 'greatest foreign policy challenges' for the Obama administration. It may be recalled that during his candidacy, Obama had highlighted the following issues:

1. That there was the need to 'shift the strategic focus from Iraq to Afghanistan'.
2. That the Iraqi adventure was a 'strategic blunder', based on 'naive neo-conservative political evangelism'.
3. That Afghanistan-Pakistan-India are interconnected parts of the 'same strategic puzzle'.

The US has increasingly been using the phrase 'smart power' which is a combination of hard and soft power. Moreover Washington visualizes the need to use 'the full Range of tools at the disposal of the US viz., diplomatic/economic/military/legal/political/cultural'. However there are serious limitations to the extent to which it can exercise leverage over Pakistan. The dilemma in the US approach is that:

1. it combines a 'politically soft' approach to Pakistan's military and the ISI.
2. a 'militarily hard' approach towards Afghanistan.
3. a 'politically confrontationist' approach towards Iran-a country that could provide a viable supply route to the war zone.

Hence there is the need for a fundamental change in US policy towards Pakistan. The Bush administration to a large extent de-hyphenated India-Pakistan ties. The rising economic strength of India also helped the Bush administration to look at India as a separate, sovereign power and not a conjoined twin of Pakistan.

**War on Terror in Pakistan and Challenges before Obama Administration**

Obama administration's policies and strategies towards Pakistan have been caught in a web of dilemmas, contradictions and challenges. The following are some of the major challenges before the Obama administration with respect to Pakistan:

- To convince their *Pakistani counterparts that the real dangers to Pakistan are the internal extremists and terrorists and definitely not India.*
- That certain elements of the Pakistani army and ISI see some militant groups as a *'hedge'* they can use against India in Afghanistan and Kashmir.
- That, training needs of the Pakistani military to fight insurgents are different from the training required to fight a ground war against India. Presently about 70 U.S. military advisers are working in Pakistan to train the Pakistani army and paramilitary forces to fight insurgents.
- The need to reduce the 'trust gap' between Washington and Islamabad. When *Richard Holbrooke, was asked recently on the 'News Hour with Jim Lehrer', whether Pakistan's security forces were committed to rooting out terrorists,* he replied bluntly-"I've rarely seen in my years in Washington an issue which is so hotly disputed internally by experts and intelligence officials."

Admiral Mike Mullen, Chairman of the Joint Chiefs of Staff recognizes that Pakistani military officers also have some grounds for 'mistrusting' Americans. According to him t*he cut-off of U.S. military aid in 1990 led to* a whole generation of Pakistani military officers who have had no contact with Americans and thus, suspect American motives. Hence Mike Mullen made numerous visits to Pakistan to confer with top military officials, as has Gen. David Petraeus, now head of Central Command. Pakistan's army chief, Gen. Kayani and the head of the ISI, Lt. Gen. Shuja Pasha, have been regularly conferring with U.S. officials in Washington.

General David Petraeus of the Central Command said on April 1, 2009 that Islamist insurgents pose a growing threat not only to Afghanistan but to Pakistan's 'very existence'. Bruce Riedel in his book 'The Search for Al Qaeda' observes that the former President General Musharraf had allowed Al Qaeda to 'regroup' in 'Pakistan's tribal lands' and Musharraf and his ISI stooges was 'more an enabler' 'than a foe' of the terrorist formation in Waziristan. Now Pakistan seems to be paying a heavy price for all its follies.

On the one hand, the Pakistani's have been nervous about U.S. predator drone strikes against al-Qaeda and Taliban targets which not only cause collateral damage but also affect public opinion and on the other; Islamabad complains that the US isn't providing the equipments they need. Hence Islamabad has been demanding cobra helicopters, night-vision equipments, jamming equipment to block radio broadcasts of the Taliban commander in Swat. They would also like 'small surveillance drones'. On the whole 'surgical military strikes' will continue to be an issue of contention in US-Pakistan relations.

**Afpak: Issues and Challenges before Obama Administration**

It may be recalled that Richard Holbrooke had invited the Defence and Foreign ministers of Afghanistan and Pakistan to Washington to give them inputs into Obama's strategic review of 'Afpak' related issues. A large number of additional troops have headed for Afghanistan in 2009. Many of these troops have been deployed in provinces close to Kabul which currently do not have a significant international presence and are largely under insurgent control. The challenge for Washington is to hold onto the territory it has gained in Afghanistan and initiate reconstruction projects so that the local population can see the benefits of their presence.

A concern expressed by western officials has pertained to the propensity on the part of some elements of the Pakistani military to support militants based on Pakistani soil, who cross into Afghanistan and launch attacks. This has long been a source of tension between the two countries, but in recent years some militants allied with the Al Qaeda have also launched a war against Pakistan. The result is that Islamabad follows a dual policy of cracking down on such militants arrayed against the Pakistani state-which includes Al Qaeda on the one hand and on the other, tolerating/backing militants covertly who restrict themselves to fighting Afghanistan.

The forty one NATO countries involved in Afghanistan - who make up roughly 55,000 of the 70,000 troops in the country - have differing rules of operation. Some refuse to deploy to combat-intensive zones and others have already set withdrawal dates. Both Pakistan and the United States must both 'do more' to fight terrorism. Alternative strategies also need to be adopted. The battle cannot be won only by military force. The response has to be multi-pronged which requires an approach that encompasses the political, economic and social as well.

To succeed, this initiative must be fought and won on both sides of the Pakistan-Afghan border. The US needs to stay focused on Afghanistan and put more pressure on the Pakistanis. Bill O'Reilly contends, *"There's no winning the Taliban war unless Pakistan cracks down on the guys that are in Pakistan."* Success in Afghanistan depends on success in Pakistan and vice versa. Many of the tribes and developmental challenges are the same on both sides of the border. AfPak will remain as long as the US does not move away from its failed policies.

**US Aid to Pakistan**

A large part of the US aid to Pakistan has gone to the Pakistan army in the hope that it will cooperate in US efforts in combating terrorism. The US has pledged huge military/financial aid to Pakistan, though this is conditional on Pakistan's cooperation on the war against terror. Between fiscal years 2002 and 2008, the US has spent more than US$ 11.2 billion. Of this amount, almost US$ 5.9 billion was from the Coalition Support Fund (CSF) program. This is strictly meant to reimburse countries for the costs incurred in support of the global war on terrorism. The funds were never intended to build 'capacity' within the armed forces of Pakistan. Washington generally pursues what Christine Fair calls 'supply-driven' aid to Pakistan. In the process large sums of money are pumped into Pakistan's coffers with 'few meaningful accountability requirements'. Pakistan has resisted such scrutiny, asserting that once such monies go into Pakistan's exchequer, they become sovereign funds (C. Christine Fair: 2009: 150-51). Coalition Support Funds account for the majority of the US assistance to Pakistan. Among all the countries receiving such funds, perhaps Pakistan is the largest recipient. Officially the fund is reimbursement for food, clothing, fuel, ammunition, billeting and medical expenses. Islamabad has been repeatedly submitting receipts to the US Central Command. Pakistan is also one of the four countries along with-Israel, Egypt and Jordan- to receive budget support from the US. The purpose of this direct cash transfer to Pakistan is to help it pay off its debt, so that it can spend more on the social sector. Needless to say that there is little accountability in the manner in which the money is being spent. (Craig

Cohen and Derek Chollet: 2007).

Most of Washington's 11 billion dollars in aid to Islamabad has gone to the Pakistani Army, in the hope that the then military-led government of former President Pervez Musharraf would fully cooperate with the U.S. to prevent the Taliban and other radical groups from returning to Afghanistan. But not only have the Taliban and its allies made a strong comeback in Afghanistan over the past two years-in part due to the safe havens they have enjoyed in the tribal regions on the Pakistani side of the border-their brand of radicalism has also spread outwards from the Federally Administered Tribal Areas (FATA), where al Qaeda's leadership is believed to be based, into the North-West Frontier Province (NWFP) and beyond even into Punjab and other parts of Pakistan's heartland (Jim Lobe: 2009).

The Obama Administration will be increasing 'non-military aid' to Pakistan. Pakistan needs to be held 'accountable for security in the border region with Afghanistan'. It may be recalled that earlier, Joe Biden, in his capacity as Chairman of the Senate Foreign Relations Committee had introduced a legislation proposing to triple non-military aid to Pakistan in the next five years; the legislation had authorized US$ 7.5 billion over a period of five years, mainly for building schools, roads and clinics. Pakistan has been keen that both Pakistan and the US move ahead with the following two legislations:

1. The 'Biden-Lugar' Legislation ('Enhanced Partnership with Pakistan Act of 2008') introduced on the July 15, 2008.
2. The 'Reconstruction of Opportunity Zones (ROZ) Legislation' (Allow duty-free access to US markets for certain types of goods produced).

As a presidential candidate, Barack Obama had advocated putting more pressure on Pakistan because he feared that Pakistan was preparing for a war against India, using US military aid given to it for fighting terrorists. Asked how Islamabad could be pressurized, Obama said,

1. "We are providing them *military aid without having enough strings attached;*
2. They are *using the military aid*-for preparing *for a war against India"*. (US Presidential Election 2008, 'Pakistan using US aid for war against India', September 5, 2008, IANS).

Washington's ties with Islamabad have grown tense. Pakistan has been unhappy about the pace of deliveries of U.S. military equipment and Congressional attempts to impose restrictions on its supply and use. "We are fighting this war today," a senior Pakistani military official said in describing U.S. assistance as slow and stingy, "What good is it two years from now?" Official and other voices have maintained that there have been long delays in the delivery of helicopters, night-vision equipments and other supplies, requested for, by the army in its ongoing offensive against Pakistan-based insurgents. In recent interviews, civil and military officials in Pakistan drew a sharp contrast between the billions of dollars of assistance that George W. Bush's administration gave, with few strings attached, to the then President Pervez Musharraf - a general who came into power in a military coup-and what they see as efforts to condition assistance to the democratically elected government of President Asif Ali Zardari. (The Nation: August 30, 2009). However the fact is that the Obama Administration has requested for a US$ 2.5 billion direct security assistance fund for Pakistan in 2010-a 25 percent increase over 2009. A US Defence official is on record to have said that General David H. Petraeus, head of the U.S. Central Command, 'personally gets a daily update-daily, mind you-on supplies shipped to Pakistan. That should give you some sense of how riveted we are on this.' However going by the past experiences, military aid to Pakistan need to be channelled through 'civilian institutions'. Given the propensity for the aid to be diverted from its original intent, perhaps the time has come for the US to be as transparent as possible about the aid it provides to Pakistan.

**Developments in the Swat and US-Pak Ties**

The rise of a 'Taliban version of Islam'-which is at variance with the subcontinent's traditional version of Islam-is a huge challenge for Pakistan. Until 2007 the SWAT had been a popular tourist destination dubbed as the 'Switzerland of Asia.' Till the recent offensive by Pakistan, about 75 percent of the valley was under the control of the Pakistani Taliban, which had 'destroyed schools' and 'terrorized the population.' If the authorities in Pakistan have been unable to tackle home-grown insurgency just hours from its seat of power, prospects for their cracking down on the Taliban and the Al-Qaeda forces along the border, are grim.('Pakistan: A Mounting Problem for Obama', By Aryn Baker and Omar Waraich/Islamabad Monday, January 26, 2009, Time World).

It may be recalled that just one week after Pakistani President Asif Ali Zardari approved the Swat Valley Peace Agreement following passage of a parliamentary resolution urging him to do so, the Taliban took over the neighbouring district of Buner in the Northwest Frontier Province (NWFP) in mid-April. On the April 24, 2009 under U.S. pressure and the pressure exerted by Pakistani public opinion, the Pakistani Army deployed paramilitary troops to the region and Chief of Army Staff (COAS) General Ashfaq Kayani sent a warning to the militants that the Army would not allow them to 'impose their way of life on the civil society of Pakistan.' The statement was a positive first step in clarifying Pakistani policy toward the militants. This was followed by aggressive military operations that have ousted the Taliban from the Swat Valley. Since then the U.S. also has stepped up its drone missile strikes in the region, apparently with the support of Pakistani intelligence (Lisa Curtis: 2009).

**Obama Administration and India-Pakistan Relations**

The Obama Administration has been keen to revive the peace process between Islamabad and New Delhi after it was derailed following the terrorist attacks in Mumbai, popularly referred to as 26/11. Taking the relationship forward could be a key factor in helping stabilize Afghanistan. At the same time the Obama administration knows that the U.S.-Pakistani relationship is too important to let the trust gap widen. Obama had argued out his case as follows,

*"I will join with our allies in insisting, not simply requesting, that Pakistan crack down on the Taliban, pursue Osama bin Laden and end its relationship with the terrorist groups. At the same time I will encourage dialogue between India and Pakistan to work towards resolving their dispute over Kashmir and between Afghanistan and Pakistan to resolve their differences and develop the Pashtun border region. If Pakistan can look towards the east (India) with confidence, it will be less likely to believe its interests are best achieved through cooperation with the Taliban" (*see Raja Mohan: 2009: 174).

In the process there is a risk that president Obama may flag-off a 'regional solution for the India-Pakistan impasse. The path to peace between India and Pakistan need not necessarily go through the Kashmir valley. New Delhi needs to be cautious of the US tendency of linking up Afghanistan's security with terrorism in Kashmir. Obama had pointed out the need to resolve the Kashmir problem to reduce nuclear dangers in South Asia, *"I will continue support of ongoing Indian and Pakistani efforts to resolve the Kashmir problem in order to address the political roots of the arms race between India and Pakistan".* Obama's comments in interviews to the *Time* magazine in October and December 2008 and the reported consideration of former President Bill Clinton as a special envoy to Kashmir were at that point of time perceived as indications of a possible pro-interventionist stance.

A few years back with Musharraf at the helm of affairs, a Pakistan scholar Hussain Haqqani surmised the situation as follows, "Fifty eight years after partition, and in the absence of any incentive or compulsion on the part of India to revise the status quo, it might be prudent for Pakistanis to give priority to normalization and stability in South Asia over settlement of the Kashmir dispute. To make that possible, the rhetoric fed to Pakistanis over Kashmir must end. Musharraf too should try to lower the rhetoric over Kashmir rather than raise his people's expectations in that regard." (Hussain Haqqani: 2005). The ISI chief Pasha told a German magazine, Der Spiegel, in January 2009, "We may be crazy in Pakistan, but we are not completely out of our minds. We know full well that terror is our enemy, not India." These are signs at the top that Pakistani security officials understand the need for change.

The U.S. must not fall into the trap of pushing for a resumption of official India-Pakistan talks as an end in itself but instead encourage changes in the dynamics of the relationship that will reduce tensions and uproot terrorism from the region. Without concerted action against the perpetrators of the Mumbai attacks it could well embolden groups like LeT to up the ante. The first step is for Pakistan to demonstrate that it will no longer tolerate the export of terrorism from its territory. If Pakistan takes decisive action to close down the LeT, India and Pakistan could pick up the threads of the dialogue they conducted from 2004 to 2007. Through this dialogue, the two sides strengthened mutual confidence by increasing people-to-people exchanges, improving annual bilateral trade to over US$1 billion, launching several cross-border bus and train services, and liberalizing visa regimes to encourage travel between the two countries. There was even progress on the vexing Kashmir issue with the two governments narrowing the gap in their rhetoric about an ultimate solution to Kashmir. Both sides referred to the idea of keeping the current boundaries intact and making the Line of Control (LOC) that divides Kashmir irrelevant and instituting some type of joint mechanism to facilitate cooperation between the Pakistani and Indian parts of Kashmir (Lisa Curtis: 2009).

**Observations**

Reducing the trust deficit between the US and Pakistan revolves around the way Pakistan deals with the militants within Pakistan. Perhaps the militants have been briefed that the Taliban is making huge inroads into Afghanistan and that they perceive it as an opportunity to take over a nuclear-armed state. President Barack Obama's decision just days after his inauguration to authorize a new round of strikes by aerial drones within FATA-particularly in Waziristan, suggests that he is unconvinced by Islamabad's promises to curb militants such as the JuD.

President Obama will have to seek 'more flexible & imaginative ways'-of managing USA's political relationship with Pakistan. The fundamentals of US policy towards Pakistan 'have to be reworked'. There is 'no easy solution'. Some prioritizing of issues would be necessary. Longer- term goals cannot be sacrificed for short-term gains. The US will have to strike a balance between short-term measures-such as frequent air strikes against Al Qaeda and Taliban targets on Pakistani soil-and the long-term goal of enhancing the 'credibility' and 'effectiveness' of Pakistan's 'civilian leadership and institutions'. The future direction of the region pivots on Pakistan's ability to overcome multiple socio-economic challenges as well as its willingness to fight terrorism in all its forms within its own borders. Washington will have to coax Pakistan into doing more against home bred terrorist havens in the tribal areas and in Pakistan occupied Kashmir. Using terrorists as a means of 'hedging' against India could only aggravate matters for Pakistan. Needless to say, it would further delay the resumption of the India-Pakistan composite dialogue. Washington's success in Afghanistan will be contingent on fixing the problems and bottlenecks in Pakistan. While cooperation between the US and Pakistan has increased manifold, 'mutual distrust' continues. Restoring trust between Washington and Islamabad will be the greatest challenge.

**References**

C. Christina Fair, "Time for Sober Realism: Renegotiating US Relations with Pakistan", The Washington Quarterly, 32:2 (April 2009), pp.149-172.

C. Raja Mohan, "How Obama Can Get South Asia Right", The Washington Quarterly, 32:2 (April 2009), pp. 173-189.

Craig Cohen and Derek Chollet, "When US$10 billion is not Enough: US Strategy Towards Pakistan", The Washington Quarterly, 30:2, pp. 7-19.

Hussain Haqqani, 'The Eternal India-Pakistan-US Triangle', Gulf News, April 6, 2005.

Jim Lobe, US-Pakistan: Obama-Tied think Tank Calls for a Dramatic shift, http://ipsnews.net/news.aspidnews=44739

Lisa Curtis, From Strategy to Implementation: Strengthening U.S.-Pakistan Relations, The Heritage Foundation, July 8, 2009. http://www.heritage.org/research/asiaandthepacific/tst070809a.cfm

Maleeha, Lodhi, "A renewed approach: finding stability in US-Pakistan relations", Harvard International Review, spring 2009 (Interview). http://www.entrepreneur.com/tradejournals/article/200271864.html

The Nation, "Obama Administration Devising Metrics to Measure Progress Under Afghanistan-Pakistan Strategy", August 30, 2009.

# 26

# India-EU Strategic Partnership: Perspectives for the 21st Century

B. Krishnamurthy

## India-EU Strategic Partnership

India and the European Union (EU) are two prominent global actors in present day international politics. Their greatest strength is unity in diversity and pluralism which bring the two entities closer. [1] Through these relations India, the largest democracy in the world joins hands with the EU, the largest cluster of democracies in the world. India was the first among the non-Community member countries to develop a close and regular official relationship with the European Community since the early 1960s. Bilateral agreements were signed in 1973 and 1981 to foster the relationship between the two entities. The relations were more economic than political till early 1990s and the Europeans tried to balance their economic relations with India with a reinforced political dialogue through the EU-India Partnership Agreement of 1993. This partnership formulated a road plan for reinforcing geo-political dialogue between the two largest democracies in terms of population and is intended to create a positive image of the EU in India and of India in Europe, and is the first of its kind entailing the involvement of the Union with any Asian country.

By the end of 1999, member states of the EU and the European Commission decided to hold summit meetings with India. The first institutionalized summit-level interaction between India and the EU was held on the June 28, 2000, in Lisbon, Portugal. This high level relationship between the two parties flows from a shared conviction in the values of democracy, fundamental freedoms, pluralism, rule of law, respect for human rights and multilateralism in the international political architecture as the means to tackle global challenges effectively. The Lisbon declaration spoke of 'a new strategic partnership founded on shared values and aspirations characterized by enhanced and multi-faceted cooperation'. The joint declaration also recognized the need to build a coalition of interests to meet the challenges of the 21$^{st}$ century, as well as recognized the EU and India as important partners in the shaping of the emerging multipolar world.

This Summit was the manifestation of the EU's will to engage India as a major player in an emerging multipolar world and a milestone in India-EU relations and this development was quite significant also for India in status as well as in substance. [2] The EU held such summit meetings with the US, Russia, Canada, China and Japan alone earlier and now India has become the sixth country. All these clearly show that the EU treats India differently from her South Asian neighbours and considers India as the primary interlocutor in this region. In its 'concentric circle' [3] of external relations, India stands at par with China and Japan in Asia.

Moreover, the Lisbon Summit Agenda for Action called for the launch of an India-EU Round Table, which continues to provide an ongoing forum for civil society cooperation and contributes to the enhancement of bilateral relations between India and the EU. It was also decided to set up an EU-India Think-Tank Network, which would bring together research institutes from both sides. It is expected that such discussions and recommendations would emanate from this that would lead to a better understanding of the concerns and priorities of the other side and would form non-binding inputs for decision making by the Government of India and the European Institutions. After the first summit the Indo-EU relations took a new upward curve. During his visit to India in November 2001 to participate in the second India-EU summit meeting, Romano Prodi, the then President of the European Commission, insisted that both the parties should work as 'poles of stability in an unstable world situation'.

In an effort to promote ties between India and the European Parliament in order to strengthen India-EU relations, a European Parliament Friends of India Group was formed in May 2003. Charles Tannock, Member of the European Parliament (MEP), became and still continues to be the Founder Chairman of this group, which remains a cross-party initiative, supported by MEPs from all EU member states. It intends to serve as a focus for those who support India as the world's largest multicultural, secular democracy, which, despite difficulties, continues to retain a tradition of democracy, an independent judiciary and respect for the rule of law. [4] The group aims at pressing the EU to have good commercial and political links with India.

By mid-2003, Javier Solana, the then High Representative of Common Foreign and Security Policy of Europe came up with the European Security Strategy in his effort to chart out a future course of the Union in its external relations and it was approved by the leaders of the EU member states in December 2003. Solana advocated two strategies, "We need to pursue our objectives both through multilateral cooperation in international organizations and through partnerships with key actors-to develop strategic partnerships with the US, Russia, Japan, China, Canada and India." [5] It is significant to note that

India formed part of EU's global security strategy.

Subsequently, the Strategic Partnership between India and the EU was launched at The Hague in November 2004 and this coziness flows from a shared belief in sanguine democratic values elaborated afore. Both the parties are determined to further strengthen the strategic partnership and to cooperate at the global level for the cause of peace, security and sustainable development for all. [6]

A Joint Action Plan was adopted at the sixth India-EU Summit at New Delhi in September 2005 and a Memorandum of Understanding was signed on the *Country Strategy Paper for India for 2007-2010*. The Union pledged to offer € 260 million to support India's efforts to achieve the Millennium Development Goals and to implement the India-EU Joint Action Plan. Subsequently, the Plan was reviewed in the 2008 summit in Marseilles and was expanded to include diverse areas for action. As such, the Joint Action Plan between the two entities has proved to be of great importance and relevance.

**India-EU Security Dialogue**

In May 2006, the first ever India-EU Strategic Dialogue was held and of late, it has emerged as a useful institutionalized mechanism for both the parties to discuss and exchange views on the security situation and security challenges existing at the global and the regional level and attempt coordination of responses; counter-terrorism responses, cooperation and intelligence sharing; conflict-resolution initiatives in troubled regions of the world; WMD proliferation and furtherance of democracy and human rights as the basis for political stability in troubled regions. [7] The second meeting under the auspices of India-EU Security Dialogue was held at Berlin in May 2007, for exchanging views on security issues, including disarmament and non-proliferation, as well as bilateral issues of mutual concern. India and the EU reaffirmed their shared interest in working together as partners in disarmament and in countering the proliferation of WMDs and their delivery systems. They regard proliferation of WMDs and their delivery systems, particularly the risk of them falling into the hands of terrorists and other Non-State actors, as a significant contemporary challenge. In this regard they emphasize the importance of full compliance by all States with their Non-Proliferation and disarmament obligations including through national implementation of effective export control measures as detailed in the UNSC Resolution 1540.

**India-EU Economic Relations**

The European Union is already India's premier partner in terms of trade and actual investment inflows and is at the forefront in the fields of economic and development cooperation. India and the EU support a rule-based international trading system which is non-discriminatory, open and equitable and both aspire for the establishment of a global economic and commercial architecture in which all countries have a stake and an equal voice. [8]

The EU is one of India's largest trading partners and accounts for 21 percent share in its total exports, followed by the US (15 percent) and the UAE (9.5 percent). India's engagement with the EU in trade of goods has increased by 2.7 times between 2000 and 2007 and currently, India's annual trade with the EU is to the tune of US$ 56.6 billion. During the course of the first nine months of 2007-08, trade had touched US$ 50 billion and was expected to reach US$ 68 billion for 2007-08. India's exports to the EU were US$ 26.8 billion in 2006-07 and it reached US$ 24.4 billion for 2007-08 (April-December). Exports have grown 2.64 times in 2006-07 over 2000-01's figure of US$ 10.6 billion. Average growth rate of India's exports to the EU was 16.1 percent for the period 2000-01 to 2006-07. India stands at the 10th position amongst the top importing partners of the EU. However, its share is only 1.98 percent of EU's world imports. India's imports from the EU were US$ 29 billion in 2006-07, and it has grown by over 190 percent against 2000-01(US$ 10 billion). On the other hand, trade deficit of India vis-à-vis EU has increased over the period. The deficit was US$ 492.63 million in the year 2001-02 and it increased to US$ 3 billion in 2006-07. Imports from the EU crossed US$ 25 billion for the period April-December, 2007-08. [9]

India's economic growth is because of the service sector and export of services is a large component of the Indian success story. In this regard, India is in an advantageous position in comparison to the EU. While in EU's case it is just 4-5 percent, in India's case it is 17 percent. However, India's share of total trade in services of the EU is just 1.4 percent, with the largest partner of the EU being the U.S in service trade. India exported services worth US$ 5.8 billion to the EU during the year 2005, while EU's total import was US$ 427 billion, implying that India's share was just 1.3 percent. India's total export of services to the world was US$ 56.1 billion in 2005 and as such, share of the EU in India's export of services to the world was 10.4 percent. India imported services worth US$ 6.3 billion from the EU which accounts for 1.27 percent share of the EU's total exports of services to the world. [10]

The EC-India Country Strategy Paper for 2002-2006 maintains that there are several factors favouring EU's FDI in India such as the high professional qualifications of its workforce, a reliable legal framework and a huge market, though problems of infrastructure, power supply and rates, a complex tax system and corruption exist as stumbling blocks. In terms of Cumulative FDI inflows to

India since April 2000, the EU ranks 2nd. In 2007, EU's investment in India rose by 266.66 percent from 2006. The EU invested US$ 13.9 billion in 2007. India's cumulative direct investments in joint ventures and wholly owned subsidiaries in the EU (from April 1996 to 2006-07) were US$ 6715.305 million; making it the largest destination of overseas investments of India. Overseas investments to the EU grew by 266 percent in 2005-06 and 687 percent in 2006-07. India's overall investment in the EU was US$ 12.19 billion in 2007, exceeding Canada, Russia, China and Brazil. [11]

**Convergences and Divergences**

Growing political and economic relations between India and the EU are mainly due to the fact that there is notable convergence between India and the EU on many issues of international politics, which has made the strategic partnership between them conceivable as well as compatible. Both emphasize on the paramount need for effective multilateralism, are committed to a rules-based international order and stress on the need to maintain a momentum in the efforts to adapt the United Nations to the needs of today's world. The Europeans insist on multilateralism and on the need for international laws, agreements, rules and institutions, which can implement and police them. They emphasize on the need to ensure that the United Nations and other institutions of global governance operate as effectively as possible and with multilateral cooperation. Chris Patten, the European Commissioner in charge of External Relations, maintains, "The main role of the EU in international affairs must be to give teeth and bite to this multilateralism". [12] "We are committed to upholding and developing International Law. The fundamental framework for international relations is the United Nations Charter. The United Nations Security Council has the primary responsibility for the maintenance of international peace and security. Strengthening the United Nations, equipping it to fulfil its responsibilities and to act effectively, is a European priority," maintains Solana in the European Security Strategy of 2003.

India and the EU are united in facing the scourge of terrorism, which constitutes one of the most serious threats to international peace and security. Both the entities condemn terrorism in all its forms and manifestations, committed by whomever, wherever and for whatever purpose and are for early finalization of a Comprehensive Convention on International Terrorism at the UN.

The EU and India agreed to work together bilaterally to accelerate their countries' transitions towards a low carbon economy. An EU-India Joint Initiative on Clean Development and Climate Change was launched to develop a joint work program covering the key areas of energy, environment, research and climate change, to promote ongoing and future cooperation. Both the parties reaffirmed the provisions and principles of the United Nations Framework Convention on Climate Change (UNFCCC), including that of common but differential responsibilities and respective capabilities and underscored the importance of its full, effective and sustained implementation and expressed hope that a global goal of significantly reducing greenhouse gas emissions by 2050 compared to the 1990 levels would be reached at Copenhagen.

On certain other issues like nuclear Non-Proliferation in which India has taken a certain stand, there is some divergence of views. Nuclear risk in South Asia is of concern to Europe and the EU Council held in Sevilla in June 2002 called on both India and Pakistan to adhere to the NPT and sign and ratify the CTBT. However, the joint press statement issued at the end of the 3rd EU-India summit in October 2002 said nothing about nuclear issues, in consideration of Indian sensitivities over this issue. [13] While India seeks time-bound global and complete nuclear disarmament, the EU is adopting an ad hoc fire fighters' approach.

Again, in the issue of climate change and the responsibility of the developing world in tackling the problem, India and EU maintain slightly different stands. India is ready to take a series of mitigation steps aimed at reducing emission intensity by 20-25 percent by 2020 on the 2005 levels, but, maintains that these steps are voluntary and not legally binding or open to international scrutiny. On the other hand, the EU pledges US$ 10 billion to the climate battle and advocates a legally binding treaty which mandates developing nations to cap their emissions and make them verifiable. [14] However, both the entities have seen to it that these differences of opinion, which are more in details than in substance, are not allowed to complicate the otherwise smooth relationship between them.

**India-EU Axis in the Triangular Relations among India, EU and the US**

India in particular perceives the EU as a 'positive influence' in international politics and a second western voice to balance American bellicosity. There is overwhelming hope that the EU as a counter-hegemonic alternative will be able to restrain the all-powerful US, which is considered as a behemoth and a menace to world peace, through its unilateral actions.

On the other hand, India, as perceived by the French scholar Dominique Moisi, "has stepped onto the world stage as both an independent and an important power. Cooperating diplomatically with the United States and making economic deals in Europe, the emerging Indian elites are displaying even more pride and optimism than their Chinese counterparts. The world's largest democracy will soon emerge as the most populous country, and it seems to know no limits". [15] In the international political scenario India is perceived by the European leaders as one among the poles of the prospective multipolar world order. Incidentally, EU's six strategic partners including India, offer the picture of a more balanced multipolar world.

**India-EU Strategic Partnership in the Context of Relations with the US**

The significance and propriety of the India-EU Strategic Partnership in the twenty-first century needs to be contextualized with regards to their relationship with the US. Both the partners need to redefine their relationship in the context of the present global system and to move beyond it, to further develop their roles as partners in shaping globalization. [16] Both India and the EU find the US an inevitable partner. The European Security Strategy acknowledges that the United States has played a critical role in European integration and European security, in particular through the NATO. At the same time it highlights the changed reality that the end of the Cold War has left the United States in a dominant position as a military actor and points out that still 'no single country is able to tackle today's complex problems on its own'. Again it adds, 'The transatlantic relationship is irreplaceable. Acting together, the European Union and the United States can be a formidable force for good in the world. Our aim should be an effective and balanced partnership with the USA'. [17]

As in the case of EU, India too has opted for close relationship with the US, leaving behind its decades-old mistrust and misgivings. Both the largest and most powerful democracies have come closer in the post-Cold War period and India has offered unconditional support to the US after 9/11, in its efforts to build up the international coalition against terrorism. The Indo-US Nuclear Deal has further strengthened the cordiality between the two powers to the extent of doubting the Indian commitment to the cause of a multipolar world order.

In spite of this cordiality and acknowledgement of the need of fostering a close relationship with the US, both India and the EU have some real problem with the latter due to its unilateral actions, born out of the American conviction that it is the sole Super Power in the post-Cold War 'unipolar era/world'. [18] On the other hand, the Europeans as well as the Indians maintain that it was and continues to be a multipolar world [19] and insist on 'multilateralism' in the face of American advocacy and practice of 'unilateralism'. [20]

The American efforts to extend their all-out war on terrorism to Iraq without proper sanctions from the UN Security Council was stoutly opposed by the 'core' members of the EU-France and Germany. The fact that other member countries like the UK, Spain and Italy and especially the new members from Central and

Eastern Europe supported the US, actually divided the EU. This cleavage was attributed to the US, when the then American Defence Secretary Donald Rumsfeld termed France and Germany as 'old' Europe against the 'new' Europe, which readily rallied behind it in its war against terrorism. [21] Moreover, the American Realists and Neo-Conservatives criticized the Europeans on their failure to perceive and react to the security threat from rogue states, which belonged to league of the terrorists and posed a real threat with their possession of Weapons of Mass Destruction. Robert Kagan maintains that the Europeans are from Venus, while the Americans are from Mars and pointed out that EU's lukewarm response to the terrorist menace is due to their military weakness and passivism. [22]

In the same way, India too has developed certain uneasiness with the US regarding the renewed pressure from the Americans that India should sign the NPT and CTBT and on contentious issues like reprocessing spent nuclear fuel. The Indians fail to understand and appreciate when the Americans project Pakistan as a front line state in the war against international terrorism and prop it up despite the Indian offer of unconditional support and unstringing offers of positive role in the reconstruction process in Afghanistan as well as Pakistan's its nefarious role in fostering and foisting terrorist attacks on their soil.

India and the EU react to the American onslaught in their own ways and generally positively. The Europeans reacted to the American criticism positively and invariably took corrective measures regarding their military weakness. Under the European Security and Defence Policy, they are making earnest efforts to build up further the Union's capabilities and increase its coherence to deal with security issues, including the establishment of a Rapid Reaction Force, greater surveillance capacity and greater readiness to take over some military operations in Europe and elsewhere. [23] In the same way, India too stuck to its guns regarding the signing of the NPT but continues to play its appointed role in Afghanistan, keeping its national interest in mind.

As this is the case, there is a need to ponder over and analyze to what extent the India-EU Strategic Partnership may be of help for both the parties in their efforts to maintain a positive and constructive relation with the US. Though doubts regarding the efficacy of India-EU Strategic Partnership in helping solve future international crises together and the sincerity of both the parties to help each other in doing so, are raised by certain quarters [24], some other analysts like Subhash Kapila maintain, "The EU-India Strategic Partnership is a multidimensional partnership and the Joint Action Plan formulated covers cooperation in every conceivable area in the realms of political, economic, scientific and technological, cultural and strategic cooperation". Again, comparing India-EU Strategic Partnership to other such partnerships, Kapila adds, "In terms of substantial progress, formulation of multi-dimensional blueprints for joint development of the strategic partnership and moving forward and establishment of institutional mechanisms to carry the blueprint further, the EU-India Strategic Partnership scores heavily in comparison with the Russia-India Strategic Partnership and the US-India Strategic Partnership. Yet another notable factor of the EU-India Strategic Partnership is that if compared to India's strategic partnership with Russia and the USA, it can be said to be more equitable as glaring power differentials do not exist between the EU and India". Kapila is not very much off the mark when he says, "The future prospects of the EU-India Strategic Partnership are bright because there are more strategic issues that unite the European Union and India than those that can divide them. More importantly, the EU-India Strategic Partnership has evolved naturally from an economic dimension to begin with and then graduated to the political and strategic dimensions to now emerge as a 'comprehensive strategic partnership." [25]

Placing EU-India relations in the context of globalization, Gunter Rinsche maintains that India and the EU should reinforce their strategic alliance for the promotion of an effective multilateral approach, peace, security, human rights and democracy in the world. In order to make India-EU relations strategic, it should have a global and not just a bilateral dimension. India and the EU are partners by choice and partners of complementarity. However, to be able to be a key pole, the EU should be able to speak in one voice and act in unison. The EU is committed to shaping the world according to its beliefs in the principles of self-determination, democracy, the rule of law, the respect for diversity, tolerance, the need for solidarity, fairness and equality in our international system. This is the case not only within the EU or with India, but also within the global system. If India and the EU want to be global players, they would be required to exhibit the political will to take on international responsibility. [26]

In the recent summit in November 2009, both India and the EU reiterated that their relations are founded on a global, strategic and mutually beneficial partnership and both the parties are determined to strengthen the strategic partnership and cooperate at the bilateral as well as at the global level for the cause of peace, security and sustainable development for all. [27]

## Conclusion

The European Security Strategy of 2003 concludes emphatically, "The European Union has the potential to make a major contribution, both in dealing with the threats and in helping realize the opportunities. An active and capable European Union would make an impact on a global scale. In doing so, it would contribute to an effective multilateral system leading to a fairer, safer and more united world". The Europeans believe that the partnership and cooperation between the EU and India is of key significance to world peace and prosperity. It is mutually beneficial to both in dealing with the US, since mutual cooperation gives added strength and weight. It is especially beneficial to India since it is increasing India's political weight in the international political arena and is a significant and strategically relevant partnership for India's emerging strategic profile.

**Notes**

1. "Relations between India and EU have grown from strength to strength". [November 7, 2004]On the eve of the India-EU Summit at the Hague, Dutch Ambassador in India Eric F. Ch. Niehe spoke about India-EU relations to Dipanjan Roy Chaudhury. http://www.icfdc.com/html/newsarchives/external/_relations_between_india_and_eu.html.
2. *The Hindu* (Chennai), June 20 and 23, 2000.
3. Christopher Hill, "The Capability-Expectations Gap, or Conceptualizing Europe's International Role" in Simon Bulmer and Andrew Scott (eds.), *Economic and Political Integration in Europe – Internal Dynamics and global Context*, Blackwell Publishers, Oxford, 1994, pp. 122-3. EU 's external relations is regulated by the concept of 'concentric circles' or the notion of the 'pyramid of privileges', whereby states like the US form the closest ring around the EU, followed by a belt including the CSCE, ASEAN, China, Japan and India, and then, another constituted by the African, Caribbean and Pacific and Asian and Latin American countries. The EU's relations with these countries vary in warmth and intensity and while with some it is simple exchange relationship, in the case of some others, economic assistance and incentives are involved aiming at long-term patterns of friendship and stability. As of now, the EU has strategic partnership with the US, Russia, Canada, Japan, China and India, which makes the relationship maintained by the Union with these countries something 'special', more intensive and rigorous..
4. http://www.charlestannock.com/pressarticle.asp?ID=160
5. "A Secure Europe in a Better World", European Security Strategy (Brussels, 12 December 2003) *www.consilium.europa.eu/uedocs/cmsUpload/78367.pdf*
6. India-EU Joint Statement, New Delhi, 30 November 2007 *www.eu2007.pt/NR/rdonlyres/...0E1B.../20071130EUIndiaStatement.pdf*
7. Subhash Kapila, European Union–India Strategic Partnership Reviewed, http://www.southasiaanalysis.org/ percent5Cpapers27 percent5Cpaper2661.html
8. A.N. Ram, "India and the European Union in the New Millennium", in Rajendra K. Jain (ed.), *India and the European Union in the 21st Century",* Radiant Publishers, New Delhi, 2002, p.11.
9. Report for the 12th EU-India Round Table on India-EU Trade and Investment- Current Status & Issues, Indian Rapporteur: Mr Amit MITRA, www.eesc.europa.eu/.../india/.../MITRA percent20Trade percent20and percent20investment.doc
10. Ibid.
11. Ibid.
12. http://europe.eu.int/comm/external_relationss/nfewss/patten/sp02_134.htm (14-06-02) Developing Europe's External Policy in the Age of Globalisation (Speech by Chris Patten,

the then European Commissioner for External Relations on April 4, 2002).

13. Jean-Luc Racine, "European Union and South Asia: An Appraisal" in *Major Powers of South Asia*, Institute of Regional Studies, Islamabad, 2004, pp. 131-162.
14. *The Hindu*, December 12-13, 2009.
15. Dominique Moïsi, "The Clash of Emotions", *Foreign Affairs*, January/February 2007.
16. http://www.ipcs.org/seminar_details.php?recNo=685
17. A Secure Europe in a Better World, European Security Strategy (Brussels, 12 December 2003. www.consilium.europa.eu/uedocs/cmsUpload/78367.pdf
18. Charles Krauthammer, 'The New Unilateralism', *Washington Post*, June 8, 2001, p. A29. He elaborated this theme later in his 'The Unipolar Moment Revisited,' *National Interest*, no. 70 (Winter 2003), p. 17.
19. Dominique Moisi, What Went Wrong with America, http://www.project-syndicate.org/commentary/moisi7
20. http://www.france.diplomatie.fr/label_france/ENGLISH/DOSSIER/2000/04puissance.html
21. "EU-US: Kiss and make up?", http://www.euractiv.com/en/security/eu-us-kiss/article-135513
22. Robert Kagan, "Power and Weakness - Why the United States and Europe see the world differently", http://www.hoover.org/publications/policyreview/3460246.html
23. B. Krishnamurthy and Geetha Ganapathi Doré (eds.), *Changing World Order: India, EU and US – A Trialogue,* Shipra, New Delhi, 2009, pp.175-6, 180-1.
24. Nadia Mushtaq Abbasi, EU-INDIA: LOOKING TOWARDS DEEPER RELATIONS, http://www.issi.org.pk/journal/2003_files/no_4/article/4a.htm
25. Kapila, n. 7.
26. http://www.ipcs.org/seminar_details.php?recNo=685
27. India-EU Joint Statement of November 6, 2009.

# 27

# India's 123 Nuclear Agreement with the US

D. Purushothaman

## Introduction

India's nuclear agreement with the US, commonly known as India-US nuclear deal is one of the most hotly debated issues in India's foreign policy. This issue became controversial in India. One of the main issues of debate was whether it served India's nuclear interest. This agreement also generated more or less the same heat in the US. An important foreign policy decision needs to be examined from the perspectives of continuity and changes as an examination of a foreign policy decision from this perspective, not only enables us to understand the policy better but also facilitates the evaluation of the decision from the perspective of national interest. Surprisingly much of the debate on this issue focused on how this agreement represented continuity and change in the foreign policy of both the countries. This paper makes an attempt to examine how this agreement represents continuity and changes in India's foreign policy.

## Background to India's Nuclear Policy

Jawaharlal Nehru, the first Prime Minister of India, laid great emphasis on complete and universal nuclear disarmament and opposed the development of all types of nuclear weapons. India advocated the prohibition of use of nuclear weapons at various international forums. [1] India, since 1959 has been voting in favour of the UNGA resolutions on the non-proliferation of nuclear weapons. After Nehru's regime, Shastri slightly changed his policy. He said that the existing policy of nuclear pacifism was deep rooted and could not predict the future. [2] Shastri took a more flexible attitude towards the development of nuclear weapons. Later when Mrs. Gandhi came to power she gave importance to national security. She kept the nuclear option open and later exercised the nuclear weapons option. [3] When the Janta party came in to power in 1977, India's nuclear policy underwent changes in a Gandhian way. [4] However, the Charan Singh government did not stay for long and Mrs. Gandhi returned to power in 1980. She said that India did not believe in making nuclear bombs, but added that India 'should be free to carryout experiments' (dual track policy). [5] Her son Rajiv Gandhi came to power in 1984. He worked towards global disarmament.

[6] During the regimes of V.P. Singh and Chandra Shekhar, the nuclear policy remained the same.

During the P.V. Narasimha Rao government, India was pressurised by the US which demanded it to cap its nuclear, missile and space programmes. [7] During the Gujral period, India committed the use of nuclear programmes to peaceful purposes, and did not close its nuclear option. In 1998, A.B. Vajpayee the Prime Minister said, "to ensure the security, territorial integrity and unity of India, we will take all necessary steps and exercise all available options. Towards the end we will re-evaluate the nuclear policy and exercise the option to induct nuclear weapons". In May 1998, India proved to the world that India was a nuclear weapon state by conducting nuclear tests. Later under the Manmohan regime, the 123 Agreement was signed between India and the US.

From this, we should understand that, India's nuclear policy has been oriented towards protecting India's autonomy in its nuclear policy, moving towards realism rather than idealism. From Nehru's era to the present period, India revolves around sustaining its autonomy in nuclear policy. India does not like other countries interfering in its nuclear policy.

**The 123 Agreement**

The Indo-U.S. civilian nuclear agreement refers to a bilateral accord on civil nuclear cooperation between India and the United States. The July 18, 2005 joint statement was the one by which Indian Prime Minister Manmohan Singh and the then U.S. President George W. Bush, under which India agreed to separate its civil and military nuclear facilities and place all its civil nuclear facilities under International Atomic Energy Agency (IAEA) safeguards. [8] The deal places under permanent safeguards those nuclear facilities that India has identified as 'civil' and permits broad civil nuclear cooperation, while excluding the transfer of 'sensitive' equipment and technologies, including civil enrichment and reprocessing items even under IAEA safeguards.

**The IAEA Approval**

The 123 Agreement crossed the IAEA hurdle without much difficulty. A proposal for amending the Nuclear Supply Group (NSG) guidelines was drafted by the Unites States, approved by India, and placed before the NSG committee. The IAEA Board of Governors and the 45-state Nuclear Suppliers Group approved the safeguards agreement on August 1, 2008. [9] The U.S. President George Bush made the necessary certifications and then sought the final approval of the U.S. Congress. Initially, there were objections from Pakistan, Iran, Ireland, Norway, Switzerland and Austria at the IAEA meeting. On August 18, 2008 the

IAEA Board of Governors approved it on February 2, 2009, India signed an India-specific safeguards agreement with the IAEA. By this agreement, 35 civilian nuclear installations will be under inspection. [10]

The nuclear deal was widely seen as a legacy-building effort by President Bush and Prime Minister Singh. But while the deal had to pass the U.S. Congress twice (once when the Hyde Act was passed in late 2006 to amend U.S. domestic law and then when the final deal-related package was approved, in October 2008), the deal became a contentious issue in India and threatened at one time, to topple Manmohan Singh's government, which survived a confidence vote in the Parliament in July 2008 by roping in a regional party as a coalition partner in place of the Leftist bloc. On August 1, 2008, the IAEA approved the safeguards agreement with India, after which the United States approached the Nuclear Suppliers Group (NSG) to grant a waiver to India to commence civilian nuclear trade. The NSG granted the waiver to India on September 6, 2008 allowing it to access civilian nuclear technology and fuel from other countries. The implementation of this waiver makes India the only known country with nuclear weapons which is not a party to the Non Proliferation Treaty (NPT), to carry out nuclear commerce with the rest of the world.

The US House of Representatives passed the bill on September 28, 2008. [11] Two days later, India and France inked a similar nuclear pact making France the first country to have such an agreement with India. On October 1, 2008 the US Senate also approved the civilian nuclear agreement allowing India to purchase nuclear fuel and technology from the United States. [12] George W. Bush, signed on October 8, 2008, the legislation on the Indo-US nuclear deal, approved by the U.S. Congress, converting it into a law, now called the United States-India Nuclear Cooperation Approval and Non-proliferation Enhancement Act. The agreement was signed by Indian External Affairs Minister Pranab Mukherjee and his counterpart, Secretary of State Condolessa Rice, on the October 10.

**Rationale behind the Agreement**

The civil nuclear agreement implicitly recognizes India's 'de facto' status even without signing the NPT. The Bush administration justifies a nuclear pact with India because it is important in helping to advance the non-proliferation framework by formally recognizing India's strong non-proliferation record even though it has not signed the NPT. [13] The former Under Secretary of State for Political Affairs, Nicholas Burns, one of the architects of the Indo-U.S. nuclear deal said, "India's trust, its credibility, the fact that it has promised to create a state-of-the-art facility, monitored by the IAEA, to begin a new export control regime in place, because it has not proliferated the nuclear technology, we can't say that about Pakistan." When asked whether the U.S. would offer a nuclear deal to Pakistan on the lines of the Indo-U.S. deal, [14] Mohammed-El-Baradei, head of the International Atomic Energy Agency, praising the proposal said, "it would also bring India closer as an important partner in the non-proliferation regime". However, members of the IAEA safeguards staff have made it clear that Indian demands of New Delhi being allowed to determine which Indian reactors may be inspected could undermine the IAEA safeguards system. The reason for this is to restrict the development of nuclear weapons and to negotiate with India indirectly to ratify the NPT using another mechanism. Likewise, the reaction in the Western academic community was mixed. While some authors praised the agreement as bringing India closer to the NPT regime, others argued that it gave India too much in determining which facilities were to be safeguarded and that it effectively rewarded India for continuously defying the Non-Proliferation Treaty by not acceding to it. [15]

**Why is it Called as the 123 Agreement?**

The Agreement gets its name with reference to Section 123 of the US Atomic Energy Act of 1954 (the 'Atomic Energy Act') which basically says that an agreement for peaceful nuclear cooperation between the US and another state should fulfil certain criteria, including, in the case of non-nuclear weapons states, International Atomic Energy Agency (IAEA) safeguards, though the President may exempt such requirements in the interests of US policy. The Nuclear Non-proliferation Treaty defines a nuclear weapon state as a state that exploded a nuclear weapon before 1967. Under US law, a non-nuclear weapon state is any state that is not a nuclear weapon state under the NPT. India therefore, is defined to be a non-nuclear weapon state and the US Senate has declared that the President cannot exempt India from Section 123 of the Atomic Energy Act. [16]

**What is the Hyde Act?**

The *Henry J. Hyde United States-India Peaceful Atomic Energy Cooperation Act of 2006*, also known as the *Hyde Act*, is the U.S. domestic law that modifies the requirements of Section 123 of the U.S. Atomic Energy Act to permit nuclear cooperation with India and in particular to negotiate a 123 Agreement to operationalize the 2005 Joint Statement. As a domestic U.S. law, the Hyde Act is binding on the United States. The Hyde Act cannot be binding on India's sovereign decisions although it can be construed as prescriptive for future U.S. reactions. As per the Vienna convention, an international treaty such as the 123 agreement cannot be superseded by an internal law such as the Hyde Act.

Under Section 104 of the Hyde Act, the US President may exempt a nuclear cooperation agreement from the requirement of IAEA safeguards under the Atomic Energy Act, if the President considers that India:

- Has provided a plan to separate civil and nuclear programs;
- Has concluded an agreement applying IAEA safeguards on India's civil nuclear facilities;
- Is working with the US on a multi-lateral treaty to stop the production of fissile material for nuclear weapons;
- Supports the US in efforts to prevent the spread of enrichment and reprocessing technology; and
- Secures nuclear material and technology through export regulation.

Although a determination by the President is ultimately discretionary, supporting material assessing India's actions needs to be submitted to the US Congress for scrutiny on an annual basis. Furthermore, an assessment of India's cooperation with the US efforts to prevent Iran from acquiring weapons of mass destruction is a key consideration for Congress in assessing the President's decision. [17]

While Congress effectively assesses India's conduct, it is important to stress that the Hyde Act does not bind India. It simply provides guidelines for the President to exercise discretion.

**Political Opposition and Resolutions Passed in India**

The internal political context within India, which led to the creation of an impasse and its later resolution, requires greater understanding. Why did the Congress-led UPA government procrastinate in dealing with its recalcitrant Left allies and later shake of their political constraints?

The Indo-US civilian nuclear agreement was met with stiff opposition by some political parties and activists in India. Although many mainstream political parties including the Congress (I) supported the deal along with regional parties like the Dravida Munnetra Kazhagam and the Rashtriya Janata Dal its realization ran into difficulties in the face of stiff political opposition in India. In November 2007, former Indian Military chiefs, bureaucrats and scientists drafted a letter to Members of Parliament expressing their support for the deal. However, opposition and criticism continued at political levels. The Samajwadi Party (SP), which was with the Left Front in opposing the deal, changed its stand, after discussions with the former president of India and scientist Dr. A.P.J. Abdul Kalam, who supported the deal. The Indian Government survived a vote of confidence by 275-256 after the Left Front withdrew their support to the government over this dispute. [18] There were heavy accusations against the

Congress Party regarding 'buying' of MPs, reportedly for Rs.250 million, to vote in favour of the deal in the vote of confidence motion.

As details were revealed about serious inconsistencies between what the Indian parliament was told about the deal and the actual facts about the agreement that were presented by the Bush administration to the US Congress, opposition to the deal grew in India. In particular, portions of the agreement dealing with guaranteeing India fuel supply or allowing India to maintain a strategic reserve of nuclear fuel appear to be diametrically opposed to what the Indian parliament was led to expect from the agreement.

Prime Minister Manmohan Singh's statement in parliament was totally at variance with the Bush Administration's communication to the House Foreign Affairs Committee, which said India would not be allowed to stockpile nuclear fuel stocks as to undercut American leverage to re-impose sanctions. To drive home this point, it said that the 123 Agreement was not inconsistent with the Hyde Act's stipulation-the little-known 'Barack Obama Amendment'-that the supply of nuclear fuel should be 'commensurate with reasonable operating requirements'. The 'strategic reserve' that is crucial to India's nuclear program is, therefore, a non-starter. [19] Furthermore, the agreement, as a result of its compliance with the Hyde Act, contains a direct linkage between shutting down US nuclear trade with India due to any potential future Indian nuclear weapons test-a point that is factually inconsistent with explicit reassurances made on this subject by Prime Minister, Manmohan Singh, during the final parliamentary debates on the nuclear deal.

On July 9, 2008, India formally submitted the safeguards agreement to the IAEA. This development came after Prime Minister Manmohan Singh returned from the 34th G8 summit meeting in Hokkaido, Japan, where he met the U.S. President George W. Bush. On July 19, 2008, the media reported that Manmohan Singh threatened to resign his position if the Left Front, whose support was crucial for the ruling United Progressive Alliance to prove its majority in the Indian parliament, continued to oppose the nuclear deal and he described their stance as irrational and reactionary. According to *the Hindu*, External Affairs Minister Pranab Mukherjee's earlier statement said, "I cannot bind the government if we lose our majority," [20] implying that the United Progressive Alliance government would not put its signature on any deal with the IAEA if it lost the majority in either a 'opposition-initiated no-confidence motion' or on failing to muster a vote of confidence in the Indian parliament after being told to prove its majority by the president. Soon after, Prakash Karat announced that the Left Front was withdrawing its support to the government over the decision by the government to go ahead on the United States-India Peaceful Atomic Energy

Cooperation Act. The Left Front had been a staunch advocate of not proceeding with this deal citing national interests.

On July 22, 2008 the UPA faced its first confidence vote in the Lok Sabha after the Communist Party of India (Marxist) led Left Front withdrew support over the issue of India approaching the IAEA for the Indo-U.S. nuclear deal. The UPA won the confidence vote with 275 votes to the opposition's 256, (10 members abstained from the vote) to record a 19-vote victory. This victory paved the way for the pursuance of the 123 Agreement.

**After the 123 Accord**

Once the 123 accord was over, the US instructed India to follow the rules and regulations under the accord, which were:

- After this Agreement USA will supply all fuel, machinery / equipment & technology to India for producing Nuclear Power.
- India is as yet producing from about 22 Nuclear Power Plants, power as well as Atom. From where which is produced, how much is produced, where it is supplied and what research is being done is to be kept as a high security secret.
- The fuel utilized to produce Atomic Power may be recycled for reuse and this plant will be under direct supervision of the IAPO.

However, if India goes for nuclear tests, this agreement gets cancelled which implies the following:

- The USA will take back all machinery/equipments/technology supplied to India.
- Those 14 plants would continue to be under the scanner irrespective of the status of the agreement.

On the other hand, if any of the US breaches any commitment, there would be no automatic cancelling of the agreement.

**Advantages**

There are a lot of advantages for India in having this accord. They are:

- The most important requirements for India's economic growth in the coming years are energy and infrastructure. By signing this agreement, we will be able to meet these demands to a certain extent.
- The Biggest advantage is that the Hyde Act does not apply to India.
- India does not become a party to the NPT or the CTBT.
- Employment Opportunities.
- Possibilities of obtaining new techniques & technologies.

- The NSG facilitates India in buying nuclear material from other countries which came to a standstill post-Pokhran II.

**Disadvantages**

At the same time, there are some drawbacks to this agreement. They are:

- If India conducts any nuclear test, there may be a chance of cancelling the 123 agreement and subsequent decisions will be taken by the US based on the circumstances on which India conducts the test.
- Nuclear power plants remain under IAEA (International Atomic Energy Agency) inspection.
- If the US breaches any provision, the Agreement does not stand cancelled.
- The Indian private sphere has been encroached upon, to some extent.
- Transfer of technology from the civil to the military sector would become impossible.
- Presently, 35 percent of the produced plutonium is being used to produce bombs. The agreement however, permits the usage of just 10 percent.

**Conclusion**

Though the 123 agreement was made between India and the US government, it has facilitated India to receive nuclear technology from the Nuclear Supplier's Group (NSG). For example, France is the first country that agreed to supply the nuclear material to India. The agreement facilitates trade not only with the US but also with the international community. This proves our nuclear autonomy simultaneously removing the idea of nuclear untouchably entailed by the NPT. It allows India to play an active role in strengthening the activities of the NPT. Continuity in India's nuclear policy has been in the protection of its continuity of nuclear autonomy carried over from the Nehruvian period. India has not surrendered its nuclear policy so far. Changes in India's Policy may be identified as (a) Convergence of Indian and US interests with regards to the safeguarding of India's autonomy in the field of nuclear policy making, which have come about due to various reasons such as the emergence of Indian markets, IT, Indian community in the US, terrorism and so on. (b) Earlier our interests lay in approaching nuclear haves, but now Indian interests lie in promoting Non-Proliferation. Now that we are new members of the nuclear club, we are changing our old strategies so as to maintain our autonomy.

**Notes**

1. Alam B. Mohamed, ed, *India's Nuclear Policy*, Delhi, Mittal Publishers, 1988, pp. 14-16.
2. Ibid, pp. 21-23.

3. Paper laid down on the House on *Evolution of India's Nuclear Policy*, Strategic Digest, New Delhi, Courtesy Government of India, vol. 28, n.7, July 1998.
4. Opcit.1, pp. 31-34.
5. Jain B.M, *Nuclear Politics in South Asia-In Search of an Alternative Paradigm*, Jaipur, Rawatt Publishers, 1994, p. 58.
6. Ibid.
7. Ibid.
8. Joint Statement between President George W. Bush and Prime Minister Manmohan Singh.
9. Text of Draft US Proposal to NSG, August 2008. Available at http://www.armscontrol.org/node/3274 (accessed on 23/09/2008). Outlookindia.com, 2/10/2008.
10. IAEA Board approves India Safeguard Agreement and INFCIRC/731.
11. *Times of India*, 2/10/2008.
12. Senate approves nuclear deal with India, CNN.COM
13. *The Economic Times*, 26/7/2008.
14. Ibnlive.com, 2/10/2008.
15. Muller, John, "The Signing of US-India Agreement Concerning Peaceful Uses of Nuclear Energy", *Gottingen Journal of International Law*, 5/4/2009, pp. 179-198.
16. HallsBury's Law, August 2008, LexisNexis.com
17. Ibid.
18. Indian Government Survives Vote.
19. Daily Pioneer.com, 2/10/2008.
20. Varadarajan Siddharth, "India Sends Safeguard Agreement to IAEA Board", www.hindu.com, 8/7/2008.

# PART VII

# INDIA AND AFRICA

# 28

# Competition for Africa: Challenges and Opportunities for Indian Foreign Policy

Vijay Prakasam G.V.

## Introduction

Traditionally, Africa has been spoken only in very pessimistic terms. The once romantic wilderness and game hunting paradise for the affluential from the western world, has today become synonymous with all the extremes of ills which one can associate with any society, be it extreme poverty, disease or conflicts. The sum of its misfortunes—its wars, its despotisms, its corruptions, its droughts-is truly daunting. No other area of the world arouses such a sense of foreboding, and very few states from within this continent have managed to escape this downward spiral.

What went wrong? How did Harold Macmillan's 'wind of change' turn into Tony Blair's 'scar on the conscience of the world'? What happened to this vast continent, so rich in resources, culture and history, to bring it so close to destitution and despair in the space of just two generations?

Though Africa's ills maybe many, a lion's share of it is owing to the long-term systematic exploitation of the continent by foreign powers. Inducements of power and wealth gave rise to multiple brutal regimes and dictatorships in the continent. As long as the resources kept flowing out unhindered, the powers that were, looked the other way.

Brutality, plundering of resources, massive trade in slave labour, were the hallmarks of the long and dark years of the colonial history of Africa. With next to nil knowledge of the vast African hinterland and its myriad traditional monarchies, chiefdoms and about various African societies that existed on the ground, colonial powers frequently resorted to drawing straight lines on the maps, when marking out the boundaries of their new territories. This resulted in the clubbing together of hundreds of diverse and independent groups with no common history, culture, language or religion. By the time the great scramble for Africa was over, some 10,000 odd African polities of various hues and colour had been amalgamated into forty odd European colonies or protectorates. The ramifications of this act, undertaken by the colonial powers is felt to this day, by the fact that 70 percent of all conflicts in Africa are ethnicity based. The most notorious examples are those between the Hutus and Tutsis in Rwanda, Darfur in Sudan and Muslim-Christian rivalries in Somalia-Ethiopia. Thus, were born the modern states of Africa.

As European colonial powers withdrew, dozens of new states were launched amid much jubilation and to the world's applause. The newly independent African states excited the attention of the world's then rival power blocs: in the Cold War era. Africa was considered too valuable a prize to lose. The post-war industrialized nations replaced the colonial powers in competing with one another for influence, hydrocarbons, minerals, precious metals etc.

Though dictatorships, corruption and exploitation continued unabated on one side, a sense of need for an 'African renaissance' began taking shape in the 1950s & 1960s. With concepts such as democracy, Human Rights etc. becoming prominent themes of discussion among nation states on the world stage, resistance from among the people increased to one-party states and military dictatorships. Combine this with other factors, prominent of which is the emergence of South Africa from the apartheid regime resulted in the formation of cooperative forums such as the OAU (Organization of African Unity, subsequently replaced by the AU or African Union in 2001) and NEPAD (New partnership for African development).

Africa is in the throes of a defining resurgence that promises to have lasting implications for global economy. Despite the global economic slowdown, the IMF has conjured up a robust future for the continent. According to the IMF, the African economy is expected to grow at an average rate of over 5 percent, which will be above the global average. A recent survey by *The Economist* reveals that 6 of the 12 fastest-growing economies are in sub-Saharan Africa. Africa has also emerged as a new oil hub that has sparked an unprecedented global interest in the continent. Oil producers like Angola, Libya, Mauritania, Republic of Congo and Sudan are some of the top-performing economies in Africa.

Against this background, this paper explores briefly the current policy directions adopted by prominent world powers such as the USA, EU and China to extend their reach and influence in Africa, and the challenges arising out of these to Indian Foreign Policy initiatives and interests in Africa. Why one may ask, to study policies of other significant powers while calibrating the dynamics and analyzing our own policy initiatives? A nation's foreign policy not only shows its broader intent and objectives towards the said region or country, but is also a reflection of that nation's innate character and inherent nature. Though objectives may dynamically change, the kind of policies adopted by each nation is by and far determined mostly by a nation's character and power (derived from its perceived strengths). From this perspective the countries considered above are by and far very different in their inherent characteristics. Hence, their respective policies on Africa are bound to clash and overlap with the interests of others.

## Significance of Africa

**Why is Africa Becoming so Strategically Important?:** From being looked upon as a subject of humanitarian concern, Africa has risen steadily in importance to the rest of the world in the recent decades, culminating in the year 2005, dubbed as the 'Year of Africa' by the G8 countries and also becoming the primary theme of its summit that year at Gleneagles, Scotland. Ambitious pledges were made at the summit which included, doubling of aid to Africa, writing off the debts of fourteen of the poorest of African nations, and making available cheaper life saving generic drugs for containing the rampant HIV epidemic in Africa.

Beyond critical humanitarian concerns, Africa has other reasons to grasp the world's attention and making it one of the major geopolitical fields having enunciated competition among the major powers. Let's look at some of them:

**Energy:** Africa holds a fraction of the world's proven oil reserves—10 percent compared to the Middle East's nearly 62 percent—but industry analysts believe it could hold significant undiscovered reserves. China receives about one-third of its oil imports from Africa, and the U.S roughly around 15 percent. Moreover, Africa is poised to double its output over the coming decade and potentially could provide as much as 25 percent of U.S. imports in the coming years. Africa's capacity to export natural gas is also growing rapidly, with American and British companies making billions of dollars of investments in Liquefied Natural Gas (LNG) plants along the Gulf of Guinea. Yet nearly all of Africa's oil reserves are in countries experiencing violence or instability, and in some cases serious violation of human rights.

Africa contributed 12.4 percent of world oil production and around 7 percent of the world natural gas production in 2008. It possessed 10 percent of the total world oil reserves and 7.9 percent of the world natural gas reserves at the end of 2008. During the period between 1998-2008, Africa has recorded nearly a 34.55 percent increase in oil production from7.64 million barrels per day (bpd) in 1998 to 10.28 million bpd in 2008. Oil and gas fields in sub-Saharan Africa are the fastest growing E&P areas in the world today, providing numerous business and investment opportunities. The major energy producers and exporters in Africa are Angola, Nigeria, Equitorial guinea, Sudan, the Democratic Republic of Congo and the region around the Gulf of Guinea.

**Metals and Minerals:** Africa is richly endowed with several mineral reserves such as bauxite, cobalt, industrial diamond, phosphate rock, platinum-group metals (PGM), vermiculite, zirconium and gold. For many African countries, mineral exploration and production constitute significant parts of their economies and remain keys to future economic growth.

African mineral reserves rank 1st or 2nd for bauxite, cobalt, diamonds, phosphate rocks, platinum-group metals (PGM), vermiculite, and zirconium. As of 2005, the percentage share of world production from African soil is as follows: Bauxite 9 percent, Aluminium 5 percent, Chromite 44 percent, Cobalt 57 percent, Copper 5 percent, Gold 21 percent, Iron ore 4 percent, Steel 2 percent, Lead (Pb) 3 percent, Manganese ore 39 percent, Zinc 2 percent, Cement 4 percent, natural Diamond 46 percent, Graphite 2 percent, Phosphate rock 31 percent, including Coal 5 percent, Mineral fuels (including coal) and Petroleum 13 percent, Uranium 16 percent, Platinum/palladium 62 percent.

**Terrorism:** Prolonged poverty, lack of opportunities etc., have directly contributed to the emergence and growth of terrorist networks in the African continent. Al Shahab, is an organization strongly rooted in the Sahel region of Africa, more notably in Somalia and is a direct affiliate of the Al Qaeda. Africa has also been a major transit and storage point for illegal arms, money laundering, narcotics and human trafficking. According to recent reports from INTERPOL and UNODC, African fighters have evolved into becoming paid mercenaries in conflicts and coups in various parts of the world. Sizeable numbers of Islamists from Libya, Algeria, Tunisia, Morocco, Egypt and even Somalia found their way into Jihadi ranks fighting in Iraq and Afghanistan. This led to the U.S declaring Africa as a major focal point in its Global war on Terror (GWOT).

**Healthcare-HIV/AIDS:** Africa is at the centre of the worldwide concern for the AIDS pandemic, with 28 million of the total of 40 million infected with HIV worldwide. The number of infected are spreading rapidly approaching the stage where it will not only lead to a steadily rising death toll but will also undermine social and political stability as well as the prospects for economic progress in the continent. Led by the United States, the annual worldwide expenditure on AIDS programmes has risen from less than US$ 1 billion in 2000 to US$ 8 billion in 2006. But estimates are that as much as US$ 22 billion will be needed annually in the next few years for AIDS alone. Whether these costs can be met without subtracting from other forms of aid for education, agriculture, etc., is very uncertain.

Africa also suffers the most number of deaths from malaria-one million per year. What the world community and various international bodies learn in Africa, and what it is able to achieve, will be critical to whether it is possible to stem this pandemic as it spreads into and across Asia and Europe.

Frequent conflicts and large scale displacement of people have also placed a huge burden on the already meagre resources of Africa. Huge sprawling refugee camps operated by various UN agencies are a common sight across almost major conflict zones in Africa; be it Sudan, Ethiopia or Rwanda. Malnutrition and hunger combined with various air and water borne diseases kill more people in these camps every year than the actual conflict from which these people have managed to flee.

**Poverty:** At the centre of all of Africa's issues and challenges lies the persistence of poverty. Africa is by far the poorest continent and is marginalized in the global trading system. Poverty adds to the potential for conflict, the vulnerability to terrorist influence, the pressures of illegal migration and the spread of disease; it constitutes a drain of worldwide aid resources.

**Global Co-operation in Multilateral Bodies:** Comprising over 54 individual nations, the African continent forms a significant voting bloc in any major international forum. It may be the UN General Assembly resolutions or WTO talks on food security and subsidies, the African countries have become more vocal in voicing their collective stand on issues directly affecting their livelihood. For example, with 40 of the World Trade Organization's 185 members, Africa demanded significant reduction in U.S. and European agricultural subsidies and tariffs in return for agreement on a new round of talks on worldwide trade improvements. Teaming up with India, Brazil and other third world countries, Africa did essentially bring the negotiations of the Doha Round to a standstill. Hence, for many major powers, it becomes crucial to cultivate this voting bloc to significantly influence agendas and outcomes on various international issues.

All the above factors clearly show that Africa is of both-Strategic as well as humanitarian significance.

## Policy Approaches of Various World Powers towards Africa

**U.S Interests and Policy on Africa: U.S Strategic Interests in Africa:** Until very recently, Africa was never considered a strategic priority by the U.S. Even during World War II, Africa was just a strategic stepping stone to the places that mattered in Europe. During the Cold War, Africa was a pawn in East-West struggles. Even as the Americans set in place several well-intentioned economic development policies aimed at the region, it was too often with the idea of trying to do good '*for Africa*', rather than to do good '*with Africa*'.

After the fall of the Soviet Union, many U.S. Policymakers considered the U.S. military's role and responsibilities on the continent to be minimal. In 1995, the Department of Defence outlined its view of Africa in its '*U.S. Security*

*Strategy for Sub-Saharan Africa'*, asserting, "ultimately we see very little traditional strategic interest in Africa." In 1998, following the terrorist attacks on two U.S. embassies in East Africa, the United States conducted a retaliatory attack against a pharmaceutical factory in Khartoum, Sudan, that Clinton Administration officials initially contended was producing precursors for chemical weapons for Al Qaeda. The embassy bombings, and the retaliatory strike against Sudan, are considered by many analysts to be a turning point in U.S. strategic policy towards the region.

Bush Administration's National Security Strategy of 2002 reflected a need for a more focused strategic approach towards the African continent-"*In Africa, promise and opportunity sit side by side with disease, war, and desperate poverty. This threatens both a core value of the United States—preserving human dignity—and our strategic priority—combating global terror.*"

To address these perceived challenges, the document asserted that **U.S. Security Strategy must focus on building indigenous security and intelligence capabilities through bilateral engagement and 'coalitions of the willing'.** The National Security Strategy paper, issued in 2006, goes further, identifying Africa as 'a high priority' and recognized that partly, American security depended upon partnering with Africans to strengthen some of their fragile and failing states and bringing ungoverned areas under the control of effective democracies.

In 2004 an advisory panel of Africa experts authorized by the Congress to propose new policy initiatives, identified five factors that have shaped increased U.S. interest in Africa in the past decade: oil, global trade, conflicts, terror, and AIDS. The above perceptions culminated in the establishment of the New Africa Command in 2007, reflecting an evolution in the policymakers' perceptions of U.S. strategic interests in Africa.

**U.S Foreign Policy Priorities in Africa**

The U.S state Department has identified four major priority areas for its policy focus in Africa. They are:

**1. Providing Security Assistance to Various African Nation States to Secure Peace:** This plan envisages working along with various African partners in developing their security preparedness and building capacities at three distinct levels:

- At the level of the African Union. (Extending support to the Strategic Planning & Management Unit at the A.U Headquarters in Addis Ababa with advisors & equipment).
- At the Regional level. (Extending assistance to Peacekeeping Training

Centres in Senegal, Ghana, South Africa, Mali, and Kenya, and providing a security advisor at ECOWAS headquarters, and supporting the ECOWAS logistics facility in Freetown, Sierra Leone.

- At the level of individual nations. (Extending specialized training programs tailor made to individual nations such as, maritime patrol exercises with Nigeria, police training to Liberia and Botswana, training of technical personnel of the Kenyan Air force etc.)

A strategically significant step was taken in early 2007 when the decision was made to create a Department of Defence Unified Combatant Command for Africa—the U.S. Africa Command, or 'AFRICOM'. Owing to the significance of Africom in the African context, it has been dealt with in detail in the subsequent section in this paper.

Notable initiatives under this plan include the International Military Education and Training (IMET) Program and the Africa Contingency Operations Training and Assistance (ACOTA) Programme. Over 100,000 African Peacekeepers have been trained under these programs since its inception which has increased the share of African contingents deployed for various UN Peacekeeping Missions in conflict zones such as Somalia, Sudan, Rwanda etc.

**2. Promoting Democracy:** This aspect envisages:

- Supporting freedom and promoting democratic values and principles throughout the continent.
- Assisting and encouraging African partners in building democratic institutions, conducting free and fair elections, and governing justly.
- Providing support to civil society and media, strengthening political parties and elections monitoring mechanisms, providing support to legislatures, building the capacity of key ministries, and encouraging political transparency.
- Working closely with African societies on the critical issues of governance, transparency, and accountability as a means of helping establish pluralistic communities.

**3. Promoting Free Market Economy and Growth:** This initiative strives to work closely with African partner nations to raise income levels, promote sustainable growth, explore new markets for African exports, reduce barriers to investment, and to identify opportunities and comparative advantages. Programs to be implemented under this initiative are:

- Millennium Challenge Account (MCA)—a foreign assistance programme that seeks to reduce poverty through sustainable economic growth by awarding sizeable grants-not loans-to countries that practice good governance, seek to take responsibility for their own development, and are committed to achieving results. Of the 18 compacts signed to date, ten totalling over US$ 3.8 billion have been signed with sub-Saharan African countries. Two other African countries, Senegal and Malawi are in the process of developing compacts.

- Enactment of the African Growth and Opportunity Act (AGOA)-a programme that allows 'responsive and responsible' partners in Africa to benefit from preferential access to American markets. Over 40 countries in Africa are presently qualified for this programme.
- Providing expertise and technical assistance to various countries in Africa to increase the productivity of staple crops, stimulate supply response, and expand the trade in staple crops.

**4. Promoting Healthcare and Social Development:**

- Funding public health initiatives targeting the prevention, care and treatment of disease, and partnering with sub-Saharan nations to fight HIV/AIDS, tuberculosis, and malaria. Through PEPFAR (President's Emergency Program for AIDS Relief), the U.S. Government has since provided close to US$ 18.8 billion in HIV/AIDS funding, with a subsequent reauthorization of up to US$ 48 billion for HIV/AIDS, tuberculosis, and malaria in the coming years.
- The President's Malaria Initiative (PMI), 2005, committed up to US$ 1.2 billion as funds to reduce malaria-related deaths by 50 percent in 15 African countries. This program is said to have benefited close to 25 million people.

However comprehensive the policy priorities may seem, U.S policymakers acknowledge that they continue to face significant challenges in the implementation of the above. One cannot help but notice that the above mentioned policy priorities involve just about every U.S government agency. Quite a few programmes cited above require immense coordination between two or more departments for effective implementation and to prevent wastage of resources. It was precisely for this, that U.S policymakers conceived a totally new geographic command, for the African continent, titled the African command or AFRICOM.

## Africom

**Mission and Mandate:** On February 6, 2007, the Bush Administration announced its intention to create a new unified combatant command, U.S. Africa Command or AFRICOM, to promote U.S. national security objectives in Africa and its surrounding waters. As defined by the Department of Defence (DOD), Africom's mission would be to promote U.S. strategic objectives by working with African states and regional organizations to help strengthen stability and security in the region through improved security capability, military professionalization, and accountable governance. The command's military operations would aim to deter aggression and respond to crises. According to DOD officials, the new command will seek greater interagency coordination with the State Department, USAID, and other government agencies and will have a larger civilian staff (possibly between one quarter to one third of the total staff) than has been traditional with other combatant commands.

The keywords used to describe Africom, are those of 'Unified Command'. What is significant about that? Africom is headed by a four-star African-American Army General 'Kipp' Ward. Apart from incorporating the conventional components of the military, which is the Army, Navy, Air Force & the Marines, Africom has in its various top executive positions represented at least 26 other US government agencies. These range from the State department, Treasury, Homeland Security, and even the FBI. This clearly shows that Africom shall act as a single-window option to coordinate and implement the entire spectrum of U.S policy objectives.

Though its primary AOR (Area of responsibility) happens to be the African continent as a whole (excluding Egypt), Africom is currently headquartered in Stuttgart, Germany. The U.S government is said to be in discussions with quite a few governments in Africa, for basing rights for Africom within Africa itself. There is still quite a lot of hesitation in the minds of most of the African nations in allowing the US to set up permanent bases within the continent. However the command operates two Forward Operating Stations (FOS)s at Ascension Island (United Kingdom) and Camp Lemonier (Djibouti).

**Strategy:** Africom's key strategy is 'sustained security engagement' focusing on military-to-military (mil-to-mil) programs on conflict and crisis 'prevention rather than reaction'.

**Interests and Objectives:** Africom in developing its command strategy, identified the following as its strategic interests:

- Preventing attacks against Americans by transnational threats emanating from Africa.
- Preventing acquisition, transfer, or transit of Weapons of Mass Destruction (WMD) material or expertise.
- Maintaining freedom of movement into and through the AOR unhindered.
- Fostering the prevention, mitigation and containment of conflict.
- Fostering sustained stability.
- Mitigating the effects of significant humanitarian crisis and disasters.

- Deterring and containing the influenza pandemic in the AOR.

**Africom's Strategic Objectives Are:**

- Defeating the Al-Qaeda terrorist organization and its associated networks.
- Ensuring that Peace Operation Capacity exists so as to respond to emerging crises and ensuring that continental peace support operations are effectively fulfilling mission requirements.
- Cooperating with identified African states in the creation of an environment inhospitable to unsanctioned possession and proliferation of WMD capabilities and expertise.
- Improving security sector governance and increasing stability through military support to comprehensive, holistic, and enduring USG efforts in designated states.
- Protecting populations from deadly contagions.

**Operations/Programmes Currently Undertaken by Africom:** Since its operationalization, Africom has undertaken as well as participated in a variety of programmes across the continent. These include, joint military exercises, training programmes, community interaction events, academic exchanges and seminars with regional scholars etc. Significant among those were:

- Operation Enduring Freedom-Transsahara-(OEF-TS) is a DOD contribution to the Trans-Sahara Counter Terrorism Partnership (TSCTP). This partnership uses the capabilities of U.S. Government (USG) Agencies to counter terrorism in North and West Africa. The OEF-TS component of TSCTP is designed to assist participating African nations as they improve control of their territories and thus deny safe havens to terrorist groups.
- Combined Joint Task Force-Horn of Africa (CJTF-HOA)-Focuses on operations in Somalia and combating piracy off the Horn of Africa.
- Operation Objective Voice (OOV)-known previously as OPERATION Assured Voice - Africa (OAV-A) - OOV is a proactive effort where multiple agencies partner with African governments to broadcast messages to counter extremist propaganda.
- International Military Education and Training (IMET) and expanded IMET (E-IMET) programs provide education and training to select military and civilian personnel from various African countries.
- Foreign Military Financing (FMF)-provides critical U.S. military equipment and services to partner countries as part of a long-term strategy to procure compatible systems that increase interoperability, effectiveness, and efficiency of training.
- Global Peace Operations Initiative (GPOI)-is a U.S. State Department-led

initiative to enhance global capabilities to conduct peace support operations, with a particular emphasis on building African capacity. This programme is expected to train 75,000 peacekeeping troops worldwide by 2010, develop a transportation and logistics architecture to facilitate peacekeeping deployments, and establish an international training centre for the training of formed police unit trainers.

- The Mil-to-Mil Contact programme.
- The National Guard State Partnership Program (SPP) - links U.S. States and territories with African countries. The SPP helps build long-term relationships, promotes access, enhances African military professionalism and capabilities, interoperability, and promotes healthy civil-military relations.

**Chinese Interests and Policies towards Africa**

**Overview of China's Engagement in Africa:** China's engagement with Africa and bilateral assistance was initiated way back in 1956 and, by its own account, has funded over 800 projects between 1957 and 2008. There are few capitals in Africa where China has not built a showpiece building, from a national sports stadium to a gleaming new ministry headquarter. Estimates of Chinese development assistance to Africa in this decade vary, but tend to fall around US$ 1-US$ 2 billion per year. This amount is still relatively modest in comparison to the annual contributions of US$ 18 billion (including debt relief) provided by the European Union (EU) and member countries, US$ 9 billion from multilateral institutions, and about US$ 5 billion from the United States Government.

China's booming economy, which has averaged annually at 9 percent for the last two decades, requires massive levels of energy to sustain its growth. Though China relies on coal for most of its energy needs, it is the second-largest consumer of oil in the world, just after the United States. Once the largest oil exporter in Asia, China became a net importer of oil in the year 1993. The International Energy Agency projects that China's net oil imports will jump to 13.1 million barrels per day by 2030 from 3.5 million barrels per day in 2006. China currently imports about half its oil supplies from the Middle East, and that percentage is projected to grow in the coming decades. Yet the extent of the country's energy demand has also compelled China to push into new markets, and particularly Africa. China currently receives about one-third of its oil requirements from Africa. China's biggest suppliers in Africa as of 2006 were Angola, the Republic of Congo, Equatorial Guinea and Sudan. It has also sought supplies from Chad, Nigeria, Algeria and Gabon.

China has developed a two-pronged strategy toward energy investments.

First, it has pursued exploration and production deals in smaller, low-visibility countries such as Gabon, Equatorial Guinea, and the Republic of Congo. Second, it has gone after the largest oil producers by offering integrated packages of aid. In Angola, which exported roughly 465,000 barrels of oil per day to China in the first six months of 2007, Beijing secured a major stake in future oil production in 2004 with a US$ 2 billion package of loans and aid that included funds for Chinese companies to build railroads, schools, roads, hospitals, bridges, and offices, lay a fibre optic network and train Angolan telecommunications workers. However China's most successful African energy investment has been in Sudan, which now sends 60 percent of its oil output to China.

Chinese interest in Africa extends beyond oil. China now ranks as the continent's second-highest trading partner, behind the United States, and ahead of France and Britain. From 2002 to 2003, trade between China and Africa doubled to US$ 18.5 billion; by 2007, it had reached US$ 73 billion. Chinese firms also import a significant amount of non-oil commodities such as timber, copper, and diamonds. China recently has begun importing some African-manufactured value-added goods, such as processed foods and household consumer goods.

Africa is also becoming an important export market for Chinese consumer goods. Small, private Chinese investors have invested millions of dollars into opening enterprises in Africa that operate in textiles, light manufacturing, construction and agriculture. Recent media attention has focused on high-profile Chinese investments in Africa, such as the Industrial and Commercial Bank of China's October 2007 purchase of a twenty-percent stake in South Africa's Standard Bank, or a US$ 9 billion loan and investment package for Congo that will be repaid in cobalt and copper from Congolese mines.

China's economic and commercial engagement in Africa has increased dramatically in recent years, after having started from a relatively low base. As of 2006, the value of China's trade with Africa was lower than that with the Middle East or Latin America and was a minute percentage of its trade with the rest of Asia. On the investment side, China's investment flow into Africa constituted only 2.9 percent of its global outward direct investment. China's total direct investment stock in Africa accounted for only 1 percent of global foreign direct investment in Africa.

**Official Chinese Policy on Africa:** The general principals and objectives as stated by the official Chinese foreign policy documents are as follows:

- Sincerity, friendship and equality-China shall adhere to the Five Principles of Peaceful Coexistence, respect African countries' independent choice of the road to development and support African countries' efforts to grow stronger through unity.

- Mutual benefit, reciprocity and common prosperity-China shall support African countries' endeavours for economic development and nation building, carry out cooperation in various forms for economic and social development, and promote simultaneously the prosperity of China and Africa.
- Mutual support and close coordination-Strengthen cooperation with Africa in the UN and other multilateral organisations by supporting each other's just demand and reasonable propositions and continue to appeal to the international community to give more attention to questions concerning peace and development in Africa.
- Learning from each other and seeking common development-Support African countries' efforts to enhance capacity building.
- The one China principle continues to be the political foundation for the establishment and development of China's relations with African countries and regional organizations.

**Components of Chinese Foreign Policy towards Africa**

**Politics:**

- Frequent high-level bilateral political visits.
- Exchanges between legislative bodies.
- Exchanges between political parties.
- Setting up consultative mechanisms.
- Cooperation in international forums on major issues.
- Exchanges & links between and at the level of provincial governments (partner cities) in China and the respective countries in Africa.

**Economics:**

- Expand bilateral trade via Duty-Free mechanisms and Free Trade Agreements.
- Encourage investments – capital, infrastructure, contracts, acquisitions etc.
- Financial & agricultural cooperation.
- Economic assistance for debt reduction and relief.

**Education, Science, Culture and Social Aspects:**

- Cooperation in Human Resources Development and Education.
- Science and Technology Cooperation.
- Enhancing tourism and cultural exchanges.
- Supporting Healthcare.
- Enhancing people-to-people exchanges and media cooperation.
- Disaster relief and humanitarian assistance.

**Peace and Security:**

- Military exchanges & training programs.
- Participation and support in Peacekeeping Operations.
- Cooperation at the Judicial & Police levels.
- Cooperation in Non-Traditional Security areas.

**Key Chinese Initiatives in Africa**

Launched in 2000, the Forum on China-Africa Cooperation (FOCAC) has become a crucial mechanism for collective dialogue and multilateral cooperation between China and Africa. Pledges made by China at this forum are:

- Provide US$ 3 billion in "preferential loans" and US$ 2 billion in "preferential buyers' credits" targeted at poor African countries by 2009.
- Establish a China-Africa Development Fund worth an eventual US$ 5 billion to encourage Chinese companies to invest in Africa and provide support to them.
- Write off the interest-free government loans due at the end of 2005 given to poor African countries that had diplomatic relations with China.
- Increase the number of items subject to Chinese Duty-Free Treatment exported by poor Africa countries having diplomatic ties with China from 190 to 440.
- Setting up to 5 SEZs in Africa for the benefit of Chinese companies setting themselves up in Africa.
- Deploy up to 100 top Chinese agricultural experts to Africa, establish 10 agricultural technology centres, build 30 hospitals, provide about US$ 40 million in grants for anti-malaria drugs, prevention, and construction of model treatment centres; deploy 300 PRC Peace Corps-like volunteers to Africa; build 100 rural schools in Africa; train 15,000 African professionals and double the number of PRC government scholarships for African students from 2,000 per year to 4,000 per year.

**EU's Policy towards Africa**

E.U's policies towards Africa are based on the following postulates:

- Engaging with a changing Africa: equality, partnership, ownership.
- Engaging with a multilayered Africa: subsidiarity and solidarity.
- Engaging with Africa on a continuous basis: political dialogue.
- Fostering Peace & Security.
- Supporting legitimate and effective governance.
- Reinforcing respect for human rights and democracy.

- Promoting gender equality.
- Creating a positive economic environment.
- Boosting agriculture and ensuring food security.
- Interconnecting Africa.
- Building an environmentally sustainable future.
- Increasing EU financing for Africa.

The Cotonou Agreement, the Trade, Development and Cooperation Agreement (TDCA), the Euro-Mediterranean Partnership and the European Neighbourhood Policy initiative provide an effective framework for EU-Africa relations. Since the E.U policy is more aligned along the US & NATO lines, E.U policy initiatives in Africa has just been mentioned brief.

## Indian Foreign Policy on Africa

**Overview of Indo-African Relationship:** India has had a long association with Africa. From the time of independence till the early 1990s, relationship between India and the African countries was, to a large extent, based on ideological complementarities and was political. India, at the time, was struggling with its own developmental problems, was itself a recipient of aid, and had hardly any leftover capital to invest outside its borders. Trade too, was directed Northwards, according to the pattern set during colonial times. The concept of South-South cooperation could hardly take root under these circumstances.

India’s economic reforms which began in the early 1990s, however, brought about a significant change in configurations-trade, aid, alignments, to mention a few. There has been unprecedented economic growth in the ongoing first decade of the twenty-first century, placing India among the middle powers of the world today with the potential to develop into a major power within the next quarter century. India now has capital to invest, finances for development, technologies for enhancing productivity and an enormous market for exports.

In this regard, India initiated several economic collaboration arrangements with the countries of Africa. These include India's membership of the African Development Bank, assistance under India's Technical and Economic Cooperation programme, credit arrangements, both through governmental channels and through the Exim Bank of India, and several initiatives within the multilateral G-15 grouping and the Indian Ocean Rim Association for Regional Cooperation.

India's re-engagement with Africa has majorly been fuelled by pragmatic concerns, namely expanding economic interdependence and meeting resource needs. Bilateral trade between India and Africa has grown from US$ 967 million in 1991 to over US$ 30 billion in 2007-2008 with intentions to double this to US$ 50 billion by 2012. Africa's share of India's global trade increased from 5.8 percent in 2002-2003 to 8 percent in 2006-2007.

India's official investment in Africa stands at US$ 2 billion in addition to US$ 5 billion from the private sector. Economic cooperation spans several sectors, including agriculture, small and medium enterprises, health, education, information technology and communications, automobiles, manufacturing and railways. Ore and metals continue to dominate India's imports from Africa although uranium may emerge as an increasingly important import from the region as India expands its civilian nuclear program.

India's trade relationship with Africa has traditionally been skewed toward East and Southern Africa although its trade with West Africa is likely to increase given its growing dependence on oil imports from the region, as 70 percent of Africa's oil production is concentrated in the Gulf of Guinea, which stretches from the Ivory Coast to Angola. India's state-owned Oil and Natural Gas Corporation Videsh (OVL) has invested US$ 2 billion in eight African countries, including Nigeria, which is the region's leading oil exporter accounting for 10 percent of India's oil imports.

India's Essar Group, Gas Authority of India Limited (GAIL), Indian Oil Corporation and Reliance Industries have also acquired interests in African energy assets. Imports now account for more than two-thirds of India's oil consumption and India's energy demands are expected to double by 2030 making it the world's third-largest net oil importer, after the US and China.

India's re-engagement with Africa has majorly been driven by its quest for 'great power' status and a desire to balance the presence of other external powers in the region, most notably regional rival China, which has made considerable inroads in recent years.

**Overview of Indian Foreign Policy on Africa**

Indian foreign policy priorities underwent a major overhaul in the 90s. The influencing factors were economic difficulties followed by liberalization and to a certain extent the Indian Nuclear Tests of 1998. 'Realism' or more specifically 'structural realism' became the guiding principle of our foreign policy pursuit. In this context the new priorities for our external relations were:

- Replacing the principle of equal treatment for all sovereign states, India now has a priority category of a dozen odd countries with which India seeks to pursue a strategic partnership or strategic dialogue.
- There is a greater economic focus in our foreign policy, including an

emphasis on trade, investment and energy security.

- India's definition of security has been broadened from the protection of its borders and territorial integrity to a wider concept of defending its national interests.
- There is a greater focus on relationships with India's immediate neighbours.

Africa fits in as a major focus area on the basis of the first three criteria. India is pursuing a strategic partnership with South Africa and Egypt, two of the most influential and significant countries in the African continent.

Africa is important for India's economic interests, especially as it is abundantly endowed with valuable minerals and hydrocarbon resources. Africa is also vital to security, being an immediate offshore neighbour across the Indian Ocean. India's stakes in the security of its sea-lanes and the Indian Ocean were dramatically demonstrated when the Indian Navy sank a Somalian pirate vessel off the coast of Oman in 2008.

**Parameters of India's Africa Policy**

**Economy:** Indo-African economic and trade relationship has seen a robust revival and growth, with bilateral (non-oil) trade going from less than US$ 1billion in 1990-91 to US$ 30 billion in 2007-08, a 30-fold increase. While this is cause for cheer, we need to recognise that our trade is still confined to a dozen countries only, and our basket of inputs and reports still follow a colonial pattern of importing raw material and exporting finished goods. This is an area which needs attention.

India had also been a significant donor to Africa via its EXIM bank and other agencies.

**Industry:** We have in the past decade established linkages with African industry. In 2006, the Exim Bank of India extended 46 lines of credit for projects in different parts of Africa. Indian industry is finally looking seriously at industrial investments in Africa. Unlike, China where till recently almost all investments were made by state owned companies, in the case of India, it was the private sector which spearheaded investments and in tapping contracts and agreements. Indian corporates have invested in a broad spectrum of industries and Joint Ventures in Africa – coal, mining, oil, telecom, pharmaceuticals, steel, minerals, refineries etc.

**RICON:** The consortium of RITES and IRCON in December 2004 had won the 25-year concession for the rehabilitation and management of the Beira railway system (SENA line). Coal India in March 2009 was awarded two coal blocks in Moatize, Tete Province through an open tender floated by the

Mozambique Government in December, 2008.

Tata Steel has entered into a joint venture with Australian company Riversdale with 35 percent stake in coal licences covering 25,000 hectares of land. Riversdale plans to start producing coal starting from 2010 from 290,000 hectares concession in Moatize Basin in the Tete province of South Africa. Jindal Steel, Videocon, Adani Group and M/s P.K. Ores of Orissa are other companies who have joined the 'coal pursuit' in Mozambique by buying coal mines from local license holders.

**Energy:** Africa's energy resources have attracted global attention. India has been a relative latecomer, and hence there is a sense of frustration in feeling left out of the energy bonanza. Even so, Indian companies like ONGC, Indian Oil and Reliance have been active in indirectly seeking avenues for exploration. India has established a presence in Libya, Sudan, Angola, Nigeria and the area around the Gulf of Guinea. Oil India and ONGC have secured three blocks for exploration in Libya. ONGC /OVL has also acquired an oil field in Nigeria through an investment of around US $2 billion. It has reserves of 300 million barrels of oil and 2.5 trillion cubic feet of gas.

**Political Relations and Interactions:** Despite all economic and trade related initiatives, Indian Foreign Policy lacked a comprehensive political engagement with individual African states or prominent regional forums such as ECOWAS, AU & SADC. This lacunae was filled when in April 2008, the first ever India-Africa Summit was held in Delhi in the presence of the leaders of 14 major African states. It was preceded by a conclave of business leaders on both sides-there were 600 business representatives from 33 African countries and 35 African ministers. They brought to the table 150 projects with a total of US$ 10 billion in investments. The areas of cooperation identified were the four core areas of Indian competence: technology, agriculture, human resources and energy. Salient outcomes of this summit have been outlined in the next section of this paper.

**Military Liaisons/Peace Keeping Operations:** Africa has been a critical region for peace keeping operations. India has a record of being among the longest and largest contributors to UN peace keeping activities. India's peace keeping roles have traditionally been guided by two distinct characteristics-'Red block principles' of consent, impartiality and minimal use of force, and secondly, strict command and control under UN auspices only. India's current force level contributions for various UN missions in Africa are shown in Table 28.1.

Apart from taking part in UN missions, India has an active military exchange and training program wherein officers from select African countries undergo staff and other specialized courses of the Indian military. India also has a modest weapons sales program in Africa. This includes offshore patrol vessels and some select munitions.

A few other noteworthy initiatives of the Indian Government towards Africa are discussed below.

**Table 28.1**

| Mission | Troops | Police | Military Observers | Total |
|---|---|---|---|---|
| MONUC | 4375 | 250 | 45 | 4670 |
| UNMEE | 845 | 0 | 8 | 853 |
| UNMIL | 0 | 125 | 0 | 125 |
| UNMIS | 2608 | 23 | 20 | 2651 |
| UNOCI | 0 | 2 | 98 | 10 |
| Total | | | | 8309 |

Source: Department of Peace keeping Operations, UN (Accessed May 2007).

**India-Africa Forum Summit:** The India-Africa Forum Summit held in New Delhi from 8-9 April 2008, was a landmark event. The Summit created a new architecture for the relationship between India and Africa for the earlier part of the 21st century. The Delhi Declaration and the Africa-India Framework for Cooperation that emerged from the Summit set out an ambitious road map.

The Prime Minister announced the doubling of the existing levels of Lines of Credit to Africa to US$ 5.4 billion over the next five years. These Lines of Credit would be utilized in such crucial areas as enhancing agricultural production, food processing, small and medium enterprises, irrigation, infrastructure, IT, energy and pharmaceutical sectors, among others. These projects will be prioritized by the African governments, reflecting their own needs. A separate grant of US$ 500 million was also announced for projects especially in the areas of capacity building and human resource development. These include an entire range of programmes, namely, doubling of educational scholarships under ITEC, general scholarship schemes of the ICCR, organization of courses in water resources, health, agriculture, mining, establishment of apex institutions in such diverse areas as trade, IT, vocational training, diamond, coal etc. These programmes will keep Africa as the largest recipient of the ITEC programme.

The Prime Minister also announced an offer of the Duty Free Tariff Preference (DFTP) Scheme for access to products from African LDCs. Out of the 50 LDCs of the world, 34 are in Africa. A number of African nations have already joined the Scheme. This was a fulfilment of a promise made by India earlier at the WTO.

**Pan-African E-Network Project:** This project seeks to assist Africa to bridge the digital divide in the 21st century. Launched in Addis Ababa in July

2007, the network will be connected by satellite and fibre optics to all the 53 nations of Africa. It will provide tele-education, tele-medicine and VVIP connectivity. It will also connect five regional universities, five regional centres and five regional super-specialty hospitals as well as cover universities and hospitals in every single country in Africa. The project will cost a mere US$ 120 million for India.

The seven Indian educational institutions associated with the project are Indian Institute of Science-Bangalore, Amity University, University of Madras, Indira Gandhi National Open University, Birla Institute of Technology and Science, University of Delhi and IIT Kanpur. Online medical consultation will be available for one hour every day to each participating African country for a period of five years in various medical disciplines. For this purpose, twelve leading Indian Super Specialty Hospitals have been enlisted in the project. They include AIIMS, Escorts Heart institute, Care Hospital, Hyderabad and Narayan Hrudayaylaya, Bangalore.

The project, being implemented by the state-run Telecommunications Consultants India Ltd., has a target of providing tele-education services to 10,00 African students in different courses. Former president A.P.J. Abdul Kalam had first offered the proposal years ago when he addressed the inaugural session of the Pan-African Parliament in Johannesburg.

**ITEC Programme:** This programme was initiated to fund and support technology transfer as well as human resource training exercises for partner countries. Over the years, ITEC has also become a powerful instrument of projecting India's soft power and its cultural diplomacy as most of these students retain a lifelong association with India, long after their brief stay in the country.

On an average, India spends about Rs 500 million (US$ 10.8 million) on varied ITEC activities. Since 1964, India has provided nearly US$ 2.5 billion worth of technical assistance to developing countries, including neighbouring countries (assistance to whom is administered separately). Today, Afro-Asian Rural Reconstruction Organisation (AARRO) and the G-15 are being helped by ITEC with training and project support, and a small beginning has also been made by cooperating with the SADC (Southern African Development Community).

Agriculture, however, remains a major focus of ITEC's project assistance. The programme has provided Ghana, Senegal, Burkina Faso, Mali and Surinam with equipment and expertise for agricultural use and generated tremendous goodwill among African countries. Vocational training in small-scale industry and entrepreneurship development are important areas of cooperation with Senegal and Zimbabwe under the ITEC. Such training enables young people to gain useful employment at comparatively low levels of capital intensity.

**Team Nine Initiatives:** Team nine envisages special cooperation amongst the eight West African Countries and India. The countries being Burkina Faso, Chad, Cote D'Ivoire, Equatorial Guinea, Ghana, Guinea Bissau, Mali, Senegal, and India. The recently held first ministerial meeting of Team 9 Nine countries in New Delhi has helped in clarifying issues of common concern and the logistics of cooperation. While India and the West African countries share similar developmental challenges, the particular developmental needs of the region were not known.

Apart from Senegal and Ghana, with whom India has a long history of political and economic cooperation, the rest are unfamiliar. India has extended credit facilities of US$ 500 million for these projects identified by the Team Nine countries.

## Implications of Various Policy Initiatives for Indian Interests

**Implications of US policy:** True to its size and pre-eminent position as the sole existing super power, USA's engagement in Africa is truly comprehensive. Its engagement covers the entire spectrum of activities from aid to military relations. Though the US tend to project AFRICOM as a purely capacity building mechanism, the recent posture statement of the command as well as statements by senior officials tend to suggest otherwise. Though currently Africom is stationed outside Africa, subsequently US could succeed in convincing an African nation for hosting rights, which would directly bring in the presence of US military in Africa.

Possible scenarios are:

- As the US seeks to acquire more energy resources in Africa it is bound to come into conflict with Chinese interests. Hence stiff energy competition between the US and China is bound to emerge in the near future.
- Potential disgruntlement and opposition to US military presence in Africa.
- Prolonged Counter-Terrorism Initiatives will have its effects on society.
- Increasing support for repressive regimes so as to gain easy access to resources will result in the emergence of new conflicts and hence will pressurize current peacekeeping missions.

## Implications of Chinese Policy

China's burgeoning economic and political engagement with Africa has elicited a range of reactions from African, U.S., and other policy makers and analysts. These range from enthusiastic or guardedly optimistic responses to growing concern over what some perceive to be an actual or potential Chinese strategic and economic threat to western, African and other Asian interests. Such concerns primarily relate to the state-centric, political-commercial mode of the PRC's engagement in Africa; to its potential negative impacts on other powers' policy goals and engagements in Africa; to the competitive impact of increased PRC's imports of raw materials from Africa and, to a lesser extent and to Chinese competition for acquiring current and future African markets.

**Possible Scenarios Are**

- China's ever increasing appetite for energy could lead it down the path of increasing competition with the west as well as with India.
- China's policy of extending aid with 'no strings attached' and its support for regimes such as that in Sudan under the guise of non interference in internal affairs of countries, has already raised eyebrows among human rights agencies and will continue to do so in future.
- China's cheap products in the African market could kill local industry.
- There has been significant concern in certain countries where Chinese companies are bringing in labour from China and not providing employment to the locals.

**Policy Options for India**

Indian policy as pursued in Africa is rather unique. India has made a promising beginning, but it is necessary to reorganise the priorities and challenges ahead. India possesses a unique soft advantage which other powers do not have. Neither Europe nor China has historical linkages or the enormous fund of goodwill that India enjoys in Africa. As the Prime Minister said at the recent Africa Summit, *"We visualise a partnership that is anchored in the fundamental principles of equality, mutual respect and mutual benefit"*. It is important that India works on this unique strength and converts it into a long-term strategic advantage.

India could further reassess and identify focal areas to better entrench and secure its fundamental strategic position in Africa. This could be broken into two possible areas:

**At the Indian end: Political/Diplomatic steps could be:**

- To enhance political contacts with various African governments.
- To identify and establish relationships with power centres across Africa. (This could include ruling and opposition political factions, prominent business leaders, religious figures, community and tribal leaders etc.)

- To increase the frequency of high profile visits both at the ministerial level as well as at the level of officials.
- To enhance the number of African specialists in the Ministry of External Affairs and resources to constantly monitor the emerging trends in the continent.
- Actively engage with the government in place as well as the prominent political entities /parties in key African countries.

**Cultural/Social Steps could be:**

- Enhancing more people-to-people contact initiatives.
- Promoting and enhancing academic exchanges and mutual visits of scholars between India and Africa.
- Promoting academic knowledge and research potential on Africa in Indian universities.
- Enhancing scholarship support programs for higher education options for African students in India.

**At the African end it could entail:**

- Engaging and actively influencing the diaspora to strive for and take up leadership positions at various levels of power.
- Sponsoring/funding research departments/think tanks in prominent African countries to engage with Indian strategic perspectives.
- Encouraging Indian investment in strategic sectors such as Media, telecom, agricultural inputs etc.
- Providing support to Indian industries in acquiring contracts and strategic acquisitions in Africa.
- Rationalizing the activities of the ITEC to make it more effective.
- Increasing aid and focusing on capacity-building areas.

The aforementioned are just recommendations. For our policy response to be comprehensive, structured and effective, it is imperative for our MEA, to outline a Strategic vision framework document for Africa. Though this was outlined at the Indo African summit, it was no means comprehensive. And this framework should include the following questions:

- What are India's strategic objectives in Africa?
- What are the policies and activities of other major powers active in Africa and what are their effects on Indian interests?
- Whether our current initiatives are in line with our objectives and whether they are delivering the desired objectives?
- Whether these require the building of a contingency plan directing future alignment and realignment, based on a detailed study of prevailing political,

social and economic conditions and policies in African nations?

## Conclusion

Though one could take heart on the fact that Indian policy towards Africa is very much on the right track, it is very much important that the said policy be regularly reassessed against developments and activities of the other powers. We just cannot be supporting in the building of hospitals roads alone. Such measures though generate goodwill, may not actually translate into strategic benefits. Most parts of Africa still do not have mature political or administrative systems and most governments there are under the influence of major transnational corporations or foreign powers. Therefore goodwill among the people may not automatically imply political goodwill or preferential contracts. Therefore India needs a comprehensive action plan for Africa backed by a long-term strategic vision. If I may borrow here Mr. Obama's phrase-"Yes, we can..."

### References

AFRICOM; *"United States Africa Command – 2009 Posture Statement"*; Text of the Statement made before the Senate Armed Forces Committee and the House Armed Services Committee by Gen. William E. Ward, USA Commander, AFRICOM; http://www.Africom.mil/pdfFiles/USAFRICOM2009PostureStatement.pdf

Charles W. Corey, Staff Writer; *"Obama's Africa Policy";* Statement by then Secretary of State–designate Hillary Clinton at her confirmation hearing before the Senate Committee; 13 January 2009.

*China's Africa Policy*; MEA, Beijing; January 2006. http://www.fmprc.gov.cn/zflt/eng/zfgx/dfzc/t481748.htm

Commission of the European Communities; *"E.U Strategy for Africa : Towards a Euro –African Pact to accelerate Africa's Development"*; 2005.; http://ec.europa.eu/development/icenter/repository/COMM_PDF_COM_2005_0489_F_EN_ACTE.pdf

Ed. By Avtar Singh Bhasin; *"India's Foreign Relations – 2008 Documents"*; Public Diplomacy Division, MEA & Geetika Publishers; March 2009. http://meaindia.nic.in/onmouse/foreignrelations2008.pdf

Exim bank, India; "*Indo–African Trade Statistics*", (accessed as on 21-10-2009).

*Forum on China – Africa Cooperation* – Beijing Action Plan (2007-2009); http://english.focacsummit.org/

Indian Technical & Economic Cooperation Program, ITEC, - www.itec.nic.in/

Lauren Ploch; *"Africa Command: U.S. Strategic Interests and the role of the U.S. Military in Africa*"; CRS Report for Congress series, July 2009. http://www.fas.org/sgp/crs/natsec/RL34003.pdf

Martin Dahle Huse & Stephen L. Muyakwa; *"China in Africa : lending, policy space and governance"*; Norwegian Council for Africa; 2008. http://www.afrika.no/noop/file.php?id=17232

Martin Meredith; *"The State of Africa – A History of Fifty Years of Independence"*; Free Press; 2006.

MIA: Thomas R. Yager, Omayra Bermudez-lugo, Philip M. Mobbs, Harold R. Newman, David R. Wilburn; *"The Mineral Resources of Africa"*. http://minerals.usgs.gov/minerals/pubs/country/ 2005/myb3-sum-2005-Africa.pdf

Ministry of External Affairs, India; *"Annual Report : 2008-2009"*; Policy Planning & Research Division, New Delhi; http://meaindia.nic.in/annualreport/12ar012009.pdf

Pan Africa E- Network – http://www.panAfricanenetwork.com/

Phillip Carter, III - Acting Assistant Secretary, Bureau of African Affairs; *"U.S. Policy in Africa in the 21st Century"* ; Speech Delivered on the topic at The Africa Centre for Strategic Studies, Washington, DC, February 9, 2009. http://www.state.gov/p/af/rls/rm/2009/117326.htm

Princeton N. Lyman and J. Stephen Morrison (Project Directors); *"More than Humanitarianism : A Strategic U.S. approach toward Africa"*; Independent Task force report sponsored by the Council on Foreign Relations, Washington D.C; 2006.; http://www.cfr.org/publication/9302/more_ than_humanitarianism.html?breadcrumb= percent2Fregion percent2F143 percent2FAfrica

Stephanie Hanson; *"China, Africa and Oil"*; CFR Publications (Backgrounders); June 2008 ; http://www.cfr.org/publication/9557/

*Team 9 opens a new innings in India – West Africa Relations"*; The Financial Express; 06 March 2004;http://www.financialexpress.com/news/team-9-opens-a-new-innings-in-indiawest-Africa-relations/87180/0

*The Africa – E.U Strategic Partnership: A joint Africa – EU Strategy*; 2007; http://ec.europa.eu/development/icenter/repository/EAS2007_joint_strategy_en.pdf

Thomas J. Christensen, Dy Asst Secretary for East Asian and Pacific affairs & James Swan, Dy Asst Secretary for African Affairs; *" Policy Statement : China in Africa – Implications for U.S. Policy"*; Statement made before the subcommittee on African affairs of the Senate foreign relations Committee; June 2008. http://china.usc.edu/ShowArticle.aspx?articleID=1084&Aspx AutoDetectCookieSupport=1

U.S. Geological Survey; *2006 Minerals Year Book*; (U.S. Government source, public domain); http://minerals.usgs.gov/minerals/pubs/country/2006/myb3-sum-2006-Africa.pdf

# Index

# Index